ORIGINAL NARRATIVES
OF EARLY AMERICAN HISTORY

REPRODUCED UNDER THE AUSPICES OF THE
AMERICAN HISTORICAL ASSOCIATION

GENERAL EDITOR, J. FRANKLIN JAMESON, Ph.D., LL.D., Litt.D.

DIRECTOR OF THE DEPARTMENT OF HISTORICAL RESEARCH IN THE
CARNEGIE INSTITUTION OF WASHINGTON

EARLY NARRATIVES OF THE NORTHWEST

1634—1699

ORIGINAL NARRATIVES
OF EARLY AMERICAN HISTORY

EARLY NARRATIVES
OF THE NORTHWEST

1634—1699

EDITED BY

LOUISE PHELPS KELLOGG, Ph.D.

OF THE RESEARCH DEPARTMENT OF THE STATE HISTORICAL SOCIETY
OF WISCONSIN

WITH A FACSIMILE AND TWO MAPS

CHARLES SCRIBNER'S SONS
NEW YORK - - - - - - 1917

COPYRIGHT, 1917, BY
CHARLES SCRIBNER'S SONS

PUBLISHED FEBRUARY, 1917

CONTENTS

EARLY NARRATIVES OF THE NORTHWEST, 1634–1699

Edited by Louise Phelps Kellogg

CONTENTS

CONTENTS

MAPS AND FACSIMILE REPRODUCTION

NOTE

The first of the illustrations in this volume is a facsimile of a page of the manuscript of Radisson's journal, photographed from the original in the Bodleian Library at Oxford (Rawlinson, A. 329). The photograph used is in the possession of the State Historical Society of Wisconsin, which has kindly lent it for the purposes of the present reproduction.

We are also indebted to the same society, and to its superintendent, Dr. M. M. Quaife, for the opportunity to reproduce the second of our illustrations, a map in the Bibliothèque Nationale in Paris, bearing the title "Carte de la nouvelle decouverte que les RR. Peres Jesuistes ont fait en l'année 1672, et continuée par le R. Pere Jacques Marquette de la mesme Compagnie, accompagné de quelques François en l'année 1673, qu'on pourra nommer la Manitoumie, a cause de la Statue qui s'est trouvée dans une belle vallée, et que les Sauvages vont reconnoistre pour leur Divinité, quils appellent Manitou, qui signifie Esprit, ou Genie." The original, a map measuring 73 by 44 centimetres, is preserved in vol. C., 17701, in the library named, and is no. 7 in Gabriel Marcel's *Cartographie de la Nouvelle France*, closely resembling no. 202 in Henry Harrisse's *Notes sur la Nouvelle France*. It has been reproduced, as no. 30, in Marcel's *Reproductions de Cartes et de Globes relatifs à la Découverte de l'Amérique*, atlas (Paris, 1893), and is discussed on pp. 106–108 of the volume of letter-press accompanying that atlas. It was evidently drawn from the description of Marquette's Mississippi River voyage, and was the prototype of the map published in Melchisédec Thévenot's *Recueil de Voyages* (Paris, 1681), a map reproduced in the late Dr. R. G. Thwaites's *Jesuit Relations*, vol. LIX., but contains additional data.

As to the name *Manitoumie* (which to be sure never adhered to the region), one who looks at the legend of the map in our facsimile, or in the original photograph, even with a magnifying glass, may easily think that the word has not precisely the form *Manitoumie*, but comparison with the duplicate will probably convince him that though the word in our map seems to end with the two letters

"-me," yet above and between them an "i" has been subsequently inserted by way of correction.

The third illustration represents a portion of Franquelin's great map of 1688, a manuscript map in the library of the Dépôt des Cartes et Plans, in Paris, one of the libraries of the Ministry of the Marine. It is designated as 4040^B (no. 227 in M. de la Roncière's *Catalogue Général* of the collection), 6 *bis*, and bears the title "Carte de l'Amérique septentrionnale depuis le 25: jusqu'au 65e deg. de latt. et environ 140: et 235 deg. de longitude, contenant les pays de Canada ou Nouvelle France, la Louisiane, la Floride, Virginie, N^{lle} Suède, N^{le} Yorc, N^{lle} Angleterre, Acadie, Isle de Terre-neuve, etc.; Le Tout, tres fidellement dressé, conformement aux observations que l'Auteur a faites luy mesme pendant plus de 16 années, par l'ordre des Gouverneurs et Intendans du Pays. . . . En l'Année 1688: Par Jean Baptiste Louis Franquelin, Hydrographe du Roy à Quebec en Canada."

Jean Baptiste Louis Franquelin, b. 1653, was employed by the French government in Canada in the making of several important maps. His large "Carte de la Louisiane" of 1684 is reproduced in Thwaites's *Jesuit Relations*, vol. LXIII. Of another large map by him, "Carte de l'Amérique Septentrionale," etc., of date about 1687, the essential portion is reproduced in A. L. Pinart's *Recueil de Cartes* (Paris, 1893), no. 12. The map of 1688 represents a more advanced state of geographical knowledge, but no complete reproduction of it has been published. A rough facsimile of a portion of it appeared in the fourth edition of E. D. Neill's *History of Minnesota* (1882), and in Winsor's *Narrative and Critical History of America*, IV. 230–231. The original measures 160 by 105 centimetres. A manuscript copy in the same dimensions, beautifully executed, is in the Map Division of the Library of Congress. Our reproduction is from a photograph of this, and embraces an area of the original measuring about 29 x 22 inches, reduced about one-half in each dimension. Acknowledgments are made to Mr. P. Lee Phillips, chief of the Map Division, for the opportunity to photograph. Careful study of the map will show how it reflects the results of the explorations made by La Salle, Perrot, and perhaps Tonty and others. Since its reproduction for this volume, a full-size photograph of the original has been acquired by the State Historical Society of Wisconsin; another is in the possession of the Michigan Historical Commission.

J. F. J.

EARLY NARRATIVES OF THE
NORTHWEST, 1634-1699

GENERAL INTRODUCTION

In the seventeenth century the term Northwest was used to designate the region of the upper Great Lakes and the northeastern part of the Mississippi Valley. It was ordinarily spoken of by the colonists of the St. Lawrence as *le pays d'en haut*—the Upper Country. The discovery and exploration of the Upper Country was accomplished by the French, who had appropriated the St. Lawrence Valley as their sphere of influence, and by the seventeenth century had begun to people it. In the first half of the century the Great Lakes were discovered; the exploration of the Mississippi Valley was the work of the second half-century.

The fitness of the French for this especial task has often been recounted. Gifted with imperial imaginations, with visions of future greatness, undaunted by obstacles, undismayed by hardships, the founders of New France planned to add to that colony an empire in the vast hinterland beyond the sources of their own great river, a region that is now fitly designated as the heart of America. The numerous tribes of aborigines dwelling in this wilderness they speedily learned to conciliate and exploit. The laborers for the expeditions were recruited from the Canadian colonists, who readily developed a woodcraft that rivalled that of the natives, paddling canoes and portaging burdens with a good humor and adaptation to emergencies that made them useful members of exploring parties. Trained to habits of obedience to superiors, they responded with alacrity and pleasure to the demands of wilderness faring.

The leaders of these expeditions were from two walks of life, military officers of the colonial troops and missionaries

3

of the Church; both of these professions were recruited chiefly from the lesser nobility and higher bourgeois class of France. Officers and missionaries vied with one another in devotion to their duties and in ardor for the service of the Crown. Thus, for the discovery and exploration of the Northwest, France enlisted religious enthusiasm, military zeal, pioneering adventure, and far-sighted patriotism, embodied in missionary, soldier, voyageur, and builder of empire.

The founder and forerunner of the great French line of discoverers and explorers was Samuel de Champlain. It was Champlain who chose the site for the capital of the colony on the rock of Quebec, who ascended the St. Lawrence and the Richelieu to the lake that still perpetuates his name. Moreover, Champlain was the discoverer of the Great Lakes, and had planted the flag of France on the shore of Lake Huron, before the English had landed on the coast of New England or appropriated its narrow, rocky shores.

Champlain was not only himself an explorer, but he carefully provided for the continuance of the work by sending promising youths to live in Indian villages, there to learn woodcraft and the native languages, and thence to accompany their Indian friends upon remote voyages for trade or war. Jean Nicolet, one of Champlain's chosen interpreters, as early as 1634 carried his discovery beyond the shores of Lake Huron, through the straits of Mackinac, out upon Lake Michigan, down its western arm, Green Bay, and landed on the farther margin of the valley of St. Lawrence in the present State of Wisconsin. With the narrative of Nicolet's voyage our volume begins.

Meanwhile in the heart of the Ontarian forests, at the foot of Georgian Bay, the Jesuits had begun a flourishing mission for the Huron tribesmen; from this as a base, in 1643, a missionary exploring party went with some Indian visitors to the strait where the waters leap down from Lake Superior.

This they christened the Sault de Ste. Marie, and on its shores Fathers Raymbault and Jogues preached to a mingled throng of the tribesmen of the upper lakes, and looked forward with longing vision to the time when they should all be sheltered within the fold of the Church. At the Sault they saw the entrance to the greatest of the Great Lakes, and thus before the seventeenth century was half-way on its course Lakes Huron, Michigan, and Superior were placed upon the map of North America. When in 1669–1670 the Sulpician missionaries, Galinée and Dollier de Casson, seeking new fields for converts, skirted the shores of Lake Ontario, wintered almost within sound of the Falls of Niagara, and the following spring navigated Lake Erie, the straits of Detroit and St. Clair, and crossing Lake Huron arrived at Sault Ste. Marie, the circuit of the Great Lakes was completed and the sources of the St. Lawrence revealed to the world.

The interior wilderness was more difficult to penetrate than these great bodies of water; the records of its discovery are less circumstantial. Some time between 1650 and 1660 two daring voyageurs, known to us as Radisson and Grosseilliers, accompanied a trading fleet of Indians to the Upper Country and spent several years upon the shores of Green Bay and Lake Superior, wandering far through inland forests, mingling with various tribesmen, trafficking for their rich stores of furs, and learning the woodland routes. Since, however, the journals of their travels were not made known until the nineteenth century, the impress of their discoveries on the progress of geographical knowledge in their own time was slight.

The Indians of the Upper Country had for some time known the value of the white men's goods and had sent annual trading fleets to Montreal and Three Rivers to secure the coveted ammunition, blankets, kettles, and trinkets, when in 1665 Nicolas Perrot conceived the plan of carrying goods into the Indian country, and of securing alliances with the tribesmen who were thickly clustered around the western end of Green Bay and its wooded streams. Perrot spent five years among the tribes in this vicinity, becoming the best-informed and most noted trader and interpreter of his time. To this same region in 1669 came Father Claude Allouez, who had previously opened a mission on Chequamegon Bay, and had skirted both the southern and the northern shores of Lake Superior and traced its coast-line for the remarkable map of that lake that was published in 1670. Father Allouez in the years succeeding his first visit to Green Bay opened missions at many of the villages on the eastward-flowing streams, and in his travels explored the waterways that inter-lace the Fox River route and lead to the waters of the Mis-sissippi. But as yet no Frenchman, if we except the untracked journeys of Radisson and Grosseilliers and the last tragic voyage of Father Ménard who is thought to have perished on the head streams of the Wisconsin, had ventured over the easy divide that separates the valley of the great river from that of the Great Lakes.

Meanwhile, the governor of New France, exulting in the discoveries already accomplished and anticipating those yet to be made, in 1671 sent his envoy, Sieur Daumont de St. Lusson, to plant upon the straits of Ste. Marie the arms and emblems of the French monarch, and before a wondering crowd of awed aborigines to proclaim in solemn conclave the sovereignty of France over the whole American Northwest.

It yet remained to discover the Mississippi. By the time of St. Lusson's pageant the existence of a great interior river had become an open secret to the missionaries and officers of the West. Only government initiative was needed to set on foot an expedition for the purpose of this discovery. The honor of conducting such an expedition was accorded by the governor to Louis Jolliet, a native-born Canadian, who had

had singular success in striking new paths through the wilderness. At the St. Ignace mission on the straits of Mackinac Jolliet secured for his proposed journey the companionship of Father Jacques Marquette, who had already spent three years at the missions of the upper lakes. After many consultations the route via Green Bay and Fox River was chosen, and at the present site of Portage, Wisconsin, the divide between the two great drainage systems was easily crossed. In the lovely, early summer days of our Western woods the canoe floated gently down the Wisconsin River to its union with the Father of Waters, which was entered the 17th of June, 1673. Thence the two explorers continued down the Mississippi to the mouth of the Arkansas, finding neither falls nor rapids to obstruct or endanger their progress. On the return journey another portage route, by way of the Illinois, Des Plaines, and Chicago rivers, was followed. Thus the easy approach to the great central valley of North America was definitely established, and its exploration and exploitation intrusted to the leaders of New France.

Among these leaders were two remarkable explorers and colonizers, Robert Cavelier de La Salle and Daniel Greysolon Duluth. Both had imperial ambitions, both sought to secure the Mississippi Valley for France and make it the seat of a noble civilization. La Salle chose for his sphere of operations the genial prairies of the Illinois. Duluth discovered the portage routes from Lake Superior to the sources of the Mississippi and planned his establishment for the headwaters of the great river among the powerful tribe of the Sioux. His plans were frustrated by the policy of the Canadian governors, who summoned him to the St. Lawrence before his task was well begun. La Salle perished at the hands of an assassin, while striving to colonize the Mississippi's mouth.

Henri de Tonty, lieutenant of La Salle, cousin of Duluth, held together for some years after the former's death the remnants of French occupation in the valley. Around his Fort St. Louis on the Illinois he gathered a small settlement of Frenchmen, and a large concourse of friendly Indians. Many times he made the arduous journey from the St. Lawrence to his inland home, transporting supplies, escorting settlers and missionaries. Vainly he sought at the Mississippi's mouth for the lost colonists of La Salle. In the valley of the Arkansas Tonty established the oldest colony in the lower valley, and thither at the very close of the century he escorted the seminary missionaries St. Cosme and Montigny. The narrative of their journey from Michilimackinac to the Arkansas post forms the closing number of our volume.

The latter years of Tonty's life were given to assisting in founding the colony of Louisiana at the mouth of the Mississippi, thus continuing La Salle's plan of interior occupation, and completing the arch of French control in North America. With one end resting upon the St. Lawrence at Quebec and the other planted on the Mississippi at New Orleans, with the keystones at the Wisconsin and Chicago portages, New France rivalled in extent and promise any colony of any European power in any part of the world. The crumbling of this arch of empire is the story of the eighteenth century.

It is our opportunity here to present the narratives of the discoverers, explorers, and founders of the French empire in North America—narratives full of the charm of brave deeds, of heroic endurance, of abiding enthusiasms, and of famous achievements. With the exception of Radisson's journal, all were originally written in French; the editors hope that the flavor, as well as the accuracy, of the originals has been preserved for our English readers.

THE JOURNEY OF JEAN NICOLET, BY FATHER VIMONT, 1634 [1642]

INTRODUCTION

THAT the French explored the heart of the North American continent while the English occupied only the Atlantic coast plain during the seventeenth century was chiefly due to the lure of the St. Lawrence River. The year after Champlain had founded his colony at the site of Quebec (1608) he had followed the great river to the Richelieu and, ascending that, had discovered the lake that bears his name. By 1615 he had penetrated to Lake Huron, explored its eastern border, and heard of the great fresh-water seas beyond, whose coasts he was not destined to see, but whose discovery was due to the zeal for exploration that he inspired. Choosing adventurous and promising youths, he sent them into the Indian villages to acquire the native languages, and the skill in woodcraft and voyaging that helped to plant the lilies of France on the farther margin of the Great Lakes. Such a disciple and agent of Champlain was Jean Nicolet.

Born in the Norman port of Cherbourg, Nicolet arrived in New France in the summer of 1618, and immediately began his novitiate among the Algonkin Indians on the upper Ottawa. His career of adventure was interrupted by the English capture of the St. Lawrence colony in 1629, whereupon Nicolet retired farther into the continent among the Huron Indians and returned to Quebec only after the Treaty of St. Germain (1632) had brought back Champlain as governor of the restored French dependency. Flushed with triumph at his return, Champlain planned to enlarge the domain of his beloved France and arranged for Nicolet to penetrate to the remotest peoples of whom rumor had reached Quebec. Thus, fourteen years after the Pilgrim fathers

11

landed on the Massachusetts coast, a French discoverer had advanced (1634) a thousand miles west, passed the straits of Mackinac, skirted the shores of Green Bay, and made his landfall in the present State of Wisconsin.

Both Champlain and his envoy supposed that the "People of the Sea," whom they sought, were dwellers in Asia, or on the shores of the western ocean; hence the provision of the damask robe, and the disappointment at finding savages instead of Moguls, fresh-water lakes instead of southern seas. During his thirteen months of absence from Quebec Nicolet may have wandered farther than we know. The Jesuit letter of 1640 says: "Sieur Nicolet, who has advanced farthest into these so distant countries, has assured me that if he had sailed three days' journey farther upon a great river which issues from this lake he would have found the sea." Does this imply the discovery of the Mississippi? We think it probable that the "great river which issues from this lake [Michigan]" was the Fox, whence in three days he might have reached a westward-flowing stream that would ultimately lead to the sea. This was his interpretation of the information from the Winnebago, whose language he but imperfectly understood. After a winter's sojourn among them, he returned to Quebec and reported the discoveries he had made.

This was his last westward journey. Settling at Three Rivers, he founded a Canadian family, among whose descendants were those who carried the flag of New France far out upon the plains of the Saskatchewan, though they never saw the western ocean. In going to Quebec in 1642 on an errand of mercy for an Indian captive, Nicolet's boat was capsized by a treacherous breeze, and he was lost in the stormy waters. His eulogist says: "This was not the first time that this man had exposed himself to death for the salvation and weal of the Savages."

We owe our knowledge of Nicolet's explorations to the

series of reports of missionary operations in North America under the auspices of the Jesuit order, that are known as the *Jesuit Relations*. After the return of the French to the shores of the St. Lawrence in 1632 all missionary enterprises in Canada were placed under the control of the Society of Jesus. Each year Jesuit missionaries wrote from their remote stations throughout the continent reports of their work, which were arranged by the superior into a continuous narrative and published at Paris in an annual volume. These small yearly volumes issued by the Parisian house of Sébastien Cramoisy were eagerly read by the pious supporters of French missions and had a wide circulation. In 1673 their issue was stopped, and later these *Relations* became exceedingly rare, accessible only in the collections of bibliophiles or in the larger libraries. Their importance for the study of Canadian history caused the Canadian Government in 1858 to issue a reprint of the entire series. No complete English edition, however, appeared until 1896, when under the editorial supervision of Dr. Reuben G. Thwaites the *Jesuit Relations and Allied Documents*, 1610–1791, began to be published by Burrows Brothers, of Cleveland, Ohio. The series was completed in 1903 and comprises seventy-three volumes. These are bilingual in form, the French (sometimes Latin) text appearing on the left-hand page, the English translation on the right. Besides a reprint of the original *Jesuit Relations*, this series contains much hitherto unpublished material from original manuscripts of Jesuit missionaries. Full bibliographical indications and illustrative material add to the value of the edition.

As a result of the reawakened interest in the *Jesuit Relations* during the latter half of the nineteenth century, the name of Jean Nicolet began to appear in our histories. John Gilmary Shea, in his *History of the Discovery of the Mississippi* (1853), cited a passage from the *Relation* of 1642 describing

Nicolet's voyage. The following year, in an article on "Indian Tribes in Wisconsin," appearing in *Wisconsin Historical Collections*, III. 125–129, Shea again called attention to Nicolet's remarkable voyage, placing it in the year 1639. This date was adopted by historians until 1876, when Benjamin Sulte, a careful student of Canadian origins, proved from church registers and other contemporary documents that Nicolet visited Wisconsin in 1634. Sulte's article was published in *Wisconsin Historical Collections*, VIII. 188–194, and his conclusions regarding the date are generally accepted. Two other articles resulting from investigations into Nicolet's life and antecedents appeared in volume XI. of the same series, pp. 1–25. Consul W. Butterfield, in his *History of the Discovery of the Northwest by Jean Nicolet in* 1634 (Cincinnati, 1881), embodied the results of careful study of all the known data on Nicolet's career.

The *Jesuit Relations* make several references to Nicolet's explorations. The selection we publish is from the *Relation* of 1642, which was written by Father Vimont, a personal friend and admirer of the great explorer. It is found in the Thwaites edition in volume XXIII., pp. 275–279.

THE JOURNEY OF JEAN NICOLET, 1634

I WILL now speak of the life and death of Monsieur Nicollet, interpreter and agent for the Gentlemen of the Company of New France. He died ten days after the Father,[1] and had lived in this region twenty-five years. What I shall say of him will aid to a better understanding of the country. He came to New France in the year 1618; and forasmuch as his nature and excellent memory inspired good hopes of him, he was sent to winter with the Island Algonquins, in order to learn their language.[2] He tarried with them two years, alone of the French, and always joined the barbarians in their excursions and journeys, undergoing such fatigues as none but eyewitnesses can conceive; he often passed seven or eight days without food, and once, full seven weeks with no other nourishment than a little bark from the trees. He accompanied four hundred Algonquins, who went during that time to make peace with the Hyroquois,[3] which he successfully accomplished; and would to God that it had never been broken, for then we should not now be suffering the calamities which move us to groans, and which must be an extraordinary impediment in the way of converting these tribes. After this treaty of peace, he went to live eight or nine years with the Algonquin Nipissiriniens,[4] where he passed for one of that nation, taking part in the very frequent councils of those tribes, having his own separate cabin and

[1] Father Charles Raymbault, for whom see the succeeding document.

[2] The "Island Algonquins" were the tribe occupying a large island in Ottawa River, known as Allumettes, ruled by a chief called Le Borgne (the one-eyed). This chieftain exacted tribute of all voyagers up or down the Ottawa, and was well known to the early French explorers.

[3] Hyroquois or Iroquois, a powerful confederation of five Indian tribes dwelling south of Lake Ontario. Nothing is known of this specific peace (or truce) save what is here narrated. The colony of New France struggled against the Iroquois during the whole first century of its existence.

[4] The Nipissing Indians were a tribe of Algonquian stock dwelling north of the lake (in the present province of Ontario) to which they gave their name.

household, and fishing and trading for himself. He was
finally recalled, and appointed agent and interpreter. While
in the exercise of this office, he was delegated to make a journey to the nation called People of the Sea,[1] and arrange peace
between them and the Hurons, from whom they are distant
about three hundred leagues westward. He embarked in the
Huron country,[2] with seven savages; and they passed by many
small nations, both going and returning. When they arrived
at their destination, they fastened two sticks in the earth,
and hung gifts thereon, so as to relieve these tribes from the
notion of mistaking them for enemies to be massacred. When
he was two days' journey from that nation, he sent one of
those savages to bear tidings of the peace, which word was
especially well received when they heard that it was a European who carried the message; they despatched several young
men to meet the Manitouiriniou—that is to say, "the wonder-
ful man." They meet him; they escort him, and carry all
his baggage. He wore a grand robe of China damask, all
strewn with flowers and birds of many colors. No sooner
did they perceive him than the women and children fled, at
the sight of a man who carried thunder in both hands—for
thus they called the two pistols that he held. The news of
his coming quickly spread to the places round about, and
there assembled four or five thousand men. Each of the
chief men made a feast for him, and at one of these banquets
they served at least sixscore beavers. The peace was concluded; he returned to the Hurons, and some time later to the
Three Rivers,[3] where he continued his employment as agent
and interpreter, to the great satisfaction of both the French and
the savages, by whom he was equally and singularly loved.

[1] The Winnebago Indians dwelling on the shore of Green Bay. The French
called them "Puants," a translation of their aboriginal name, which signified
"ill-smelling or dirty water," a variation of the word applied to the sea. The
Winnebago were of Dakotan stock, and before Nicolet's day had occupied all
of southern Wisconsin and northern Illinois.

[2] The Huron, of Iroquoian origin, occupied the peninsula between Lake
Erie and the southern end of Georgian Bay. The earliest French missions were
founded in their villages and were familiar to early westward explorers.

[3] Three Rivers (Trois Rivières), on the St. Lawrence, at the mouth of St.
Maurice River, was the third post of importance in the colony of New France.

THE JOURNEY OF RAYMBAULT AND JOGUES
TO THE SAULT, BY FATHER LALEMANT, 1641

INTRODUCTION

DURING the early part of the seventeenth century the Huron mission was the centre for Western enterprise and discovery. This mission was founded in 1615 by the Recollect fathers, who in 1625 called Jesuit missionaries to their aid. During the occupation of New France by the English (1629–1632) this mission served as a refuge for the interpreters and adventurers scattered among the interior tribes, and after the reoccupation by the French (1632) was assigned to the exclusive care of the Jesuits. They maintained the mission with great effectiveness, until its disastrous overthrow at the hands of the Iroquois in 1649 and 1650. The Huron country was situated between Georgian Bay and Lake Simcoe, along the Wye and Severn rivers, bordering on Matchedash and Nottawasaga bays, in the present province of Ontario. The Huron were docile and gentle, and village after village became the home of a "black-gown" missionary, and the site of a rude bark chapel. In 1639 a central station, named Ste. Marie, was established upon the Wye; this was a large, substantially built village surrounded by a moat whose outlines are visible to the present day. From Ste. Marie attempts were made to discover distant tribes and open the way for further missionary enterprises. As younger Jesuits sought the promising American field, plans were made to preach the gospel to the Algonquian tribes who surrounded the Huron on every side. Among those chosen for this new enterprise was Father Charles Raymbault, a Norman youth, who, after a novitiate at Rouen, arrived in Canada in the summer of 1637. Three years he tarried in the colony to make himself master of the Algonquian tongue, being stationed for a time at Quebec and for a time at Three Rivers. Late in the autumn of 1640 he arrived at Huronia and was assigned to his field of labor among the Nipissing Indians, whose winter hunting-grounds lay adjacent to the villages of the Huron, the two tribes being on friendly terms. From one camp to another, throughout the cold of a Canadian winter, Father Raymbault wandered, willing to starve or freeze might he but snatch some souls from the gates of Hell. With the coming of the tardy spring, the Nipissing returned to their villages on the northern shore of Lake Nipissing, accompanied by their faithful missionary.

Meanwhile in the Huron mission was laboring Father Isaac Jogues, a friend and early comrade of Raymbault, who, originally from Orleans, had made his novitiate at Rouen and Paris. He had come to New France a year earlier than his colleague, and, assigned at once to Huronia, had greatly aided in the founding of Ste. Marie. After its completion he had attempted an unsuccessful mission to the Petun or Tobacco Huron, ancestors of the modern Wyandot Indians. Upon his return he found Raymbault en route to his sojourn among the Nipissing. The latter mission was terminated for the time by the resolve of that tribe to celebrate an elaborate ceremony known as the feast for the dead. Invitations had been sent throughout the Algonquian Northwest; and on the shore of Lake Huron, sixty miles northwest of the Huron villages, there assembled by the 1st of September, 1641, two thousand savages from the region of the upper lakes. Thither Father Raymbault came with his Nipissing, while from the Huron villages the other "black gowns" sought the concourse.

Under the vivid pen of the Jesuit historian the description of this festival reads like a page strayed from a Grecian epic —so mighty were the combats, so virile the games, so plaintive the chants, and so agile the dances of these barbarians. This is a picture of the primitive Indians, before the white man's fire-water and epidemics had enfeebled their bodies and lowered their morals. Among their amusements we even find the greased pole of our own rude forefathers; and under the guise of mourning their dead they displayed many feats of valor and indulged in hearty feasts.

Among the participants in the festival were a tribe of Indians who had come from a distance of a hundred or more leagues and who reported themselves to be dwellers beside the great strait where the waters leap from the upper or "Superior" lake into the basin of Lake Huron. The Jesuit fathers, having eagerly made friends with these distant tribesmen, were invited to accompany them to their village, whereupon Raymbault and Jogues were chosen for the honor of the voyage. In the following pages the narrative of their journey is told—the first description of the Sault Ste. Marie and its aborigines, whose name yet remains as a memorial of the expedition.

After returning to Huronia Raymbault essayed a further mission to the Nipissing, but his enfeebled condition made rest imperative. Jogues begged to be allowed to accompany him to Quebec. There the invalid missionary passed away, October 22, 1642. For Jogues was reserved a martyr's fate and fame. Captured by the Iroquois on his return route to the Huron mission, he was tortured as a prisoner until rescued by the Dutch of Albany, who sent him back to France. Thence in June, 1644, he again sought Quebec, and was finally massacred by the Iroquois when he essayed a mission to their country. The portion of his biography which forms a part of the history of New York is set forth, in connection with portions of his narrative writings, in an earlier volume of this series, *Narratives of New Netherland*, pp. 235–263.

The following account of the discovery of Sault Ste. Marie in 1641 is taken from the second part of the *Jesuit Relation* of 1642, which was written from the country of the Huron by Father Jerome Lalemant. In all probability he had with him, as he wrote, the original narratives of the discoverers themselves. Certainly the narrative must be regarded as first-hand material, since the writer was present both at the departure and at the return of Raymbault and Jogues, and heard their adventures from their own lips. The passage we here present is from Thwaites, *Jesuit Relations*, XXIII. 223–227.

THE JOURNEY OF RAYMBAULT AND JOGUES
TO THE SAULT, 1641

In this gathering of so many assembled nations,[1] we strove to win the affections of the chief personages by means of feasts and presents. In consequence of this, the Pauoiti-goueieuhak invited us to go and see them in their own country. (They are a nation of the Algonquin language, distant from the Hurons a hundred or a hundred and twenty leagues towards the west, whom we call the inhabitants of the Sault.)[2] We promised to pay them a visit, to see how they might be disposed, in order to labor for their conversion, especially as we learned that a more remote nation whom they call Pou-teatami[3] had abandoned their own country and taken refuge with the inhabitants of the Sault, in order to remove from some other hostile nation who persecuted them with endless wars. We selected Father Charles Raymbaut to undertake this journey; and as, at the same time, some Hurons were to be of the party, Father Isaac Jogues was chosen, that he might deal with them.

They started from our house of Ste. Marie,[4] about the

---

[1] This refers to the feast for the dead described in the Introduction, *ante.*

[2] Pauoitigoueieuhak is one form of the native name of this tribe, and means "dwellers at the falls." The French translated this name into their own language and called the tribe Saulteurs (Sauteux). They are known to us as the Chippewa, one of the largest tribes of Algonquian stock. This tribe still dwells in northern Wisconsin and Minnesota, and in Ontario along the northern shore of Lake Superior.

[3] The Potawatomi in language and customs are nearly allied to the Chippewa. From their temporary refuge at Sault Ste. Marie they removed to the entrance of Green Bay, and gradually spread along the western shore of Lake Michigan, occupying the sites of Milwaukee and Chicago, and doubling around the southern end of Lake Michigan into northern Indiana and southwest Michigan. By successive cessions in the early nineteenth century they sold their lands and removed to Kansas and Oklahoma, where remnants of the tribe are now living.

[4] See Introduction, *ante,* for this mission village.

end of September, and after seventeen days of navigation on the great lake or fresh-water sea that bathes the land of the Hurons, they reached the Sault, where they found about two thousand souls, and obtained information about a great many other sedentary nations, who have never known Europeans and have never heard of God—among others, of a certain nation, the Nadouessis,[1] situated to the northwest or west of the Sault, eighteen days' journey farther away. The first nine days are occupied in crossing another great lake that commences above the Sault; during the last nine days one has to ascend a river that traverses those lands.[2] These peoples till the soil in the manner of our Hurons, and harvest Indian corn and tobacco. Their villages are larger, and in a better state of defense, owing to their continual wars with the Kiristinons, the Irinions, and other great nations who inhabit the same country.[3] Their language differs from the Algonquin and Huron tongues.

The captains of this nation of the Sault invited our Fathers to take up their abode among them. They were given to understand that this was not impossible, provided that they were well disposed to receive our instruction. After having held a council, they replied that they greatly desired that good fortune—that they would embrace us as their Brothers, and would profit by our words. But we need laborers for that purpose; we must first try to win the peoples that are nearest to us, and meanwhile pray Heaven to hasten the moment of their conversion.

Father Charles Raymbaut had no sooner returned from

[1] This was the Algonquian name for the Sioux Indians. It signified the "enemy," and indicates the hostile spirit that existed for generations between the Chippewa and the Sioux. The habitat of the latter was at the western end of Lake Superior, about the headwaters of the Mississippi, thence west to the Missouri, where several large branches of their tribe dwelt. They are still on reservations in the Dakotas along the tributaries of the Missouri.

[2] This is a description, from the reports of the Indians, of the route to the Sioux via Lake Superior, St. Louis River, and by various portages to the lakes of the upper Mississippi.

[3] Kiristinons (Christinaux) are the tribe now known as the Cree, a northern Algonquian people who roamed the plains north and west of Lake Superior to the shores of Lake Winnipeg and beyond. "Irinions" refers to the Illinois, then the largest tribe between the Ohio, the Mississippi, and Lake Michigan.

this journey to the Saut than he reëmbarked in another canoe, to seek the Nipissiriniens at their winter quarters and to continue instructing them. Father René Menard,[1] who had recently come to our assistance, went with him, for we deemed it advisable to retain Father Claude Pijart,[2] so as not to abandon entirely a number of other Algonquin bands who come here every year to winter with the Hurons.

The lake was so agitated, the winds so contrary, and the storms so great, that the canoe was compelled to put back to our port, whence it had started ; and, as the ice formed immediately afterward, it rendered the voyage impossible. Father Charles Raymbaut thereupon fell seriously ill, and has not had one day's good health since.

A great many Algonquins landed at the same time near our house, with the intention of spending the winter here. God wished to give employment to the two Fathers who knew the Algonquin language, and who remained in health, so as thereby to save some souls that he had chosen for Heaven ; for disease carried off several children, and I do not think that a single one of them died without having received baptism, whatever opposition the parents may often have shown thereto.

[1] René Ménard entered the Jesuit order in 1624 at the age of nineteen; sixteen years later he came to Quebec, and in 1641 was sent to the Huron country as a missionary for the Algonquian tribes. This was his first attempt to winter among the savages; the next spring, however, he and Pijart began a Nipissing mission that was maintained for eighteen months. Returning to Huronia, he labored there until the ruin of that mission. In 1660 he visited Lake Superior, and during the following summer, somewhere in the wilderness of northern Wisconsin, was lost in the woods and never found.

[2] Claude Pijart came to Canada three years before Ménard, was assigned to the Algonquian mission, became, in 1653, superior of his order, and acted as pastor for the town of Quebec, where he died November 16, 1680.

RADISSON'S ACCOUNT OF HIS THIRD
JOURNEY, 1658–1660 [1654–1656 ?]

INTRODUCTION

AFTER the voyages described in the preceding documents nearly twenty years elapsed before any recorded expeditions of discovery and exploration into the Northwest took place. This was due in large measure to the harassing of New France by wars with the Iroquois—raids which resulted in the complete overthrow of the flourishing Huron missions, and rendered extremely hazardous all journeying in the Upper Country.

The Iroquois, after destroying the tribes south of Lake Erie, turned their arms against the villages of the Huron, capturing numbers whom they either put to torture or transported to their own country and incorporated into their confederacy. The Jesuit missionaries were forced to flee before this storm of war, and with a few of their neophytes took refuge at Quebec. Even here they were not safe from the fury of their enemies. The island of Orleans at the foot of the Quebec bluff was raided and many Huron carried captive. All the waterways were infested by war parties. It was no longer safe to journey from Quebec up the St. Lawrence, much less to venture forth into the great wilderness of the Northwest. Nor did the Western Indians dare to bring to the colony the peltry they gathered in the northern regions; New France, whose economic life rested on the fur trade, was on the verge of ruin. Means were sought to escape the Iroquois by roundabout routes; some tribesmen crossing the network of lakes in northern Canada came down the St. Maurice to the little post at Three Rivers.

At this post there dwelt two young Frenchmen whose

exploits of exploration and discovery were to create a new epoch for the French colony in the New World. Médart Chouart, Sieur des Grosseilliers, had been born in eastern France, somewhere in the region of the Marne, so lately scarred and torn by battling armies. In 1637 he arrived in New France, and having entered the Jesuit service as a *donné* or assistant, spent nine years in the Huron mission. About the middle of the seventeenth century he removed to Three Rivers, where in 1653 he married Marguerite, widowed sister of Pierre Esprit Radisson. Radisson and Grosseilliers soon formed a congenial partnership which endured through many years of association in adventure. Radisson, although the younger, appears to have been the leader in their expeditions, and to his fertile mind and dauntless spirit we may attribute the success of their explorations.

Radisson had reached New France in the summer of 1651. The following spring, while exploring the environs of Three Rivers, he was taken prisoner by a party of Iroquois and carried to their villages, where adoption saved him from the stake. On a visit to Albany he was rescued from the savages by some Dutch merchants, who sent him home to France; thence he returned to Three Rivers in the summer of 1654. Notwithstanding his rough treatment at the hands of the Iroquois he accompanied, in 1657, a colony into their country, to escape only with difficulty in the following year.

Meanwhile Radisson yearned to see the mysterious West, whence the caravans of furs arriving at Three Rivers brought news of great lakes and streams, gentle people, and game untold. Perchance traditions of Nicolet's voyage, lingering at Three Rivers, whetted his desire to venture in the footsteps of the earlier explorer. As for Grosseilliers, his sojourn among the Huron had certainly made him familiar with the peoples of the West and taught him something of their languages and customs.

The two brothers (as they called themselves) secured the governor's permission to return with one of the trading fleets of Indian canoes that during a lull in Iroquois hostilities had, to the great joy of the colonists, reached the St. Lawrence unmolested. The voyage—known as the third Radisson voyage, the two to the Iroquois being the first and second respectively—is described in the following pages.

The date of this third voyage or rather *first Western* voyage is much in doubt; it has usually been referred to the years 1658 to 1660. The *Jesuit Relation* of 1656, however, mentions the return in that year of two nameless travellers, who had spent two years in the interior of the country; and since no mention can be found of Radisson or Grosseilliers in the register of Three Rivers during those years, some scholars assume that they were the anonymous voyagers of the *Relation*. The question of the date cannot be determined from the sources now available.

The two discoverers made a second journey to the West, in the course of which they visited Lake Superior and the headwaters of the Mississippi, and seem to have journeyed overland to Hudson Bay. They returned to New France with an immense fortune in furs, and, angered by some unjust treatment, left the colony and offered their services as explorers to the English king, Charles II. Under his patronage they made several voyages to Hudson Bay; aided in founding the great fur company of that name; returned once more to the French service and revisited Canada, where Grosseilliers thenceforth remained. Radisson, however, deserted once more to the English service, made several more voyages to Hudson Bay, and, having married an English wife, lived in London on his pension from the Hudson's Bay Company until his death about the year 1710.

The manuscripts of Radisson's narratives have had almost as adventurous a career as their author. The journals of the first four voyages to the Iroquois country and to the Northwest were written, not for publication, but for the edification and entertainment of Charles II. of England, whose patronage Radisson desired. They were written in English, the English of an unaccustomed foreigner. They came into the hands of Samuel Pepys, the diarist, who was secretary of the Admiralty under Charles II. and his brother James. Part of Pepys's manuscripts were secured by a London shopkeeper, who was using them for waste paper when, in 1750, Richard Rawlinson rescued the remnants, among them the narrative of Radisson. Rawlinson's collection came into the possession of the Bodleian Library at Oxford, where the Radisson manuscripts (Rawlinson A. 329) remained unnoticed until the last quarter of the nineteenth century. Interest having been aroused in Radisson as the founder of the Hudson's Bay Company, and the records of his voyages thither having been found in the British Museum, the Bodleian journals were brought to light, and in 1885 published under the editorship of Gideon D. Scull for the Prince Society in Boston. They awakened much interest among students of Western history, both for the charm of the narrative, for the vivid description of natural objects, and for the great daring of the adventurers. Discussion of the probable route and extent of the discovery has been voluminous, since they were the first white men known to have penetrated into the country beyond the Great Lakes. Thus they probably were the discoverers of Iowa, Minnesota, and the Canadian Northwest. They are likewise claimed as the first French discoverers of the Mississippi River. The difficulty of interpreting Radisson's text, written in a language unfamiliar to himself and some years after the completion of his journeys, adds to the differences of opinion with regard to the route and the locations described. Nevertheless the essential facts of his discovery are clear, and as the earliest description we now possess of the country beyond the upper lakes, these pages have an especial significance.

We reprint by permission of the Prince Society from their edition of Radisson's *Journals*, pp. 134–172.

RADISSON'S ACCOUNT OF HIS THIRD
JOURNEY, 1658–1660 [1654–1656?]

*Now followeth the Auxoticiat Voyage into the Great and filthy
Lake of the Hurrons, Upper Sea of the East, and Bay of
the North.*

BEING come to the 3 rivers, where I found my brother who
the yeare before came back from the lake of the Hurrons with
other french, both weare upon the point of resolution to
make a journey a purpose for to discover the great lakes
that they heard the wild men[1] speak off; yea, have seene
before, For my brother made severall journeys when the
Fathers lived about the lake of the hurrons, which was upon
the border of the sea. So my brother seeing me back from
those 2 dangerous voyages, so much by the cruelties of the
barbars as for the difficulties of the wayes, for this reason
he thought I was fitter and more faithfull for the discovery
that he was to make. He plainly told me his minde. I knowing it, longed to see myselfe in a boat. There weare severall
companies of wild men Expected from severall places, because
they promissed the yeare before, and [to] take the advantage
of the Spring (this for to deceive the Iroquoits, who are allwayes in wait for to destroy them), and of the rivers which is
by reason of the melting of the great snows, which is onely
that time, For otherwise no possibility to come that way because for the swift streams that runs in summer, and in other
places the want of watter, so that no boat can come through.
We soone see the performance of those people, For a company came to the 3 rivers where we weare. They tould us
that another company was arrived att Mont Royal,[2] and that
2 more weare to come shortly, the one to the Three Rivers, the

---

[1] The French habitually spoke of the Indians as "sauvages," savages;
Radisson, whose use of English was not idiomatic, translates the idea into the
term "wild" (or uncivilized) men.

[2] Montreal, named from the peak that dominates its site, was founded in
1642 as a religious colony by Maisonneuve and his associates. It became the
great fur-trade market of New France.

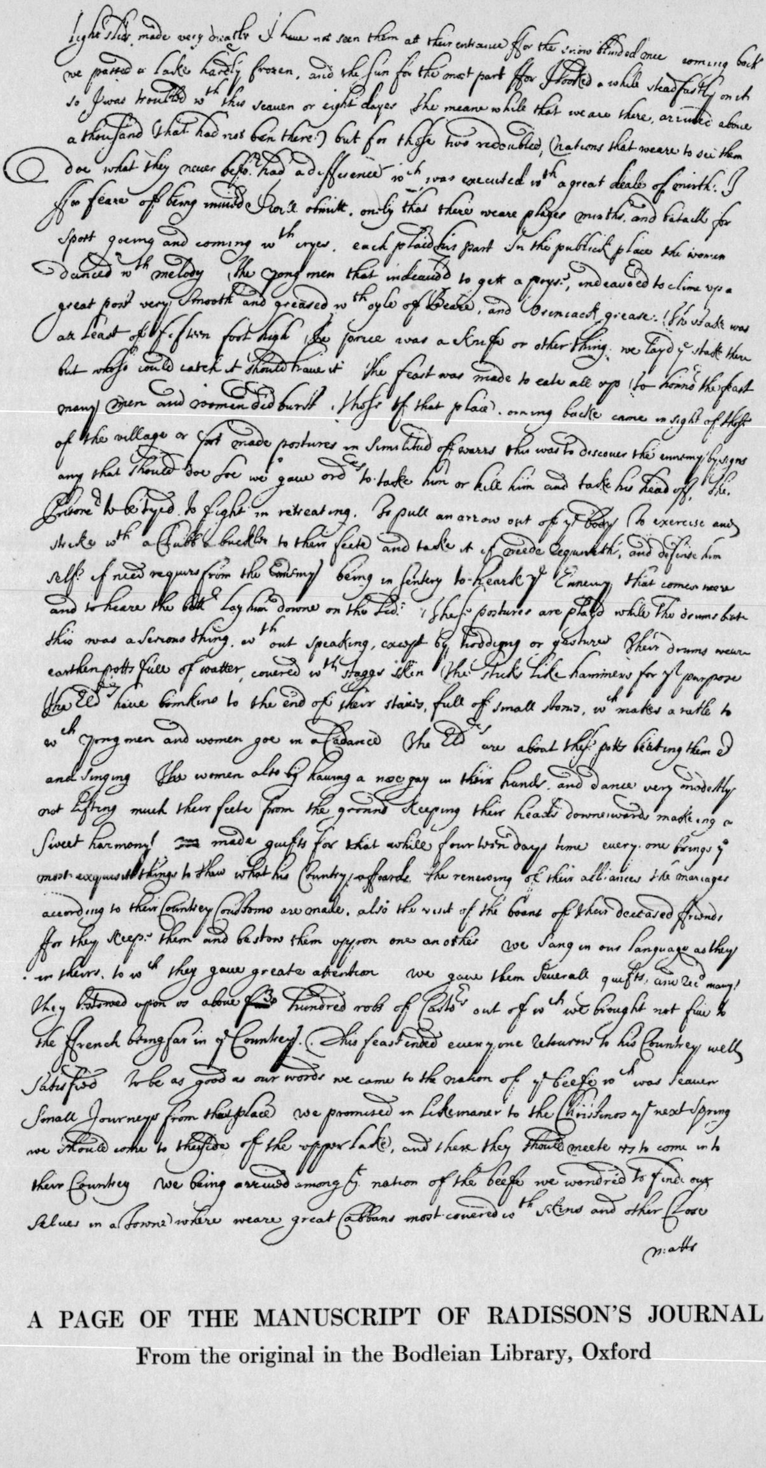

other to Saegne, a river of Tudousack,[1] who arrived within
2 dayes after.   They divided themselves because of the scant
of provision; For if they weare together they could not have
victualls enough.   Many goes and comes to Quebecq for
to know the resolution of mr Governor, who together with the
Fathers thought fitt to send a company of French to bring
backe, if possible, those wildmen the next yeare, or others,
being that it is the best manna of the countrey by which the
inhabitants doe subsist, and makes the French vessells to
come there and goe back loaden with merchandises for the
traffique of furriers who comes from the remotest parts of the
north of America.

As soone as the resolution was made, many undertakes the
voyage; for where that there is lucre there are people enough
to be had.   The best and ablest men for that businesse weare
chosen.   They make them goe up the 3 rivers with the band
that came with the Sacques.   There take those that weare
most capable for the purpose.   Two Fathers weare chosen to
conduct that company, and endeavoured to convert some of
those foraigners of the remotest country to the Christian
faith.   We no sooner heard their designe, but saw the effects
of the businesse, which effected in us much gladnesse for the
pleasure we could doe to one another, and so abler to oppose
an ennemy if by fortune we should meet with any that would
doe us hurt or hinder us in our way.

About the midle of June we began to take leave of our
company and venter our lives for the common good.   We
find 2 and 30 men, some inhabitants, some Gailliards[2] that
desired but doe well.   What fairer bastion then a good tongue,
especially when one sees his owne chimney smoak, or when
we can kiss our owne wives or kisse our neighbour's wife with
ease and delight?   It is a strange thing when victualls are
wanting, worke whole nights and dayes, lye downe on the
bare ground, and not allwayes that hap, the breech in the watter, the feare in the buttocks, to have the belly empty, the
wearinesse in the bones, and drowsinesse of the body by the
bad weather that you are to suffer, having nothing to keepe
you from such calamity.

[1] The River Saguenay, at whose mouth is the port Tadoussac.
[2] "Gaillard" means a merry fellow or a jolly companion.

Att last we take our journey to see the issue of a prosperous adventure in such a dangerous enterprise. We resolved not to be the first that should complaine. The French weare together in order, the wildmen also, saving my brother and I that weare accustomed to such like voyages, have foreseene what happened afterwards. Before our setting forth we made some guifts, and by that means we weare sure of their good will, so that he and I went into the boats of the wild men. We weare nine and twenty french in number and 6 wildmen. We embarked our traine in the night, because our number should not be knowne to some spyes that might bee in some ambush to know our departure; For the Iroquoits are allwayes abroad. We weare 2 nights to gett to mont royall, where 8 Octanac[1] stayed for us and 2 French. If not for that company, we had passed the river of the meddowes,[2] which makes an isle of Mont royall and joines itselfe to the lake of St. Louis, 3 leagues further then the hight of that name.

We stayed no longer there then as the french gott themselves ready. We tooke leave without noise of Gun. We cannot avoid the ambush of that eagle, which is like the owle that sees better in the night then in the day. We weare not sooner come to the first river, but our wildmen sees 5 sorts of people of divers countrys laden with marchandise and gunns, which served them for a shew then for defence if by chance they should be sett on. So that the glorie begins to shew itsselfe, no order being observed among them. The one sings, the other before goes in that posture without bad encounter. We advanced 3 dayes. There was no need of such

[1] The Ottawa Indians were a branch of the Algonquian stock, first encountered by the French on the islands in Lake Huron. Later they fled westward before the pressure of the Iroquois, and after brief sojourns at Mackinac and in the interior of Wisconsin located for a time on Chequamegon Bay. Still later they returned to the vicinity of Mackinac, which became their permanent habitat. A remnant of this tribe lives at present on Little Traverse Bay. The Ottawa were traders, and acted as middlemen between the French and the farther tribesmen. Hence the great flotillas coming down to Canada with furs were said to come from the Ottawa, while the region of the upper lakes was known as the Ottawa country.

[2] This stream is still called River des Prairies, separating Montreal and Jesus islands.

a silence among us. Our men composed onely of seaven score men, we had done well if we had kept together, not to goe before in the river,[1] nor stay behind some 2 or 3 leagues. Some 3 or 4 boats now and then to land to kill a wild beast, and so putt themselves into a danger of their lives, and if there weare any precipice the rest should be impotent to helpe. We warned them to looke to themselves. They laughed att us, saying we weare women; that the Iroquoits durst not sett on them. That pride had such power that they thought themselves masters of the earth; but they will see themselves soone mistaken. How that great God that takes great care of the most wild creatures, and will that every man confesses his faults, and give them grace to come to obedience for the preservation of their lives, sends them a remarquable power and ordnance, which should give terrour and retinue to those poore misled people from the way of assurance.

As we wandered in the afforesaid manner all a sunder, there comes a man alone out of the wood with a hattchett in his hand, with his brayer, and a cover[2] over his shoulders, making signes aloud that we should come to him. The greatest part of that flock shewed a palish face for feare att the sight of this man, knowing him an ennemy. They approached not without feare and apprehension of some plot. By this you may see the boldnesse of those buzards, that think themselves hectors when they see but their shadowes, and tremble when they see a Iroquoit. That wild man seeing us neerer, setts him downe on the ground and throwes his hattchett away and raises againe all naked, to shew that he hath no armes, desires them to approach neerer for he is their friend, and would lose his life to save theirs. Hee shewed in deed a right captayne for saveing of men that runned to their ruine by their indiscretion and want of conduct; and what he did was out of meere piety, seeing well that they wanted wit, to goe so like a company of bucks, every one to his fancy, where his litle experience leads him, nor thinking that danger wherin they

---

[1] The adventurers were ascending Ottawa River, the usual route to the Upper Country. Some commentators have asserted that Radisson and Grosseilliers took the St. Lawrence route through the lower lakes; but that view is now generally discarded.

[2] The Indian was clad in a blanket (cover) and breech-cloth (brayer).

weare, shewing by their march they weare no men, for not fearing. As for him, he was ready to die to render them service and prisoner into their hands freely. "For," saith he, "I might have escaped your sight, but that I would have saved you. I feare," sayth he, "not death"; so with that comes downe into the watter to his midle. There comes many boats about him, takes him into one of the boats, tying a coard fast about his body. There is he fastned. He begins to sing his fatal song that they call a nouroyall. That horrid tone being finished, makes a long, a very long speech, saying,

Brethren, the day the sunne is favourable to mee, appointed mee to tell you that yee are witlesse before I die, neither can they escape their ennemys, that are spred up and downe everywhere, that watches all moments their coming to destroy them. Take great courage, brethren, sleepe not; the ennemy is att hand. They wait for you; they are soe neare that they see you, and heare you, and are sure that you are their prey. Therefore I was willing to die to give you notice. For my part that what I have ben I am a man and commander in the warrs, and tooke severall prisoners; yet I would put meselfe in death's hands to save your lives. Believe me; keepe you altogether; spend not your powder in vaine, thinking to frighten your enemys by the noise of your guns. See if the stoanes of your arrowes be not bent or loose; bend your bowes; open your ears; keepe your hattchetts sharpe to cutt trees to make you a fort; doe not spend soo much greas to greas yourselves, but keep it for your bellies. Stay not too long in the way. It 's robbery to die with conduct.

That poore wretch spake the truth and gave good instructions, but the greatest part did not understand what he said, saving the hurrons that weare with him, and I, that tould them as much as I could perceive. Every one laughs, saying he himself is afraid and tells us that story. We call him a dogg, a woman, and a henne. We will make you know that we weare men, and for his paines we should burne him when we come to our country. Here you shall see the brutishnesse of those people that think themselves valliant to the last point. No comparison is to be made with them for vallour, but quite contrary. They passe away the rest of that day with great exclamations of joy, but it will not last long.

That night wee layd in our boats and made not the ketle boyle, because we had meat ready dressed. Every boat is tyed up in the rushes, whether out of feare for what the prisoner told them, or that the prisoner should escape, I know not. They went to sleepe without any watch. The French began to wish and moane for that place from whence they came from. What will it be if wee heare yeatt cryes and sorrows after all? Past the breake of day every one takes his oare to row; the formost oares have great advantage. We heard the torrent rumble, but could not come to the land that day, although not farr from us. Some twelve boats gott afore us. These weare saluted with guns and outcrys. In the meane while one boat runs one way, one another; some men lands and runs away. We are all put to it; non knowes where he is, they are put to such a confusion. All those beasts gathers together againe frighted. Seeing no way to escape, gott themselves all in a heape like unto ducks that sees the eagle come to them.

That first feare being over a litle, they resolved to land and to make a fort with all speed, which was done in lesse then two houres. The most stupidest drowsy are the nimblest for the hattchett and cutting of trees. The fort being finished, every one maketh himselfe in a readiness to sustaine the assault if any had tempted. The prisoner was brought, who soone was despatched, burned and roasted and eaten. The Iroquoits had so served them, as many as they have taken. We mist 20 of our company, but some came safe to us, and lost 13 that weare killed and taken in that defeat. The Iroquoite finding himselfe weake would not venture, and was obliged to leave us least he should be discovered and served as the other. Neverthelesse they shewed good countenances, went and builded a fort as we have done, where they fortified themselves and feed on human flesh which they gott in the warres. They weare afraid as much as we, but far from that; For the night being come, every one imbarks himselfe, to the sound of a low trumpet, by the help of the darknesse. We went to the other side, leaving our marchandises for our ransome to the ennemy that used us so unkindly. We made some cariages that night with a world of paines. We mist 4 of our boats, so that we must alter our equipages. The wildmen complained much that the French could not swime, for that they might be together. The French seeing that they weare not able to undergo such a voyage, they consult together and for conclusion resolved to give an end to such labours and dangers; moreover, found themselves incapable to follow the wildmen who went with all the speed possible night and day for the feare that they weare in. The Fathers, seeing our weaknesse, desired the wildmen that they might have one or two to direct them, which by no means was granted, but bid us doe as the rest. We kept still our resolution, and knowing more tricks then they, would not goe back, which should be but disdainful and prejudiciall. We told them so plainly that we would finish that voyage or die by the way. Besides that the wildmen did not complaine of us att all, but incouraged us. After a long arguing, every one had the liberty to goe backwards or forwards, if any had courage to venter himselfe with us. Seeing the great difficulties, all with one consent went back againe, and we went on.

The wildmen weare not sorry for their departure, because of their ignorance in the affaire of such navigation. It 's a great alteration to see one and 30 reduced to 2. We encouraged one another, both willing to live and die with one another; and that [is] the least we could doe, being brothers. Before we [went] to the lake of the hurrons we had crosses enough, but no encounter. We travelled onely in the night in these dangerous places, which could not be done without many vexations and labours. The vanity was somewhat cooler for the example we have seene the day before. The hungar was that tormented us most; for him we could not goe seeke for some wild beasts. Our chiefest food was onely some few fishes which the wildmen caught by a line, may be two dozens a whole day, no bigger then my hand.

Being come to the place of repose, some did goe along the water side on the rocks and there exposed ourselves to the rigour of the weather. Upon these rocks we find some shells, blackish without and the inner part whitish by reason of the heat of the sun and of the humidity. They are in a maner glued to the rock;[1] so we must gett another stone to

---

[1] Apparently the punctuation should be, a period after " whitish " and a comma after " humidity."

gett them off by scraping them hard. When we thought to
have enough [we] went back again to the Cottages, where
the rest weare getting the litle fishes ready with trips,[1] gutts
and all. The kittle was full with the scraping of the rocks,
which soone after it boyled became like starch, black and clam-
mie and easily to be swallowed. I think if any bird had
lighted upon the excrements of the said stuff, they had stuckt
to it as if it weare glue. In the fields we have gathered severall
fruits, as goosberyes, blackberrys, that in an houre we
gathered above a bushell of such sorte, although not as yett
full ripe. We boyled it, and then every one had his share.
Heere was daintinesse slighted. The belly did not permitt us
to gett on neither shoos nor stockins, that the better we
might goe over the rocks, which did [make] our feet smart [so]
that we came backe. Our feet and thighs and leggs weare
scraped with thorns, in a heape of blood. The good God
looked uppon those infidels by sending them now and then a
beare into the river, or if we perceived any in an Isle forced
them to swime, that by that means we might the sooner kill
them. But the most parts there abouts is so sterill that there
is nothing to be seene but rocks and sand, and on the high
wayes but deale trees that grow most miraculously, for that
earth is not to be seene than can nourish the root, and most of
them trees are very bigg and high. We tooke a litle refreshment in a place called the lake of Castors, which is some 30
leagues from the first great lake.[2] Some of those wildmen hid
a rest[3] as they went down to the French; but the lake was
so full of fishes we tooke so much that served us a long while.

We came to a place where weare abundance of Otters, in
so much that I believe all gathered to hinder our passage.
We killed some with our arrows, not daring to shoote because
we discovered there abouts some tracks, judging to be our
ennemy by the impression of their feet in the sand. All
knowes there one another by their march, for each hath his

---

[1] "Tripe des roches." This is a species of lichen that in extremity of
hunger is scraped from rocks and eaten. While unpalatable, it is capable of sus-
taining life.

[2] Lake of Castors (Beaver Lake) is the present Lake Nipissing, en route to
the "first great lake" (Huron).

[3] *I. e.*, made a cache.

proper steps, some upon their toes, some on their heele, which is natural to them, for when they are infants the mother warpeth them to their mode. Heer I speake not of the horrid streams we passed, nor of the falls of the water, which weare of an incredible height. In some parts most faire and delicious, where people formerly lived onely by what they could gett by the bow and arrows. We weare come above 300 leagues allwayes against the streame, and made 60 carriages, besides drawing,[1] besides the swift streams we overcame by the oares and poles to come to that litle lake of Castors which may be 30 or 40 leagues in compasse. The upper end of it is full of Islands, where there is not time lost to wander about, finding wherewith all to make the kettle boyle with venison, great bears, castors and fishes, which are plenty in that place. The river that we goe to the great lake is somewhat favorable.[2] We goe downe with ease and runing of the watter, which empties itsselfe in that lake in which we are now coming in. This river hath but 8 high and violent streams, which is some 30 leagues in length. The place where we weare is a bay all full of rocks, small isles, and most between wind and water with an infinite [number] of fishes, which are seene in the water so cleare as christiall. That is the reason of so many otters, that lives onely uppon fish. Each of us begins to looke to his bundle and merchandizes and prepare himselfe for the bad weather that uses to be on that great extent of water. The wildmen finds what they hid among the rocks 3 months before they came up to the french.[3] Heere we are stiring about in our boats as nimble as bees and divided ourselves into 2 companys. Seaven boats went towards west norwest and the rest to the South.

After we mourned enough for the death of our deare countrymen that weare slained coming up, we take leave of each other with promise of amitie and good correspondence

[1] Radisson here distinguishes between portages (carriages), when all canoes were unloaded and dragged around the obstruction, and *décharges* (drawings), when the canoe's load was lightened so that it could in that condition be drawn over the shallows or through the rapids.

[2] Formerly Rivière des Français, it is now known as French River, emptying into Georgian Bay.

[3] Radisson means before they came down to the French merchants at Three Rivers.

one with another, as for the continuance of peace, as for the assistance of strength, if the enemy should make an assault. That they should not goe to the french without giving notice one to another and soe goe together. We that weare for the South went on severall dayes merily, and saw by the way the place where the Fathers Jesuits had heretofore lived; a delicious place, albeit we could but see it afarre off.[1] The coast of this lake is most delightfull to the minde. The lands smooth, and woods of all sorts. In many places there are many large open fields wherein, I believe, wildmen formerly lived before the destruction of the many nations which did inhabit, and tooke more place then 600 leagues about; for I can well say that from the river of Canada to the great lake of the hurrons, which is neere 200 leagues in length and 60 in breadth, as I guesse, for I have [been] round about it, plenty of fish. There are banks of sand 5 or 6 leagues from the waterside, where such an infinite deale of fish that scarcely we are able to draw out our nett. There are fishes as bigg as children of 2 years old. There is sturgeon enough and other sorte that is not knowne to us. The South part is without isles, onely in some bayes where there are some. It is delightfull to goe along the side of the watter in summer where you may pluck the ducks.

We must stay often in a place 2 or 3 dayes for the contrary winds; For [if] the winds weare anything high, we durst not venter the boats against the impetuosity of the waves, which is the reason that our voyages are so long and tedious. A great many large deep rivers empties themselves in that lake, and an infinit number of other small rivers, that cann beare boats, and all from lakes and pools which are in abundance in that country.

After we travelled many dayes we arrived att a large island[2] where we found their village, their wives and children. You must know that we passed a strait some 3 leagues beyond that place. The wildmen give it a name; it is another lake, but not so bigg as that we passed before. We calle it the lake of the staring hairs, because those that live

---

[1] The southern shore of Georgian Bay, the country of the Huron mission. See narrative of Raymbault and Jogues, *ante*.

[2] Probably Manitoulin Island, where the French first found Ottawa villages.

about it have their hair like a brush turned up. They all have a hole in their nose, which is done by a straw which is above a foot long. It barrs their faces. Their ears have ordinarily 5 holes, where one may putt the end of his finger. They use those holes in this sort : to make themselves gallant they passe through it a skrew of coper with much dexterity, and goe on the lake in that posture. When the winter comes they weare no capes[1] because of their haire tourned up. They fill those skrews with swan's downe, and with it their ears covered; but I dare say that the people doe not for to hold out the cold, but rather for pride, For their country is not so cold as the north, and other lakes that we have seene since.

It should be difficult to describe what variety of faces our arrivement did cause, some out of joy, others out of sadnesse. Neverthelesse the numbers of joyfull exceeded that of the sorrowfull. The season began to invite the lustiest to hunting. We neither desire to be idle in any place, having learned by experience that idlenesse is the mother of all evil, for it breeds most part of all sicknesse in those parts where the aire is most delightfull. So that they who had most knowledge in these quarters had familiarity with the people that live there about the last lake.

The nation that we weare with had warrs with the Iroquoits, and must trade. Our wildmen out of feare must consent to their ennemy to live in their land. It 's true that those who lived about the first lake had not for the most part the conveniency of our french merchandise, as since, which obliged most of the remotest people to make peace, considering the enemy of theirs that came as a thunder bolt upon them, so that they joyned with them and forgett what was past for their owne preservation. Att our coming there we made large guifts, to dry up the tears of the friends of the deceased. As we came there the circumjacent neighbours came to visit us, that bid us welcome, as we are so. There comes newes that there weare ennemy in the fields, that they weare seene att the great field. There is a councell called, and resolved that they should be searched and sett uppon them as [soon as] possible may be, which [was] executed speedily. I offered my service, soe went and looked for them 2 dayes;

---

[1] Caps.

finding them the 3d day, gave them the assault when they least thought off it. We played the game so furiously that none escaped.

The day following we returned to our village with 8 of our enemys dead and 3 alive. The dead weare eaten and the living weare burned with a small fire to the rigour of cruelties, which comforted the desolat to see them revenged of the death of their relations that was so served. We weare then possessed by the hurrons and Octanac; but our minde was not to stay in an island, but to be knowne with the remotest people. The victory that we have gotten made them consent to what we could desire, and because that we shewed willing[ness] to die for their defence. So we desired to goe with a company of theirs that was going to the nation of the stairing haires.

We weare wellcomed and much made of, saying that we weare the Gods and devils of the earth; that we should fournish them, and that they would bring us to their ennemy to destroy them. We tould them [we] were very well content. We persuaded them first to come peaceably, not to destroy them presently, and if they would not condescend, then would wee throw away the hattchett and make use of our thunders. We sent ambassadors to them with guifts. That nation called Poutouatemick [1] without more adoe comes and meets us with the rest, and peace was concluded. Feasts were made and dames with guifts came of each side, with a great deale of mirth.

We visited them during that winter, and by that means we made acquaintance with an other nation called Escotecke, which signified fire, a faire proper nation; they are tall and bigg and very strong.[2] We came there in the spring. When we arrived there weare extraordinary banquetts. There they never have seen men with beards, because they pull their

---

[1] The Potawatomi Indians, for whom see p. 23 *ante*, note 3.

[2] This tribe was probably the Mascoutin, an Algonquian tribe, allied to the Miami and Illinois. Their original habitat appears to have been in southeast Michigan; thence about the middle of the seventeenth century they migrated to Wisconsin and had a large village on upper Fox River. In the eighteenth century they migrated to the Wabash, and dwindled in number until they became as a tribe extinct.

haires as soone as it comes out; but much more astonished when they saw our armes, especially our guns, which they worshipped by blowing smoake of tobacco instead of sacrifice. I will not insist much upon their way of living, For of their ceremonys heere you will see a pattern.

In the last voyage that wee made I will lett you onely know what cours we runned in 3 years' time. We desired them to lett us know their neighboring nations. They gave us the names, which I hope to describe their names in the end of this most imperfect discours, at least those that I can remember. Among others they told us of a nation called Nadouecero-non,[1] which is very strong, with whome they weare in warres with, and another wandering nation, living onely uppon what they could come by. Their dwelling was on the side of the salt watter in summer time, and in the land in the winter time, for it 's cold in their country. They calle themselves Chris-tinos, and their confederats from all times, by reason of their speech, which is the same, and often have joyned together and have had companys of souldiers to warre against that great nation. We desired not to goe to the North till we had made a discovery in the South, being desirous to know what they did. They told us if we would goe with them to the great lake of the stinkings,[2] the time was come of their trafick, which was of as many knives as they could gett from the french nation, because of their dwellings, which was att the coming in of a lake called Superior, but since the destructions of many neighboring nations they retired themselves to the height of the lake. We knewed those people well. We went to them almost yearly, and the company that came up with us weare of the said nation, but never could tell punc-tually where they lived because they make the barre of the Christinos from whence they have the Castors that they bring to the french. This place is 600 leagues off, by reason of the circuit that we must doe. The hurrons and the Octa-nacks, from whence we came last, furnishes them also, and comes to the furthest part of the lake of the Stinkings, there to have light earthen pots, and girdles made of goat's hairs,

[1] Sioux.

[2] Green Bay, the habitat of the Winnebago (stinkards). See p. 16, *ante*, note 1.

and small shells[1] that grow att the sea side, with which they trim their cloath made of skin.

We finding this opportunity would not lett it slippe, but made guifts, telling that the other nation would stand in feare of them because of us. We flattered them, saying none would dare to give them the least wrong, in so much that many of the Octanacks that weare present to make the same voyage. I can assure you I liked noe country as I have that wherein we wintered; For whatever a man could desire was to be had in great plenty; viz. staggs, fishes in abundance, and all sort of meat, corne enough. Those of the 2 nations would not come with us, but turned back to their nation. We neverthelesse put ourselves in hazard, for our curiosity, of stay 2 or 3 years among that nation. We ventured, for that we understand some of their idiome and trusted to that.

We embarked ourselves on the delightfullest lake of the world. I tooke notice of their Cottages and of the journeys of our navigation, for because that the country was so pleasant, so beautifull and fruitfull that it grieved me to see that the world could not discover such inticing countrys to live in. This I say because that the Europeans fight for a rock in the sea against one another, or for a sterill land and horrid country, that the people sent heere or there by the changement of the aire ingenders sicknesse and dies thereof. Contrarywise those kingdoms are so delicious and under so temperat a climat, plentifull of all things, the earth bringing foorth its fruit twice a yeare, the people live long and lusty and wise in their way. What conquest would that bee att litle or no cost; what laborinth of pleasure should millions of people have, instead that millions complaine of misery and poverty! What should not men reape out of the love of God in converting the souls heere, is more to be gained to heaven then what is by differences of nothing there, should not be so many dangers committed under the pretence of religion! Why so many thoesoever are hid from us by our owne faults, by our negligence, covetousnesse, and unbeliefe. It's true, I confesse, that the accesse is difficult, but must say that we are like the Cockscombs of Paris, when first they begin to have

---

[1] The original wampum was made from sea-shells, bored by the Indians. After the coming of French goods, porcelain beads took the place of shell wampum.

wings, imagining that the larks will fall in their mouths roasted;[1] but we ought [to remember] that vertue is not acquired without labour and taking great paines.

We meet with severall nations, all sedentary, amazed to see us, and weare very civil. The further we sejourned the delightfuller the land was to us. I can say that [in] my lifetime I never saw a more incomparable country, for all I have ben in Italy; yett Italy comes short of it, as I think, when it was inhabited, and now forsaken of the wildmen. Being about the great sea, we conversed with people that dwelleth about the salt water,[2] who tould us that they saw some great white thing sometimes uppon the water, and came towards the shore, and men in the top of it, and made a noise like a company of swans; which made me believe that they weare mistaken, for I could not imagine what it could be, except the Spaniard; and the reason is that we found a barill broken as they use in Spaine. Those people have their haires long. They reape twice a yeare; they are called Tatarga, that is to say, buff.[3] They warre against Nadoueceronons, and warre also against the Christinos. These 2 doe no great harme to one another, because the lake is betweene both. They are generally stout men, that they are able to defend themselves. They come but once a year to fight. If the season of the yeare had permitted us to stay, for we intended to goe backe the yeare following, we had indeavoured to make peace betweene them. We had not as yett seene the nation Nadoueceronons. We had hurrons with us. Wee persuaded them to come along to see their owne nation that fled there, but they would not by any means. We thought to gett some castors there to bring downe to the French, seeing [it] att last impossible to us to make such a circuit in a twelve month's time. We weare every where much made of; neither wanted victualls, for all the different

[1] The reference is to the fabled land of Cockaigne.

[2] This is supposed to mean that somewhere near Lake Superior (the great sea) they met Indians that had been as far as Hudson Bay and had there seen ships.

[3] Buffalo Indians. There is no distinct tribe with this appellation; probably it here refers to the Indians of the plains who hunt the buffalo and war with both Sioux and Cree. Some editors think it refers to the Teton branch of the Sioux. "Tetanka" is the Siouan word for buffalo.

nations that we mett conducted us and furnished us with all necessaries. Tending to those people, went towards the South and came back by the north.

The Summer passed away with admiration by the diversity of the nations that we saw, as for the beauty of the shore of that sweet sea. Heere we saw fishes of divers, some like the sturgeons and have a kind of slice att the end of their nose some 3 fingers broad in the end and 2 onely neere the nose, and some 8 thumbs long, all marbled of a blakish collor. There are birds whose bills are two and 20 thumbs long. That bird swallows a whole salmon, keeps it a long time in his bill. We saw alsoe shee-goats very bigg. There is an animal somewhat lesse then a cow whose meat is exceeding good. There is no want of Staggs nor Buffes. There are so many Tourkeys that the boys throws stoanes att them for their recreation. We found no sea-serpents as we in other laks have seene, especially in that of d'Ontario and that of the stairing haires. There are some in that of the hurrons, but scarce, for the great cold in winter. They come not neere the upper lake. In that of the stairing haires I saw yong boy [who] was bitten. He tooke immediately his stony knife and with a pointed stick and cutts off the whole wound, being no other remedy for it. They are great sorcerors and turns the wheele.[1] I shall speake of this at large in my last voyage. Most of the shores of the lake is nothing but sand. There are mountains to be seene farre in the land. There comes not so many rivers from that lake as from others; these that flow from it are deeper and broader, the trees are very bigg, but not so thick. There is a great distance from one another, and a quantitie of all sorts of fruits, but small. The vines grows all by the river side; the lemons are not so bigg as ours, and sowrer. The grape is very bigg, greene, is seene there att all times. It never snows nor freezes there, but mighty hot; yett for all that the country is not so unwholsom, For we seldome have seene infirmed people. I will

---

[1] This is probably a reference to the wheel of feathers that is attached to the calumet, or ceremonial pipe. In the journal of his so-called fourth voyage Radisson in describing the calumet says: "There is tyed to it the tayle of an eagle all painted over with severall coulours and open like a fan, or like that makes a kind of wheele when he shuts."

speake of their manners in my last voyage, which I made in October.

We came to the strait of the 2 lakes of the stinkings and the upper lake, where there are litle isles towards Norwest, Few towards the southest, very small. The lake towards the North att the side of it is full of rocks and sand, yett great shipps can ride on it without danger. We being of 3 nations arrived there with booty, disputed awhile, For some would returne to their country. That was the nation of the fire, and would have us backe to their dwelling. We by all means would know the Christinos. To goe backe was out of our way. We contented the hurrons to our advantage with promises and others with hope, and persuaded the Octonack to keepe his resolution, because we weare but 5 small fine dayes from those of late that lived in the sault of the coming in of the said upper lake, from whence that name of salt, which is *panoestigonce* in the wild language, which heerafter we will call the nation of the salt.[1]

Not many years since that they had a cruell warre against the Nadoueseronons. Although much inferiour in numbers, neverthelesse that small number of the salt was a terror unto them, since they had trade with the French. They never have seene such instruments as the French furnished them withall. It is a proude nation, therfore would not submitt, although they had to doe with a bigger nation 30 times then they weare, because that they weare called ennemy by all those that have the accent of the Algonquin language, that the wild men call Nadoue, which is the beginning of their name. The Iroquoits have the title of bad ennemy, Maesocchy Nadoue. Now seeing that the Christinos had hattchetts and knives, for that they resolved to make peace with those of the sault, that durst not have gon hundred of leagues uppon that upper lake with assurance. They would not hearken to anything because their general resolved to make peace with those of the Christinos and an other nation that gott gunns, the noise of which had frighted them more then the bulletts that weare in them. The time approached, there came about 100 of the nation of the Sault to those that lived towards the north. The christinos gott a bigger company and fought a

---

[1] The Saulteurs or Chippewa, for whom see note 2, on p. 23, *ante*.

batail. Some weare slaine of both sids. The Captayne of
these of the Sault lost his eye by an arrow. The batail being
over he made a speech, and said that he lost his sight of one
side, and of the other he foresee what he would doe; his courage being abject by that losse, that he himselfe should be ambassador and conclud the peace.

He seeing that the Iroquoits came too often, a visit I must
confesse very displeasing, being that some [of] ours looses
their lives or liberty, so that we retired ourselves to the
higher lake neerer the nation of the Nadoueceronons, where
we weare well receaved, but weare mistrusted when many
weare seene together. We arrived then where the nation of
the Sault was, where we found some french men that came
up with us, who thanked us kindly for to come and visit them.
The wild Octanaks that came with us found some of their nations slaves, who weare also glad to see them. For all they
weare slaves they had meat enough, which they have not in
their owne country so plentifull, being no huntsmen, but altogether Fishers. As for those towards the north, they are
most expert in hunting, and live uppon nothing else the most
part of the yeare. We weare long there before we gott acquaintance with those that we desired so much, and they in
lik maner had a fervent desire to know us, as we them. Heer
comes a company of Christinos from the bay of the North
sea, to live more at ease in the midle of woods and forests, by
reason they might trade with those of the Sault and have the
Conveniency to kill more beasts.

There we passed the winter and learned the particularitie
that since wee saw by Experience. Heere I will not make a
long discours during that time, onely made good cheere and
killed staggs, Buffes, Elends, and Castors.[1] The Christinos
had skill in that game above the rest. The snow proved
favourable that yeare, which caused much plenty of every
thing. Most of the woods and forests are very thick, so that
it was in some places as darke as in a cellar, by reason of the
boughs of trees. The snow that falls, being very light, hath
not the strenght to stopp the eland, which is a mighty strong
beast, much like a mule, having a tayle cutt off 2 or 3 or 4

[1] Deer, buffalo, moose, and beaver. *Eland* was then the Dutch name for
the European elk.

thumbes long, the foot cloven like a stagge. He has a muzzle mighty bigge. I have seene some that have the nostrills so bigg that I putt into it my 2 fists att once with ease. Those that uses to be where the buffes be are not so bigg, but about the bignesse of a coach horse. The wildmen call them the litle sort. As for the Buff, it is a furious animal. One must have a care of him, for every yeare he kills some Nadoueseronons. He comes for the most part in the plaines and meddows; he feeds like an ox, and the Oriniack so but seldom he galopps. I have seene of their hornes that a man could not lift them from of the ground.[1] They are branchy and flatt in the midle, of which the wildman makes dishes that can well hold 3 quarts. These hornes fall off every yeare, and it's a thing impossible that they will grow againe. The horns of Buffs are as those of an ox, but not so long, but bigger, and of a blackish collour; he hath a very long hairy taile; he is reddish, his haire frized and very fine. All the parts of his body much [like] unto an ox. The biggest are bigger then any ox whatsoever. Those are to be found about the lake of the Stinkings and towards the North of the same. They come not to the upper lake but by chance. It's a pleasur to find the place of their abode, for they tourne round about compassing 2 or 3 acres of land, beating the snow with their feete, and coming to the center they lye downe and rise againe to eate the bows of trees that they can reach. They go not out of their circle that they have made untill hunger compells them.

We did what we could to have correspondence with that warlick nation and reconcile them with the Christinos. We went not there that winter. Many weare slained of both sides the summer last. The wound was yett fresh, wherfore it was hard to conclude peace between them. We could doe nothing, For we intended to turne back to the French the summer following. Two years weare expired. We hoped to be att the 2 years end with those that gave us over for dead, having before to come back at a year's end. As we are once in those remote countreys we cannot doe as we would. Att last we declared our mind first to those of the Sault, encourag-

---

[1] This entire description applies to the moose, which Radisson calls both "eland" and "oriniack." The latter term is a variation of *orignal*, the present French-Canadian term for moose.

ing those of the North that we are their brethren, and that we would come back and force their enemy to peace or that we would help against them. We made guifts one to another, and thwarted a land of allmost 50 leagues before the snow was melted. In the morning it was a pleasur to walke, for we could goe without racketts.[1] The snow was hard enough, because it freezed every night. When the sun began to shine we payd for the time past. The snow sticks so to our racketts that I believe our shoes weighed 30 pounds, which was a paine, having a burden uppon our backs besides.

We arrived, some 150 of us, men and women, to a river side, where we stayed 3 weeks making boats. Here we wanted not fish. During that time we made feasts att a high rate. So we refreshed ourselves from our labours. In that time we tooke notice that the budds of trees began to spring, which made us to make more hast and be gone. We went up that river 8 dayes till we came to a nation called Poutouate-nick and Matouenock; that is, the scrattchers. There we gott some Indian meale and corne from those 2 nations, which lasted us till we came to the first landing Isle. There we weare well received againe. We made guifts to the Elders to encourage the yong people to bring us downe to the French. But mightily mistaken; For they would reply, "Should you bring us to be killed? The Iroquoits are every where about the river and undoubtedly will destroy us if we goe downe, and afterwards our wives and those that stayed behinde. Be wise, brethren, and offer not to goe downe this yeare to the French. Lett us keepe our lives." We made many private suits, but all in vaine. That vexed us most that we had given away most of our merchandises and swapped a great deale for Castors. Moreover they made no great harvest, being but newly there. Beside, they weare no great huntsmen. Our journey was broaken till the next yeare, and must per force.

That summer I went a hunting, and my brother stayed where he was welcome and putt up a great deale of Indian corne that was given him. He intended to furnish the wildmen that weare to goe downe to the French if they had not enough. The wild men did not perceive this; For if they

[1] Snowshoes.

wanted any, we could hardly kept it for our use. The winter passes away in good correspondence one with another, and sent ambassadors to the nations that uses to goe downe to the french, which rejoyced them the more and made us passe that yeare with a greater pleasur, saving that my brother fell into the falling sicknesse,[1] and many weare sorry for it. That proceeded onely of a long stay in a new discovered country, and the idlenesse contributs much to it. There is nothing comparable to exercise. It is the onely remedy of such diseases. After he languished awhile God gave him his health againe.

The desire that every one had to goe downe to the French made them earnestly looke out for castors. They have not so many there as in the north part, so in the beginning of spring many came to our Isle. There weare no lesse, I believe, then 500 men that weare willing to venter themselves. The corne that my brother kept did us a world of service. The wildmen brought a quantity of flesh salted in a vesell. When we were ready to depart, heere comes strang news of the defeat of the hurrons, which news, I thought, would putt off the voyage. There was a councell held, and most of them weare against the goeing downe to the French, saying that the Iroquoits weare to barre this yeare, and the best way was to stay till the following yeare. And now the ennemy, seeing himselfe frustrated of his expectation, would not stay longer, thinking thereby that we weare resolved never more to go downe, and that next yeare there should be a bigger company, and better able to oppose an ennemy. My brother and I, seeing ourselves all out of hopes of our voyage, without our corne, which was allready bestowed, and without any merchandise, or scarce having one knife betwixt us both, so we weare in a great apprehension least that the hurrons should, as they have done often, when the Fathers weare in their country, kill a frenchman.

Seeing the equipage ready and many more that thought long to depart thence for marchandise, we uppon this resolved to call a publique councell in the place; which the Elders hearing, came and advised us not to undertake it, giving many faire words, saying, "Brethren, why are you such

[1] Epilepsy.

ennemys to yourselves to putt yourselves in the hands of those
that wait for you? They will destroy you and carry you
away captives. Will you have your brethren destroyed that
loves you, being slained? Who then will come up and baptize our children? Stay till the next yeare, and then you
are like to have the number of 600 men in company with you.
Then you may freely goe without intermission. Yee shall
take the church along with you, and the Fathers and mothers
will send their children to be taught in the way of truth of
the Lord."[1] Our answer was that we would speake in publique, which granted, the day appointed is come. There
gathered above 800 men to see who should have the glorie
in a round. They satt downe on the ground. We desired
silence. The elders being in the midle and we in their midle,
my brother began to speak. "Who am I? am I a foe or a
friend? If I am a foe, why did you suffer me to live so long
among you? If I am friend, and if you take so to be, hearken
to what I shall say. You know, my uncles and brethren,
that I hazarded my life goeing up with you; if I have no
courage, why did you not tell me att my first coming here?
And if you have more witt then we, why did not you use it
by preserving your knives, your hattchetts, and your gunns,
that you had from the French? You will see if the ennemy
will sett upon you that you will be attraped like castors in
a trappe; how will you defend yourselves like men that is
not courageous to lett yourselves be catched like beasts?
How will you defend villages? with castors' skins? how will you
defend your wives and children from the ennemy's hands?"

Then my brother made me stand up, saying, "Shew them
the way to make warrs if they are able to uphold it." I
tooke a gowne of castors' skins that one of them had uppon
his shoulder and did beat him with it. I asked the others if I
was a souldier. "Those are the armes that kill, and not your
robes. What will your ennemy say when you perish without
defending yourselves? Doe not you know the French way?

[1] Grosseilliers, who had lived among the Jesuits, seems to have had some
idea of Christianizing these distant nations. The *Jesuit Relation* for 1660, describing the return of Radisson and Grosseilliers, says: "They passed the winter
on the shores of Lake Superior and were fortunate enough to baptize there two
hundred little children." *Jes. Rel.*, XLV. 235.

We are used to fight with armes and not with robes. You say that the Iroquoits waits for you because some of your men weare killed. It is onely to make you stay untill you are quite out of stocke, that they dispatch you with ease. Doe you think that the French will come up here when the greatest part of you is slained by your owne fault? You know that they cannot come up without you. Shall they come to baptize your dead? Shall your children learne to be slaves among the Iroquoits for their Fathers' cowardnesse? You call me Iroquoit. Have not you seene me disposing my life with you? Who has given you your life if not the French? Now you will not venter because many of your confederates are come to visit you and venter their lives with you. If you will deceave them you must not think that they will come an other time for shy words nor desire. You have spoaken of it first, doe what you will. For myne owne part, I will venter choosing to die like a man then live like a beggar. Having not wherewithall to defend myselfe, farewell; I have my sack of corne ready. Take all my castors. I shall live without you." And then departed that company.

They weare amazed of our proceeding; they stayed long before they spoake one to another. Att last sent us some considerable persons who bid us cheare up. "We see that you are in the right; the voyage is not broaken. The yong people tooke very ill that you have beaten them with the skin. All avowed to die like men and undertake the journey. You shall heare what the councell will ordaine the morrow. They are to meet privatly and you shall be called to it. Cheare up and speake as you have done; that is my councell to you. For this you will remember me when you will see me in your country; For I will venter meselfe with you." Now we are more satisfied then the day before. We weare to use all rhetorique to persuade them to goe downe, For we saw the country languish very much, For they could not subsist, and moreover they weare afraid of us. The councell is called, but we had no need to make a speech, finding them disposed to make the voyage and to submitt. "Yee women gett your husbands' bundles ready. They goe to gett wherewithall to defend themselves and you alive."

Our equipage was ready in 6 days. We embarked ourselves. We weare in number about 500, all stout men. We had with us a great store of castors' skins. We came to the South. We now goe back to the north, because to overtake a band of men that went before to give notice to others. We passed the lake without dangers. We wanted nothing, having good store of corne and netts to catch fish, which is plentyfull in the rivers. We came to a place where 8 Iroquoits wintered. That was the company that made a slaughter before our departure from home. Our men repented now they did not goe sooner, For it might be they should have surprised them.

Att last we are out of those lakes. One hides a caske of meale, the other his campiron, and all that could be cumbersome. After many paines and labours wee arrived to the Sault of Columest,[1] so called bccause of the Stones that are there very convenient to make tobacco pipes. We are now within 100 leagues of the french habitation, and hitherto no bad encounter. We still found tracks of men which made us still to have the more care and guard of ourselves. Some 30 leagues from this place we killed wild cowes and then gott ourselves into cottages, where we heard some guns goe off, which made us putt out our fires and imbark ourselves with all speed. We navigated all that night. About the breake of day we make a stay, that not to goe through the violent streames for feare the Ennemy should be there to dispute the passage. We landed and instantly sent 2 men to know whether the passage was free. They weare not halfe a mile off when we see a boat of the ennemy thwarting the river, which they had not done without discovering our boats, having nothing to cover our boats nor hide them. Our lightest boats shewed themselves by pursueing the ennemy. They did shoot, but to no effect, which made our two men come back in all hast. We seeing ourselves but merchandmen, so we would not long follow a man of warre, because he runned swifter then ours.

We proceeded in our way with great diligence till we came to the carriage place, where the one halfe of our men weare in readinesse, whilst the other halfe carried the baggage and the boats. We had a great alarum, but no hurt done. We

[1] Calumet Rapids of Ottawa River.

saw but one boat, but have seene foure more going up the river. Methinks they thought themselves some what weake for us, which persuaded us [of] 2 things : 1st, that they weare afraid ; 2ndly, that they went to warne their company, which thing warned us the more to make hast.

The 2nd day att evening after we landed and boyled an horiniack[1] which we killed. We then see 16 boats of our ennemy coming. They no sooner perceived us but they went on the other side of the river. It was a good looke[2] for us to have seene them. Our wildmen did not say what they thought, For they esteemed themselves already lost. We encouraged them and desired them to have courage and not [be] afraid, and so farr as I think we weare strong enough for them, that we must stoutly goe and meet them, and they should stand still. We should be alltogether, and put our castors' skins upon pearches, which could keepe us from the shott, which we did. We had foure and 20 gunns ready, and gave them to the hurrons, who knewed how to handle them better then the others. The Iroquoits seeing us come, and that we weare 5 to 1, could not imagine what to doe. Neverthelesse they would shew their courage ; being that they must passe, they putt themselves in array to fight. If we had not ben with some hurrons that knewed the Iroquoits' tricks, I believe that our wild men had runned away, leaving their fusiques[3] behind. We being neere one another, we commanded that they should row with all their strength towards them. We kept close one to another to persecut what was our intent. We begin to make outcryes and sing. The hurrons in one side, the Algonquins att the other side, the Ottanak, the panoestigons, the Amickkoick, the Nadouicenago, the ticacon,[4] and we both encouraged them all, crying out with a loud noise. The Iroquoits begin to shoot, but we made ours to goe one forwards without any shooting, and that it was the onely way of fighting. They indeed turned their backs and we followed them awhile. Then was it that we weare called devils, with great thanks and incouragements that they gave us, attributing to us the masters of warre and

---

[1] Moose.   [2] Luck.   [3] Fusees.
[4] Huron, Algonkin, Ottawa, Chippewa, Beaver, Sioux, and Kiskakon (an Ottawa clan) Indians.

the only Captaynes. We desired them to keepe good watch
and sentry, and if we weare not surprized we should come
safe and sound without hurt to the French. The Iroquoite
seeing us goe on our way, made as if they would leave us.

We made 3 carriages that day, where the ennemy could
doe us mischief if they had ben there. The cunning knaves
followed us neverthelesse pritty close. We left 5 boats behind that weare not loaden. We did so to see what inven-
tion our enemy could invent, knowing very well that his
mind was to surprise us. It is enough that we are warned
that they follow us. Att last we perceived that he was before us, which putt us in some feare; but seeing us resolut,
did what he could to augment his number. But we weare
mighty vigilent and sent some to make a discovery att every
carriage through the woods. We weare told that they weare
in an ambush, and there builded a fort below the long Sault,
where we weare to passe. Our wildmen said doubtlesse they
have gott an other company of their nation, so that some
minded to throw their castors away and returne home. We
told them that we weare almost att the gates of the French
habitation, and bid [them] therefore have courage, and that
our lives weare in as great danger as theirs, and if we weare
taken we should never escape because they knewed us, and I
because I runned away from their country having slained
some of their brethren,[1] and my brother that long since was
the man that furnished their enemy with arms.

They att last weare persuaded, and landed within a mile
of the landing place, and sent 300 men before armed. We
made them great bucklers that the shot could not pearce in
some places. They weare to be carryed if there had ben occasion for it. Being come neere the torrent, we finding the
Iroquoits lying in ambush, who began to shoot. The rest of
our company went about cutting of trees and making a fort,
whilst some brought the boats; which being come, we left
as few men as possible might bee. The rest helped to carry
wood. We had about 200 men that weare gallant souldiers.
The most weare hurrons, Pasnoestigons, and Amickkoick frequented the French for a time. The rest weare skillfull in
their bows and arrows. The Iroquoits perceiving our device,

---

[1] See Introduction, *ante*, for Radisson's experiences among the Iroquois.

resolved to fight by forceing them to lett us passe with our arms. They did not know best what to doe, being not so munished nor so many men above a hundred and fifty. They forsooke the place and retired into the fort, which was underneath the rapide. We in the meane while have slained 5 of theirs, and not one of ours hurted, which encouraged our wildmen. We bid them still to have good courage, that we should have the victory. Wee went and made another fort neere theirs, where 2 of our men weare wounded but lightly.

It is a horrid thing to heare [of] the enormity of outcryes of those different nations. The Iroquoits sung like devils, and often made salleys to make us decline. They gott nothing by that but some arrows that did incommodat them to some purpose. We foresee that such a batail could not hold out long for want of powder, of shott and arrows; so by the consent of my brother and the rest, made a speech in the Iroquoit language, indueing meselfe with armours that I might not be wounded with every bullet or arrow that the ennemy sent perpetually. Then I spoake. "Brethren, we came from your country and bring you to ours, not to see you perish unlesse we perish with you. You know that the French are men, and maks forts that cannot be taken so soone therefore cheare upp, For we love you and will die with you." This being ended, nothing but howling and crying. We brought our castors and tyed them 8 by 8, and rowled them before us. The Iroquoits finding that they must come out of their fort to the watterside, where they left their boats, to make use of them in case of neede, where indeed made an escape, leaving all their baggage behind, which was not much, neither had we enough to fill our bellyes with the meat that was left; there weare kettles, broaken gunns, and rusty hattchetts.

They being gone, our passage was free, so we made hast and endeavoured to come to our journey's end; and to make the more hast, some boats went downe that swift streame without making any carriage, hopeing to follow the ennemy; but the bad lacke was that where my brother was the boat turned in the torrent, being seaven of them together, weare in great danger, For God was mercifull to give them strength to save themselves, to the great admiration, for few can speed so well in such precipices. When they came to lande they cutt rocks. My brother lost his booke of annotations of the last yeare of our being in these foraigne nations. We lost never a castor, but may be some better thing. It 's better [that one] loose all then lose his life.

We weare 4 moneths in our voyage without doeing any thing but goe from river to river. We mett severall sorts of people. We conversed with them, being long time in alliance with them. By the persuasion of som of them we went into the great river that divides itselfe in 2, where the hurrons with some Ottanake and the wild men that had warrs with them had retired.[1] There is not great difference in their language, as we weare told. This nation have warrs against those of [the] forked river. It is so called because it has 2 branches, the one towards the west, the other towards the South, which we believe runns towards Mexico, by the tokens they gave us. Being among these people, they told us the prisoners they take tells them that they have warrs against a nation, against men that build great cabbans and have great beards and had such knives as we have had. Moreover they shewed a Decad of beads and guilded pearls that they have had from that people, which made us believe they weare Europeans. They shewed one of that nation that was taken the yeare before. We understood him not; he was much more tawny then they with whome we weare. His armes and leggs weare turned outside; that was the punishment inflicted uppon him. So they doe with them that they take, and kill them with clubbs and doe often eat them. They doe not burne their prisoners as those of the northern parts.

We weare informed of that nation that live in the other river. These weare men of extraordinary height and biggnesse, that made us believe they had no communication with them. They live onely uppon Corne and Citrulles,[2]

---

[1] This paragraph is thought by some scholars to be out of place, that it belongs to the description of the Wisconsin territory, p. 45, *ante*. Others suppose it to be in the nature of a summary of their discovery of the Mississippi, which is usually thought to be indicated by the "forked river."

[2] Citruelles are pumpkins, frequently raised by Indians.

which are mighty bigg.   They have fish in plenty throughout
the yeare.   They have fruit as big as the heart of an Oriniak,
which grows on vast trees which in compasse are three arme-
full in compasse.   When they see litle men they are affraid
and cry out, which makes many come help them.   Their arrows are not of stones as ours are, but of fish boans and other
boans that they worke greatly, as all other things.   Their
dishes are made of wood.   I having seene them, could not
but admire the curiosity of their worke.   They have great
calumetts of great stones, red and greene.   They make a
store of tobacco.   They have a kind of drink that makes them
mad for a whole day.   This I have not seene, therefore you
may believe as you please.

When I came backe I found my brother sick, as I said before.   God gave him his health, more by his courage then
by any good medicine, For our bodyes are not like those of
the wildmen.   To our purpose; we came backe to our carriage, whilst wee endeavoured to ayde our compagnions in
their extremity.   The Iroquoits gott a great way before, not
well satisfied to have stayed for us, having lost 7 of their
men; 2 of them weare not nimble enough, For our bulletts
and arrows made them stay for good and all.   Seaven of our
men weare sick, they have ben like to be drowned, and the
other two weare wounded by the Iroquoits.

The next day we went on without any delay or encounter.
I give you leave if those of mont Royall weare not overjoyed
to see us arrived where they affirme us the pitifull conditions
that the country was by the cruelty of these cruell barbars,
that perpetually killed and slaughtered to the very gate of
the French fort.   All this hindered not our goeing to the
French att the 3 rivers after we refreshed ourselves 3 dayes,
but like to pay dearly for our bold attempt.   20 inhabitants
came downe with us in a shawlopp.   As we doubled the
point of the river of the meddows we weare sett uppon by
severall of the Iroquoits, but durst not come neare us, because
of two small brasse pieces that the shalop carryed.   We tyed
our boats together and made a fort about us of castors' skins,
which kept us from all danger.   We went downe the streame
in that posture.   The ennemy left us, and did well; for our
wildmen weare disposed to fight, and our shaloupp could not

come neare them because for want of watter. We came to Quebecq, where we are saluted with the thundring of the guns and batteryes of the fort, and of the 3 shipps that weare then att anchor, which had gon back to france without castors if we had not come. We weare well traited for 5 dayes. The Governor made guifts and sent 2 Brigantins to bring us to the 3 rivers, where we arrived the 2nd day of, and the 4th day they went away.

That is the end of our 3 years' voyage and few months. After so much paine and danger God was so mercifull [as] to bring us back saf to our dwelling, where the one was made much off by his wife, the other by his friends and kindred. The ennemy that had discovered us in our goeing downe gott more company, with as many as they could to come to the passages, and there to waite for the retourne of those people, knowinge well that they could not stay there long because the season of the yeare was almost spent; but we made them by our persuasions goe downe to Quebecq, which proved well, For the Iroquoits thought they weare gone another way. So came the next day after our arrivall to make a discovery to the 3 rivers, where being perceived, there is care taken to receive them.

The French cannot goe as the wildmen through the woods, but imbarks themselves in small boats and went along the river side, knowing that if the ennemy was repulsed, he would make his retreat to the river side. Some Algonquins weare then att the habitation, who for to shew their vallour disposed themselves to be the first in the poursuit of the enemy. Some of the strongest and nimblest French kept them company, with an other great number of men called Ottanacks, so that we weare soone together by the ears. There weare some 300 men of the enemy that came in the space of a fourteen night together; but when they saw us they made use of their heels. We weare about 500; but the better to play their game, after they runned half a mile in the wood they turned againe, where then the batail began most furiously by shooting att one another.

That uppermost nation, being not used to shooting nor heare such noise, began to shake off their armours, and tooke their bows and arrows, which indeed made [more] execution then all the guns that they had brought. So seeing 50 Algonquins and 15 French keep to it, they resolved to stick to it also, which had not long lasted; For seeing that their arrows weare almost spent and they must close together, and that the enemy had an advantage by keeping themselves behind the trees, and we to fall uppon we must be without bucklers, which diminished much our company that was foremost, we gave them in spight us place to retire themselves, which they did with all speed. Having come to the watter side, where their boats weare, saw the French all in a row, who layd in an ambush to receive them, which they had done if God had not ben for us; For they, thinking that the enemy was att hand, mistrusted nothing to the contrary. The French that weare in the wood, seeing the evident danger where their countrymen layd, encouraged the Ottanaks, who tooke their armes againe and followed the enemy, who not feared that way arrived before the French weare apprehended, by good looke.

One of the Iroquoits, thinking his boat would be seene, goes quickly and putts it out of sight, and discovers himselfe, which warned the French to hinder them to goe further uppon that score. Our wildmen made a stand and fell uppon them stoutly. The combat begins a new; they see the French that weare uppon the watter come neere, which renforced them to take their boats with all hast, and leave their booty behind. The few boats that the french had brought made that could enter but the 60 French, who weare enough. The wildmen neverthelesse did not goe without their prey, which was of three men's heads that they killed att the first fight; but they left Eleven of theirs in the place, besides many more that weare wounded. They went straight to their countrey, which did a great service to the retourne of our wildmen, and mett with non all their journey, as we heard afterwards.

They went away the next day, and we stayed att home att rest that yeare. My brother and I considered whether we should discover what we have seene or no; and because we had not a full and whole discovery, which was that we have not ben in the bay of the north, not knowing anything but by report of the wild Christinos, we would make no mention of it for feare that those wild men should tell us a fibbe. We would have made a discovery of it ourselves and have an assurance, before we should discover anything of it.

The ende of the Auxotacicac voyage,
which is the third voyage.

ADVENTURES OF NICOLAS PERROT,
BY LA POTHERIE, 1665–1670

INTRODUCTION

THE year 1665 is marked by the re-establishment of the profitable fur trade of New France with the Northwest, which (as we have seen in the introduction to Radisson's *Journal, ante*) had been almost destroyed by the raids of the hostile Iroquois. The king in that summer sent his famous Carignan regiment, 1400 strong, to subdue the hostile bands and protect the pathways of commerce. Therefore a great flotilla from the Upper Country appeared upon the St. Lawrence, bringing hundreds of tribesmen to exchange their furs for the iron implements and weapons of the French, and for the much-prized blankets and silver ornaments offered by the white traders. After the great fair at Montreal had been held, and promises had been made that the Iroquois should be subdued, the great fleet of canoes prepared to return to the Upper Country, and with them went such adventurous Frenchmen as the love of gain or the lure of the unknown tempted to endure the hardships of wilderness life. Among these rangers of the woods was Nicolas Perrot, who began a life among the Indians that was destined to continue for thirty-five years and make him one of the most influential and best-informed men of his time on Indian habits and history.

Perrot had but just attained his majority when he set forth on his eventful voyage. The date of his arrival in New France is not known, but at the time of his departure he had acquired the Algonquian language and was versed in the art of winning the red men's good-will. The *Jesuit Relation* for 1665 speaks of a "Frenchman who went up the year before." This may possibly have been Perrot, but his first recorded voyage is narrated below, when he sought the Potawatomi tribesmen at Green Bay. His address and influence soon secured this important nation for the French alliance, whereupon Perrot visited the other tribes in this locality, winning alliances, good-will, and a vast influence over all the Western aborigines.

The descriptions of his adventures, although not presented in chronological form, appear to have covered the first five years (1665–1670) of Perrot's life in the Western country. In 1670 he visited the colony once more, where the governor asked him to remain in order to form part of the escort of Sieur de St. Lusson, who was preparing to go the next spring to take formal possession of all the Northwest. The record of the expedition forms a later division of this volume.

After the Sault Ste. Marie pageant of 1671 we hear no more of Perrot's activities until 1683, when he was sent to Wisconsin as accredited government agent. The following year he led a large detachment of Indian warriors from the banks of the Mississippi to reinforce Governor La Barre's unfortunate expedition into the Iroquois country. He returned to the Northwest in the spring of 1685 as commissioned commandant for Green Bay and all its dependencies, built several posts on the Mississippi, discovered the presence of lead in southwestern Wisconsin, and finally, in 1689, at Fort St. Antoine upon Lake Pepin, took possession for King Louis of all the upper Mississippi region and the country of the Sioux. It was in this period that he presented to the mission at Green Bay the beautiful silver ostensorium, the oldest relic of French occupation in the West, now in the possession of the Wisconsin Historical Society.

It was at the Green Bay mission that a great disaster overtook Perrot's fortunes, for while he was absent on Denonville's military campaign of 1687, the mission house in which $40,000 worth of his furs was stored was burned by hostile tribesmen and the means of settling with his creditors was lost.

After the departure of Denonville and the return to Canada of Count de Frontenac, in 1689, Perrot was again employed as government agent among the Northwestern tribes, whose languages and alliances he so well understood. In spite, however, of his ascendancy over these fierce warriors he was, in 1695, in great danger of being burned by the Miami, and was rescued just in time by the Foxes, who had always been his friends. He later directed his efforts toward adjusting local quarrels and rendering the Upper Country safe for traders and travellers, until the edict of 1696 recalled all commandants from the Northwest and overthrew the labor of years.

Once more, in 1701, the services of Perrot were utilized as interpreter at the great peace conference held at Montreal between the Iroquois and the nations of the upper lakes. The declining years of his life seem to have been passed at Montreal, where he was occupied in writing his *Mémoire sur les Mœurs, Coustumes et Relligion des Sauvages de l'Amérique Septentrionale*, and where he died in 1718.

His *Mémoire* remained in manuscript until 1864, when it was edited by Rev. Jules Tailhan and published at Paris. An English translation appears in E. H. Blair, *Indian Tribes of the Upper Mississippi and Region of the Great Lakes* (Cleveland, 1911), I. 25–272.

In addition to this *Mémoire* Perrot apparently kept journals of his adventures and experiences that have disappeared, but were extensively used by early Canadian historians. The one who most freely owns his debt to information from Perrot is La Potherie.

Charles Claude le Roy, sieur Bacqueville de la Potherie, was a West Indian Creole, who had influential connections at the court of Louis XIV., and received official appointments therefrom. In 1697 he was sent with the French fleet to

Hudson Bay, and on that voyage met Canadian adventurers and heroes, notably Iberville and his brothers. The succeeding year he was appointed to an important post in Canada, and arrived just in time to meet the great governor Frontenac before his death. La Potherie spent about five years in the colony, and was present in person at the great peace treaty of 1701, where all the tribes from the North and West gathered to negotiate and exchange prisoners with the Iroquois. At that assembly La Potherie and Perrot are known to have met, and without doubt the former secured from the latter both the narrative of his adventures and such notes and diaries as Perrot could furnish for the history La Potherie proposed to write. To the completion of this work Perrot's material contributed largely. The volumes appeared at Paris in 1716 under the title *Histoire de l'Amérique Septentrionale*. It acquired some measure of popularity and subsequent editions appeared in 1722 and 1753. Of the four small volumes, the second and third appear to be almost wholly reproductions of the lost journals of Nicolas Perrot, and give much fuller descriptions of his relations to the Western Indians and life among them than may be found in Perrot's own *Mémoire*. Miss Blair has incorporated an English translation of these two volumes of La Potherie in her *Indian Tribes*, as above cited. We have chosen for reproduction (with permission of the publishers, the Arthur H. Clark Company) the selection from volume I., pp. 307–339, which recounts Perrot's first years in Wisconsin, and describes the tribes as he saw them before they had been changed by the influence of white men.

ADVENTURES OF NICOLAS PERROT,
BY LA POTHERIE, 1665-1670

CHAPTER VIII

. . . ALL the Outaouak peoples[1] were in alarm. While we were waging war with the Iroquois, those tribes who dwelt about Lake Huron fled for refuge to Chagoüamikon,[2] which is on Lake Superior; they came down to Montreal only when they wished to sell their peltries, and then, trembling. The trade was not yet opened with the Outaouaks. The name of the French people gradually became known in that region, and some of the French made their way into those places where they believed that they could make some profit; it was a Peru for them.[3] The savages could not understand why these men came so far to search for their worn-out beaver robes;[4] meanwhile they admired all the wares brought to them by the French, which they regarded as extremely precious. The knives, the hatchets, the iron weapons above all, could not be sufficiently praised; and the guns so astonished them that they declared that there was a spirit within the gun, which caused the loud noise made when it was fired. It is a fact that an Esquimau from Cape Digue,[5] at 60° latitude, in the strait of Hudson Bay, displayed so

[1] As explained in note 1 on p. 36, *ante*, the Ottawa were a specific tribe of Algonquian stock; but the term here employed, "all the Outouak peoples," refers to the several Algonquian tribes that dwelt in the Upper Country, such as the Ottawa, Chippewa, Potawatomi, Menominee, Foxes, Sauk, Mascoutin, etc.

[2] Now called Chequamegon Bay, on the northern shore of Wisconsin.

[3] A reference to the immense treasure and profit secured by the Spanish from the native empire of Peru.

[4] The beaver pelts most desired by the traders were those that had been worn by the Indians, since the oil they used upon their persons rendered the furs more supple and valuable.

[5] This illustration of Esquimaux life at Cape Diggs (Digue) on Hudson Strait was derived from La Potherie's personal experience. See Introduction, *ante*.

73

much surprise to me when he saw a *gode*[1] suddenly fall, covered with blood, as the result of a gunshot, that he stood motionless with the wonder caused by a thing which seemed to him so extraordinary. The Frenchmen who traded with the Canadian tribes were often amused at seeing those people in raptures of this sort. The savages often took them [the Frenchmen] for spirits and gods; if any tribe had some Frenchmen among them, that was sufficient to make them feel safe from any injuries by their neighbors; and the French became mediators in all their quarrels. The detailed conversations which I have had with many voyageurs in those countries have supplied me with material for my accounts of those peoples; all that they have told me about them has so uniformly agreed that I have felt obliged to give the public some idea of that vast region.

Sieur Perot has best known those peoples; the governors-general of Canada have always employed him in all their schemes; and his acquaintance with the savage tongues, his experience, and his mental ability have enabled him to make discoveries which gave opportunity to Monsieur de la Salle to push forward all those explorations in which he achieved so great success. It was through his agency that the Mississippi became known.[2] He rendered very important services to the colony, made known the glory of the king among those peoples, and induced them to form an alliance with us. On one occasion, among the Pouteouatemis, he was regarded as a god. Curiosity induced him to form the acquaintance of this nation, who dwelt at the foot of the Bay of Puans. They had heard of the French, and their desire to become acquainted with them in order to secure the trade with them had induced these savages to go down to Montreal, under the guidance of a wandering Outaouak who was glad to conduct them thither.[3] The French had been described

---

[1] *Gode* is a sea-bird, probably the murre or awk, common in the North Atlantic and in the Gulf of St. Lawrence.

[2] Perrot probably saw the Mississippi before La Salle had done so; whether he had made it known before the voyage of Jolliet and Marquette in 1673 is questionable.

[3] Perrot would seem to imply that he was the first Frenchman the Potawatomi had ever seen. Either he was ignorant of the visit of Radisson and Grosseilliers and other early adventurers, or he purposely magnifies his own discoveries.

to them as covered with hair (the savages have no beards),
and they believed that we were of a different species from
other men.   They were astonished to see that we were made
like themselves, and regarded it as a present that the sky
and the spirits had made them in permitting one of the celestial beings to enter their land.   The old men solemnly smoked
a calumet[1] and came into his presence, offering it to him as
homage that they rendered to him.

After he had smoked the calumet, it was presented by
the chief to his tribesmen, who all offered it in turn to one
another, blowing from their mouths the tobacco-smoke over
him as if it were incense.   They said to him: "Thou art
one of the chief spirits, since thou usest iron; it is for thee
to rule and protect all men.   Praised be the Sun, who has
instructed thee and sent thee to our country."   They adored
him as a god; they took his knives and hatchets and incensed them with the tobacco-smoke from their mouths;
and they presented to him so many kinds of food that he
could not taste them all.   "It is a spirit," they said; "these
provisions that he has not tasted are not worthy of his lips."
When he left the room, they insisted on carrying him upon
their shoulders; the way over which he passed was made
clear; they did [not] dare look in his face; and the women
and children watched him from a distance.   "He is a spirit,"
they said; "let us show our affection for him, and he will
have pity on us."   The savage who had introduced him to
this tribe was, in acknowledgment thereof, treated as a captain.   Perot was careful not to receive all these acts of ado-
ration, although, it is true, he accepted these honors so far
as the interests of religion were not concerned.   He told
them that he was not what they thought, but only a Frenchman; that the real Spirit who had made all had given to the
French the knowledge of iron, and the ability to handle it
as if it were paste.   He said that that Spirit, desiring to show
his pity for his creatures, had permitted the French nation
to settle in their country in order to remove them from the

---

[1] The calumet was the sacred pipe of the Indians and was used in all forms
of worship and negotiation.   The word is supposed to be derived from the
Norman-French "chalumet," meaning a reed.   The heads of the calumets are
made of pipestone, the stems of hollow wood, with fantastic decorations.

blindness in which they had dwelt, as they had not known the true God, the author of nature, whom the French adored; that, when they had established a friendship with the French, they would receive from the latter all possible assistance; and that he had come to facilitate acquaintance between them by the discoveries of the various tribes which he was making. And, as the beaver was valued by his people, he wished to ascertain whether there were not a good opportunity for them to carry on trade therein.

At that time there was war between that tribe and their neighbors, the Malhominis.[1] The latter, while hunting with the Outagamis, had by mistake slain a Pouteouatemi, who was on his way to the Outagamis.[2] The Pouteouatemis, incensed at this affront, deliberately tomahawked a Malhomini who was among the Puans.[3] In the Pouteouatemi village there were only women and old men, as the young men had gone for the first time to trade at Montreal; and there was reason to fear that the Malhominis would profit by that mischance. Perot, who was desirous of making their acquaintance, offered to mediate a peace between them. When he had arrived within half a league of the village, he sent a man to tell them that a Frenchman was coming to visit them; this news caused universal joy. All the youths came at once to meet him, bearing their weapons and their warlike adornments, all marching in file, with frightful contortions and yells; this was the most honorable reception

[1] The Menominee (Malhominis) were an important tribe of Algonquian people, who have, so far as known, always dwelt in Wisconsin. When first noticed they appear to have lived on the shore of Lake Superior, whence they passed southward to the northwest shore of Green Bay. Their name was derived from the wild rice which was plentiful in their habitat and formed one of their standard articles of food. They still live in Wisconsin, either on the Keshena reservation or on farms that have been allotted to them. Many tribal members have made great progress toward civilized life.

[2] Outagami was the aboriginal name for the tribe called by the French les Reynards, by the English the Foxes. They were recent comers in Wisconsin, having been driven thither by Iroquois enmity. A valiant tribe, devoted to their own customs, they became to New France a great source of danger in the eighteenth century through a series of disastrous wars. In the course of these they removed their habitat to the Mississippi and later to Iowa, where a portion of the tribe still dwells.

[3] The Winnebago, for whom see p. 16, note 1, ante.

that they thought it possible to give him. He was not uneasy, but fired a gun in the air as far away as he could see
them; this noise, which seemed to them so extraordinary,
caused them to halt suddenly, gazing at the sun in most
ludicrous attitudes. After he had made them understand
that he had come not to disturb their repose, but to form an
alliance with them, they approached him with many gesticulations. The calumet was presented to him; and, when he
was ready to proceed to the village, one of the savages stooped
down in order to carry Perot upon his shoulders; but his
interpreter assured them that he had refused such honors
among many tribes. He was escorted with assiduous attentions; they vied with one another in clearing the path,
and in breaking off the branches of trees which hung in the
way. The women and children, who had heard "the spirit"
(for thus they call a gun), had fled into the woods. The men
assembled in the cabin of the leading war chief, where they
danced the calumet to the sound of the drum. He had them
all assemble next day, and made them a speech in nearly
these words:

Men, the true Spirit who has created all men desires to put
an end to your miseries. Your ancestors would not listen to him;
they always followed natural impulses alone, without remembering
that they had their being from him. He created them to live in
peace with their fellow-men. He does not like war or disunion;
he desires that men, to whom he has given reason, should remember
that they all are brothers, and that they have only one God, who
has formed them to do only his will. He has given them dominion
over the animals, and at the same time has forbidden them to make
any attacks on one another. He has given the Frenchmen iron,
in order to distribute it among those peoples who have not the use
of it, if they are willing to live as men, and not as beasts. He is
angry that you are at war with the Pouteouatemis; even though it
seemed that they had a right to avenge themselves on your young
man who was among the Puans, God is nevertheless offended at
them, for he forbids vengeance, and commands union and peace.
The sun has never been very bright on your horizon; you have always been wrapped in the shadows of a dark and miserable existence, never having enjoyed the true light of day, as the French
do. Here is a gun, which I place before you to defend you from
those who may attack you; if you have enemies, it will cause them

terror. Here is a porcelain collar,[1] by which I bind you to my body: what will you have to fear, if you unite yourselves to us, who make guns and hatchets, and who knead iron as you do pitch? I have united myself with the Pouteouatemis, on whom you are planning to make war. I have come to embrace all the men whom Onontio,[2] the chief of all the French who have settled in this country, has told me to join together, in order to take them under his protection. Would you refuse his support, and kill one another when he desires to establish peace between you? The Pouteouatemis are expecting many articles suited to war from the hands of Onontio. You have been so evenly matched [with them; but now] would you abandon your families to the mercy of their [fire] arms, and be at war with them against the will of the French? I come to make the discovery of [new] tribes, only to return here with my brothers,[3] who will come with me among those people who are willing to unite themselves to us. Could you hunt in peace if we give [weapons of] iron to those who furnish us beaver-skins? You are angry against the Pouteouatemis, whom you regard as your enemies, but they are in much greater number than you; and I am much afraid that the prairie people [4] will at the same time form a league against you.

The father of the Malhomini who had been murdered by the Pouteouatemis arose and took the collar that Perot had given him; he lighted his calumet, and presented it to him, and then gave it to the chief and all who were present, who smoked it in turn; then he began to sing, holding the calumet in one hand, and the collar in the other. He went out of the cabin while he sang, and, presenting the calumet and collar toward the sun, he walked sometimes backwards, sometimes forward; he made the circuit of his own cabin, went past a great number of those in the village, and finally returned to that of the chief. There he declared that he attached himself wholly to the French; that he believed in the living Spirit, who had, in behalf of all the spirits, domination over all other men who were inferior to him; that all

[1] A belt of wampum, called by the French *porcelaine*.

[2] *Onontio* was the title given by the tribesmen to the governor of New France; sometimes this term was used to refer to the king, who was called the "Great Onontio." The governor at this time was Daniel de Remy, sieur de Courcelles.

[3] Brothers is used figuratively, denoting other Frenchmen.

[4] Probably the Mascoutin, for whom see note 2 on p. 45, *ante*.

his tribe had the same sentiments; and that they asked only the protection of the French, from whom they hoped for life and for obtaining all that is necessary to man.

The Pouteouatemis were very impatient to learn the fate of their people who had gone trading to Montreal; they feared that the French might treat them badly, or that they would be defeated by the Iroquois. Accordingly, they had recourse to Perot's guide, who was a master juggler. That false prophet built himself a little tower of poles, and therein chanted several songs, through which he invoked all the infernal spirits to tell him where the Pouteouatemis were. The reply was that they were at the Oulamanistik River,[1] which is three days' journey from their village; that they had been well received by the French; and that they were bringing a large supply of merchandise. This oracle would have been believed if Perot, who knew that his interpreter had played the juggler, had not declared that he was a liar. The latter came to Perot, and heaped upon him loud reproaches, complaining that he did not at all realize what hardships his interpreter had encountered in this voyage, and that it was Perot's fault that he had not been recompensed for his prediction. The old men begged that Perot himself would relieve them from their anxiety. After telling them that such knowledge belonged only to God, he made a calculation, from the day of their departure, of the stay that they would probably make at Montreal, and of the time when their return might be expected; and determined very nearly the time when they could reach home. Fifteen days later, a man fishing for sturgeon came to the village in great fright, to warn them that he had seen a canoe, from which several gunshots had proceeded; this was enough to make them believe that the Iroquois were coming against them. Disorder prevailed throughout the village; they were ready to flee into the woods or to shut themselves into their fort. There was no probability that these were Iroquois, who usually make their attacks by stealth; Perot conjectured that they were probably their own men, who were thus displaying their joy as they came near the village. In fact, a young man

[1] Manistique River, a tributary of Green Bay in the Upper Peninsula of Michigan.

who had been sent out as a scout came back, in breathless haste, and reported that it was their own people who were returning. If their terror had caused general consternation, this good news caused no less joy throughout the village. Two chiefs, who had seen Perot blow into his gun at the time of the first alarm, came to let him know of the arrival of their people, and begged him always to consult his gun. All were eager to receive the fleet. As they approached, the new-comers discharged a salvo of musketry, followed by shouts and yells, and continued their firing as they came toward the village. When they were two or three hundred paces from the shore, the chief rose in his canoe and harangued the old men who stood at the water's edge; he gave an account of the favorable reception which had been accorded them at Montreal. An old man informed them, meanwhile praising the sky and the sun who had thus favored them, that there was a Frenchman in the village who had protected them in several times of danger; at this, the Pouteouatemis suddenly flung themselves into the water, to show their joy at so pleasing an occurrence. They had taken pleasure in painting themselves in a very peculiar manner; and the French garments, which had been intended to make them more comfortable, disfigured them in a ludicrous fashion. They carried Perot with them, whether or no he would, in a scarlet blanket (Monsieur de la Salle was also honored with a like triumph at Huron Island), and made him go around the fort, while they marched in double files in front and behind him, with guns over their shoulders, often firing volleys. This cortège arrived at the cabin of the chief who had led the band, where all the old men were assembled; and a great feast of sturgeon was served. This chief then related a more detailed account of his voyage, and gave a very correct idea of French usages. He described how the trade was carried on; he spoke with enthusiasm of what he had seen in the houses, especially of the cooking; and he did not forget to exalt Onontio, who had called them his children and had regaled them with bread, prunes, and raisins, which seemed to them great delicacies.

CHAPTER IX.

Those peoples were so delighted with the alliance that they had just made that they sent deputies in every direction to inform the Islinois, Miamis, Outagamis, Maskoutechs, and Kikabous that they had been at Montreal, whence they had brought much merchandise; they besought those tribes to visit them and bring them beavers. Those tribes were too far away to profit by this at first; only the Outagamis came to establish themselves for the winter at a place thirty leagues from the bay,[1] in order to share in the benefit of the goods which they could obtain from the Pouteouatemis. Their hope that some Frenchmen would come from Chagouamikon induced them to accumulate as many beavers as possible. The Pouteouatemis took the southern part of the bay, the Sakis[2] the northern; the Puans, as they could not fish, had gone into the woods to live on deer and bears. When the Outagamis had formed a village of more than six hundred cabins, they sent to the Sakis, at the beginning of spring, to let them know of the new establishment that they had formed. The latter sent them some chiefs, with presents, to ask them to remain in this new settlement; they were accompanied by some Frenchmen. They found a large village, but destitute of everything. Those people had only five or six hatchets, which had no edge, and they used these, by turns, for cutting their wood; they had hardly one knife or one bodkin to a cabin, and cut their meat with the stones which they used for arrows; and they scaled their fish with mussel-shells. Want rendered them so hideous that they aroused compassion. Although their bodies were large,

[1] This was probably the village where the Jesuit missionaries first found the Outagami or Foxes. Its exact location is not known, but it is believed to have been on Wolf River, somewhere in Waupaca or Outagami County, Wisconsin.

[2] The Sauk tribe was closely allied to the Foxes, but preserved a separate tribal existence until about 1733, when the two united and have since been known as Sauk and Foxes. The chief Sauk village was first at Green Bay, then on the Wisconsin near the present Sauk City, thence removed to the mouth of Rock River. The Sauk war under the chief Black Hawk occurred in 1832; at its close the tribe was removed beyond the Mississippi.

they seemed deformed in shape; they had very disagreeable faces, brutish voices, and evil aspects. They were continually begging from our Frenchmen who went among them, for those savages imagined that whatever their visitors possessed ought to be given to them gratis; everything aroused their desires, and yet they had few beavers to sell. The French thought it prudent to leave to the Sakis for the winter the trade in peltries with the Outagamis, as they could carry it on with the former more quietly in the autumn.

All the tribes at the bay went to their villages after the winter, to sow their grain. A dispute occurred between two Frenchmen and an old man, who was one of the leading men among the Pouteouatemis; the former demanded payment for the goods, but he did not show much inclination to pay; sharp words arose on both sides, and they came to blows. The Frenchmen were vigorously attacked by the savages, and a third man came to the aid of his comrades. The confusion increased; that Frenchman tore the pendants from the ears of a savage, and gave him a blow in the belly which felled him so rudely that with difficulty could he rise again. At the same time the Frenchman received a blow from a war-club on his head, which caused him to fall motionless. There were great disputes among the savages in regard to the Frenchman who had just been wounded, who had rendered many services to the village. There were three families interested in this contention—those of the Red Carp, of the Black Carp, and of the Bear.[1] The head of the Bear family—an intimate friend of the Frenchman, and whose son-in-law was the chief of the Sakis—seized a hatchet and declared that he would perish with the Frenchman, whom the people of the Red Carp had slain. The Saki chief, hearing the voice of his father-in-law, called his own men to arms; the Bear family did the same; and the wounded Frenchman began to recover consciousness. He calmed the Sakis, who were greatly enraged; but the savage who had

---

[1] Indian clans were designated by some natural object, usually some animal. The clan was an intermediate organization between the single family and the tribe; it took its inheritance through the mother, and persons of the same clan were not permitted to marry. The animal or tutelary being was worshipped in common by all the group.

maltreated him was compelled to abandon the village. These same Frenchmen's lives were in danger on still another occasion. One of them, who was amusing himself with some arrows, told a Saki who was bathing at the water's edge to ward off the shaft that he was going to let fly at him. The savage, who held a small piece of cloth, told him to shoot; but he was not adroit enough to avoid the arrow, which wounded him in the shoulder. He immediately called out that the Frenchman had slain him; but another Frenchman hastened to the savage, made him enter his cabin, and drew out the arrow. He was pacified by giving him a knife, a little vermilion to paint his face, and a piece of tobacco. This present was effectual; for when, at the Saki's cry, several of his comrades came, ready to avenge him on the spot, the wounded man cried, "What are you about? I am healed. Metaminens" (which means "little Indian corn"—this name they had given to the Frenchman, who was Perot himself) "has tied my hands by this ointment which you see upon my wound, and I have no more anger," at the same time showing the present that Perot had given him. This presence of mind checked the disturbance that was about to arise.

The Miamis, the Maskoutechs, the Kikabous, and fifteen cabins of Islinois came toward the bay in the following summer, and made their clearings thirty miles away, beside the Outagamis, toward the south. These peoples, for whom the Iroquois were looking, had gone southward along the Mississippi after the combat which I have mentioned.[1] Before that flight, they had seen knives and hatchets in the hands of the Hurons who had had dealings with the French, which induced them to associate themselves with the tribes who already had some union with us. They are very sportive when among their own people, but grave before strangers; well built; lacking in intelligence, and dull of apprehension; easily persuaded; vain in language and behavior, and extremely selfish. They consider themselves much braver than their neighbors; they are great liars, employing every kind of baseness to accomplish their ends; but they are industrious, indefatigable, and excellent pedestrians. For this

---

[1] This refers to a prehistoric enmity between the Winnebago and Illinois described by La Potherie in an earlier chapter.

last reason, they are called Metousceprinioueks, which in their language means "Walkers."

After they had planted their fields in this new settlement, they went to hunt cattle. They wished to entertain the people at the bay; so they sent envoys to ask the Pouteoua-temis to visit them, and to bring the Frenchmen, if they were still with them. But those savages were careful not to let their guests know how desirous their neighbors were to become acquainted with the French; so they went away without telling the latter, and came back at the end of a fortnight, loaded with meat and grease. With them were some of those new settlers, who were greatly surprised to see the French—whom they reproached for not having come to visit them with the Pouteouatemis. The French saw plainly that the latter were jealous, and they recognized the importance of becoming acquainted with those peoples, who had come to the bay on purpose to trade more conveniently with us. The Pouteouatemis, when they saw that the French desired to go away with a Miami and a Maskoutech, made representations to them that there were no beavers among those people—who, moreover, were very boorish—and even that they were in great danger of being plundered. The French took their departure, notwithstanding these tales, and in five days reached the vicinity of the village.[1] The Maskoutech sent ahead the Miami, who had a gun, with orders to fire it when he arrived there; the report of the gun was heard soon afterward. Hardly had they reached the shore when a venerable old man appeared, and a woman carrying a bag in which was a clay pot filled with cornmeal porridge. More than two hundred stout young men came upon the scene; their hair was adorned with headdresses of various sorts, and their bodies were covered with tattooing in black, representing many kinds of figures; they carried arrows and war-clubs, and wore girdles and leggings of braided work. The old man held in his hand a calumet of red stone, with a long stick at the end; this was ornamented in its whole length with the heads of birds, flame-colored, and had in the middle a bunch of feathers colored a bright red, which resembled a great fan.

[1] This village site has been identified near the town of Berlin, Wisconsin, on the upper Fox River.

As soon as he espied the leader of the Frenchmen, he presented to him the calumet, on the side next to the sun; and uttered words which were apparently addressed to all the spirits whom those peoples adore. The old man held it sometimes toward the east, and sometimes toward the west; then toward the sun; now he would stick the end in the ground and then he would turn the calumet around him, looking at it as if he were trying to point out the whole earth, with expressions which gave the Frenchman to understand that he had compassion on all men. Then he rubbed with his hands Perot's head, back, legs, and feet, and sometimes his own body. This welcome lasted a long time, during which the old man made a harangue, after the fashion of a prayer, all to assure the Frenchman of the joy which all in the village felt at his arrival.

One of the men spread upon the grass a large painted ox-skin,[1] the hair on which was as soft as silk, on which he and his comrade were made to sit. The old man struck two pieces of wood together, to obtain fire from it; but as it was wet he could not light it. The Frenchman drew forth his own fire-steel, and immediately made fire with tinder. The old man uttered loud exclamations about the iron, which seemed to him a spirit; the calumet was lighted, and each man smoked; then they must eat porridge and dried meat, and suck the juice of the green corn. Again the calumet was filled, and those who smoked blew the tobacco-smoke into the Frenchman's face, as the greatest honor that they could render him; he saw himself smoked like meat, but said not a word. This ceremony ended, a skin was spread for the Frenchman's comrade. The savages thought that it was their duty to carry the French guests; but the latter informed the Maskoutechs that, as they could shape the iron, they had strength to walk, so they were left at liberty. On the way, they rested again, and the same honors were paid to him as at the first meeting. Continuing their route, they halted near a high hill, at the summit of which was the village; they made their fourth halt here, and the ceremonies were repeated. The great chief of the Miamis came to meet them, at the head of more than three thousand men, accom-

---

[1] A buffalo robe; the French called buffaloes oxen or wild cattle.

panied by the chiefs of other tribes who formed part of the village. Each of these chiefs had a calumet, as handsome as that of the old man; they were entirely naked, wearing only shoes, which were artistically embroidered like buskins; they sang, as they approached, the calumet song, which they uttered in cadence. When they reached the Frenchmen, they continued their songs, meanwhile bending their knees, in turn, almost to the ground. They presented the calumet to the sun, with the same genuflexions, and then they came back to the principal Frenchman, with many gesticulations. Some played upon instruments the calumet songs, and others sang them, holding the calumet in the mouth without lighting it. A war chief raised Perot upon his shoulders, and, accompanied by all the musicians, conducted him to the village. The Muskoutech who had been his guide offered him to the Miamis, to be lodged among them; they very amiably declined, being unwilling to deprive the Maskoutechs of the pleasure of possessing a Frenchman who had consented to come under their auspices. At last he was taken to the cabin of the chief of the Maskoutechs; as he entered, the lighted calumet was presented to him, which he smoked; and fifty guardsmen were provided for him, who prevented the crowd from annoying him. A grand repast was served, the various courses of which reminded one of feeding-troughs rather than dishes; the food was seasoned with the fat of the wild ox. The guards took good care that provisions should be brought often, for they profited thereby.

On the next day, the Frenchman gave them, as presents, a gun and a kettle; and made them the following speech, which was suited to their character:

Men, I admire your youths; although they have since their birth seen only shadows, they seem to me as fine-looking as those who are born in regions where the sun always displays his glory. I would not have believed that the earth, the mother of all men, could have furnished you the means of subsistence when you did not possess the light of the Frenchman, who supplies its influences to many peoples; I believe that you will become another nation when you become acquainted with him. I am the dawn of that light, which is beginning to appear in your lands, as it were, that which precedes the sun, who will soon shine brightly and will cause you to be born again, as if in another land, where you will find, more easily and in greater abundance, all that can be necessary to man. I see this fine village filled with young men, who are, I am sure, as courageous as they are well built; and who will, without doubt, not fear their enemies if they carry French weapons. It is for these young men that I leave my gun, which they must regard as the pledge of my esteem for their valor; they must use it if they are attacked. It will also be more satisfactory in hunting cattle and other animals than are all the arrows that you use. To you who are old men I leave my kettle; I carry it everywhere without fear of breaking it. You will cook in it the meat that your young men bring from the chase, and the food which you offer to the Frenchmen who come to visit you.

He tossed a dozen awls and knives to the women, and said to them: "Throw aside your bone bodkins; these French awls will be much easier to use. These knives will be more useful to you in killing beavers and in cutting your meat than are the pieces of stone that you use." Then, throwing to them some rassade:[1] "See; these will better adorn your children and girls than do their usual ornaments." The Miamis said, by way of excuse for not having any beaver-skins, that they had until then roasted those animals.

That alliance began, therefore, through the agency of Sieur Perot. A week later the savages made a solemn feast, to thank the sun for having conducted him to their village. In the cabin of the great chief of the Miamis an altar had been erected, on which he had caused to be placed a Pindi-ikosan. This is a warrior's pouch, filled with medicinal herbs wrapped in the skins of animals, the rarest that they can find; it usually contains all that inspires their dreams.[2] Perot, who did not approve this altar, told the great chief that he adored a God who forbade him to eat things sacrificed to evil spirits or to the skins of animals. They were greatly surprised at this, and asked if he would eat provided they shut up their Manitous;[3] this he consented to do. The chief begged Perot to consecrate him to his Spirit, whom he

---

[1] A French term for the ordinary round beads of glass or porcelain, which soon superseded the Indians' bone and shell ornaments.

[2] The common "medicine-bag" of the North American Indian, containing objects of his veneration, is well described by Perrot.

[3] Manitou was the Algonquian term for spirit; in this instance it was applied to the medicine-bag which was supposed to be the abode of the personal god of each owner.

would thenceforth acknowledge; he said that he would prefer that Spirit to his own, who had not taught them to make hatchets, kettles, and all else that men need; and he hoped that by adoring him they would obtain all the knowledge that the French had. This chief governed his people as a sort of sovereign; he had his guards, and whatever he said or ordered was regarded as law.[1]

The Pouteouatemis, jealous that the French had found the way to the Miamis, secretly sent a slave to the latter, who said many unkind things about the French; he said that the Pouteouatemis held them in the utmost contempt, and regarded them as dogs. The French, who had heard all these abusive remarks, put him into a condition where he could say no more outrageous things; the Miamis regarded the spectacle with great tranquillity. When it was time to return to the bay, the chiefs sent all their young men to escort the Frenchmen thither, and made them many presents. The Pouteouatemis, having learned of the Frenchman's arrival, came to assure him of the interest they felt in his safe return, and were very impatient to know whether the tribes from whom he had come had treated him well. But when they heard the reproaches which he uttered for their sending a slave who had said most ungenerous things regarding the French nation, they attempted to make an explanation of their conduct, but fully justified the poor opinion which he already had of them. The savages have this characteristic, that they find a way to free themselves from blame in any evil undertaking, or to make it succeed without seeming to have taken part in it.

Chapter X.

It was for the interest of the Pouteouatemis to keep on good terms with the French; and they had been too well received at Montreal not to return thither. Indeed, after having presented to Perot a bag of Indian corn, that he might, they said, "eat and swallow the suspicion that he

[1] The position of a chief among the Miami was unusually prominent for North American Indians. The Jesuit missionaries represent the great Miami chief as having more influence and being attended with more guards and surrounded with more ceremony than the chief of any other tribe in the Northwest.

felt toward them," and five beaver robes to serve as an emetic
for the ill-will and vengeance which he might retain in his
heart, they sent some of their people on a journey to Montreal. When they came in sight of Michilimakinak, which
then was frequented only by them and the Iroquois, they
perceived smoke. While they were trying to ascertain what
this meant, they encountered two Iroquois, and saw another
canoe off shore. Each party was alarmed at the other; as
for the Iroquois, they took to flight, while the Pouteouatemis,
plying their paddles against contrary winds, fled to their
own village; they felt an extraordinary anxiety, for they
knew not what measures to take for protection against the
Iroquois. All the peoples of the bay experienced the same
perplexity. Their terror was greatly increased when, a fortnight later, they saw large fires on the other shore of the bay,
and heard many gun-shots. As a climax to their fears, the
scouts whom they had sent out brought back the news that
they had seen at night many canoes made in Iroquois fashion,
in one of which was a gun, and a blanket of Iroquois material; and some men, who were sleeping by a fire. All those
canoes came in sight the next morning, and each one fled,
at the top of his speed, into the forest; only the most courageous took the risk of awaiting, with resolute air, the Iroquois
in their fort, where they had good firearms. As we were at
peace with the Iroquois, some of the bolder spirits among
our Frenchmen offered to go to meet that so-called army,
in order to learn the motive which could have impelled them
to come to wage war against the allies of Onontio. They
were greatly surprised to find that it was a fleet of Outaouaks,
who had come to trade; these people had, while travelling
across the country, built some canoes which resembled those
of the Iroquois. The men whom the Pouteouatemis had seen
at Michilimakinak were really Iroquois; but they had feared
falling into the hands of the Pouteouatemis quite as much
as the latter had feared them. The Iroquois, while fleeing,
fell into an ambuscade of forty Sauteurs, who carried them
away to the Sauteur village; they had come from a raid
against the Chaouanons[1] near Carolina, and had brought

[1] *Chaouanon* was the French word for the Shawnee, an important Algonquian tribe, whose name means "Southerners." When first known to whites

with them a captive from that tribe, whom they were going to burn. The Sauteurs set him at liberty, and enabled him to return to the bay by entrusting him to the Sakis. This man gave them marvellous notions of the South Sea, from which his village was distant only five days' journey—near a great river which, coming from the Islinois, discharges its waters into that sea. The tribes of the bay sent him home with much merchandise, urging him to persuade his tribesmen to come and visit them.

These peoples held several councils, to deliberate whether they should go down to Montreal; they hesitated at first, because they had so few beavers. As the savages give everything to their mouths, they preferred to devote themselves to hunting such wild beasts as could furnish subsistence for their families, rather than seek beavers, of which there were not enough; they preferred the needs of life to those of the state. Nevertheless, they reflected that if they allowed the Frenchmen to go away without themselves going down to trade, it might happen that the latter would thereafter attach themselves to some other tribes; or, if they should afterward go to Montreal, the governor would feel resentment against them because they had not escorted these Frenchmen thither. They decided that they would go with the Frenchmen; preparations for this were accordingly made, and a solemn feast was held; and on the eve of their departure a volley of musketry was fired in the village. Three men sang incessantly, all night long, in a cabin, invoking their spirits from time to time. They began with the song of Michabous;[1] then they came to that of the god of lakes, rivers, and forests, begging the winds, the thunder, the storms, and the tempests to be favorable to them during the voyage. The next day, the crier went through the village, inviting the men to the cabin where the feast was to be prepared. They found no difficulty in going thither, each furnished

---

they were residing in Tennessee on the Cumberland River. Later they gathered in southern Ohio, where they formed the most intractable barrier to American advance. Tecumseh was a Shawnee chief, and his tribe opposed the Americans until the close of the War of 1812. They were removed, first to Missouri, later to Oklahoma.

[1] "Michabous" is one form of the name of the Great Spirit, which all Indian tribesmen invoke as their highest deity.

with his Ouragan and Mikouen.[1] The three musicians of
the previous night began to sing; one was placed at the entrance of the cabin, another in the middle, and the third at
its end; they were armed with quivers, bows, and arrows, and
their faces and entire bodies were blackened with coal. While
the people sat in this assembly, in the utmost quiet, twenty
young men—entirely naked, elaborately painted, and wearing
girdles of otter-skin, to which were attached the skins of
crows, with their plumage, and gourds—lifted from the fires
ten great kettles; then the singing ceased. The first of these
actors next sang his war-song, keeping time with it in a dance
from one end to the other of the cabin, while all the savages cried in deep guttural tones, "Hay, hay!" When the
musician ended, all the others uttered a loud yell, in which
their voices gradually died away, much as a loud noise dis-
appears among the mountains. Then the second and the
third musicians repeated, in turn, the same performance;
and, in a word, nearly all the savages did the same, in alter-
nation—each singing his own song, but no one venturing to
repeat that of another, unless he were willing deliberately to
offend the one who had composed the song, or unless the
latter were dead (in order to exalt, as it were, the dead man's
name by appropriating his song). During this, their looks
were accompanied with gestures and violent movements;
and some of them took hatchets, with which they pretended
to strike the women and children who were watching them.
Some took firebrands, which they tossed about everywhere;
others filled their dishes with red-hot coals, which they threw
at each other. It is difficult to make the reader understand
the details of feasts of this sort, unless he has himself seen
them. I was present at a like entertainment among the
Iroquois at the Sault of Montreal,[2] and it seemed as if I
were in the midst of hell. After most of those who had been
invited to this pleasant festival had sung, the chief of the

---

[1] Dish and spoon; it was customary for each guest at the feast to come provided with his own utensils.

[2] A mission colony of Iroquois was established at Sault St. Louis or the
village of Caughnawaga, on the south bank of the St. Lawrence not far from
Montreal. La Potherie is comparing Perrot's account of the feast among the
Miami with one he has himself witnessed.

feast, who had given the dance, sang a second time; and he said at the end of his song (which he improvised) that he was going to Montreal with the Frenchmen, and was on that account offering these prayers to their God, entreating him to be propitious to him on the voyage, and to render him acceptable to the French nation.   The young men who had taken off the kettles took all the dishes, which they filled with food, while the three chanters repeated their first songs, not finishing their concert until everything had been eaten —a feat which did not take long to accomplish.   An old man arose and congratulated, in the most affable manner, the chief of the feast on the project which he had formed, and encouraged the young men to follow him.   All those who wished to go on the voyage laid down a stick; there were enough people to man thirty canoes.   At the Sault,[1] they joined seventy other canoes, of various tribes, all of whom formed a single fleet.

[1] Sault Ste. Marie.

FATHER ALLOUEZ'S JOURNEY TO LAKE SUPERIOR, 1665–1667

INTRODUCTION

THE Jesuit missions to the Western tribes that had begun so auspiciously in the early years of the seventeenth century were completely wrecked in the middle of the century (1649) by the hostile incursions of the Iroquois, and the death or flight of the Indian neophytes. The tribes that had dwelt on the shores of Lake Huron, the islands of Georgian Bay, and the lower peninsula of Michigan fled like leaves before a northern blast and sought refuge on the distant shores of Lake Superior, or hid themselves in the dense forests of northwestern Wisconsin. Driven from their former habitats, lurking in hidden coverts of the woods, the remnant of the Huron tribes and their Algonquian neighbors wandered through the northern wilderness, stopping here and there as chance brought them respite to build temporary villages or raise an occasional crop of corn.

The Jesuit fathers, of whom some had suffered martyrdom with their Huron converts, and others had fled to the settled parts of the colony, sought in vain for more than a decade to re-establish their ruined missions. In 1654 Father Léonard Garreau courageously set forth from Montreal to accompany an Algonquian fleet to the western country; but only a short distance up the Ottawa River he fell into an Iroquois ambuscade and was killed. Father René Ménard, a refugee from the Huron mission, succeeded in 1660 in reaching the shores of Lake Superior, where, after wintering in a wretched hut at the bottom of Keweenaw Bay, he started in the early summer of 1661 to visit some refugee Huron upon the headwaters of Black River. Somewhere upon the Wisconsin River he was lost in the dense woods, and his fate was never known.

Jean Claude Allouez, unterrified by the martyrdom of these early apostles to the Northwestern tribes, accompanied the returning fleet of 1665, somewhere in which was the trader and explorer Nicolas Perrot.   At the Sault they parted company, and Allouez after skirting the shores of Lake Superior finally arrived at the Ottawa village on Chequamegon Bay, where he founded the mission of the Holy Spirit.

Even as a youth in his home in southern France, Allouez had ardently longed to seek the mission fields in foreign lands; great had been his joy, therefore, when he had been assigned by the superiors of his order to work upon the distant banks of the St. Lawrence.   There seven years had been passed in acquiring the Algonquian language and learning Indian lore, before he finally reached his chosen field of labor on the shores of the northern inland sea.   With vivid pen he pictures for us in the passage that follows his outward journey and his first two dismal winters at this remote post on Chequamegon Bay.   Then by another long and toilsome journey, he returned in the summer of 1667 to Quebec to tarry but two days in the house of his friends, duty driving him again to the distant north.   The next year (1668) the Algonquian tribes largely abandoned Chequamegon Bay, and Father Allouez founded a flourishing mission at the Sault, which for many years served as headquarters for the Jesuits of the Upper Country.   Thence he visited Wisconsin, and after 1669 for nearly a decade devoted his services to the numerous tribes about Green Bay.   Heedless of fatigue or hunger, cold or heat, he travelled over snow and ice, swollen streams or dangerous rapids, seeking distant Indian villages, counting it all joy if by any means he could win a few savages for a heavenly future.

Allouez was a keen observer and had a ready pen; his

descriptions are graphic, his incidents vivid. Zealot though he may have been with regard to his mission enterprises, Wisconsin historians owe him an undying debt of gratitude for his faithful portrayal of our earliest history. In 1671 he was with St. Lusson, at his great pageant at Sault Ste. Marie; while the next year we find him again in the Wisconsin mission, where he had the misfortune to have his cabin burned, December 22, 1672, and his diary and papers lost. About this time he built the mission house of St. Francis Xavier at De Pere. When he was reinforced by the arrival of other Jesuits, he left to them the missions around the bay, and chose for himself a more severe field of labor among the distant Mascoutin and Foxes.

It was from the mission house at De Pere that Father Marquette in 1674 set forth on his second journey to the Illinois, a voyage which was to end only with his death. Thereafter Allouez adopted the Illinois mission as his own, and while temporarily abandoning it during La Salle's régime, was later found at Fort St. Louis of the Illinois when Tonty was in command of that post. In 1689 this devoted servant of the cross died at the Miami village on St. Joseph River. A second St. Francis Xavier, Allouez is said during his twenty-four years of service to have instructed a hundred thousand Western savages and baptized at least ten thousand.

The first selection we have made from Allouez's writings is taken from the *Jesuit Relation* of 1668, first published in that year at Paris by Sébastien Cramoisy. In the Thwaites edition it is found in volume L., pp. 249–311, and volume LI., pp. 21–69. It describes the outward journey to Chequamegon Bay and the experiences of the missionary during the years 1665–1667.

FATHER ALLOUEZ'S JOURNEY TO LAKE SUPERIOR, 1665–1667

CHAPTER II.

Journal of Father Claude Allouez's Voyage into the Outaouac Country.

Two years ago, and more, Father Claude Allouez set out for that great and arduous mission, in behalf of which he has journeyed, in all his travels, nearly two thousand leagues through these vast forests, enduring hunger, nakedness, shipwreck, weariness by day and night, and the persecutions of the idolaters; but he has also had the consolation of bearing the torch of the Faith to more than twenty different infidel nations.

We cannot gain a better knowledge of the fruits of his labors than from the Journal which he was called upon to prepare.

The narrative will be diversified by the description of the places and lakes that he passed, the customs and superstitions of the peoples visited, and by various incidents of an unusual nature and worthy of relation. He begins as follows:

"On the eighth of August, in the year 1665, I embarked at Three Rivers with six Frenchmen, in company with more than four hundred savages of various nations, who, after transacting the little trading for which they had come, were returning to their own country.

"The Devil offered all conceivable opposition to our journey, making use of the false prejudice held by these savages, that baptism causes their children to die. One of their chief men declared to me, in arrogant and menacing terms, his intention, and that of his people, to abandon me on some desert island if I ventured to follow them farther. We had then proceeded as far as the rapids of the River des Prairies, where the breaking of the canoe that bore me made me apprehensive of the threatened disaster. We promptly set about repairing our little vessel; and, although the savages did not trouble themselves either to aid us or to wait for us, we were so expeditious as to join them near the Long Sault,[1] two or three days after we started.

"But our canoe, having been once broken, could not long be of service, and our Frenchmen, already greatly fatigued, despaired of being able to follow the savages, who were thoroughly accustomed to such severe exertions. Therefore, I resolved to call them all together, in order to persuade them to receive us separately into their canoes, showing them that our own was in so bad a condition as to be thenceforth useless to us. They agreed to this; and the Hurons promised, although with much reluctance, to provide for me.

"On the morrow, accordingly, when I came down to the water's edge, they at first received me well, and begged me to wait a very little while, until they were ready to embark. After I had waited, and when I was stepping down into the water to enter their canoe, they repulsed me with the assertion that there was no room for me, and straightway began to paddle vigorously, leaving me all alone with no prospect of human succor. I prayed God to forgive them, but my prayer was unanswered; for they were subsequently wrecked, and the divine Majesty turned my abandonment on the part of men to the saving of my life.

"Finding myself, then, entirely alone, forsaken in a strange land—for the whole fleet was already a good distance away—I had recourse to the blessed Virgin, in whose honor we had performed a novena which gained for us from that Mother of Mercy a very manifest daily protection. While I was praying to her I saw, quite contrary to my hopes, some canoes in which were three of our Frenchmen. I hailed them, and resuming our old canoe, we proceeded to paddle with all our strength, in order to overtake the fleet. But we had long since lost sight of it, and knew not whither to

---

[1] The Long Sault of Ottawa River is about forty-five miles above Montreal. It is now avoided by means of the Grenville Canal. It is famous in Canadian history for the defense (1660) by a handful of French led by Dollard against a horde of Iroquois. It thus became the Thermopylae of New France. See Francis Parkman, *The Old Régime in Canada* (Boston, 1875), pp. 72–82.

go, it being very difficult to find a narrow detour which must
be taken in order to gain the portage of Cat Rapids (as that
part is called).[1] We should have been lost had we missed
this narrow channel; but it pleased God, owing to the blessed
Virgin's intercessions, to guide us directly, and almost without our realizing it, to this portage. Here, as I saw two more
canoes, belonging to the savages, I leaped into the water, and
hastened to intercept them by land on the other side of the
portage, where I found six canoes. 'How is this?' said I to
them; 'do you thus forsake the French? Know you not
that I hold Onnontio's voice in my hands, and that I am to
speak for him, through the presents he entrusted to me, to
all your nations?' These words forced them to give us aid,
so that we joined the bulk of the fleet toward noon.

"Upon landing, I felt that I must, in that critical state of
affairs, use every possible and most effective means for the
glory of God. I spoke to them all, and threatened them with
the displeasure of Monsieur de Tracy, whose spokesman I
was.[2] Fear of disobliging that great Onnontio impelled one
of the chief men among them to take the word, and harangue
long and forcibly to persuade us to turn back. The weakness
of this discontented man was turned to account by the evil
spirit for closing the way against the Gospel. None of the
others were better disposed; so that, although our Frenchmen found places for themselves without much difficulty, no
one would be burdened with me—all declaring that I had
neither skill at the paddle, nor strength to carry loads on my
shoulders.

"In this abandoned state I withdrew into the woods,
and, after thanking God for making me so acutely sensible

[1] Cat Rapids, now called Les Chats, lie at the head of the widening of the
Ottawa known as Lake des Chaudières, not far above the city of Ottawa.

[2] Alexandre de Prouville, Marquis de Tracy (1603–1670), was a French
general who had served in the West Indies, and was appointed in November,
1663, governor-general of all the French possessions in the New World. He
arrived in Canada in June, 1665, and took such vigorous measures against the
Mohawk Indians that the colony secured a temporary peace. Allouez had been
commissioned by Governor Tracy to announce to the visiting Algonquian Indians the arrival of the Carignan regiment, designed to protect New France and
its Algonquian allies against Iroquois aggression. Tracy returned to France
in August, 1667.

of my slight worth, confessed before his divine Majesty that I was only a useless burden on the earth. My prayer ended, I returned to the water's edge, where I found the disposition of that savage who had repulsed me with such contempt entirely changed; for, unsolicited, he invited me to enter his canoe, which I did with much alacrity, fearing he would change his mind.

"No sooner had I embarked than he put a paddle in my hand, urging me to use it, and assuring me it was an honorable employment, and one worthy of a great captain. I willingly took the paddle and, offering up to God this labor in atonement for my sins, and to hasten those poor savages' conversion, I imagined myself a malefactor sentenced to the galleys; and, although I became entirely exhausted, yet God gave me sufficient strength to paddle all day long, and often a good part of the night. But this application did not prevent my being commonly the object of their contempt and the butt of their jokes; for, however much I exerted myself, I accomplished nothing in comparison with them, their bodies being large and strong, and perfectly adapted to such labors. The slight esteem in which they held me caused them to steal from me every article of my wardrobe that they could; and I had much difficulty in retaining my hat, the wide rim of which seemed to them peculiarly fitted for defense against the excessive heat of the sun. And when evening came, as my pilot took away a bit of blanket that I had, to serve him as a pillow, he forced me to pass the night without any covering but the foliage of some tree.

"When hunger is added to these discomforts, it is a severe hardship, but one that soon teaches a man to find a relish in the bitterest roots and the most putrid meat. God was pleased to make me suffer from hunger, on Fridays especially, for which I heartily thank him.

"We were forced to accustom ourselves to eat a certain moss growing upon the rocks. It is a sort of shell-shaped leaf which is always covered with caterpillars and spiders; and which, on being boiled, furnishes an insipid soup, black and viscous, that rather serves to ward off death than to impart life.[1]

---

[1] Tripe de roche, for which see p. 41, note 1, *ante*.

"One morning, we found a stag that had been dead four or five days. It was a lucky accident for poor starvelings. I was given a piece of it, and although its offensive odor deterred some from eating any, hunger made me take my share; but my mouth had a putrid taste, in consequence, until the next day.

"Amid all these hardships, whenever we came to any rapids I carried as heavy burdens as I could; but I often succumbed under them, and that made our savages laugh and mock me, saying they must call a child to carry me and my burden. Our good God did not forsake me utterly on these occasions, but often wrought on some of the men so that, touched with compassion, they would, without saying anything, relieve me of my *chapelle* [1] or of some other burden, and would help me to journey a little more at my ease.

"It sometimes happened that, after we had carried our loads and plied our paddles all day long, and even two or three hours into the night, we went supperless to bed on the ground, or on some rock, to begin over again the next day with the same labors. But everywhere the Divine Providence mingled some little sweetness and relief with our fatigue.

"We endured these hardships for nearly two weeks; and after passing the Nipissirinien Lake, as we were descending a little river,[2] we heard cries of lamentation and death-songs. Approaching the spot whence came these outcries, we saw eight young savages of the Outaouacs, frightfully burned by a direful accident, a spark having by inadvertence fallen into a keg of powder. Four among them were completely scorched, and in danger of dying. I comforted them and prepared them for baptism, which I would have conferred had I had time to see them sufficiently fitted for it; for, despite this disaster, we had to keep on our way, in order to reach the entrance to the Lake of the Hurons, which was the rendezvous of all these travellers.

"They arrived there on the twenty-fourth of this month, to the number of a hundred canoes; and then they applied

---

[1] The sacred vessels, collectively, which were used in the celebration of the mass.

[2] Lake Nipissing and French River. See p. 15, note 4, and p. 92, note 2, *ante*.

themselves to the healing of these poor burned men, using on them all their superstitious remedies.

"I was made well aware of this on the following night by the singing of certain jugglers, which filled the air, and by a thousand other ridiculous ceremonies employed by them. Others offered a sort of sacrifice to the Sun, to effect the cure of these patients; for, sitting in a circle, ten or twelve in number, as if to hold a council, on the point of a rocky islet, they lighted a little fire, with the smoke of which they sent up into the air confused cries, which ended with a speech addressed to the Sun by the oldest and most influential man among them.

"I could not endure the invocation of any of their imaginary divinities in my presence; and yet I saw myself quite alone, and at the mercy of all these people. I wavered for some time, in doubt whether it would be more fitting for me to withdraw quietly, or to offer opposition to their superstitious practices. The completion of my journey depended upon them; if I incensed them the Devil would make use of their anger in closing against me the door to their country, and in preventing their conversion. Besides, I had already perceived how little weight my words had with them, and knew that I should turn them still more against me by opposing them. Despite all these reasons, I believed that God demanded this little service from me; and accordingly I went forward, leaving the result to his Divine Providence. I accosted the chief jugglers, and, after a long talk, sustained by each side, God was pleased to touch the sick man's heart so that he promised me to permit no superstitious ceremonies for his cure; and, addressing God in a short prayer, he invoked him as the author of life and of death.

"This victory is not to be regarded as slight, being gained over the Evil One in the heart of his empire, and on ground where, for so many ages, he had been obeyed and worshipped by all those tribes. Hence he resented it soon after, and sent us the juggler, who howled about our cabin like a desperate man, and seemed bent on venting his rage upon our Frenchmen. I prayed our Lord that his vengeance might not fall on any one but me, and my prayer was not in vain: we lost only our canoe, which that wretch broke in pieces.

"I had at the same time the grief to learn of the death of one of those poor burned men, without being able to attend him. Still I hope that God may have shown him mercy, in consequence of the acts of faith and contrition and the few prayers which I made him recite, the first time I saw him, which was also the last.

"Toward the beginning of September, after coasting along the shores of the Lake of the Hurons, we reached the Sault : for such is the name given to a half-league of rapids that are encountered in a beautiful river which unites two great lakes—that of the Hurons, and Lake Superior.

"This river is pleasing, not only on account of the islands intercepting its course and the great bays bordering it, but because of the fishing and hunting, which are excellent there. We sought a resting-place for the night on one of these islands, where our savages thought they would find provision for supper upon their arrival; for, as soon as they landed, they put the kettle on the fire, expecting to see the canoe laden with fish the moment the net was cast into the water. But God chose to punish their presumption, and deferred giving any food to the starving men until the following day.

"On the second of September, then, after clearing this Sault—which is not a waterfall, but merely a very swift current impeded by numerous rocks—we entered Lake Superior, which will henceforth bear Monsieur de Tracy's name, in recognition of indebtedness to him on the part of the people of those regions.[1]

"The form of this lake is nearly that of a bow, the southern shore being much curved, and the northern nearly straight. Fish are abundant there, and of excellent quality; while the water is so clear and pure that objects at the bottom can be seen to the depth of six *brasses*.[2]

"The savages revere this lake as a divinity, and offer it sacrifices, whether on account of its size—for its length is two hundred leagues, and its greatest width eighty[3]—or be-

---

[1] The name was used only temporarily, quickly reverting to the earlier form, Superior (or Upper) Lake.

[2] *Brasse* was a French linear measure amounting to 5.318 English feet.

[3] Its extreme length from east to west is 412 miles, its extreme breadth 167.

cause of its goodness in furnishing fish for the sustenance of all these tribes, in default of game, which is scarce in the neighborhood.

"One often finds at the bottom of the water pieces of pure copper, of ten and twenty pounds' weight. I have several times seen such pieces in the savages' hands; and, since they are superstitious, they keep them as so many divinities, or as presents which the gods dwelling beneath the water have given them, and on which their welfare is to depend. For this reason they preserve these pieces of copper, wrapped up, among their most precious possessions. Some have kept them for more than fifty years; others have had them in their families from time immemorial, and cherish them as household gods.

"For some time, there had been seen a sort of great rock, all of copper, the point of which projected from the water; this gave passers-by the opportunity to go and cut off pieces from it. When, however, I passed that spot, nothing more was seen of it; and I think that the storms—which here are very frequent, and like those at sea—have covered the rock with sand. Our savages tried to persuade me that it was a divinity, who had disappeared for some reason which they do not state.

"This lake is, furthermore, the resort of twelve or fifteen distinct nations—coming, some from the north, others from the south, and still others from the west; and they all betake themselves either to the best parts of the shore for fishing, or to the islands, which are scattered in great numbers all over the lake. These peoples' motive in repairing hither is partly to obtain food by fishing, and partly to transact their petty trading with one another, when they meet. But God's purpose was to facilitate the proclaiming of the Gospel to wandering and vagrant tribes—as will appear in the course of this journal.

"Having, then, entered Lake Tracy, we spent the whole month of September in coasting along its southern shore—where, finding myself alone with our Frenchmen, I had the consolation of saying holy mass, which I had been unable to do since my departure from Three Rivers.

"After I had consecrated these forests by this holy ceremony, God led me to the water-side, and, to crown my joy, made me chance upon two sick children, who were being placed in canoes for a journey into the interior. I felt strongly inspired to baptize them, and, after all necessary precautions, did so in view of the danger to which I saw them exposed, of dying during the winter. All my past fatigues were as nothing to me thenceforth; and I was thoroughly inured to hunger, which ever followed us in close pursuit, our provision consisting only of what our fishermen's skill, which not always met with success, could furnish us from day to day.

"We then crossed the bay named for Saint Theresa[1] by the late Father Menard. There this brave missionary spent a winter, laboring with the same zeal which afterward made him sacrifice his life in the quest of souls. I found, at no great distance thence, some remnants of his labors, in the persons of two Christian women who had always kept the faith, and who shone like two stars amid the darkness of that infidelity. I made them pray to God, after I had refreshed their memory concerning our mysteries.

"The Devil, doubtless filled with jealousy at this glory which, in the heart of his estates, is paid to God, did what he could to prevent my coming up hither; and, having failed in his object, he vented his spite on some writings I had brought with me, designed for the instruction of these infidels. I had enclosed them, with some medicines for the sick, in a little chest, which the evil spirit, seeing that it would be of great service to me in the savages' salvation, tried to make me lose. Once it was wrecked in the eddies of some rapids; again it was left behind at the foot of a portage; it changed hands seven or eight times; and, finally, it fell into those of that sorcerer whom I had censured at the entrance to the Lake of the Hurons, and who, after removing the lock, took what he chose, and then left it all open to the rain and exposed to passers-by. God was pleased to confound the evil spirit and to make use of the greatest juggler of these regions—a man with six wives, and of a dissolute life—for its preservation. This man put it into my hands

---

[1] Father Ménard arrived at Keweenaw Bay of Lake Superior, March 1, 1661, the day of Ste. Thérèse, to whom he dedicated his new abode. For a sketch of this missionary see p. 25, note 1, *ante*.

when I had given it up as lost, assuring me that the theriac[1] and some other medicines, together with the images that were in the chest, were so many manitous or demons, who would make him die if he dared touch them. I learned, by subsequent experience, how serviceable these writings in the languages of the country were to me in converting the people."

Chapter III.

Of the Missionary's Arrival and Sojourn at the Bay of Saint Esprit, called Chagouamigong.

"After coasting a hundred and eighty leagues along the southern shore of Lake Tracy, where it was our Lord's will often to test our patience by storms, famine, and weariness by day and night, finally, on the first day of October, we arrived at Chagouamigong, whither our ardent desires had been so long directed.

"It is a beautiful bay, at the head of which is situated the great village of the savages, who there cultivate fields of Indian corn and lead a settled life. They number eight hundred men bearing arms, but are gathered together from seven different nations, living in peace, mingled one with another.

"This large population made us prefer this place to all others for our usual abode, that we might apply ourselves most advantageously to the instruction of these infidels, build a chapel, and enter upon the functions of the Christian religion.

"At first, we could find shelter only under a bark roof, where we were so frequently visited by these people, most of whom had never seen any Europeans, that we were overwhelmed; and my efforts to instruct them were constantly interrupted by persons going and coming. Therefore I decided to go in person to visit them, each in his cabin, where I told them about God more at my ease, and instructed them more at leisure in all the mysteries of our faith.

"While I was occupied in these holy pursuits, a young

[1] Theriac was a much-prized remedy in mediæval times, composed of opium flavored with various spices, such as nutmeg, cinnamon, or mace.

savage—one of those who had been burned during our journey—came to seek me, and asked for my prayers, assuring
me of his earnest desire to become a Christian. He told me
something that had happened to him, of which the reader
may think what he chooses. 'I had no sooner obeyed thee,'
said he to me, 'by sending away that sorcerer who was bent
on curing me with his jugglery, than I saw the Creator of all
things, of whom thou hast so often told me. He said to me
in a voice which I heard distinctly : "Thou shalt not die, for
thou didst listen to the black gown." He had no sooner
spoken than I felt singularly strengthened, and found myself
filled with a great confidence that I should regain my health,
as, indeed, here I am, perfectly cured.' I have strong hopes
that He who has wrought for the saving of the body, will not
neglect that of the soul; and I feel all the more confidence
that He will not, since this savage has come of his own free
will to seek me, in order to learn the prayers and receive the
necessary instruction.

"Soon afterward, I learned that we had sent to Heaven
an infant in swaddling-clothes, its death having occurred two
days after I gave it holy baptism. St. Francis, whose name it
bore, has doubtless presented that innocent soul to God, as
the first-fruits of this mission.

"I know not what will happen to another child, which
I baptized immediately after its birth. Its father, an Outaouac by nation, summoned me as soon as it was born, even
coming to meet me, to tell me that I must baptize it at once,
in order to insure it a long life. This was an admirable
course of action for one of these savages, who formerly believed that baptism caused their children to die, and now are
persuaded of its necessity for insuring them long lives. That
belief gives me easier access to these children, who often come
to me in troops to satisfy their curiosity by looking at a
stranger, but much more to receive, without thinking about
it, the first seeds of the Gospel, which will in time bear fruit
in those young plants."

CHAPTER IV.

General Council of the Nations of the Outaouac Country.

Upon the Father's arrival in the country of the Outa-ouacs, he found their minds filled with alarm at a fresh war in which they were about to engage with the Nadouessi, a warlike nation, using no other arms in its wars than the bow and the club.

A detachment of young warriors was already forming under the lead of a chief who, having suffered an injury, did not consider whether the vengeance which he was bent on exacting would cause the ruin of all the villages of his country.

To forestall such a disaster, the elders called a general council of ten or twelve circumjacent nations, all interested in this war, in order to stay the hatchets of these rash ones by the presents which they should give them in so important an assembly.

To promote this end, the Father was invited to attend, and did so, that he might at the same time address all these people in the name of Monsieur de Tracy, from whom he bore a speech in three clauses, with three presents to serve as their interpreters.[1]

All this great assembly having given him audience, "My brothers," said he to them, "the motive that brings me to your country is very important, and makes it fitting that you should listen to my words with more than usual attention. Nothing less is concerned than the preservation of your entire land, and the destruction of all your enemies." As the Father found them all, at these words, well disposed to listen to him attentively, he told them about the war that Monsieur de Tracy was undertaking against the Iroquois— how, by means of the King's arms, he was about to compel them to assume a respectful demeanor, and was going to make commerce safe between us and the Algonquin peoples, cleansing all the highways from those river pirates, and forcing them to observe a general peace or see themselves totally destroyed.

---

[1] The Indians were accustomed to present or receive a gift, or a string of wampum, with every important measure proposed in council.

And here the Father took occasion to expatiate upon the piety of his Majesty, who wished God to be acknowledged throughout all his domains, and who received into his allegiance no peoples who did not submit to the Creator of all the universe. He next explained to them the chief articles of our faith, and spoke to them earnestly concerning all the mysteries of our religion. In short, he preached Jesus Christ to all those nations.

It is assuredly a very great consolation to a poor missionary, after a journey of five hundred leagues amid weariness, dangers, famines, and hardships of all sorts, to find himself listened to by so many different peoples, while he proclaims the Gospel and gives out to them the words of salvation, whereof they have never heard mention.

Those are seeds that remain for a time in the ground, and do not at once bear fruit. One must go and gather it in the cabins, in the forests, and on the lakes; and that is what the Father did, being present everywhere—in their cabins, at their embarkations, on their journeys—and everywhere finding children to baptize, sick persons to prepare for the sacraments, Christians of long standing to hear in confession, and infidels to instruct.

One day, it is true, while he was reviewing in his mind the obstacles encountered by the faith, in consequence of the depraved customs of all those peoples, he felt inwardly impelled, during the holy sacrifice of the mass, to ask of God, by the intercession of St. Andrew the Apostle, whose festival the Church was that day celebrating,[1] that it might please his divine Majesty to show him some light for the establishment of Jesus Christ's kingdom in those regions in the place of paganism. From that very day God made him recognize the formidable obstacles he should there encounter, in order that he might more and more brace himself against those difficulties—of which the following chapter will give a tolerable conception.

[1] November 30.

Chapter V.

Of the False Gods and some Superstitious Customs of the Savages of that Country.

Following is what Father Allouez relates concerning the customs of the Outaouacs and other peoples, which he has studied very carefully, not trusting the accounts given him by others, but having been himself an eye-witness and observer of everything described in this manuscript.

"There is here," he says, "a false and abominable religion, resembling in many respects the beliefs of some of the ancient pagans. The savages of these regions recognize no sovereign master of Heaven and Earth, but believe there are many spirits, some of whom are beneficent, as the Sun, the Moon, the lake, rivers, and woods; others malevolent, as the adder, the dragon, cold, and storms. And, in general, whatever seems to them either helpful or hurtful they call a Manitou, and pay it the worship and veneration which we render only to the true God.

"These divinities they invoke whenever they go out hunting, fishing, to war, or on a journey, offering them sacrifices, with ceremonies appropriate only for sacrificial priests.

"One of the leading old men of the village discharges the function of priest, beginning with a carefully-prepared harangue addressed to the Sun, if the eat-all feast,[1] which bears a certain resemblance to a holocaust, is held in its honor. He declares in a loud voice that he pays his thanks to that luminary for having lighted him so that he could successfully kill some animal or other, praying and exhorting it by this feast to continue its kind care of his family. During this invocation, all the guests eat, even to the last morsel; after which a man appointed for the purpose takes a cake of tobacco, breaks it in two, and throws it into the fire. Every one cries aloud while the tobacco burns and the smoke rises aloft; and with these outcries the whole sacrifice ends.

---

[1] The literature of Indian customs contains many descriptions of this kind of feast, which had something of a religious significance, and was supposed to bring good fortune in hunting. The name describes its character; it was the established etiquette to eat every morsel provided, hence it frequently became a disgusting orgy.

"I have seen," continues the Father, "an idol set up in the middle of a village; and to it, among other presents, ten dogs were offered in sacrifice, in order to prevail on this false god to send elsewhere the disease that was depopulating the village. Every one went daily to make his offerings to this idol, according to his needs.

"Besides these public sacrifices, they have some that are private and domestic; for often in their cabins they throw tobacco into the fire, with a kind of outward offering which they make to their false gods.

"During storms and tempests, they sacrifice a dog, throwing it into the lake. 'That is to appease thee,' they say to the latter; 'keep quiet.' At perilous places in the rivers, they propitiate the eddies and rapids by offering them presents; and so persuaded are they that they honor their pretended divinities by this external worship, that those among them who are converted and baptized observe the same ceremonies toward the true God, until they are disabused.

"As, moreover, these people are of gross nature, they recognize no purely spiritual divinity, believing that the Sun is a man, and the Moon his wife; that snow and ice are also a man, who goes away in the spring and comes back in the winter; that the evil spirit is in adders, dragons, and other monsters; that the crow, the kite, and some other birds are genii, and speak just as we do; and that there are even people among them who understand the language of birds, as some understand a little that of the French.

"They believe, moreover, that the souls of the departed govern the fishes in the lake; and thus, from the earliest times, they have held the immortality, and even the metempsychosis, of the souls of dead fishes, believing that they pass into other fishes' bodies. Therefore they never throw their bones into the fire, for fear that they may offend these souls, so that they will cease to come into their nets.

"They hold in very special veneration a certain fabulous animal which they have never seen except in dreams, and which they call Missibizi, acknowledging it to be a great genius, and offering it sacrifices in order to obtain good sturgeon-fishing.[1]

---

[1] The same as "Michibous," for whom see p. 90, note 1, *ante*.

"They say also that the little nuggets of copper which they find at the bottom of the water in the lake, or in the rivers emptying into it, are the riches of the gods who dwell in the depths of the earth.

"I have learned," says the Father who has brought to light all these follies, "that the Iliniouek, the Outagami, and other savages toward the south, hold that there is a great and excellent genius, master of all the rest, who made Heaven and Earth; and who dwells, they say, in the East, toward the country of the French.

"The fountain-head of their religion is libertinism; and all these various sacrifices end ordinarily in debauches, indecent dances, and shameful acts of concubinage. All the devotion of the men is directed toward securing many wives, and changing them whenever they choose; that of the women, toward leaving their husbands; and that of the girls, toward a life of profligacy.

"They endure a great deal on account of these ridiculous deities; for they fast in their honor, for the purpose of learning the issue of some affair. I have," says the Father, "seen with compassion men who had some scheme of war or hunting pass a whole week, taking scarcely anything. They show such fixity of purpose that they will not desist until they have seen in a dream what they desire—either a herd of moose, or a band of Iroquois put to flight, or something similar—no very difficult thing for an empty brain, utterly exhausted with hunger, and thinking all day of nothing else.

"Let us say something about the art of medicine in vogue in this country. Their science consists in ascertaining the cause of the ailment, and applying the remedies.

"They deem the most common cause of illness to come from failure to give a feast after some successful fishing or hunting excursion; for then the Sun, who takes pleasure in feasts, is angry with the one who has been delinquent in his duty, and makes him ill.

"Besides this general cause of sickness, there are special ones, in the shape of certain little spirits, malevolent in their nature, who thrust themselves of their own accord, or are sent by some enemy, into the parts of the body that are most diseased. Thus, when any one has an aching head, or arm, or stomach, they say that a manitou has entered this part of the body, and will not cease its torments until it has been drawn or driven out.

"The most common remedy, accordingly, is to summon the juggler, who comes attended by some old men, with whom he holds a sort of consultation on the patient's ailment. After this, he falls upon the diseased part, applies his mouth to it, and, by sucking, pretends to extract something from it, as a little stone, or a bit of string, or something else, which he has concealed in his mouth beforehand, and which he displays, saying: 'There is the manitou; now thou art cured, and it only remains to give a feast.'

"The Devil, bent on tormenting those poor blind creatures even in this world, has suggested to them another remedy, in which they place great confidence. It consists in grasping the patient under the arms, and making him walk barefoot over the live embers in the cabin; or, if he is so ill that he cannot walk, he is carried by four or five persons, and made to pass slowly over all the fires, a treatment which often enough results in this, that the greater suffering thereby produced cures, or induces unconsciousness of, the lesser pain which they strive to cure.

"After all, the commonest remedy, as it is the most profitable for the physician, is the holding of a feast to the Sun, which is done in the belief that this luminary, which takes pleasure in liberal actions, being appeased by a magnificent repast, will regard the patient with favor, and restore him to health."

All this shows that those poor people are very far from God's kingdom; but He who is able to touch hearts as hard as stone, in order to make of them children of Abraham and vessels of election, will also be abundantly able to make Christianity spring up in the bosom of idolatry, and to illumine with the lights of the Faith those barbarians, plunged although they are in the darkness of error, and in an ocean of debauchery. This will be recognized in the account of the missions undertaken by the Father in that extremity of the world, during the first two years of his sojourn there.

CHAPTER VI.

Relation of the Mission of Saint Esprit on Lake Tracy.

After a hard and fatiguing journey of five hundred leagues, during which all kinds of hardships were encountered, the Father, after pushing on to the head of the great lake, there found opportunity, in founding the missions of which we are about to speak, to exercise the zeal which had made him eagerly undergo so many fatigues. Let us begin with the mission of Saint Esprit,[1] which is the place of his abode. He speaks as follows:

"This part of the lake where we have halted is between two large villages, and forms a sort of centre for all the nations of these regions, because of its abundance of fish, which constitutes the chief part of these peoples' sustenance.

"Here we have erected a little chapel of bark,[2] where my entire occupation is to receive the Algonkin and Huron Christians, and instruct them; baptize and catechize the children; admit the infidels, who hasten hither from all directions, attracted by curiosity; speak to them in public and in private; disabuse them of their superstitions, combat their idolatry, make them see the truths of our Faith; and suffer no one to leave my presence without implanting in his soul some seeds of the Gospel.

"God has graciously permitted me to be heard by more than ten different nations; but I confess that it is necessary, even before daybreak, to entreat him to grant patience for the cheerful endurance of contempt, mockery, importunity, and insolence from these barbarians.

"Another occupation that I have in my little chapel is the baptism of the sick children, whom the infidels themselves bring hither, in order to obtain from me some medicine; and as I see that God restores these little innocents to health

---

[1] Usually spoken of as La Pointe de St. Esprit, because of the long point (now an island) protecting the eastern side of the bay.

[2] The location of Allouez's bark chapel is thought by local antiquaries to have been on the mainland of Chequamegon Bay on its southwest side, not far from the mouth of Whittlesey's Creek. See full discussion in *Wisconsin Historical Collections*, XIII. 419, 437–440.

after their baptism, I am led to hope that it is His will to make them the foundation, as it were, of His Church in these regions.

"I have hung up in the chapel various pictures, as of Hell and of the universal Judgment, which furnish me themes for instruction well adapted to my hearers; nor do I find it difficult then to engage their attention, to make them chant the *Pater* and *Ave* in their own tongue, and to induce them to join in the prayers which I dictate to them after each lesson. All this attracts so many savages that, from morning till evening, I find myself happily constrained to give them my whole attention.

"God blesses these beginnings; for the young people's debauches are no longer so frequent; and the girls, who formerly did not blush at the most shameless acts, hold themselves in restraint, and maintain the modesty so becoming to their sex.

"I know many who boldly meet the overtures made to them, with the reply that they have learned to pray, and that the black gown forbids them such acts of licentiousness.

"A little girl, ten or twelve years old, coming one day to request my prayers, I said to her: 'My little sister, you do not deserve them; you well know what was said about you some months ago.' 'It is true,' she replied, 'that I was not a good girl then, and that I did not know such actions were naughty; but since I have begun to pray, and you have told us that such things were wicked, I have stopped doing them.'

"The first days of the year 1666 were spent in presenting a very acceptable new-year's gift to the little Jesus, consisting of a number of children brought to me by their mothers, through a divine inspiration altogether extraordinary, to be baptized. Thus, little by little, this church was growing; and as I saw it already imbued with our mysteries, I deemed the time had come to transfer our little chapel to the midst of the great village, which lay three-quarters of a league from our abode, and which embraces forty-five or fifty large cabins of all nations, containing fully two thousand souls.[1]

---

[1] This was a very large population for an Indian village; it was probably due to the refugees from various tribes that had fled thither. There are local evidences that the site of this village was at the bottom of Chequamegon Bay, on the present Fish Creek.

"It was just at the time of their great revels; and I can say, in general, that I saw in that Babylon a perfect picture of libertinism. I did not fail to carry on there the same pursuits as in our first abode, and with the same success; but the Evil Spirit, envying the good there wrought by the grace of God, caused some diabolical jugglery to be carried on daily, very near our chapel, for the cure of a sick woman. It was nothing but superstitious dances, hideous masquerades, horrible yells, and apish tricks of a thousand kinds. Yet I did not fail to visit her daily; and, in order to win her with kindness, I made her a present of some raisins. At length, the sorcerers having declared that her soul had departed, and that they gave up hope, I went to see her on the morrow, and assured her that this was false; and that I even hoped for her recovery, if she would believe in Jesus Christ. But I could produce no effect on her mind, and that made me determine to appeal to the very sorcerer who was attending her. He was so surprised to see me at his house that he seemed quite overcome. I showed him the folly of his art, and that he was hastening the death of his patients rather than their recovery. In reply, he threatened to make me feel its effects by a death that should be beyond dispute; and beginning his operations soon after, he continued them for three hours, calling out from time to time, in the midst of his ceremonies, that the black gown would die through them. But it was all in vain, thanks to God, who was able even to make good come out of evil; for, this very man having sent me two of his children, who were ill, to be baptized, they received, through these sacred waters, the cure of soul and body at the same time.

"On the following day, I visited another famous sorcerer, a man with six wives and living the disorderly life that can be imagined from such a company. Finding in his cabin a little army of children, I wished to fulfill my ministry, but in vain; and that was the first time in those regions that I saw Christianity scoffed at, especially in matters concerning the resurrection of the dead and the fires of Hell. I came out with this thought: *Ibant Apostoli gaudentes à conspectu concilii, quoniam digni habiti sunt pro nomine Jesu contumeliam pati.*[1]

[1] Acts v. 41.

"The insults offered me in this cabin soon became known outside, and caused the others to treat me with the same insolence. Already a part of the bark—that is, of the walls —of our church had been broken; already a beginning had been made in stealing from me all my possessions; the young people were becoming more and more numerous and insolent; and the word of God was listened to only with scorn and mockery. I was therefore compelled to abandon this post, and withdraw again to our customary abode, having this consolation upon leaving them, that Jesus Christ had been preached and the Faith proclaimed, not only publicly, but to each savage in private; for, besides those who filled our chapel from morn till eve, the others, who remained in their cabins, were taught by those who had heard me.

"I have myself overheard them in the evening, after all had retired, repeating audibly and in the tone of a captain all the instruction which I had given them during the day. They freely acknowledged that what I teach them is very reasonable; but license prevails over reason, and, unless grace is very strong, all our teachings are of slight effect.

"Upon the occasion of a visit from one of them for the purpose of being instructed, at the first words I spoke to him, about his having two wives, 'My brother,' he rejoined, 'thou speakest to me on a very delicate subject; it is enough for my children to pray; teach them.'

"After I had left that village of abomination, God led me two leagues from our dwelling, where I found three adult sick persons; these I baptized, after adequate instruction, and two of them died after their baptism. God's mysterious ways excite our admiration, and I could cite many very similar illustrations of them which show the loving care of Providence for its elect."

CHAPTER VII.

Of the Mission to the Tionnontateheronnons.

"The Tionnontateheronnons of the present day are the same people who were formerly called the Hurons of the tobacco nation.[1] They, like the rest, were forced to leave their country to escape from the Hyroquois, and to retire to the head of this great lake, where distance and scarcity of game furnish them an asylum against their foes.

"They formerly constituted a part of the flourishing church of the Hurons, and had as pastor the late Father Garnier, who gave his life so courageously for his dear flock; therefore they cherish his memory with very marked veneration.[2]

"Since their country's downfall, they have received no Christian nurture; whence it results that they are Christians rather by calling than by profession. They boast of that fair name, but the intercourse which they have so long had with infidels has nearly effaced from their minds all vestiges of religion, and has made them resume many of their former customs. Their village is at no great distance from our abode, which has enabled me to apply myself to this mission with greater assiduity than to the other more distant ones.

"I have, accordingly, tried to restore this church to its pristine state by preaching the word of God, and administering the sacraments. I conferred baptism upon a hundred children during the first winter I spent with them; and upon

[1] This tribe, which was known as Petun by the French, was originally settled in Nottawasaga township of Simcoe County, Ontario, where its members raised much tobacco. Defeated and massacred by the Iroquois in 1649 they fled to the forests of Wisconsin, then migrated to the vicinity of Mackinac, whence Cadillac induced them to remove to Detroit River. Under the name of Wyandot they were prominent in the Northwestern Indian wars of the eighteenth century. A remnant still remains on their reservation near Amherstburg, Ont.

[2] Charles Garnier was born May 25, 1606, took his Jesuit novitiate at Paris, and came to New France in 1636. In November, 1639, he accompanied Isaac Jogues to the Tobacco Huron, but was received unfavorably, and driven away. Only after the third effort in 1647 did Garnier succeed in founding his mission, which became very flourishing, until the attack of the Iroquois in December, 1649. Garnier was murdered while attempting to rally and succor his flock.

others subsequently, during my two years of intercourse with them. The adults partook of the sacrament of penance, attended the holy sacrifice of the mass, prayed in public and in private; in short, as they had been very well taught, it was a matter of no great difficulty for me to restore piety to their hearts, and make them put forth once more the pious sentiments they formerly had for the Faith.

"Of all these baptized children, God chose to take but two, who winged their way to Heaven after their baptism. As for the adults, there were three of them for whose salvation God seems to have sent me hither.

"The first was an old man, Ousaki[1] by birth, formerly of importance among his own people, and ever held in esteem by the Hurons, by whom he had been taken captive in war. A few days after my arrival in this country, I learned that he was lying ill four leagues from here. I went to see him, and instructed and baptized him; and three hours later he died, leaving me every possible proof that God had shown him mercy.

"Even although my journey from Quebec should bear no further fruits than the saving of this poor old man, I would deem all the steps that I had taken only too well rewarded, inasmuch as the Son of God did not begrudge him even His last drop of blood.

"The second person I have to mention was a woman, far advanced in years, who was confined, two leagues from our abode, by a dangerous illness, occasioned by the unexpected ignition of a bag of powder in her cabin. Father Garnier had promised her baptism more than fifteen years before, and was on the point of conferring it, when he was killed by the Iroquois. That good Father was unwilling to break his promise, and like a good pastor he brought it about, by his intercession, that I should arrive here before she died. I visited her on All Saints' Day,[2] and, after refreshing her memory concerning all our mysteries, found that the seeds of God's word, implanted in her soul so many years before, had there borne fruits which awaited only the baptismal waters in order to attain their perfection. Accordingly I conferred this sacrament upon her, after I had thoroughly

---

[1] A Sauk Indian; see p. 81, note 2, *ante*.   [2] November 1.

prepared her; and on the very night of her receiving this grace she rendered up her soul to her Creator.

"The third person was a girl, fourteen years of age, who applied herself very assiduously to all the catechisms and prayers which I caused to be recited, and of which she had learned a great portion by heart. She fell ill; her mother, who was not a Christian, called in the sorcerers, and made them go through all the fooleries of their infamous calling. I heard about it and went to see the girl, broaching to her the subject of baptism. She was overjoyed to receive it; and after that, mere child although she was, she made opposition to all the jugglers' practices, which they were bent on executing in her presence. She declared that by her baptism she had renounced all superstitions; and in this courageous contest she died, praying to God until her very last breath."

CHAPTER VIII.

Of the Mission to the Outaouacs, Kiskakoumac, and Outaouasinagouc.[1]

"I group these three nations together because they have the same tongue, the Algonquin, and form collectively one village, which corresponds to that of the Tionnontateheron-nons, among whom we are dwelling.

"The Outaouacs claim that the great river[2] belongs to them, and that no nation can launch a boat on it without their consent. Therefore all who go to trade with the French, although of widely different nations, bear the general name of Outaouacs, under whose auspices they make the journey.

"The old home of the Outaouacs was a district on the Lake of the Hurons, whence the fear of the Iroquois had driven them, and whither all their longings are directed as to their native land.

"These peoples have very little inclination to receive

---

[1] These are three of the divisions of the Ottawa people. Kiskakon is a word that means "Cut Tails"; the Ottawa-Sinago were the squirrel clan of the tribe.

[2] The Ottawa River was frequently called the Grand or Great River by the people of New France.

the faith, since they are extremely addicted to idolatry, superstitions, legends, polygamy, unstable marriages, and every sort of licentiousness, which makes them renounce all natural shame. All these obstacles did not deter me from preaching to them the name of Jesus Christ, and proclaiming the Gospel in all their cabins and in our chapel. The latter was filled from morning till night, and there I gave constant instruction in our mysteries and in God's commandments.

"In the first winter that I spent with them I had the consolation to baptize about eighty children, including some boys and girls between eight and ten years old, who, by their assiduity in coming to offer prayer to God, showed themselves worthy of this blessing. A circumstance greatly facilitating the baptism of these children is the belief, now very common, that those sacred waters not only do not cause death, as was formerly held, but even give health to the sick and restore the dying to life. Indeed, as a matter of fact, of all those children that were baptized, God was pleased to take to himself only six, leaving the rest to serve as a foundation for this new church.

"As for the adults, I did not see fit to baptize many, because their superstitions, being so firmly rooted in their minds, offer a serious hindrance to their conversion. Of four whom I considered well prepared for this sacrament, the Divine Providence made itself clearly manifest in the case of one poor sick man, who lived two leagues from our dwelling. I knew not that he was in such a state, and yet felt inwardly prompted, despite my scanty strength and ill health, to go and see him. Accordingly, I made my way to a hamlet distant a good league from us, but found no sick people there. I learned, however, that there was another hamlet farther on; and, notwithstanding my weakness, felt that God demanded of me that I should repair thither. I did so with much difficulty, and found that dying savage only waiting for baptism, which I gave him after the necessary instruction. He was fortunate in having shared in the instructions that I gave during the winter, when he visited our chapel with the rest; and in having, by his attention, shown himself deserving of God's mercy.

"In the summer of that same year I was occupied chiefly

in attending the sick of this mission; three whom I found in
danger I baptized, and two of them died in the profession of
Christianity. Again God led me into the cabins, just in
time to confer baptism on eleven sick children, who had not
yet the use of their reason; of these, five have gone to enjoy
God. Of seventeen more children whom I baptized there,
during the autumn and winter following, but one died, who
ascended to Heaven almost at the same time when a good
old blind man breathed his last, three days after his baptism."

CHAPTER IX.

Of the Mission to the Pouteouatamiouec.

"The Pouteouatami are a people speaking the Algonquin
tongue, but in a dialect much harder to understand than
that of the Outaouacs. Their country lies along the Lake of
the Ilimouek, a large lake which had not before come to
our knowledge, adjoining the Lake of the Hurons, and that
of the Stinkards, in a southeasterly direction.[1] These people are warlike, and they engage in hunting and fishing. Their
country is excellently adapted to raising Indian corn, and
they have fields covered with it, to which they are glad to
have recourse, to avoid the famine that is only too common
in these regions. They are extremely idolatrous, clinging
to their ridiculous legends, and are addicted to polygamy.
We have seen them all here, to the number of three hundred
men bearing arms. Of all the people with whom I have
mingled in these regions, they are the most docile, and the
best disposed toward the French. Their wives and daughters
are more modest than those of the other nations. They
observe among themselves a certain sort of civility, and also
show it toward strangers, which is rare among our barbarians.
Once when I went to see one of their elders, his eyes fell upon
my shoes, which were made after the French fashion; and
curiosity moved him to ask leave to take them, in order to
examine them easily. Upon returning them to me, he would
not permit me to put them on myself, but obliged me to al-

[1] Allouez terms Lake Michigan, Lake of the Ilimouek (Illinois Indians),
adjacent to Lake Huron and to the Lake of the Stinkards (Green Bay).

low him to perform that service, even insisting on fastening the thongs, and showing the same marks of respect that servants do to their masters upon rendering them this service. Kneeling at my feet, he said to me, 'It is in this way that we treat those whom we honor.'

"On another occasion when I went to see him, he arose from his seat to yield it to me, with the same formalities that politeness demands of gentlefolk.

"I proclaimed the Faith to them publicly in the general council held a few days after my arrival in this country, and privately in their cabins during their month's sojourn here, and afterward throughout the following autumn and winter, during which I baptized thirty-four of their children, nearly all of this number being in the cradle. I may say, too, for the consolation of this mission, that the first one of all these people to take possession of Heaven in the name of all his countrymen, was a Pouteouatami child whom I baptized soon after my arrival, and who died immediately afterward.

"During the same winter I received into the church five adults, of whom the first was an aged man, about a hundred years old, who was regarded by the savages as a sort of divinity. He was wont to fast twenty days at a time, and had visions of God, that is, according to these people, of the Maker of the Earth. Nevertheless, he fell ill; and he was attended in his sickness by two of his daughters, who showed an assiduity and love above the capacity of savages. Among other services rendered him by them was that of repeating to him, in the evening, the instructions which they had heard during the day in our chapel. God was pleased to make use of their piety for their father's conversion; for, when I visited him, I found him versed in our mysteries, and, the Holy Ghost operating in his heart through the ministry of his daughters, he passionately asked to be made a Christian. I granted his request by baptizing him—a ceremony which I did not think it advisable to defer, seeing that he was in danger of death. Thenceforth, he would not allow in his presence any juggler's ceremonies for his cure; he would have no conversation, except on the saving of his soul; and once, when I was urging upon him frequent prayer to God, 'Know, my brother,' said he, 'that I am continually throwing tobacco into the fire, and saying, "Thou maker of Heaven and Earth, I would honor thee." ' I contented myself with making him understand that it was not necessary to honor God in that way, but merely to speak to him with the heart and the mouth. Then, the time having come when the savages ask the fulfillment of their desires in a ceremony much resembling the Bacchanalia or carnival, our good old man caused search to be made in all the cabins for a piece of blue cloth, declaring his wish therefor because it was the color of Heaven, 'to which,' said he, 'I would keep my heart and thoughts ever directed.' Never have I seen a savage more given to prayer than he; among other prayers, he was wont to repeat the following with unusual fervor: 'My Father who art in Heaven, my Father, hallowed be your name,'— finding more sweetness in those words than in the ones I taught him, 'Our Father who art in Heaven.' One day, taking thought of his extreme old age, he exclaimed of his own accord, in the sentiments of St. Augustine: 'Too late have I come to know you, O God, too late have I come to love you.' I doubt not that his death, which was not long delayed, was precious in God's sight, who for so many years left him in idolatry, and reserved for him so few days for closing his life in so Christian a manner.

"I must not omit here a rather strange circumstance: on the day after his death his relatives, contrary to all usage of this country, burned his body and reduced it entirely to ashes.[1] The cause of this is found in a legend which passes here for truth.

"It is held beyond dispute that this old man's father was a hare, an animal which runs over the snow in winter, and that thus the snow, the hare, and the old man are of the same village, that is, are relatives. It is further said that the hare told his wife that he disapproved of their children's remaining in the depths of the earth, as that did not befit their condition, they being relatives of the snow, whose country is above, toward the sky; and, if it ever occurred that they were put into the ground after their death, he would pray the snow, his relative, in order to punish the people for this

---

[1] Cremation is not usual among the North American aborigines; when used it is due to some superstition, or is the custom of a particular clan.

offense, to fall in such quantities and so long that there should be no spring. And, to confirm this story, it is added that three years ago the brother of our good old man died, in the beginning of the winter; and, after he had been buried in the usual manner, snow fell to such an extent, and the winter was so long, that people despaired of seeing the spring in its season. Meanwhile, all were dying of hunger, and no remedy could be found for this general suffering. The elders assembled, and held many councils, but all in vain; the snow still continued. Then some one of the company said he remembered the threats which we have related. Straightway they went and disinterred the dead man, and burned him; when immediately the snow ceased, and spring followed. Who would think that people could give credence to such absurd stories? And yet they regard them as true beyond dispute.

"Our good old man was not the only one of his house to whom God showed mercy. His two daughters, who were the cause of his salvation, were undoubtedly drawn to Heaven by his prayers; for, one of them being seized with an ailment which lasted but five days, God guided my steps so fortunately for her eternal happiness that, although I could not reach her until the evening before her death, I had leisure to prepare her for holy baptism, which she received in time to go and bear her good father company in the glory which she had obtained for him. The third daughter, surviving both the others, seems to have inherited their piety. I found this woman so discreet, so modest, and so well disposed toward the Faith, that I did not hesitate to admit her into the Church through partaking of the sacraments. The entire family of that good neophyte—and it is a large one—feel the effects of this goodness, which seems natural to them. They all have a tender regard for me, and, from a feeling of respect which they bear me, call me by no other name than 'uncle.' I hope that God will show mercy to all of them, for I see them more inclined to prayer than is usual among savages.

"We can also relate, among the marvels that God has wrought in this church, what happened in regard to another family of this nation. A young man, in whose canoe I had a place on my journey to this country, was seized, toward the close of the winter, with the contagious disease that was prevalent. I tried to show him as much kindness as he had shown me ill usage on the journey. As he was a man of considerable importance, no kind of jugglery was spared for his cure; and it was carried so far that at length they came to tell me that they had extracted from his body two dog's teeth. 'That is not what causes his illness,' said I to them, 'but rather the tainted blood which he has in his body,' for I judged that he had the pleurisy. Meanwhile, I began to instruct him in good earnest; and on the next day, finding him well prepared, I gave him holy baptism with the name of Ignace, hoping that great saint would confound the evil spirit and the jugglers. Indeed, I bled him; and, showing the blood to the juggler, who was present, 'There,' said I to him, 'is what is killing this sick man. Thou shouldst, with all thy affected arts, have drawn from him every drop of this corrupt blood, and not some alleged dog's teeth.' But he, perceiving the relief which this bleeding had afforded the sick man, determined to have the glory of his cure; and, to that end, made him take a kind of medicine, which produced such an ill effect that the patient remained for three whole hours as one dead. This result was proclaimed throughout the village, and the juggler, much surprised by the turn of affairs, confessed that he had killed the poor man, and begged me not to forsake him. He was not, in truth, forsaken by his patron, Saint Ignatius, who restored him to life, in order to confound the superstitions of these infidels.

"This young man was not yet cured when his sister fell ill of the same disease. We enjoyed greater freedom in the discharge of our functions, in view of what had occurred in her brother's case, and I had every opportunity to prepare her for baptism; and besides that grace, the blessed Virgin, whose name she bore, procured her recovery.

"But hardly was she out of danger when the same disease seized her cousin, in the same cabin. He appeared to me more dangerously ill than the two others had been, which made me hasten to baptize him, after the necessary instruction. He was already feeling better, in consequence of this sacrament, when his father took it into his head to make a feast, or, rather, a sacrifice to the Sun, to ask the latter for his son's recovery. I came upon them in the midst of the ceremony, and hastened to embrace my sick neophyte, and convince him that God alone was the master of life and death. He immediately acknowledged his error, and made atonement to God by the sacrament of penance; but I, addressing his father and all the sacrificers, said to them: 'I despair now of this patient's recovery, since you have had recourse to others than Him who has in His hands both life and death. You have killed this poor man by your impiety, and I give up all hope for him.' He died, in fact, some time afterward; and I trust that God may have accepted his temporal death as penance for his offense, so that He will not deprive him of the everlasting life which this man will have obtained by the intercessions of Saint Joseph, whose name he bore.

"The gain is more assured in regard to children, of whom I baptized seventeen toward the close of this mission, which I was forced to bring to an end by the departure of these people, as they returned to their own country after harvesting their Indian corn. On taking leave, they gave me a very pressing invitation to visit them in the following spring. May God be forever glorified in the minds of those poor barbarians, who have at last acknowledged Him, after recognizing, from the earliest times, no divinity greater than the Sun."

CHAPTER X.

Of the Mission to the Ousakiouek and Outagamiouek.[1]

"I next add these two nations because they are mingled with and allied to the preceding, and have, besides, the same language, the Algonquin, although differing greatly in various idioms, a fact which makes it very difficult to understand them. Nevertheless, after some labor on my part, they understand me now, and I understand them, sufficiently for their instruction.

"The country of the Outagami lies southward toward the Lake of the Ilimouek. They are a populous tribe, of about a thousand men bearing arms, and given to hunting and war-

[1] Sauk and Outagami.

fare. They have fields of Indian corn, and live in a country
offering excellent facilities for the hunting of the wildcat,
stag, wild ox, and beaver. Canoes they do not use, but
commonly make their journeys by land, bearing their packages and their game on their shoulders. These people are as
much addicted to idolatry as the other nations. One day,
on entering the cabin of an Outagamy, I found his parents
dangerously ill; and when I told him that bleeding would
cure them, the poor man took some powdered tobacco and
sprinkled it completely over my gown, saying to me: 'Thou
art a spirit; come now, restore these sick people to health;
I offer thee this tobacco in sacrifice.' 'What art thou doing,
my brother?' said I; 'I am nothing, but He who made all
things is the master of our lives, while I am but His servant.'
'Well, then,' he rejoined, scattering some tobacco on the
ground, and raising his eyes on high, 'to Thee, then, who
madest Heaven and earth I offer this tobacco. Give these
sick persons health.'

"These people are not very far removed from the recognition of the Creator of the world; for it is they who told
me what I have already related, namely, that they acknowledge in their country a Great Spirit, the maker of Heaven
and earth, who dwells toward the country of the French.
It is said of them and of the Ousaki that, when they find a
man alone and at a disadvantage, they kill him, especially
if he is a Frenchman; for they cannot endure the beards of
the latter people. Cruelty of that kind makes them less
docile, and less inclined to receive the Gospel, than are the
Pouteouatami. Still I failed not to proclaim it to nearly
six-score persons, who passed a summer here. I found none
among them sufficiently well prepared for baptism, though I
conferred it on five of their sick children, who then recovered
their health.

"As for the Ousaki, they above all others can be called
savages. They are very numerous, but wandering and
scattered in the forests, without any fixed abode. I have
seen nearly two hundred of them, to all of whom I have published the Faith, and have baptized eighteen of their children,
to whom the sacred waters were salutary for both soul and
body."

Chapter XI.

Of the Mission to the Ilimouec, or Alimouek.

"The Ilimouec speak Algonquin, but a very different dialect from those of all the other tribes.[1] I understand them only slightly, because I have talked with them only a very little. They do not live in these regions, their country being more than sixty leagues hence toward the south, beyond a great river—which, as well as I can conjecture, empties into the sea somewhere near Virginia. These people are hunters and warriors, using bows and arrows, rarely muskets, and never canoes. They used to be a populous nation, divided into ten large villages; but now they are reduced to two, continual wars with the Nadouessi on one side and the Iroquois on the other having well-nigh exterminated them.

"They acknowledge many spirits to whom they offer sacrifice. They practise a kind of dance, quite peculiar to themselves, which they call 'the dance of the tobacco-pipe.' It is executed thus: they prepare a great pipe, which they deck with plumes, and put in the middle of the room, with a sort of veneration. One of the company rises, begins to dance, and then yields his place to another, and this one to a third; and thus they dance in succession, one after another, and not together. One would take this dance for a pantomime ballet; and it is executed to the beating of a drum. The performer makes war in rhythmic time, preparing his arms, attiring himself, running, discovering the foe, raising the cry, slaying the enemy, removing his scalp, and returning home with a song of victory, and all with an astonishing exactness, promptitude and agility. After they have all danced, one after the other, around the pipe, it is taken and offered to the chief man in the whole assembly, for him to smoke; then to another, and so in succession to all. This ceremony resembles in its significance the French custom of drinking, several out of the same glass; but, in addition, the pipe is left in the keeping of the most honored man, as a sacred trust,

[1] The language of the Illinois-Miami division of the Algonquian stock differs considerably from that of the northern tribes with whom Allouez was familiar.

and a sure pledge of the peace and union that will ever subsist among them as long as it shall remain in that person's hands.

"Of all the spirits to whom they offer sacrifice, they honor with a very special worship one who is preëminent above the others, as they maintain, because he is the maker of all things. Such a passionate desire have they to see him that they keep long fasts to that end, hoping that by this means God will be induced to appear to them in their sleep; and if they chance to see Him, they deem themselves happy, and assured of a long life.

"All the nations of the south have this same wish to see God, which, without doubt, greatly facilitates their conversion; for it only remains to teach them how they must serve Him in order to see Him and be blessed.

"I have proclaimed the name of Jesus Christ here to eighty people of this nation, and they have carried it and published it with approbation to the whole country of the south; consequently I can say that this mission is the one where I have labored the least and accomplished the most. They honor our Lord among themselves in their own way, putting His image, which I have given them, in the most honored place on the occasion of any important feast, while the master of the banquet addresses it as follows: 'In Thy honor, O Man-God, do we hold this feast; to Thee do we offer these viands.'

"I confess that the fairest field for the Gospel appears to me to be yonder. Had I had leisure and opportunity, I would have pushed on to their country, to see with my own eyes all the good things there of which they tell me.

"I find all those with whom I have mingled affable and humane; and it is said that whenever they meet a stranger, they give a cry of joy, caress him, and show him every possible evidence of affection. I have baptized but one child of this nation. The seeds of the Faith which I have sown in their souls will bear fruit when it pleases the master of the vine to gather it. Their country is warm, and they raise two crops of Indian corn a year. There are rattlesnakes there, which cause many deaths among them, as they do not know the antidote. They hold medicines in high esteem, offering sacrifice to them as to great spirits. They have no forests in their country, but vast prairies instead, where oxen, cows, deer, bears, and other animals feed in great numbers."

CHAPTER XII.

Of the Mission to the Nadouesiouek.

"These are people dwelling to the west of this place, toward the great river named Messipi.[1] They are forty or fifty leagues from this place, in a country of prairies, rich in all kinds of game. They cultivate fields, sowing therein not Indian corn, but only tobacco; while Providence has furnished them a kind of marsh rye which they go and harvest toward the close of summer in certain small lakes that are covered with it. So well do they know how to prepare it that it is highly appetizing and very nutritious.[2] They gave me some when I was at the head of Lake Tracy, where I saw them. They do not use muskets, but only bows and arrows, with which they shoot very skillfully. Their cabins are not covered with bark, but with deerskins, carefully dressed, and sewed together with such skill that the cold does not enter. These people are, above all the rest, savage and wild, appearing abashed and as motionless as statues in our presence. Yet they are warlike, and have conducted hostilities against all their neighbors, by whom they are held in extreme fear. They speak a language that is utterly foreign, the savages here not understanding it at all. Therefore I have been obliged to address them through an interpreter, who, being an infidel, did not accomplish what I might well have wished. Still I succeeded in wresting from the demon one innocent soul of that country, a little child, who went to Paradise soon after I had baptized it. *A solis ortu usque ad occasum laudabile nomen Domini.*[3] God will give us some opportunity to

---

[1] This is the first mention in the *Jesuit Relations* of the Mississippi River by this name.

[2] The wild oats or wild rice that grows so plentifully in the streams and lakes of Wisconsin and Minnesota forms a nourishing food of great value in Indian economy.

[3] Psalm cxiii. 3.

announce His word there, and glorify His holy name, when it shall please his divine Majesty to show mercy to those people. They are well-nigh at the end of the earth, so they say. Farther toward the setting Sun there are nations named Karezi, beyond whom, they maintain, the earth is cut off, and nothing is to be seen but a great lake whose waters are ill-smelling, for so they designate the sea.

"Toward the northwest there is a nation which eats meat uncooked, being content to hold it in the hand and expose it to the fire, while beyond these people lies the North Sea. On this side are the Kilistinons, whose rivers empty into Hutston's Bay.[1] We have, besides, some knowledge of the savages inhabiting the regions of the south, as far as the sea; so that only a little territory and few people are left to whom the Gospel has not been proclaimed—if we credit the reports often given us by the savages."

Chapter XIII.

Of the Mission to the Kilistinouc.

"The Kilistinouc have their usual abode on the shores of the North Sea, and their canoes ply along a river emptying into a great bay, which we think is, in all probability, the one designated on the map by the name of Hutson. For those whom I have seen from that country have told me that they had known of a ship; and one of their old men declared to me that he had himself seen, at the mouth of the River of the Assinipoualac,[2] some peoples allied to the Kilistinouc, whose country is still farther northward.

"He told me further that he had also seen a house which the Europeans had built on the mainland, out of boards and pieces of wood; and that they held books in their hands, like the one he saw me holding when he told me this. He made mention of another nation, adjoining the Assinipoualac, who eat human beings, and live wholly on raw flesh; but these people, in turn, are eaten by bears of frightful size,

---

[1] The Christinaux Indians, for whom see p. 24, note 3, *ante*. They ranged as far northward as Hudson Bay.

[2] The present Assiniboine River.

all red, and with prodigiously long claws.[1] It is deemed highly probable that they are lions.

"Concerning the Kilistinouc, they appear to me extremely docile, and show a kindness uncommon among these barbarians. They are much more nomadic than any of the other nations, having no fixed abode, no fields, no villages; and living wholly on game and a small quantity of oats which they gather in marshy places. They pay idolatrous worship to the Sun, to which they are wont to offer sacrifice by fastening a dog to the top of a pole and leaving it thus suspended until it rots.

"They speak nearly the same tongue as do the people formerly called Poissons-blancs,[2] and as the savages of Tadoussac. By the grace of God I understand them, and they me, sufficiently for their instruction. They had never heard of the Faith, and this novelty, together with their docility of temperament, made them very attentive to me. They have promised me to render homage henceforth only to the Creator of the Sun and of the world. The wandering and vagrant life which they lead made me postpone baptizing those whom I saw to be best prepared, and I only baptized a new-born girl-baby.

"I hope this mission will some day bear fruit commensurate with the labors which will be bestowed upon it when our Fathers go and winter with the people, as they do with the savages from Tadoussac,[3] at Quebec. They have invited me thither, but I cannot give myself wholly to some while depriving so many others of the succor I owe them, as being the nearest to this place and the best fitted to receive the Gospel."

[1] The Assiniboin are a Siouan tribe, offshoot from the Yankton family of the Sioux. Their habitat was on Lake Winnipeg and the river of their name. They traded with the Christinaux and were frequently supplied from Hudson Bay. The animals here described are grizzly bears.

[2] *Poissons-blancs* (whitefish) was the French appellation of the Attikamègue Indians who lived on the upper waters of St. Maurice River. Allouez speaks of them in the past tense, for they were nearly extinct at this time because of the attacks of the Iroquois and the ravages of small-pox.

[3] Tadoussac lies at the mouth of Saguenay River, where the Jesuits had a mission.

CHAPTER XIIII.

Of the Mission to the Outchibouec.[1]

"They are called *sauteurs* by the French, because their abode is the *sault* by which Lake Tracy empties into the Lake of the Hurons. They speak the common Algonquin, and are easily understood. I have proclaimed the Faith to them on various occasions, but especially when I sojourned with them at the head of our great lake for a whole month. During that time, I instructed them in all our mysteries; I also baptized twenty of their children, and an adult who was sick; this man died on the day after his baptism, bearing to Heaven the first-fruits of his nation."

CHAPTER XV.

Of the Mission to the Nipissiriniens, and Father Alloues's Journey to Lake Alimibegong.

"The Nipissiriniens formerly received instruction from our Fathers who sojourned in the country of the Hurons.[2] These poor people, many of whom were Christians, were compelled by the incursions of the Iroquois to flee for refuge even to Lake Alimibegong, only fifty or sixty leagues from the North Sea.[3]

"For nearly twenty years they have neither seen a pastor nor heard the name of God. I thought that I ought to bestow a part of my labors on that old-time church, and that a journey undertaken to their new country would be attended with Heaven's blessings.

"On the sixth day of May of this year, 1667, I embarked in a canoe with two savages to serve me as guides, throughout this journey. Meeting on the way two-score savages from the North Bay, I conveyed to them the first tidings of the Faith, for which they thanked me with some politeness.

"Continuing our journey, on the seventeenth we crossed

---

[1] A variant for the Chippewa tribe, for whom see p. 23, note 2, *ante*.

[2] See Introduction to Raymbault and Jogues, *ante*.

[3] Lake Nipigon, north of Lake Superior, emptying into it by a river of the same name.

a portion of our great lake, paddling for twelve hours without dropping the paddle from the hand. God rendered me very sensible aid; for, as there were but three of us in our canoe, I was obliged to paddle with all my strength, together with the savages, in order to make the most of the calm, without which we should have been in great danger, utterly spent, as we were, with toil and lack of food. Nevertheless, we lay down supperless at nightfall, and on the morrow contented ourselves with a frugal meal of Indian corn and water; for the wind and rain prevented our savages from casting their net.

"On the nineteenth, invited by the beautiful weather, we covered eighteen leagues, paddling from daybreak until after sunset, without respite and without landing.

"On the twentieth, finding nothing in our nets, we continued our journey, munching some grains of dry corn. On the following day, God refreshed us with two small fishes, which gave us new life. Heaven's blessings increased on the next day, our savages catching so many sturgeon that they were obliged to leave part of them at the water's edge.

"Coasting along the northern shore of this great lake on the twenty-third, we passed from island to island, these being very frequent. There is one, at least twenty leagues long, where are found pieces of copper, which is held by the Frenchmen who have examined it here to be true red copper.[1]

"After accomplishing a good part of our journey on the lake, we left it on the twenty-fifth of this month of May, and consigned ourselves to a river, so full of rapids and falls that even our savages could go no farther; and learning that Lake Alimibegong was still frozen over, they gladly took the two days' rest imposed upon them by necessity.

"As we drew near our journey's end, we occasionally met Nipissirinien savages, wandering from their homes to seek a livelihood in the woods. Gathering together a considerable number of them, for the celebration of Whitsuntide,[2] I prepared them by a long instruction for hearing the holy sacrifice of the mass, which I celebrated in a chapel of foliage. They listened with as much piety and decorum as do our

---

[1] Isle Royale, now under the jurisdiction of Keweenaw County, Michigan.

[2] Whitsunday fell on May 29 in 1667.

savages of Quebec in our chapel at Sillery;[1] and to me it was the sweetest refreshment I had during that journey, entirely removing all past fatigue.

"Here I must relate a remarkable circumstance which occurred not long ago. Two women, mother and daughter, who had always had recourse to God from the time of their instruction, and had received from Him unfailing and extraordinary succor, very recently learned by experience that God never forsakes those who put their trust in Him. They had been captured by the Iroquois, and had happily escaped from the fires and cruelties of those barbarians; but had soon afterward fallen a second time into their clutches, and were, consequently, left with no hope of escape. Yet one day, when they found themselves alone with a single Iroquois, who had remained behind to guard them while the rest went out to hunt, the girl told her mother that the time had come to rid themselves of this guard, and flee. To this end she asked the Iroquois for a knife to use on a beaver-skin that she was ordered to dress; and at the same time, imploring Heaven's aid, she plunged it into his bosom. The mother, on her part, arose and struck him on the head with a billet of wood, and they left him for dead. Taking some food, they started forth with all haste, and at length reached their own country in safety.

"We spent six days in paddling from island to island, seeking some outlet; and finally, after many detours, we reached the village of the Nipissiriniens on the third day of June. It is composed of savages, mostly idolaters, with some Christians of long standing. Among them I found twenty who made public profession of Christianity. I did not lack occupation with both classes during our two weeks' sojourn in their country, and I worked as diligently as my health, broken by the fatigues of the journey, allowed. I found more resistance here than anywhere else to infant baptism; but the more the Devil opposes us, the more must we strive to confound him. He is hardly pleased, I think, to see me make this latest journey, which is nearly five hundred leagues in length, going and coming, including the detours we were obliged to make."

[1] A mission colony not far from Quebec.

FATHER ALLOUEZ'S WISCONSIN JOURNEY
1669–1670

INTRODUCTION

In our last selection Allouez, in the summer of 1667, was left at his farthest north on Lake Nipigon; the following narrative commences with the autumn of 1669. Within the two years unrecorded here, he had visited the St. Lawrence twice, had secured more workers for the Western field, and had established permanent headquarters at Sault Ste. Marie. At this place Father Claude Dablon had been made superior of all the Western missions; while Father Jacques Marquette had taken Allouez's former place at the Bay of Chequamegon.

Allouez was eager to begin new work among the Wisconsin tribes, many from among whose members had paid him short visits in his hut on Chequamegon Bay. No sooner had he reached the Sault, after the long fatiguing canoe journey of a thousand miles, than he began preparations for a voyage to Green Bay and the villages upon its shores. The succeeding narrative is especially interesting to the student of Western history, since by this journey Allouez opened the way for the later exploration of Father Marquette, and in his accurate and detailed descriptions portrays with careful hand the Wisconsin of the aborigines.

The extract that follows is from the *Jesuit Relation* of 1669–1670, first published at Paris in 1671. It is found in the Thwaites edition in volume LIV., pp. 197–214.

FATHER ALLOUEZ'S JOURNEY INTO WISCONSIN, 1669–1670

Chapter XII.

Of the Mission of Saint François Xavier on the "Bay of Stinkards," or rather "of Stinking Waters."

Letter from Father Allouez, who has had charge of this Mission, to the Reverend Father Superior.

My Reverend Father, Pax Christi.

I SEND to Your Reverence the journal of our winter's campaign, wherein you will find how the Gospel has been proclaimed, and Jesus Christ preached, to peoples that worship only the Sun, or some imaginary idols.

On the third of November, we departed from the Sault, I and two others. Two canoe-loads of Prouteouatamis wished to conduct me to their country; not that they wished to receive instruction there, having no disposition for the Faith, but that I might curb some young Frenchmen, who, being among them for the purpose of trading, were threatening and maltreating them.[1]

We arrived on the first day at the entrance to the Lake of the Hurons, where we slept under the shelter of the islands. The length of the journey and the difficulty of the way, because of the lateness of the season, led us to have recourse to Saint Francis Xavier, patron of our mission; this obliged me to celebrate holy mass, and my two companions to receive communion on the day of the feast,[2] in his honor, and still further to invoke him, twice every day, by reciting his orison.

On the fourth, toward noon, we doubled the cape which

---

[1] See Perrot's account of the disorder and license of the early *coureurs des bois*, p. 82, *ante*.

[2] December 3 was the feast-day of St. Francis Xavier; see p. 145, *post*.

forms the detour,[1] and is the beginning of the strait or the gulf of Lake Huron, which is well known, and of the Lake of the Ilinois, which up to the present time is unknown, and is much smaller than Lake Huron. Toward evening the contrary wind, which was about to cast our canoe upon the shoals of rocks, obliged us rather to finish our journey.

On the 5th, upon waking, we found ourselves covered with snow, and the surface of the canoe coated with ice. This little beginning of crosses which our Lord was pleased to allot us invited us to offer ourselves for greater ones. We were compelled to embark with all the baggage and provisions, with great difficulty, our bare feet in the water, in order to keep the canoe afloat, which otherwise would have broken. After leaving a great number of islands to the northward,[2] we slept on a little island, where we were detained six days by the bad weather. The snow and frosts threatening us with ice, my companions had recourse to Saint Anne, to whom we entrusted our journey, praying her, together with St. Francis Xavier, to take us under her protection.

On the eleventh we embarked, notwithstanding the contrary wind, and crossed to another island, and thence to the mainland, where we found two Frenchmen with several savages. From them we learned of the great dangers to which we were about to expose ourselves, by reason of the storms that are frequent on this lake, and the ice which would soon be afloat. But all that was not sufficient to shake the confidence that we had reposed in our protectors. After invoking them, we launched the canoe, and then doubled successfully enough the cape[3] which makes a detour to the west, having left in our rear a large island named Michilimakinak, celebrated among the savages. Their legends about this island are pleasing.

They say that it is the native country of one of their gods, named Michabous—that is to say, "the Great Hare," Ouisaketchak, who is the one that created the earth; and that it was in these islands that he invented nets for catch-

[1] Still called Detour, in Chippewa County, Mich.

[2] The Cheneaux Islands of Mackinac County, now utilized for summer homes.

[3] Cape St. Ignace, directly west of Mackinac Island.

ing fish, after he had attentively considered the spider while she was working at her web in order to catch flies in it. They believe that Lake Superior is a pond made by beavers, and that its dam was double, the first being at the place called by us the Sault, and the second five leagues below. In ascending the river, they say, this same god found that second dam first and broke it down completely; and that is why there is no waterfall or whirlpools in that rapid. As to the first dam, being in haste, he only walked on it to tread it down; and, for that reason, there still remain great falls and whirlpools there.

This god, they add, while chasing a beaver in Lake Superior, crossed with a single stride a bay of eight leagues in width. In view of so mighty an enemy, the beavers changed their location, and withdrew to another lake, Alimibegoung, whence they afterward, by means of the rivers flowing from it, arrived at the North Sea,[1] with the intention of crossing over to France; but, finding the water bitter, they lost heart, and spread throughout the rivers and lakes of this entire country. And that is the reason why there are no beavers in France, and the French come to get them here.[2] The people believe that it is this god who is the master of our lives, and that he grants life only to those to whom he has appeared in sleep. This is a part of the legends with which the savages very often entertain us.

On the fourteenth, God delivered us from two great dangers, through the intercession of our protectors. While we were taking a little rest, our canoe was borne away from us by a gust of wind, which carried it to the other side of the river; then it was brought back to us by another gust of wind, when, awakened by the noise it made, we were thinking of making a raft, in order to go and get it. Toward evening, after making a long day's journey and finding no place

[1] Lake Nipigon discharges into Lake Superior, but the portages between its tributaries and Albany River—an affluent of Hudson Bay—are very short and easy; thus Allouez, who had been at Lake Nipigon, thought of it as directly communicating with the North Sea.

[2] Either the missionary put his own interpretation upon this myth, or it was of very recent growth, since the Indians of that region had known of white men only in their own generation. This is an interesting example of the constant adaptation of the old myths to new conditions.

for disembarking, by reason of the inaccessible banks, we were forced to remain out in the stream during the night; but, being surprised by an unusual gust of wind, we were obliged to land among rocks, where our canoe would have been shattered if God in His Providence had not taken charge of our guidance. In this second danger we appealed to Him by the mediation of our intercessors, and afterward said mass in thanksgiving.

After we had continued our voyage until the twenty-fifth, amid continual dangers, God indemnified us for all our hardships by causing us to chance upon a cabin of Pouteoua-tamis, who were engaged in fishing and hunting at the edge of the wood. They regaled us with all that they had, but especially with *fené*, which is the nut of the beech-tree, which they roast, and pound into flour. I had leisure to instruct them, and to confer baptism upon two little sick children.

On the twenty-seventh, while we were trying to paddle with the utmost vigor possible, we were perceived by four cabins of savages named Oumalouminek,[1] who forced us to land; but as they were pressed with hunger, and we were at the end of our provisions, we could not remain long together.

On the twenty-ninth, as the mouth of the river which we were to enter was frozen over, we were in great difficulty. We thought of making the rest of the journey to the rendezvous by land; but, a furious wind having arisen during the night, we found ourselves enabled, owing to the breaking-up of the ice, to continue our voyage. We finished it on the second of December, on the eve of Saint Francis Xavier's day, when we arrived at the place where the French were; and they helped us to celebrate his day with the utmost solemnity in our power, thanking him for the succor that he had procured for us during our voyage, and entreating him to be the patron of that mission, which we were about to start under his protection.

On the following day, I celebrated holy mass, at which the French, to the number of eight, paid their devotions. As the savages had gone into winter quarters, I found here only one village of different nations—Ousaki, Pouteouatami, Outagami, Ovenibigoutz—about six hundred souls. A league

---

[1] The Menominee Indians, for whom see p. 76, note 1, *ante.*

and a half away was another, of a hundred and fifty souls; four leagues distant, one of a hundred souls; and eight leagues from here, on the other side of the bay, one of about three hundred souls.[1]

All these nations have their fields of Indian corn, squashes, beans, and tobacco. On this bay, in a place that they call Ouestatinong,[2] twenty-five leagues away, there is a large nation named Outagami, and a day's journey from them there are two others, Oumami and Makskouteng.[3] Of all these peoples, a portion gained a knowledge of our Faith at Saint Esprit Point, where I instructed them; we shall do so more fully, with Heaven's help.

In the matter of our sustenance, we have had a good deal of trouble. Scarcely have we found material to make our cabin; all that we have had for food has been only Indian corn and acorns; the few fish that are seen here, and that but seldom, are very poor; and the water of this bay and of the rivers is like stagnant ditch-water.

The savages of this region are more than usually barbarous; they are without ingenuity, and do not know how to make even a bark dish or a ladle; they commonly use shells. They are grasping and avaricious to an extraordinary degree, and sell their little commodities at a high price, because they have only what is barely necessary. The season in which we arrived among them was not favorable for us: they were all in a needy condition, and very little able to give us any assistance, so that we suffered hunger. But blessed be God, who gives us all these opportunities and richly recompenses, besides, all these hardships by the consolation that He makes us find, amid the greatest afflictions, in the quest of so many poor savages' souls, which are not less the work of His hands and the price of the blood of Jesus Christ, His Son, than those of the princes and sovereigns of the earth.

[1] Allouez's mission during the winter of 1669–1670 at the mixed village of Sauk, Potawatomi, Fox, and Winnebago, is believed to have been located on Oconto River, probably at the rapids where the city of Oconto, Wis., now stands. The village a league and a half away would have been on the Pensaukee; that of four leagues distant at Peshtigo, where an Indian village existed until comparatively recent times.

[2] The site of this village is noted on p. 81, note 1, *ante*.

[3] This village is located on p. 84, note 1, *ante*.

Of the Mission to the Ousaki.

The village of the Ousaki is the first where I began to give instruction. As soon as we were provided with a cabin there, I assembled all the elders, to whom, after relating the news of the peace with the Iroquois, I expatiated on the purpose of my journey, which was naught else than their instruction. I explained to them the principal articles of our belief, which they heard with approval, appearing to me very well disposed toward Christianity. Oh, if we could succor them in their poverty, how flourishing our Church would be! The rest of that month, I labored for their instruction, and gave baptism to several sick children,—having the consolation of seeing one of these, some time afterward, leave the Church Militant, which had received him into the number of her children, to enter the Church Triumphant, there to sing eternally the mercies of God toward him, and to be an advocate for the conversion of the people of his nation.

Among those who had not heard about our mysteries were some irreligious persons, who made fun of them. God put into my mouth words wherewith to check them; and I hope that, strengthened by Grace, we shall, with time and patience, have the consolation of winning some of them to Jesus Christ. Those who are Christians have come punctually every Sunday to prayers and to instruction, where we have the *Pater* and *Ave* chanted in their language.

In the month of January I purposed to go and carry the Gospel to another village, but it was impossible for me to go and settle down among them. I tried to make up for this by frequent visits.

Of the Mission to the Pouteouatamis.

On the seventeenth of February I repaired to the village of the Pouteouatamis, which is eight leagues from this place, on the other side of the lake.[1] After walking all day without

---

[1] The site of the Potawatomi village is thought to have been on the east shore of Green Bay, about six miles from the mouth of Fox River, not far from Point Sable. This seems to have been the village where Perrot also first encountered the Potawatomi.

halting, we arrived there at sunset, sustained by some small bit of frozen meat that hunger made us eat. On the day after my arrival, they made us a present of all the fat of a bear, with many manifestations of affection.

On the nineteenth, I assembled the council, and, after relating the news, informed them of the purpose that had brought me to their country, reserving for the following day a fuller discourse on our religion. This I carried out with success and the divine blessing, causing them, of their own accord, to draw this conclusion, that, since the Faith was so necessary for avoiding Hell, they wished to pray, and hoped that I would procure them a missionary to instruct them, or else would myself stay and do them that kindness.

In the days following, I visited all the cabins, and instructed the inmates very fully in private, with satisfaction on both sides. I had the consolation of conferring baptism there on two new-born babes and on a young man who was dying, who exhibited an excellent disposition.

On the twenty-third, we set out to return thence; but the wind, which froze our faces, and the snow, compelled us to halt, after we had gone two leagues, and to pass the night on the lake. On the following day, the severity of the cold having diminished, although very little, we continued our journey with much suffering. On my part, I had my nose frozen, and I had a fainting fit that compelled me to sit down on the ice, where I should have remained, my companions having gone on ahead, if, by a divine providence, I had not found in my handkerchief a clove, which gave me strength enough to reach the settlement.

At the opening of the month of March, the great thaws having begun, the savages broke up their settlements to go in quest of the means to sustain life, after being for some time pressed with hunger.

I was very sorry not to have been able to go through all the villages, by reason of the remoteness of some of them, and the little inclination of others to receive me. I resolved to try at least to establish Christianity firmly in a neighboring village, composed for the most part of Pouteouatamis. Calling the men together twice, I explained to them fully our mysteries and the obligation resting upon them to embrace our Faith; and that this was the sole reason that had brought me to their country in the autumn. They received very favorably all that I said to them, and I often visited them in their cabins, to inculcate in the inmates what I had taught them in public. I baptized some sick children there, and received great consolation in the assurance which certain persons gave me that, since hearing me five years ago at the Point of Saint Esprit, on Lake Superior, they had always invoked the true God. They said that they had been very appreciably protected by Him; that they had always succeeded in their hunting and fishing; that they had not been ill, and that, in their families, death did not occur so frequently as was usual before they adopted prayer. On another day, I taught the catechism to the girls and women, our cabin being entirely filled. These poor people are very well disposed, and show great good will; many of them question me on various matters, in order to receive instruction, propounding to me their difficulties, which arise only from their high idea of Christianity, and from their fear of not being able to fulfill its obligations. Our stay was not long, as hunger was pressing them, and they were forced to go in search of provisions. We withdrew full of consolation, praising and blessing God that His holy name had been respected, and the holy Faith well received, by these barbarian peoples.

On the 21st of that month, I took the sun's altitude, and found that this was about 46 degrees, 40 minutes; and its elevation from the pole, or the complement of the above, was about 43 degrees, 20 minutes.[1]

The ice did not break up here until the 12th of April, the winter having been extremely severe this year; and consequently navigation was much impeded.

On the 16th of April, I embarked to go and begin the mission to the Outagamis, a people of considerable note in all these regions. We slept at the head of the bay, at the mouth of the River des Puans, which we have named for

---

[1] In 1902 a combined sun-dial and compass of French manufacture was found on the site of this village. It apparently dates from the seventeenth century, and on the reverse contains notes of the latitude of principal places in New France. It was with some similar instrument that Allouez took his observation. The true latitude is about 44° 31'.

Saint Francis.[1] On our way we saw clouds of swans, bustards, and ducks. The savages set snares for them at the head of the bay, where they catch as many as fifty in one night, this game seeking in autumn the wild oats that the wind has shaken off in the month of September.

On the 17th, we ascended the River Saint François, which is two, and sometimes three, arpents wide.[2] After proceeding four leagues, we found the village of the savages called Saky, whose people were beginning a work that well deserves to have its place here. From one bank of the river to the other they make a barricade by driving down large stakes in two brasses of water, so that there is a kind of bridge over the stream for the fishermen, who, with the help of a small weir, easily catch the sturgeon and every other kind of fish, —which this dam stops, although the water does not cease to flow between the stakes.[3] They call this contrivance *Mitihikan*, and it serves them during the spring and a part of the summer.

On the eighteenth we passed the portage called by the natives Kekaling,[4] our sailors dragging the canoe among rapids, while I walked on the river-bank, where I found apple-trees and vine-stocks in great numbers.

On the 19th, our sailors ascended the rapids for two leagues by the use of poles, and I went by land as far as the other portage, which they call Ooukociting, that is to say, "the bank."[5] We observed on this same day the eclipse of the sun predicted by the astrologers, which lasted from noon until two o'clock; a third of the sun's disk, or nearly that, appeared to be eclipsed, the other two-thirds making

[1] Fox River was first known as Rivière des Puans; after the removal of the Outagami or Fox Indians to its banks (about 1680) it acquired their name, which in varying forms it has since retained.

[2] The French arpent was an area a little larger than an acre, or about 220 feet square. The meaning is that the river is 400, or at times 600, feet wide.

[3] This primitive weir was at the rapids later called De Pere from the establishment there of the Jesuit mission. The place is now covered by a government dam.

[4] This rapid was at the site of the modern Kaukauna, which is a variation of the Indian name. In all early navigation of the Fox, these rapids had to be portaged.

[5] Probably Grand Chute, at the site of the present city of Appleton.

a crescent.[1] We arrived in the evening at the entrance to Lake des Puans, which we have named Lake Saint François; it is about twelve leagues long and four wide, extends from the north-northeast to the south-southwest, and abounds in fish, but is uninhabited, on account of the Nadouecis, who are there held in fear.[2]

On the twentieth, which was Sunday, I said mass, after voyaging five or six leagues on the lake, after which we came to a river, flowing from a lake bordered with wild oats; this stream we followed, and found at the end of it the river that leads to the Outagamis, in one direction, and that which leads to the Machkoutenck, in the other. We entered this first stream, which flows from a lake;[3] there we saw two turkeys perched on a tree, male and female, resembling perfectly those of France—the same size, the same color, and the same cry. Bustards, ducks, swans, and geese are in great number on all these lakes and rivers, the wild oats, on which they live, attracting them thither. There are large and small stags, bears, and beavers in great abundance.

On the twenty-fourth, after turning and doubling several times in various lakes and rivers, we arrived at the village of the Outagamis.

This people came in crowds to meet us, in order to see, as they said, the Manitou, who was coming to their country. They accompanied us with respect as far as the door of the cabin, which we were made to enter.

This nation is renowned for being populous, the men who bear arms numbering more than four hundred; while the number of women and children there is the greater on account of the polygamy which prevails among them, each man having commonly four wives, some having six, and others

---

[1] The solar eclipse of April 19, 1670, was total in the northernmost parts of North America. A description of the phenomena observed at Quebec occurs in this *Relation* just after the portion we extract.

[2] This lake still retains the tribal name Winnebago. It is the largest in Wisconsin, about thirty miles long by eleven at its widest part. The Nadouecis were the Sioux tribes. See p. 24, note 1, *ante*.

[3] After crossing Lake Winnebago to the site of Oshkosh, the missionary entered upper Fox River; thence through Lake Butte des Morts, a widening of the stream, he reached the entrance of Wolf River, whose course he followed to the Outagami village.

as many as ten. Six large cabins of these poor people were put to rout this month of March by eighteen Iroquois from Tsonnontouan,[1] who, under the guidance of two fugitive Iroquois slaves of the Pouteouatamis, made an onslaught, and killed all the people, except thirty women whom they led away as captives. As the men were away hunting, they met with but little resistance, there being only six warriors left in the cabins, besides the women and children, who numbered a hundred or thereabout. This carnage was committed two days' journey from the place of our winter quarters, at the foot of the Lake of the Ilinioues, which is called Machihiganing.[2]

On the twenty-fifth, I called together the elders in a large assembly, with the purpose of giving them the first acquaintance with our mysteries. I began with the invocation of the Holy Ghost, to whom we had made our appeal during our journey, to pray for His blessing upon our labors. Then, when I had, by means of a present which I thought I ought to make them, dried the tears which the remembrance of the massacre perpetrated by the Iroquois caused them to shed, I explained to them the principal articles of our Faith, and made known the law and the commandments of God, the rewards promised to those that shall obey Him, and the punishments prepared by Him for those that shall not obey Him. They understood me without my having need of an interpreter, and that, too, with attention; but, oh, my God! what ideas and ways contrary to the Gospel these poor people have, and how much need there is of very powerful grace to conquer their hearts! They accept the unity and sovereignty of God, Creator of all things; for the rest, they have not a word to say.

An Outagami told me, in private, that his ancestor had come from Heaven, and that he had preached the unity and the sovereignty of a God who had made all the other gods; that he had assured them that he would go to Heaven after his death, where he should die no more; and that his body would not be found in the place where it had been buried,

---

[1] This is the Algonquian-French appellation of the Seneca tribe of the Iroquois confederacy.

[2] Lake Michigan. This Iroquois attack occurred near the site of Chicago.

which was verified, said this Outagami, the body being no
longer found where it had been put. These are fables which
God uses for their salvation; for after the man had finished
telling me everything, he added that he was dismissing all
his wives, retaining only one, whom he would not change;
and that he was resolved to obey me and pray to God. I
hope that God will show him mercy. I tried to visit the
people in their cabins, which are in very great number, sometimes for the purpose of instructing them in private, and
at other times to go and carry them some little medicine,
or, rather, something sweet for their little sick children, whom
I was baptizing. Toward the end, they brought them to
me voluntarily in the cabin where I lodged.

I spoke their language, in the assurance they gave me
that they understood me; it is the same as that of the Satzi.[1]
But alas, what difficulty they have in apprehending a law that
is so opposed to all their customs!

These savages withdrew to those regions to escape the
persecution of the Iroquois, and settled in an excellent country, the soil, which is black there, yielding them Indian corn
in abundance. They live by hunting during the winter, returning to their cabins toward its close, and living there on
Indian corn that they had hidden away the previous autumn;
they season it with fish. In the midst of their clearings they
have a fort, where their cabins of heavy bark are situated, for
resisting all sorts of attacks. On their journeys, they make
themselves cabins with mats. They are at war with the Na-
douecious, their neighbors. Canoes are not used by them;
and, for that reason, they do not make war on the Iroquois,
although they are often killed by them. They are held in
very low estimation, and are considered by the other nations
as stingy, avaricious, thieving, choleric, and quarrelsome.
They have poor opinion of the French, ever since two traders
in beaver-skins appeared among them; if these men had be-
haved as they ought, I should have had less trouble in giving these poor people other ideas of the whole French
nation, which they are beginning to esteem, since I explained
to them the principal and only motive that brought me to
their country.

[1] Misprint for Saki (Sauk).

On the twenty-sixth, the elders came into the cabin where I was lodging, to hold council there. The assembly having been convened, the captain, after laying at my feet a present of some skins, harangued in the following terms: "We thank thee," he said, "for having come to visit and console us in our affliction; and we are the more obliged to thee, inasmuch as no one has hitherto shown us that kindness." They added that they had nothing further to say to me, except that they were too dispirited to speak to me, being all occupied in mourning their dead. "Do thou, black gown, who art not dispirited and who takest pity on people, take pity on us as thou shalt deem best. Thou couldst dwell here near us, to protect us from our enemies, and teach us to speak to the great Manitou, the same as thou teachest the savages of the Sault. Thou couldst cause to be restored to us our wives, who were led away prisoners. Thou couldst stay the arms of the Iroquois, and speak to them of peace in our behalf for the future. I have no sense to say anything to thee; only take pity on us in the way thou shalt judge most fitting. When thou seest the Iroquois, tell them that they have taken me for some one else. I do not make war on them, I have not eaten their people; but my neighbors took them prisoners and made me a present of them; I adopted them, and they are living here as my children." This speech has nothing of the barbarian in it. I told them that in the treaty of peace which the French had made with the Iroquois, no mention had been made of them; that no Frenchman had then been here, and that they were not known; that, as to other matters, I much approved what their captain had said; that I would not forget it, and that in the following autumn I would render them an answer. Meanwhile, I told them to fortify themselves in their resolution to obey the true God, who alone could procure them what they asked for, and infinitely more.

In the evening four savages, of the nation of the Oumamis,[1] arrived from a place two days' journey hence, bring-

---

[1] The Miami (Oumami) Indians were closely allied in language and customs to the Illinois. Their habitat was in northern Indiana and eastern Illinois, whence they had been driven by the Iroquois into Wisconsin, and had formed a village with the Mascoutin (Machkoutench) on the upper Fox. La Salle found the Miami on St. Joseph River in 1678. By the eighteenth century

ing three Iroquois scalps and a half-smoked arm, to console
the relatives of those whom the Iroquois had killed a short
time before.

On the twenty-seventh, we took our departure, commending to the good angels the first seed sown in the hearts
of these poor people, who listened to me with respect and
attention. There is a glorious and rich harvest for a zealous and patient missionary. We named this mission after
Saint Mark, because on his day the Faith was proclaimed
there.[1]

Of the Mission to the Oumamis and Machkoutench.

On the twenty-ninth, we entered the river which leads to
the Machkoutench, who are called by the Hurons *Assista
Ectaeronnons*, "Nation of Fire." This river is very beautiful,
without rapids or portages, and flows toward the southwest.[2]

On the thirtieth, landing opposite the village and leaving
our canoe at the water's edge, after walking a league through
beautiful prairies, we perceived the fort. The savages,
espying us, immediately gave the cry in their village, hastened
to meet us, and accompanied us with honor into the cabin
of the chief, where refreshments were straightway brought
to us, and the feet and legs of the Frenchmen with me were
anointed with oil. Afterward a feast was prepared, which
was attended with the following ceremonies. When all were
seated, and after some had filled a dish with powdered tobacco, an old man arose and, turning to me, with both hands
full of tobacco which he took from the dish, harangued me as
follows : "This is well, black gown, that thou comest to visit
us. Take pity on us; thou art a Manitou; we give thee
tobacco to smoke. The Nadouessious and the Iroquois are
eating us; take pity on us. We are often ill, our children
are dying, we are hungry. Hear me, Manitou; I give thee
tobacco to smoke. Let the earth give us corn, and the rivers

they had migrated to Ohio, where the Maumee, Great and Little Miami Rivers
perpetuate their memory.

[1] St. Mark's day is April 25.

[2] Fox River comes from the southwest, not flows toward it. Allouez was
advancing toward the southwest.

yield us fish ; let not disease kill us any more, or famine treat us any longer so harshly !'' At each desire the old men who were present uttered a loud "Oh!" in response. I had a horror of this ceremony, and, begging them to hear me, I told them it was not I to whom their vows must be addressed ; that in our necessities I had recourse to prayer to Him who is the only and the true God ; that it was in Him that they ought to place their trust ; I told them that He was the sole Master of all things, as well as of their lives, I being only His servant and envoy ; that He was my sovereign Lord, as well as my host's ; and that wise men nevertheless willingly honored and listened to the black gown, as being a person who is heard by the great God and is His interpreter, His officer, and His domestic. They offered us a veritable sacrifice like that which they make to their false gods.

Toward evening, I gathered them together, and made them a present of glass beads, knives, and hatchets, that I might say to them : "Become acquainted with the black gown. I am not the Manitou who is the master of your lives, and has created Heaven and Earth ; I am His creature, I obey Him, and I bear His word through all the earth." I then explained to them the articles of our holy Faith, and God's commandments. These good people only half understood me ; but, before I left them, I had the consolation of seeing that they comprehended our principal articles of belief ; they received the Gospel with respect and awe, and showed themselves well satisfied to have a knowledge of the true God.

The savages named Oumamis are here only in very small numbers, their main body having not yet come in from their hunting ; therefore I say almost nothing about them in detail. Their language is in harmony with their disposition : they are gentle, affable, sedate ; they also speak slowly. This whole nation was to arrive in sixteen days ; but, obedience calling me to the Sault, I was not at liberty to wait for them.

These people are settled in a very attractive place, where beautiful plains and fields meet the eye as far as one can see. Their river leads by a six days' voyage to the great river named Messi-Sipi, and it is along the former river that the other populous nations are situated. Four leagues from here

are the Kikabou and the Kitchigamich, who speak the same
language as the Machkouteng.[1]

On the first of May, I went to visit them in their cabins;
and I instructed them, speaking their language sufficiently to
make myself understood by them. They heard me with respect, admired the main features of our Faith, and were
eager to lavish on me all the best things they had. Those
poor mountaineers are kind beyond all power of belief; but
they do not fail to have their superstitions, and to practise
polygamy, as is customary with the savages.

The courtesies that they showed me kept me busy almost all day : they came to my cabin to give me an invitation, conducted me to their own, and, after making me sit
down on a fine new piece of fur, presented me a handful of
tobacco, which they placed at my feet; and brought me a
kettle full of fat, meat, and Indian corn, accompanying it
with a speech or a compliment. I always took occasion
thereupon to inform them of the truths of our Faith, while
God, by His grace, never failed to make me understood,
their language being the same as that of the Saki.

I baptized there five children who were in danger of dying,
whom they themselves brought to me that I might give them
medicine. When, at times, I sought retirement for the purpose of praying, they would follow me, and, from time to
time, come and interrupt me, saying to me in a suppliant tone,
"Manitou, take pity on us!" In truth, they taught me the
respect and affection with which I ought to address God.

On the second of May, the elders came to our cabin to
hold a council; they thanked me, by an address and by some
gift, for having come to their country; and they exhorted me
to come thither often. "Guard our land," they said; "come
often, and teach us how we are to speak to that great Manitou whom thou hast made us know." This people appears
very docile. See there a mission all in readiness, and capable
of giving, in conjunction with the two neighboring nations,
full occupation to a missionary. As we were pressed for time,

[1] The Kickapoo (Kikabou) were kindred to the Mascoutin (Machkouteng);
they later dwelt with them on the Wabash. A remnant of the tribe is extant.
The Kitchigamich are not positively identified. They may have been a wandering portion of the Michigamea, for whom see Marquette's narrative, *post*.

I set out to return to the place whence I had come; and arrived there safely, proceeding by way of the River Saint François, in three days.

On the sixth, I paid a visit to the Oumalouminek, eight leagues distant from our cabin, and found them at their river [1] in small numbers, the young people being still in the woods. This nation has been almost exterminated by the wars. I had difficulty in understanding them, but in time made the discovery that their language is Algonquin, although much corrupted. They succeeded in understanding me better than I understood them. After making a little present to the elders, I proclaimed the Gospel to them, which they admired and heard with respect.

On the ninth, the elders invited me to their council, and there made me a present, with an expression of thanks for my having come to visit them in order to give them a knowledge of the true God. "Take heart," they said to me; "instruct us often, and teach us to speak to Him who has made all things." This mission we have named after Saint Michael, as well as the river where they dwell.

On the tenth, when I arrived at the settlement, a Pouteouatami, not daring to ask me for news, addressed our dog in these words: "Tell me, O captain's dog, what is the state of affairs among the Oumacouminetz? Thy master has told thee, thou hast followed him everywhere. Do not conceal the matter from me, for I dare not ask him about it." I saw well what his design was.

On the thirteenth I crossed the bay to go to find the Ovenibigoutz[2] in their clearings, where they were assembling. The next day, I held council with the old men and the youth, and proclaimed the Gospel to them, as I had done to the others. About thirty years ago, all the people of this nation were killed or taken captive by the Iliniouek, with the exception of a single man who escaped, shot through the body with an arrow. When the Iliniouetz had sent back his

---

[1] The Menominee River is now the boundary between Wisconsin and Michigan.

[2] The Winnebago tribe. Allouez in the following paragraph refers to the traditional Illinois-Winnebago war, which was waged early in the seventeenth century, and which greatly weakened the Winnebago.

captive countrymen to inhabit the country anew, he was made captain of his nation, as having never been a slave.

They speak a peculiar language which the other savages do not understand; it resembles neither the Huron nor the Algonquin. There are, they say, only certain tribes of the southwest who speak as they do. I learned some words from them, but more especially the Catechism, the *Pater*, and the *Ave*.

I visited them in their cabins and instructed them, doing the same to the Pouteouatamis who live with them; and both asked me, with gifts, to come and instruct them in the following autumn.

Condition of the Christians.

We cannot make our Christians live strictly up to their profession of Christianity, on account of the way in which we are obliged to live among them in the beginning; having only a cabin, after their own mode, we cannot instruct them, or perform the other exercises of religion at stated times, as is done in a chapel. We have, however, tried to call them together every Sunday, to teach them the Catechism and make them pray to God. We have here seven adult Christians and forty-eight others, either children or persons almost grown up, whom we baptized when they were dangerously ill, a part of them at the Point of Saint Esprit, and a part in these districts during the past winter. I do not count those who have died, who are about seventeen in number. I have received consolation this winter from seeing the fervor of our Christians, but especially that of a girl named Marie Movena, who was baptized at the Point of Saint Esprit. From last spring up to the present time, she has resisted her relatives: despite all the efforts they have made to compel her to marry her stepbrother, she has never consented to do it. Her brother has often struck her, and her mother has frequently refused her anything to eat, sometimes reaching such a pitch of anger that she would take a firebrand and burn her daughter's arms with it. This poor girl told me about all this bad treatment; but her courage could never be shaken, and she willingly made an offering of all her sufferings to God.

As far as concerns the infidels hereabout, they greatly

fear God's judgments and Hell's torments. The unity and sovereignty of God are very satisfying to their minds. Oh, if these poor people had the aids and the means that Europeans have in abundance for accomplishing their salvation, they would soon be good Christians. Oh, if they saw something of the magnificence of our churches, of the devotion with which they are frequented, of the extensive charities that are maintained for the benefit of the poor in the hospitals, I am sure that they would be greatly affected thereby.

On the twentieth, I embarked with a Frenchman and a savage to go to Sainte Marie du Sault, whither obedience called me, leaving all these peoples in the hope that we should see them again next autumn, as I had promised them.

In conclusion we add here that, as a reënforcement to the workers in so large a mission, there have been sent to it Father Gabriel Drouillette, one of the oldest and most influential missionaries; and Father Louys André, who arrived here last year and was at the very outset assigned to this mission.[1] He accordingly arrived there after having served a novitiate of a year here, as missionary among the Algonquins who make their abode in these parts.

[1] Gabriel Druillettes (1610–1681) arrived in Canada in 1643, and was employed at the Abenaki mission in Maine, at Tadoussac, and at various Algonquian missions along the St. Lawrence. He came to Sault Ste. Marie in 1671 and remained there nearly ten years. Louis André, born in 1631, reached New France in June, 1669. He remained at the upper missions about thirteen years, doing good service in Wisconsin and at St. Ignace. After a professorship of some years at Quebec, he died there in 1715.

THE JOURNEY OF DOLLIER AND GALINÉE, BY GALINÉE, 1669–1670

INTRODUCTION

ZEALOUS and devoted as were the Jesuit missionaries of New France, they were not the only religious order to whom the great adventure appealed, nor the only priests to seek for converts in the heart of the American continent.

In the midst of old Montreal still stands by the waterside the grim, gray seminary of St. Sulpice, whose founders were the seigneurs of the city and who still own much of its landed territory. The brothers of St. Sulpice, an order founded in Paris in 1641, were brave and gallant men, many of them of noble birth and lofty ideals. They dreamed of an empire in New France that should be the Kingdom of God upon the earth, and with the coming to Montreal of the Western Indians for their yearly barter, fair opportunities opened to the Sulpicians for mission work among the tribesmen. Already the brother of the great Fénelon had begun a mission on the north shore of Lake Ontario, when a chance came to open new mission territory in the Far Southwest. The governor of New France fostered the enterprise for the exploration's sake, and in midsummer of 1669 a brave little flotilla of seven birch-bark canoes set off from the water-gate of St. Sulpice to seek a new route into the Western unknown.

Three remarkable men, all in the vigor of early life, were leaders of this expedition. François Dollier de Casson, powerful in frame, erect and soldierly of bearing, was a Breton of noble family, who had served as cavalry captain under the great Turenne. Although but thirty-three years old, he had been three years in Canada, and had learned the Algonquian tongue by wintering in the huts of the savages. Burning with a desire

163

for their conversion, he had persuaded his superior to permit him to explore for unknown tribes who might listen to the gospel message with more docility than those who had been longer in contact with the French. In 1671 he became superior of St. Sulpice at Montreal, and the head of its religious interests, and there he died in September, 1701.

Dollier de Casson was the originator and leader of the expedition. At the last moment it was decided to associate with him a newly-arrived member of the order, René de Bréhant de Galinée, likewise of a noble Breton family. He had reached Montreal in the late summer of 1668, and, being an expert mathematician, was chosen to accompany the expedition as map-maker and chronicler. A shrewd observer and ready writer, possessed of a keen sense of the picturesque, Galinée gives us in the following pages one of the most interesting narratives of travel that has survived from the seventeenth century. His New World experiences were limited. In 1671 he returned to France, never again to visit the great wilderness whose waterways he so vividly described.

The third member of the expedition was still younger than the two priests, but destined to leave a permanent impress on the history of North America. Robert René Cavalier, Sieur de La Salle, was a Norman from Rouen, where his father was a wealthy burgher interested in the fortunes of the Company of New France. Robert's elder brother Jean had preceded him to Canada, where as a member of the Sulpician order he was in a position to aid his younger brother. Upon the latter's arrival, in 1666, he had secured for him a seigneury on the upper end of Montreal Island, named, in derision of his ambition for Western exploration, La Chine. That it might lead to the discovery of a new water-route to China was apparently La Salle's earliest hope. With a quick and comprehensive mind he readily mastered the Algonquian language, and the winter before his first journey entertained upon his fief two Seneca

Indians, from whom he learned of the existence of south-westerly-flowing streams.

Filled with his project, he sought the governor at Quebec, who consented to his expedition, prudently stipulating, however, that La Salle himself should bear the necessary expense. To provide for this La Salle resold his seigneury to the priests of St. Sulpice, and at the governor's instance joined forces with them in their projected expedition.

So far as is recorded, this was the first journey from the lower Great Lakes to the upper ones, the first expedition to come within sound, if not within sight, of the cataract of Niagara, the first to map the shores of Lakes Ontario and Erie. The incidents of the voyage are so graphically given by Galinée that the reader can follow the travellers with ease. La Salle accompanied them only to the head of Lake Ontario; into the vexed question of his further route we need not here enter.

After a winter near Port Dover, in southern Ontario, the two priests set forth in March for their Western journey. In May they arrived at the Jesuit mission at Sault Ste. Marie; by June they were again at St. Sulpice in Montreal, having made the grand tour of the Great Lakes during an absence of a little less than a year.

Galinée's manuscript account of their voyage is in the Bibliothèque Nationale at Paris, in the Renaudot collection, whose founder was a friend of the Sulpitian missionaries. It is a small manuscript of forty-eight pages, evidently written upon the author's return to Montreal, while every incident was fresh in his memory. Dollier de Casson generously commends it, saying: "I wrote a long account of [the voyage], but as it is much inferior to that of M. de Galinée I have thought best to omit it, because M. de Galinée's description will give you much more satisfaction."

The manuscript was found in 1847, in the library named, by Pierre Margry, who had it copied and furnished transcripts to Parkman and several Canadian historians.   In 1875 the Historical Society of Montreal published a version from which several important paragraphs were omitted, and in which many verbal changes were made.   Margry republished it in his *Découvertes et Établissements des Français dans l'Amérique Septentrionale*, I. 112–166.   This was collated with the original manuscript, and first translated into English, by James H. Coyne, who published the narrative bilingually in the Ontario Historical Society *Papers and Records*, vol. IV.   We reprint from this edition the English version, pp. 1–75.   The original manuscript at the Bibliothèque Nationale is in vol. 30 of the Collection Renaudot.

THE JOURNEY OF DOLLIER AND GALINÉE, 1669–1670

Narrative of the Most Noteworthy Incidents in the Journey of Messieurs Dollier and Galinée.

IN the year 1669 M. Dollier spent part of the winter with a Nipissing chief named Nitarikyk in order to learn in the woods the Algonkin language. The chief had a slave the Ottawas had presented to him in the preceding year, from a very remote tribe in the southwest. This slave was sent by his master to Montreal on some errand. He came and saw here the Abbé de Queylus,[1] in whose presence he gave so naïve a description of the route to his country that he made everybody believe he was thoroughly familiar with it, and could easily conduct any persons that should wish to go there with him.

The Abbé de Queylus, who is very zealous for the salvation of the Indians of this country, saw that the man might be of great service in the conversion of his countrymen, who, he said, were very numerous. So he thought he could not do better than write M. Dollier by this same slave, that if he was still of the same disposition that he had long since manifested to him, to labor for the salvation of the Indians, he believed God was presenting an excellent opportunity by means of this slave. The latter would be able to conduct him amongst tribes hitherto unknown to the French, and perhaps more tractable than those we have hitherto known, amongst whom, so far, it has been found impossible to produce any result.

M. Dollier, who was actually intending to sacrifice himself

[1] Gabriel, Abbé de Queylus, the head of the Montreal establishment of Sulpicians, arrived in New France in the summer of 1657; during his term as vicar general he made three voyages to France, returning permanently in 1671, and dying there in 1677. His relations with the Jesuit order were not cordial, and he desired to rival their missionary work among the Western Indians.

in some of the missions of this country, seized this opportunity as if it had been sent him from God, and made great friends with the slave, endeavoring to acquire from him some knowledge of his native tongue. In short, he managed so well with the man that he extracted a promise from him to conduct him to his own country.

With this purpose in view M. Dollier returned from the woods in advance of the Indians with whom he was sojourning, in order to go to Quebec to buy the necessary supplies for the undertaking, after receiving the necessary orders from M. de Queylus.

It was at this place that M. de Courcelles[1] requested him to unite with M. de la Salle, a brother of M. Cavelier, in order that they might together make the journey M. de la Salle had been long premeditating towards a great river, which he had understood (by what he thought he had learned from the Indians) had its course towards the west, and at the end of which, after seven or eight months' travelling, these Indians said the land was "cut," that is to say, according to their manner of speaking, the river fell into the sea. This river is called, in the language of the Iroquois, "Ohio."[2] On it are settled a multitude of tribes, from which as yet no one has been seen here, but so numerous are they that, according to the Indians' report, a single nation will include fifteen or twenty villages. The hope of beaver, but especially of finding by this route the passage into the Vermillion Sea, into which M. de la Salle believed the River Ohio emptied, induced him to undertake this expedition, so as not to leave to another the honor of discovering the passage to the South Sea, and thereby the way to China.[3]

M. de Courcelles, the governor of this country, was willing to support this project, in which M. de la Salle showed him some probability by a great number of fine speeches, of which

[1] Daniel de Rémy, Sieur de Courcelles, was governor of New France from 1665 to 1672. He imposed a peace upon the Iroquois after an invasion of the Mohawk lands in central New York.

[2] The word "Ohio" is said to mean beautiful, therefore the French usually called the stream La Belle Rivière.

[3] The Vermillion Sea was the Gulf of California, leading to the South Sea, now the Pacific Ocean, thence across to China, the goal of early New World exploration.

he has no lack.   But in short, this expedition tended to a
discovery, that could not be otherwise than glorious to the
person under whose government it was made, and, moreover,
it was costing him nothing.

The project having been authorized by the Governor,
letters patent were despatched to M. de la Salle, granting
permission to search in all the forests, and all the rivers and
lakes of Canada, to see if there might not be something good
in them, and requesting the governors of provinces in which
he might arrive, such as Virginia, Florida, etc., to allow him
passage, and render assistance as they would wish us to do
for them in like case.   It was to help on this project, moreover, that M. Dollier was requested by the Governor to turn
his zeal towards the tribes dwelling on the River Ohio and to
agree to accompany M. de la Salle.   Permission, moreover,
was given to soldiers who wished to undertake this expedition
to leave the ranks.   At all events, the expedition made a great
noise.

Messieurs Dollier and de la Salle went up to Montreal
again, after making their purchases at Quebec, and bought
all the canoes they could, in order to be able to take as large
a party as possible.   M. Barthélemy was intended to be a
member of the party, and had, as well as M. Dollier, received
authority from the Bishop of Canada.[1]   Accordingly, towards
the end of the month of June, 1669, everybody was preparing
in good earnest to set out.   M. de la Salle wished to take five
canoes and fourteen men, and Messieurs Dollier and Barthélemy three canoes and seven men.

The talk was already of starting as soon as possible, and
every one had done his packing, when it occurred to the Abbé
de Queylus that M. de la Salle might possibly abandon our
gentlemen, and that his temper, which was known to be rather
volatile, might lead him to quit them at the first whim, perhaps when it was most necessary to have some one with a
little skill in finding his bearings for the return journey, or

---

[1] François de Laval de Montmorency was the first bishop of Canada.
Born near Chartres in 1622, he was educated as a Jesuit, came to Canada in
1659 as vicar apostolic, was chosen bishop of Quebec in 1674, resigned in 1685,
and died at Quebec in 1708.   A patron of education, the Seminary of Quebec was
his legacy to Canada.

acquainted with the situation of known countries, in order not to get them into difficulties through imprudence; and, besides, it was desirable to have some trustworthy map of the route that was contemplated.

It was from these considerations that the Abbé de Queylus permitted me to accompany M. Dollier when I asked his leave. I had already some smattering of mathematics, enough to construct a map in a sort of fashion, but still sufficiently accurate to enable me to find my way back again from any place I might go to in the woods and streams of this country. Besides, they were glad to leave some person here who knew Algonkin, to serve as an interpreter to the Ottawas, when they come here. Accordingly I was accepted for the expedition in the place of M. Barthélemy, who, from his perfect knowledge of the Algonkin language, could be more useful at this place than myself.

I had only three days to get my crew together. I took two men and a canoe, with some goods suitable to barter for provisions with the tribes through which we were to pass, and was ready to embark as soon as the rest. The precipitancy with which my journey was decided upon did not permit me to write the Bishop and the Governor.

Our fleet, consisting of seven canoes, each with three men, left Montreal on the 6th of July, 1669, under the guidance of two canoes of Seneca Iroquois,[1] who had come to Montreal as early as the autumn of the year 1668 to do their hunting and trading. These people whilst here had stayed a long time at M. de la Salle's, and had told him so many marvels of the River Ohio, with which they said they were thoroughly acquainted, that they inflamed in him more than ever the desire to see it. They told him that this river took its rise three days' journey from Seneca, that after a month's travel one came upon the Honniasontkeronons and the Chiouanons,[2] and that, after passing the latter, and a great cataract or waterfall that there is in this river, one found the Outagame

---

[1] The Seneca, called by the French Sonontouans (or Tsonontouans), was the most westerly division of the Iroquois.

[2] The latter tribe was that of the Shawnee; the former probably a subdivision of that tribe, whom the Iroquois called Ontonagannhas, meaning the rude, barbarous people.

and the country of the Iskousogos,[1] and finally a country so abundant in roebucks and wild cattle that they were as thick as the woods, and so great a number of tribes that there could not be more.

M. de la Salle reported all these things to M. Dollier, whose zeal became more and more ardent for the salvation of these poor Indians, who perhaps would have made good use of the word of God, if it had been proclaimed to them; and the greatness of this zeal prevented M. Dollier from remarking that M. de la Salle, who said that he understood the Iroquois perfectly, and had learned all these things from them through his perfect acquaintance with their language, did not know it at all, and was embarking upon this expedition almost blindly, scarcely knowing where he was going. He had been led to expect that by making some present to the village of the Senecas he could readily procure slaves of the tribes to which he intended to go, who might serve him as guides.

As for myself, I would not start from here unless I could take with me a man who knew Iroquois. I have applied myself to Algonkin since I have been here; but I should have been very glad at that time to know as much Iroquois as Algonkin. The only person I could find who could serve me for this purpose was a Dutchman. He knows Iroquois perfectly, but French very little. At length, unable to find any other, I embarked. M. Dollier and I intended to call at Kenté to obtain intelligence of our gentlemen who are on mission there,[2] but our guides were of the great village of Seneca, and we dared not leave them lest we should be unable to find any others.

With the outfit I have mentioned, we left Montreal on the 6th of July, 1669, and the same day ascended the St. Louis Rapids, which are only a league and a half away. Navigation above Montreal is quite different from that below. The latter is made in ships, barks, launches, and boats, because the

---

[1] The country of the Outagami and Mascoutin (Iskousogos) before their migration to Wisconsin was not far from the western end of Lake Erie.

[2] A Sulpician mission had been begun in 1668 on the north shore of Lake Ontario at the present Bay of Quinté (Kenté) not far from the modern Kingston. The two missionaries were Claude Trouvé and François, Abbé de Fénelon. This mission was maintained until 1673.

River St. Lawrence is very deep, as far up as Montreal, a distance of 200 leagues; but immediately above Montreal one is confronted with a rapid or waterfall amidst numerous large rocks, that will not allow a boat to go through, so that canoes only can be used. These are little birch-bark canoes, about twenty feet long and two feet wide, strengthened inside with cedar floors and gunwales, very thin, so that one man carries it with ease, although, the boat is capable of carrying four men and eight or nine hundred pounds' weight of baggage. There are some made that carry as many as ten or twelve men with their outfit, but it requires two or three men to carry them.

This style of canoes affords the most convenient and the commonest mode of navigation in this country, although it is a true saying that when a person is in one of these vessels he is always, not a finger's breadth, but the thickness of five or six sheets of paper, from death. These canoes cost Frenchmen who buy them from Indians nine or ten crowns in clothes, but from Frenchmen to Frenchmen they are much dearer. Mine cost me eighty livres. It is only the Algonkin-speaking tribes that build these canoes well. The Iroquois use all kinds of bark except birch for their canoes. They build canoes that are badly made and very heavy, which last at most only a month, whilst those of the Algonkins, if taken care of, last five or six years.

You do not row in these canoes as in a boat. In the latter the oar is attached to a rowlock on the boat's side; but here you hold one hand near the blade of the oar and the other at the end of the handle, and use it to push the water behind you, without the oar touching the canoe in any way. Moreover, it is necessary in these canoes to remain all the time on your knees or seated, taking care to preserve your balance well; for the vessels are so light that a weight of twenty pounds on one side more than the other is enough to overturn them, and so quickly that one scarcely has time to guard against it. They are so frail that to bear a little upon a stone or to touch it a little clumsily is sufficient to cause a hole, which can, however, be mended with resin.

The convenience of these canoes is great in these streams, full of cataracts or waterfalls, and rapids through which it is impossible to take any boat. When you reach them you load canoe and baggage upon your shoulders and go overland until the navigation is good; and then you put your canoe back into the water, and embark again. If God grants me the grace of returning to France, I shall endeavor to take over one of these canoes, to show it to those who have not seen them. I see no handiwork of the Indians that appears to me to merit the attention of Europeans, except their canoes and their rackets for walking on snow. There is no conveyance either better or swifter than that of the canoe; for four good canoe-men will not be afraid to bet that they can pass in their canoe eight or ten rowers in the fastest launch that can be seen.

I have made a long digression here upon canoes because, as I have already said, I have found nothing here more beautiful or more convenient. Without them it would be impossible to navigate above Montreal or in any of the numerous rivers of this country. I know none of these without some water-fall or rapid, in which one would inevitably get wrecked if he wished to run them.

The inns or shelters for the night are as extraordinary as the vehicles, for after paddling or portaging the entire day you find towards evening the fair earth all ready to receive your tired body. When the weather is fine, after unloading your canoe, you make a fire and go to bed without otherwise hous-ing yourself; but when it is wet, it is necessary to go and strip some trees, the bark of which you arrange upon four small forks, with which you make a cabin to save you from the rain. The Algonkins carry with them pieces of birch-bark, split thin and sewed together so that they are four fathoms in length and three feet wide. These roll up into very small compass, and under three of these pieces of bark hung upon poles eight or nine men can be easily sheltered. Even winter cabins are made with them that are warmer than our houses. Twenty or thirty poles are arranged lengthwise so that they all touch each other at the top, and the bark is spread over the poles, with a little fire in the centre. Under these strips of bark I have passed days and nights where it was very cold, with three feet of snow upon the ground, without being ex-traordinarily inconvenienced

As to the matter of food, it is such as to cause all the

books to be burned that cooks have ever made, and themselves to be forced to renounce their art. For one manages in the woods of Canada to fare well without bread, wine, salt, pepper, or any condiments. The ordinary diet is Indian corn, called in France Turkey wheat, which is ground between two stones and boiled in water; the seasoning is with meat or fish, when you have any. This way of living seemed to us all so extraordinary that we felt the effects of it. Not one of us was exempt from some illness before we were a hundred leagues from Montreal.

We took the Lake Ontario route, our guides conducting us along the River St. Lawrence. The route is very difficult as far as Otondiata,[1] about forty leagues from here, for it is necessary to be almost always in the water dragging the canoes. Up to that place there are only thirteen or fourteen leagues of good sailing, in Lake St. Francis and Lake St. Louis. The river banks are of fairly good land here and there, but commonly it is mere sand or rocks. It is true the fishing is pretty good in all these rapids, for most frequently we had only to throw the line into the water to catch forty or fifty fish of the kind called here *barbue* (catfish). There is none like it in France. Travellers and poor people live on it very comfortably, for it can be eaten, and is very good cooked in water without any sauce. It is also full of a very good oil, which forms admirable seasoning for sagamite, the name given to porridge made of Indian corn.

We took two moose in Lake St. Francis, which were the beginning of our hunting. We fared sumptuously on them. These moose are large animals, like mules and shaped nearly like them, except that the moose has a cloven hoof, and on his head very large antlers which he sheds every winter, and which are flat like those of the fallow deer. Their flesh is very good, especially when fat, and the hide is very valuable. It is what is commonly called here the *orignal*. The hot weather and our scanty experience of living in the woods made us lose a good part of our meat.

The mode of curing it in the woods, where there is no salt, is to cut it in very thin slices and spread it on a gridiron raised

---

[1] Otondiata was Grenadier Island, not far from Oswegatchie River, at whose mouth now stands Ogdensburgh, New York.

three feet from the ground, covered with small wooden switches
on which you spread your meat. Then a fire is made underneath the gridiron, and the meat is dried in the fire and smoke
until there is no longer any moisture in it and it is as dry as a
piece of wood.[1] It is put up in packages of thirty or forty,
rolled up in pieces of bark, and thus wrapped up it will keep
five or six years without spoiling. When you wish to eat it
you reduce it to powder between two stones and make a broth
by boiling with Indian corn. The loss of our meat resulted
in our having nothing to eat but Indian corn with water for
nearly a month, for generally we were not in fishing spots,
and we were not in the season of good hunting.

At last, with all our misery, we discovered Lake Ontario
on the second day of August, which comes in sight like a great
sea, with no land visible but what you coast along. What
seems land on the lake-shore is merely sand and rocks. It
is true that in the depth of the woods fine land is remarked,
especially along some streams that empty into the lake. It
is by this route that the reverend Jesuit Fathers go to their
Iroquois missions, and on the river of Onondaga that they
intend to make their principal establishment.[2] They have
eight or ten men there now for the purpose of building a
house and making clearings to sow grain. Before this year
there were only one Father and one man for each nation, but
this year they have sent a considerable shipment of men and
merchants to begin a permanent establishment to which the
missionaries may retire from time to time to renew their
spiritual and bodily strength, for, to tell the truth, the life
of missionaries in this country is the most dissipating life
that can be imagined. Scarcely anything is thought of but
bodily necessities, and the constant example of the savages,
who think only of satisfying their flesh, brings the mind into
an almost inevitable enervation, unless one guards against it.

There are rivers flowing into Lake Ontario that lead into

[1] This method of preparing meat is called by frontiersmen "jerking,"
and the dried product is known as "jerk."

[2] This settlement, called Ste. Marie, was on the eastern side of Onondaga
Lake, between Syracuse and Liverpool, New York. The mission to the Onon-
daga, begun by Jogues in 1646, was re-established nine years later and named
Mission of St. Jean Baptiste.

the forests of the Five Iroquois Nations, as you will see them marked on the map. On the 8th of August we arrived at an island where a Seneca Indian has made a sort of country house, to which he retires in summer to eat with his family a little Indian corn and squash that he grows there every year. He has concealed himself so well, that unless one knew the spot one would have a great deal of difficulty in finding it. They are obliged to conceal themselves in this way when they leave their villages, lest their enemies, who are always around for the purpose of surprising and killing them, should discover them.

The good man received us well and entertained us hospitably with squashes boiled in water. Our guide would stay two days with him, after which, leaving us to go to notify the village of our arrival, we were not in entire security for our lives in the vicinity of this tribe, and many reasons gave us ground for apprehending something disagreeable.

In the first place, the peace had been made very shortly before, and these barbarians had often broken it with us when it seemed still more assured than this one, and all the more easily, as there are no authorities amongst them, everyone being perfectly free in his actions, so that all that is necessary is for a young ruffian, to whom the peace is not acceptable, or who remembers that one of his relations was killed in the preceding wars, to come and commit some act of hostility, and so break the treaty that has been made by the old men.

Secondly, the Antastogué or Antastouais, who are the Indians of New Sweden,[1] that are at war with the Senecas, are continually roving about in the outskirts of their country, and had shortly before killed ten men in the very spot where we were obliged to sojourn an entire month.

Thirdly, a week or a fortnight before our departure from Montreal, three of the soldiers in garrison there, having gone to trade, found a Seneca Indian who had a quantity of furs, to get which they made up their minds to murder the Indian, and in fact did so. Happily for us the matter was discovered

---

[1] The Andastes were of Iroquoian stock, occupying the valley of the Susquehanna River. The English called them Susquehannocks, Minquas, or Conestoga Indians. See A. C. Myers, *Narratives of Early Pennsylvania, West New Jersey, and Delaware* (Original Narratives Series), pp. 103, 104.

five or six days before our departure, and the criminals, being convicted, were put to death in presence of several Seneca Indians that were here at the time, and who were appeased at the sight of this justice; for they had resolved, in order to avenge the deceased, who was a man of importance, to kill just as many Frenchmen as they could catch away from the settlements. Judge for yourselves whether it would have had a good result for us in this country if we had left Montreal before those criminals had been executed. But nevertheless, although the bulk of the nation was appeased by this execution, the relatives of the deceased did not consider themselves satisfied, and wished at all hazards to sacrifice some Frenchmen to their vengeance, and loudly boasted of it. On this account we performed sentry duty every night, and constantly kept all our weapons in good condition.

However, I can assure you, that for a person who sees himself in the midst of all these alarms and who must, moreover, add the constant fear of dying of hunger or disease in the midst of a forest, without any help—in the midst, I say, of all these alarms, when one believes he is here by the will of God, and in the thought that what one suffers is agreeable to Him and will be able to serve for the salvation of some one of these poor Indians, not only is one free from sadness, but, on the contrary, one tastes a very appreciable joy in the midst of all these hardships.

This is what we experienced many times, but especially M. Dollier, who was sick near Seneca with a continued fever, that almost carried him off in a short time. He said to me at the time, "I am well pleased, and even rejoice, to see myself destitute as I am of all spiritual and corporal aid." "Yes," said he, "I would rather die in the midst of this forest in the order of the will of God, as I believe I am, than amongst all my brethren in the Seminary of Saint Sulpice."

At length, after thirty-five days of very difficult navigation, we arrived at a small stream, called by the Indians Karontagouat,[1] which is at the part of the lake nearest to Seneca, about one hundred leagues southwestward from Montreal. I took the altitude at this place with the Jacob's-staff that I had brought, on the 26th August, 1669, and as I had a

---

[1] The present Irondequoit River of central New York.

very fine horizon to the north, for no more land is seen there than in the open sea, I took the altitude from behind, which is the most accurate. I found the sun then distant from the zenith 33 degrees, to which I added 10 degrees 12 minutes, being the sun's north declination for that day. The equinoctial was distant from the zenith, and consequently the north pole elevated above the horizon, at this place, 43 degrees 12 minutes, which is its actual latitude, and agreed pretty well with the latitude I found I had obtained by dead reckoning, following the practice of sailors, who do not fail to get the latitude they are in although they have no instrument for taking altitude.[1]

No sooner had we arrived at this place than we were visited by a number of Indians who came to make us small presents of Indian corn, squashes, blackberries, and blueberries, fruits that they have in abundance. We returned the compliment by making them also a present of knives, awls, needles, glass beads, and other things which they esteemed and with which we were well provided.

Our guides requested us to wait at this place until the next day, and informed us that the principal persons would not fail to come in the evening with provisions to escort us to the village. And, in fact, the evening was no sooner come than we saw a large band of Indians arriving with a number of women loaded with provisions, who came and camped near us and made bread for us of Indian corn and fruits. They would not speak there in form of council, but told us we were expected at the village, and that word had been sent through all the cabins to assemble all the old men for the council, which was to be held to learn the reason of our coming.

Thereupon M. Dollier, M. de la Salle, and I consulted together to know in what manner we should act, what should be offered as presents, and how many should be made. It was resolved that I should go to the village with M. de la Salle to try to get a slave of the tribes to which we wished to go for the purpose of conducting us thither, and that we should take eight of our Frenchmen with us. The rest were to remain

---

[1] This observation was very accurate, being about the true latitude of the entrance to Irondequoit River. The Jacob's-staff, or cross-staff, was a rude predecessor of the quadrant.

with M. Dollier in charge of the canoes. The business was carried out in this way, and no sooner had daylight appeared, on the next day, the 12th August, than we were notified by the Indians that it was time to start. We set out accordingly, ten Frenchmen with 40 or 50 Indians, who obliged us every league to take a rest for fear of tiring us too much. About half way, we found another band of Indians coming to meet us who made us a present of provisions and joined us in order to return to the village. When we were about a league away the halts were more frequent and the crowd kept adding to our escort more and more until at last we saw ourselves in sight of the great village, which is in the midst of a large clearing about two leagues in circumference.[1]

In order to reach it, it is necessary to ascend a small hill, on the brow of which the village is situated. As soon as we had climbed this hill, we perceived a large number of old men seated on the grass waiting for us, who had left a good place for us opposite them, where they invited us to sit down, which we did. At the same time an old man, who could scarcely see and hardly hold himself up, so old was he, rose and in a very animated tone made us an oration, in which he assured us of his joy at our arrival, that we might regard the Senecas as our brothers and they regarded us as theirs, and that, feeling thus, they requested us to enter their village, where they had prepared a cabin for us whilst waiting until we should broach our purpose. We thanked them for their civilities and informed them through our interpreter that on the following day we should tell them the object of our journey.

Thereupon an Indian, who had the office of introducer of ambassadors, presented himself to conduct us to our lodging. We followed him, and he took us to the largest cabin of the village, where they had prepared our abode, with orders to the women of the cabin to let us lack for nothing. And in truth they were always very faithful whilst we were there to attend to our kettles, and bring us the necessary wood to light up during the night.

This village, like all those of the Indians, is nothing but a lot of cabins, surrounded with palisades of poles twelve or

[1] This was the Seneca village on the site of Boughton Hill, about one mile south of Victor in Ontario County, New York.

thirteen feet high, fastened together at the top and planted in the ground, with great piles of wood the height of a man behind these palisades, the curtains being not otherwise flanked, merely a simple enclosure, perfectly square, so that these forts are not defensible. Besides, they scarcely ever take care to settle on the bank of a stream or spring, but on some hill, where, as a general rule, they are some distance from water. By the evening of the 12th, we saw all the principal persons of the other villages arriving to attend the council, which was to be held next day.

The Seneca nation is the most numerous of all the Iroquois. It is composed of four villages, two of which contain one hundred and fifty cabins each, and the other two about thirty cabins, in all, perhaps, a thousand or twelve hundred men capable of bearing arms. The two large villages are about six or seven leagues apart, and both are six or seven leagues from the lake shore.

The country between the lake and the large village,[1] farthest to the east, to which I was going, is for the most part beautiful, broad meadows, on which the grass is as tall as myself. In the spots where there are woods, these are oak plains, so open that one could easily run through them on horseback. This open country, we were told, continues eastward more than a hundred leagues. Westward and southward it extends so far that its limit is unknown, especially towards the south, where treeless meadows are found more than one hundred leagues in length, and where the Indians who have been there say very good fruits and extremely fine Indian corn are grown.

At last, the 13th of August having arrived, the Indians assembled in our cabin to the number of fifty or sixty of the principal persons of the nation. Their custom is, when they come in, to sit down in the most convenient place they find vacant, regardless of rank, and at once get some fire to light their pipes, which do not leave their mouths during the whole time of the council. They say good thoughts come whilst smoking.

When we saw the assembly was numerous enough, we began to talk business, and it was then M. de la Salle admitted he was unable to make himself understood. On the other hand, my

---

[1] On the site of the present city of Geneva, New York.

interpreter said he did not know enough French to make himself thoroughly understood by us. So we deemed it more convenient to make use of Father Frémin's man to deliver our address and interpret to us what the Indians should say; and it was actually done in this way. It is to be remarked that Father Frémin [1] was not then at the place of his mission, but had gone a few days before to Onondaga for a meeting that was to be held there of all the Jesuits scattered among the five Iroquois nations. At that time there was no one but Father Frémin's man, who served as our interpreter.

Our first present was a double-barrelled pistol worth sixty livres, and the word we joined to the present was that we regarded them as our brothers, and in this character were so strong in their interest that we made them a present of this double-barrelled pistol, so that with one shot they could kill the Loups,[2] and with the other the Andostoues, two tribes against whom they wage a cruel war.

The second present consisted of six kettles, six hatchets, four dozen knives, and five or six pounds of large glass beads, and the word was that we came on the part of Onontio (so they call the Governor) to confirm the peace.

Lastly, the third present was two capotes, four kettles, six hatchets, and some glass beads; and the word was that we came on the part of Onontio to see the tribes called by them the Touguenha,[3] living on the River Ohio, and we asked of them a slave from that country to conduct us thither. They decided that our proposition should be considered. So they waited until next day before answering us. These tribes have this custom, that they do not speak of any business without making some present, as if to serve as a reminder of the speech they deliver.

Early next morning they all proceeded to our cabin, and the

[1] Father Jacques Frémin (1628–1691) entered the Jesuit order in 1646; coming to Canada about nine years later he became in 1669 superior of the Jesuit missions to the Iroquois. In later life he served at the mission colonies on the St. Lawrence, dying at Quebec. He was the author of several of the *Jesuit Relations.*

[2] The Delaware Indians, called the Loups (Wolves) by the French. Their habitat was along the river of their name.

[3] This was an Iroquois word for the Shawnee tribe. See another form of the word, p. 170, note 2, *ante.*

head chief amongst them presented a wampum belt, to assure us we were welcome amongst our brothers. The second present was a second wampum belt, to tell us they were firmly resolved to keep the peace with the French and their nation had never made war on the French; they would not begin it in a time of peace. For the third present they told us they would give us a slave, as we asked for one, but begged us to wait until their people came back from the trade with the Dutch, to which they had taken all their slaves, and then they would give us one without fail. We asked them not to keep us waiting more than a week, because the season was getting late, and they promised us. Thereupon everybody went off home.

Meanwhile they treated us in the best way they could, and everyone vied with his neighbor in feasting us after the fashion of the country. I must confess that several times I had more desire to give back what I had in my stomach than to put anything new into it. The great dish in this village, where they seldom have fresh meat, is a dog, the hair of which they singe over coals. After scraping it well, they cut it in pieces and put it into the kettle. When it is cooked, they serve you a piece of three or four pounds' weight in a wooden platter that has never been rubbed with any other dishcloth than the fingers of the lady of the house, which appear all smeared with the grease that is always in their platter to the thickness of a silver crown. Another of their greatest dishes is Indian meal cooked in water and then served in a wooden bowl with two fingers of bear's grease or oil of sun-flowers or of butternuts upon it. There was not a child in the village but was eager to bring us now stalks of Indian corn, at another time squashes, or it might be other small fruits that they go and gather in the woods.

We passed the time in this way for seven or eight days, waiting until some slave should return from the trading to be given to us. During the interval, to while away the time, I went with M. de la Salle under the guidance of two Indians, about four leagues south of the village we were in, to see an extraordinary spring.[1] It forms a small brook as it issues

[1] This spring, which yields sulphuretted hydrogen gas, is situated in Bristol township of Ontario County, about half-way between Honeoye and Canandaigua.

from a rather high rock. The water is very clear, but has a bad odor, like that of Paris mud, when the mud at the bottom of the water is stirred with the foot. He put a torch in it, and immediately the water took fire as brandy does, and it does not go out until rain comes. This flame is, amongst the Indians, a sign of abundance, or of scarcity when it has the opposite qualities. There is no appearance of sulphur or saltpetre, or any other combustible matter. The water has no taste even; and I cannot say or think anything better than that this water passes through some aluminous earth, from which it derives this combustible quality.

During that time, also, brandy was brought to the village from the Dutch, on which several Indians got drunk. Several times relations of the man who had been killed at Montreal a few days before we left, threatened us in their drunkenness that they would break our heads. It is a somewhat common custom amongst them when they have enemies, to get drunk and afterwards go and break their heads or stab them to death, so as to be able to say afterward that they committed the wicked act when they were not in their senses. It is actually their custom not to mourn for those who have died in this manner, for fear of causing pain to the living by reminding him of his crime. However, we always kept so well on our guard that no accident happened to us.

Lastly, it was during that time that I saw the saddest spectacle I ever saw in my life. I was told one evening that some warriors had arrived, that they had brought in a prisoner, and he had been put in a cabin not far from our own. I went to see him, and found him seated with three women, who were striving to outdo each other in bewailing the death of their kinsman, who had been killed on the occasion on which this man had been made prisoner.

He was a young fellow of eighteen or twenty years, very well formed. They had dressed him from head to foot since his arrival, and had done him no harm since his capture. They had not even given him the salutation of blows with sticks, which it is their custom to give their prisoners on entering the village. So I thought I should have time to ask for him in order that he might be our guide; for it was said he was one of the Touguenhas. I went accordingly to M. de la Salle for that purpose, who told me the Senecas were men of their word; as they had promised us a slave they would give us one, and it mattered little to us whether it was this man or another, and it was best not to press them. I gave myself no further trouble accordingly. Night came on and we went to bed. The light of next day had no sooner appeared than a large company entered our cabin, to tell us the prisoner was to be burned, and had asked to see some of the Mistigouch. I ran to the public square to see him, and found him already on the scaffold, where they were fastening him, hand and foot, to a stake. I was astonished to hear from him some Algonkin words, which I recognized, although from his manner of pronouncing them they seemed somewhat hard to make out. At last he made me understand that he would be glad if his execution were put off till the next day. If he had spoken good Algonkin I should have understood him, but his language differed from Algonkin even more than that of the Ottawas. So I understood him but very little.

I sent word to the Iroquois by our Dutch interpreter, but he told me the prisoner had been given to an old woman in place of her son, who had been killed: that she could not bear to see him live, and all her relations were so much concerned in her grief that they could not delay his execution. The irons were in the fire to torture the poor wretch. As for myself, I told my interpreter to ask for him as the slave that had been promised, and I would make a present to the old woman to whom he belonged; but our interpreter never would make this proposition, saying it was not the custom amongst them, and the matter was too important. I went so far as to threaten him in order to make him say what I wished, but could effect nothing, because he was obstinate like a Dutchman, and ran away from me.

I remained alone accordingly near the poor sufferer, who saw before him the instruments of his execution. I endeavored to make him understand that he must no longer have recourse to anyone but God, and should offer Him this prayer, "Thou who madest all, have pity on me; I am sorry I have not obeyed Thee; but if I live I will obey Thee entirely." He understood me better than I understood him, because all the tribes bordering on the Ottawas understand Algonkin. I did not think I could baptize him, not only because I did not understand him sufficiently to know his frame of mind, but also because the Iroquois were urging me to leave him, in order to begin their tragedy; and, moreover, I believed that the act of contrition which I was persuading him to make might save him. Certainly, if I had foreseen this accident the evening before, I would have baptized him, because I should have had time to instruct him during the night; but I could do nothing at the time but encourage him to suffer patiently, and to offer to God his torments, saying often to him, "Thou who madest all, have pity on me," which he repeated, with his eyes raised to heaven.

At the same time I saw the principal relative of the deceased approach with a gun-barrel red-hot up to the middle. This obliged me to withdraw. The others began to find fault with me for encouraging him, the more so because amongst them it is a bad omen for a prisoner to endure torture patiently. I retired therefore with grief, and scarcely had I turned my head when this barbarian of an Iroquois applied his red-hot gun-barrel to the top of his feet, which made the poor wretch utter a loud cry, and forced me to turn towards him. I saw that Iroquois with a grave and steady hand applying the iron slowly along his feet and legs, and other old men smoking round the scaffold, with all the young people leaping for joy to see the contortions that the violence of the fire compelled the poor sufferer to make.

Meanwhile I retired to the cabin in which we lodged, filled with grief at not being able to save this poor slave, and it was then I recognized more than ever how important it was not to engage one's self amongst the tribes of these countries without knowing their language or being sure of one's interpreter; and I may say that the lack of an interpreter under our own control prevented the entire success of our expedition.

I was in our cabin praying to God and very sorrowful. M. de la Salle came to tell me he feared, in the tumult he saw the whole village was in, there was reason to apprehend some insult might be offered to us; there were many persons getting drunk that day, and finally he was resolved to get away to the place where the canoes and the rest of our people were. I told him I was ready to follow him, and that remaining with him I had difficulty in getting that pitiful spectacle out of my mind.

We told seven or eight of our men who were with us at the time to withdraw for that day to a little village half a league from the large one in which we were, for fear of some insult, and M. de la Salle and I came away and found M. Dollier six good leagues from the village.

There were some of our men barbarous enough to wish to see the torture of the poor Toaguenha from beginning to end. They reported next day that he had been burned with hot irons over his whole body for the space of six hours, until there was not a single spot on him that was not roasted. After that they had required him to run six courses through the square where the Iroquois awaited him armed with large flaming brands, with which they kept urging him on and knocking him down when he would come near them. Many took kettles full of coals and hot cinders, with which they covered him the instant that, by reason of his exhaustion and weakness, he wished to rest for a single moment. At last, after two hours of this barbarous amusement, they killed him with a stone, and afterwards, everyone throwing himself upon him, tore him to pieces. One carried off his head, another an arm, a third some other limb, and everyone hurried away to put it in the kettle to feast on it. Several presented portions of his flesh to the French, telling them there was no better eating in the world; but no one would try the experiment. Towards evening everybody assembled in the square, each with a small stick in his hand, with which they began to beat the cabins on all sides with a very great clatter, to drive away, as they said, the dead man's soul, which might have hidden itself in some corner to do them harm.

We returned to the village some time afterward to collect amongst the cabins the supply of Indian corn that we needed for our expedition, which the women of the village brought to us, each according to her means. We had to carry it on our necks six good leagues, the distance from the village to the place where we were encamped.

During our sojourn at the village we had made careful enquiry as to the road we must take to reach the River Ohio, and everybody had told us that in order to get to it from Seneca, it was six days' journey by land of about twelve leagues each. This made us think it was not possible for us to get to it that way, as we could hardly carry anything for so long a journey but the mere necessaries of life—carrying our baggage being out of the question. But at the same time we were told that in going to Lake Erie by canoe we should have only three days' portage to get to that river,[1] much nearer the tribes we were seeking than we should find it going by Seneca.

But what prevented us more than all was that the Indians told our Dutch interpreter he had no sense to wish to go to the Toaguenha, who were an extremely wicked people, that would endeavor to discover our fire in the evening, and afterwards come in the night and kill us with their arrows, with which they would have us covered before we could perceive them; that furthermore, we ran a great risk along the Ohio River of encountering the Antastoez, who would unquestionably break our heads; that for this reason the Senecas were unwilling to come with us, for fear people might think they were the cause of the Frenchmen's death, and they had much difficulty in making up their minds to give us a guide, for fear Onontio should impute our death to them and afterward come to make war upon them in order to avenge it.

This kind of talk was going on without our knowing anything about it, but I was quite astonished to see the ardor of my Dutchman abating, who kept dinning into my ears that the Indians, where we wished to go, were no good and would kill us without fail. When I told him there was nothing to fear as long as we kept proper sentry, he answered me that the sentry, being near the fire, would not be able to perceive those coming in the night under cover of the trees and underbrush. In short, by all his talk, he showed me he was frightened. In fact, he no longer prosecuted the business of the guide with as much ardor as before, and, moreover, the Indians were given the cue. So they kept putting us off from day to day, saying that their people were slower in returning from trade than they expected. We suffered a great deal from this delay, because we were losing the favorable season for navigation, and could not hope to winter with any tribe if we delayed longer, a contingency that M. de la Salle regarded

---

[1] This was the route via Erie (formerly Presque Isle) and French Creek to the Allegheny River, which was sometimes called the Ohio, as being the headwaters of that stream.

as certain death, because we were not certain of being able to subsist in the woods. However, thank God, we experienced the contrary.

We were extricated from all these difficulties by the arrival of an Indian who came from the Dutch and camped at the place where we were. He was from a village of Iroquois of the Five Nations, collected at the end of Lake Ontario for the convenience of hunting roebuck and bear, which are plentiful at that place. This Indian assured us we should have no difficulty in finding a guide; there were a number of slaves there from the nations to which we desired to go, and he would willingly take us there. We thought it well to adopt this course, both because we were always making headway and nearing the place we wished to go to, and because, the village consisting of only eighteen or twenty cabins, we persuaded ourselves we should all the more easily become its masters and make them do through fear a part of what they would not be willing to do for friendship.

In that hope, we quitted the Senecas. We discovered a river one-eighth of a league wide and extremely rapid, which is the outlet or communication from Lake Erie to Lake Ontario.[1] The depth of this stream (for it is properly the River St. Lawrence) is prodigious at this spot; for at the very shore there are fifteen or sixteen fathoms of water, which fact we proved by dropping our line. This outlet may be forty leagues in length, and contains, at a distance of ten or twelve leagues from its mouth in Lake Ontario, one of the finest cataracts or waterfalls in the world; for all the Indians to whom I have spoken about it said the river fell in that place from a rock higher than the tallest pine trees; that is, about two hundred feet. In fact, we heard it from where we were. But this fall gives such an impulse to the water that, although we were ten or twelve leagues away, the water is so rapid that one can with great difficulty row up against it. At a quarter of a league from the mouth, where we were, it begins to contract and to continue its channel between two steep and very high rocks, which makes me think it would be navigable with difficulty as far as the neighborhood of the falls. As to the part above the falls, the water draws from a considerable

[1] The River Niagara.

distance into that precipice, and very often stags and hinds, elks and roebucks, suffer themselves to be drawn along so far in crossing this river that they find themselves compelled to take the leap and to see themselves swallowed up in that horrible gulf.

Our desire to go on to our little village called Ganastogué Sonontoua Outinaouatoua[1] prevented our going to see that wonder, which I regarded as so much the greater, as the River St. Lawrence is one of the largest in the world. I leave you to imagine if it is not a beautiful cascade, to see all the water of this great river, which at its mouth is three leagues in width, precipitate itself from a height of two hundred feet with a roar that is heard not only from the place where we were, ten or twelve leagues distant, but actually from the other side of Lake Ontario, opposite this mouth, from which M. Trouvé[2] told me he had heard it. We passed this river, accordingly, and at last, after five days' voyage, arrived at the end of Lake Ontario, where there is a fine large sandy bay, at the bottom of which is the outlet of another little lake discharging itself. This our guides made us enter about half a league, and then unload our canoes at the place nearest the village, which is, however, five or six good leagues away.

It was at that place, whilst waiting for the principal persons of the village to come to us with some men to carry our baggage, that M. de la Salle, having gone hunting, brought back a high fever which pulled him down a great deal in a few days. Some say it was at the sight of three large rattlesnakes he found in his path whilst climbing a rock that the fever seized him. It is certainly, after all, a very ugly sight; for these animals are not timid like other serpents, but wait for a man, putting themselves at once in a posture of defence, coiling half the body from the tail to the middle as if it were a cable, holding the rest of the body quite erect, and darting sometimes as much as three or four paces, all the time

[1] This small village is thought to have been situated in the Beverly swamp, near the village of Westover, Ontario. It is usually spoken of as Tinawatawa, see *post*.

[2] Claude Trouvé was one of the Sulpitian fathers who had charge of the mission on the Bay of Quinté. A native of Tours, he came to Canada in 1667, was five years at the Lake Ontario mission (1668–1673), later on the lower St. Lawrence.

making a great noise with the rattle that they carry at the end of their tails. There are a great many of them at this place, as thick as one's arm, six or seven feet long, entirely black. The rattle that they carry at the end of the tail, and shake very rapidly, makes a noise like that which a number of melon or squash seeds would make, if shut up in a box.

At last, after three days' waiting, the principal persons and almost everyone in the village came to find us. We held council in our camp, where my Dutchman succeeded better than we had done at the large village. We made two presents in order to obtain two slaves, and a third to get our packs carried to the village. The Indians made us two presents; the first of fourteen or fifteen dressed deer-skins, to tell us they were going to take us to their village, but were only a handful of people, incapable of resisting us, and begged us to do them no harm and not to burn them as the French had burnt the Mohawks.[1] We assured them of our good-will. They made us another present of about five thousand wampum beads, and, lastly, of two slaves for guides. One was from the nation of the Shawanons and the other from the Nez-Percés.[2] I have thought since that he was from a nation near the Pottawattamies; however, both were good hunters and showed that they were well disposed. The Shawanon fell to M. de la Salle and the other to us. They told us, besides, that on the following day they would help us to carry our baggage to their village, in order to go on from there to take us to the bank of a river, where we could embark for the purpose of entering Lake Erie.

We were very much pleased with the inhabitants of this little village, who entertained us to the best of their ability. M. Dollier could not contain the joy that he had in seeing himself with so favorable a prospect of arriving soon amongst the tribes to whom he wished to consecrate the rest of his days, for he had resolved never to return if he could find any nation willing to receive him. We conversed with our guide,

---

[1] Reference is here made to the signal punishment for treachery that Tracy in 1666 inflicted upon the Mohawk tribesmen.

[2] Nez Percés was one of the names given to the Ottawa Indians, for whom see p. 36, note 1, *ante*. This tribe should not be confused with the Nez Percés of the Far West, who are of the Shahaptian family.

who assured us that in a month and a half of good travelling
we should be able to reach the first nations on the River Ohio
. . . in the woods, because there was no means of reaching
any nation before the snows. We devoured, in spirit, all these
difficulties, and made no account of anything, provided we
could go where we thought we were called of God.

We set out from this place with more than fifty Indians,
male or female, about the 22nd of September, and our Indians,
sparing us, obliged us to take two days in making our portage
as far as the village, which was only, however, about five
leagues away. We camped, accordingly, in the vicinity of
the village, where our Indians went hunting and killed a roebuck, and it was in that place that we learned there had arrived
two Frenchmen at the village we were going to, who were on
their way from the Ottawas and were taking back an Iroquois
prisoner belonging to the latter.

This news surprised us, because we did not think there
was any Frenchman out on service in that direction. However, two of the most influential persons left us to go to receive these new guests, and we pursued our journey next day
with the fatigue you may imagine; sometimes in the water up
to mid-leg, besides the inconvenience of the packs, which get
caught in the branches of trees and make you recoil three or
four paces. But, after all, one is hardly sensible of those
fatigues when he thinks that by them he is pleasing God and
able to render Him service.

At last we arrived at Tinawatawa on the 24th of September, and found that the Frenchman who had arrived the
day before was a man named Jolliet,[1] who had left Montreal
before us with a fleet of four canoes loaded with goods for the
Ottawas, and had orders from the Governor to go up as far
as Lake Superior to discover the situation of a copper mine,
specimens from which are seen here that scarcely need refin-
ing, so good and pure is the copper. After finding this mine

---

[1] Louis Jolliet was Canadian born, baptized at Quebec in September,
1645. He had been a student at the Jesuit college until 1666, took minor orders
and served as clerk of the church. In 1667, however, he abandoned an eccle-
siastical career, paid a visit to France, and on his return made the voyage of
exploration here described. His later career will appear in subsequent pages
of this volume.

he was to find out an easier route than the ordinary one to transport it to Montreal. M. Jolliet had not been able to see this mine, because time pressed him for his return; but having discovered amongst the Ottawas some Iroquois prisoners that these tribes had taken, he told them that Onontio's intention was that they should live at peace with the Iroquois, and persuaded them to send one of their prisoners to the Iroquois as a token of the peace they wished to have with them.

It was this Iroquois who showed M. Jolliet a new route, heretofore unknown to the French, for returning from the Ottawas to the country of the Iroquois. However, the fear this Indian had of falling again into the hands of the Antastoes led him to tell M. Jolliet he must leave his canoe and walk overland sooner than would have been necessary. Indeed, but for this terror on the part of the Indian, M. Jolliet could have come by water as far as Lake Ontario, by making a portage of half a league to avoid the great falls of which I have already spoken. In the end he was obliged by his guide to make fifty leagues by land and to abandon his canoe on the shore of Lake Erie.

Meanwhile M. de la Salle's illness was beginning to take away from him the inclination to push further on, and the desire to see Montreal was beginning to press him. He had not spoken of it to us, but we had clearly perceived it. Moreover, the route M. Jolliet had taken, with the news he brought us—that he had sent some of his party in search of a very numerous nation of Ottawas called the Pottawattamies, amongst whom there never had been any missionaries, and that this tribe bordered on the Iskoutegas and the great river that led to the Shawanons—induced M. Dollier and me to wish to go and search for the river into which we wished to enter by way of the Ottawas rather than by that of the Iroquois, because the route seemed to us much easier and we both knew the Ottawa language.

Another accident confirmed us in this thought, which was, that after we had equipped the Indian, who was to serve as our guide, with a capote, a blanket, kettle, and knife, there arrived an Indian from the Dutch, who brought brandy, of which these people are very fond, and our guide took a strong desire to drink of it. Not having the wherewithal to trade, he gave his capote in order to obtain six mouthfuls of it from a keg with a reed, and then threw it up into a wooden platter.

I was informed of this affair, which did not please me, because our guide, having traded his capote, would certainly ask us for another to get through the winter, and we had no more left. So I thought, that in order to make sure of our guide, it was necessary to put a stop to this business. I went to the cabin where the bar was kept, and there actually found our trader, from whose hands I took away the capote which he had already virtually pledged, causing him to be informed that I would return it to him when he was no longer drunk. The man was so angry at this affair that he went and hunted up all we had given him and handed it back to us; but he had no sooner left us than a Shawanon presented himself to conduct us, whom we took at the word. However, as this act had been noised about, the principal persons assembled, and came to make us a present of two thousand wampum beads so that we might not remember what had passed. We promised, and they feasted us handsomely.

If M. Dollier's mission had not been for the Ottawas, to the exclusion of the Iroquois, he would have stopped in this village, where he was indeed urged with all imaginable protestations to apply himself to prayers in good earnest. But we had to pass on, without being able to do them any good further than to confirm them in the good intentions they had, and we promised them that the black robes of Kenté should come to see them next winter; and in fact we wrote about it to M. de Fénelon,[1] who was carrying on a successful mission at Kenté, and M. Trouvé did us the favor to fulfil the promise we had given them and to come there to announce the Word of God as early as the month of November following. M. Jolliet offered us a description he had made of his route from the Ottawas, which I accepted, and I reduced it at the time to a marine chart, which gave us a good deal of information as to our way, God having deprived us of our second guide in the manner I shall mention hereafter.

[1] François de Salignac, Abbé de Fénelon (1641–1679), came to Canada in 1667; after his five years at the Quinté mission he taught an Indian school, but having displeased Frontenac was in 1674 sent back to France.

At last M. de la Salle, seeing us determined to depart in two or three days, in order to proceed to the bank of the river that was to take us to Lake Erie, explained himself to us, and told us that the state of his health no longer permitted him to think of the journey he had undertaken along with us. He begged us to excuse him if he abandoned us to return to Montreal, and added that he could not make up his mind to winter in the woods with his men, where their lack of skill and experience might make them die of starvation.

The last day of September, M. Dollier said holy mass for the second time in this village, where most of us, as well on M. de la Salle's side as on ours, received the sacrament in order to unite in our Lord at a time when we saw ourselves on the point of separating. Hitherto we had never failed to hear holy mass three times a week, which M. Dollier said for us on a little altar prepared with paddles on forked sticks and surrounded with sails from our canoes. We took the greatest possible care not to be seen by the Indians, who would perhaps have made a mockery of our holy ceremony. So we have had the happiness and the honor of offering the holy sacrifice of the mass in more than two hundred places where it never had been offered.

We had no trouble in persuading our men to follow us. There was not one at that time who desired to leave us; and it may be said with truth that more joy was remarked in those who were going to expose themselves to a thousand perils than in those who were turning back to a place of safety, although the latter regarded us as people who were going to expose themselves to death; as indeed they announced as soon as they arrived here, and caused a great deal of pain to those who took some interest in our welfare. M. Jolliet was kind enough to inform me likewise of the place where his canoe was, because mine was now almost worthless, which made me resolve to endeavor to get it at the earliest possible moment, for fear Indians should carry it off from us.

We set out then from Tinaouataoua on the 1st of October, 1669, accompanied by a good number of Indians, who helped us to carry our canoes and baggage, and after making about nine or ten leagues in three days we arrived at the bank of the river which I call the Rapid, because of the violence of its current, although it had not much water, for in many places we did not find enough to float our canoes, which did not draw a foot of water.[1]

Holy mass was said on the fourth, St. Francis' Day, and that same day I asked all our men which of them would go by land as far as the place where the canoe was that had been given me, as it was impossible for twelve of us to embark in three canoes on a river where there is so little water as in this. My Dutchman offered himself, and said to me that he had thoroughly understood the route to go there and would find it without fail. As I knew none in our party more intelligent than he, I was glad he had proposed the thing to me. I told him to take our Shawanon Indian and the one we had from Montreal, with provisions and ammunition, and go on and wait for us at the place where the canoe was, and we should soon join him.

They left us that same day, the 3rd of October, and the rest of us set out on the 4th of the same month, two in each canoe, and the rest by land. It is marvellous how much difficulty we had in descending this river, for we had to be in the water almost all the time dragging the canoe, which was unable to pass through for lack of water, so that although this river is not more than forty leagues in length, we took eight whole days to descend it. We had very good hunting there.

At last we arrived, on the 13th or 14th, at the shore of Lake Erie, which appeared to us at first like a great sea, because there was a great south wind blowing at the time. There is perhaps no lake in the whole country in which the waves rise so high, which happens because of its great depth and its great extent. Its length lies from east to west, and its north shore is in about 42 degrees of latitude. We proceeded three days along this lake, seeing land continually on the other side about four or five leagues away, which made us think that the lake was only of that width; but we were undeceived when we saw that this land, that we saw on the other side, was a peninsula separating the little bay in which we were from the great lake, whose limits cannot be seen when one is in the peninsula. I have shown it on the map I send you pretty nearly as I saw it.

[1] Grand River of Ontario.

At the end of three days, during which we made only 21 or 22 leagues, we found a spot which appeared to us so beautiful, with such an abundance of game, that we thought we could not find a better in which to pass our winter. The moment we arrived we killed a stag and a hind, and again on the following day two young stags. The good hunting quite determined us to remain in this place. We looked for some favorable spot to make a winter camp, and discovered a very pretty river, at the mouth of which we camped, until we should send word to our Dutchman of the place we had chosen.[1] We sent accordingly two of our men to the place of the canoe, who returned at the end of a week, and told us they had found the canoe but seen neither the Dutchman nor the Indians. This news troubled us very much, not knowing what to decide. We thought we could not do better than wait in this place, which was very conspicuous, and which they must necessarily pass to go to find the canoe.

We hunted meanwhile and killed a considerable number of stags, hinds, and roebucks, so that we began to have no longer any fear of leaving during the winter. We smoked the meat of nine large animals in such a manner, that it could have kept for two or three years, and with this provision we awaited the winter with tranquillity whilst hunting and making good provision of walnuts and chestnuts, which were there in great quantities. We had indeed in our granary 23 or 24 minots[2] of these fruits, besides apples, plums and grapes, and alizes[3] of which we had an abundance during the autumn.

I will tell you, by the way, that the vine grows here only in sand, on the banks of lakes and rivers, but although it has no cultivation it does not fail to produce grapes in great quantities as large and as sweet as the finest of France. We even made wine of them, with which M. Dollier said holy mass all winter, and it was as good as vin de Grave. It is a heavy, dark wine like the latter. Only red grapes are seen here, but in so great quantities, that we found places where one could easily have made 25 or 30 hogsheads of wine.

[1] The exact site was identified in 1900 by the Ontario Historical Society, on Patterson's Creek, near Port Dover, Ontario.

[2] The *minot* was equivalent to about a bushel and a quarter.

[3] Cranberries.

I leave you to imagine whether we suffered in the midst of this abundance in the earthly Paradise of Canada; I call it so, because there is assuredly no more beautiful region in all Canada. The woods are open, interspersed with beautiful meadows, watered by rivers and rivulets filled with fish and beaver, an abundance of fruits, and what is more important, so full of game that we saw there at one time more than a hundred roebucks in a single band, herds of fifty or sixty hinds, and bears fatter and of better flavor than the most savory pigs of France. In short, we may say that we passed the winter more comfortably than we should have done in Montreal.

We stayed a fortnight on the lake shore waiting for our men; but seeing that we were at the beginning of November, we thought they had certainly missed the way, and so we could do nothing else than pray to God for them. We could not pass the winter on the lake shore because of the high winds by which we should have been buffeted. For this reason we chose a beautiful spot on the bank of a rivulet, about a quarter of a league in the woods, where we encamped. We erected a pretty altar at the end of our cabin, where we had the happiness to hear holy mass three times a week without missing, with the consolation you may imagine of finding ourselves with our good God, in the midst of the woods, in a land where no European had ever been. Monsieur Dollier often told us that that winter ought to be worth to us, as regards our eternal welfare, more than the best ten years of our life. We confessed often, received communion as well. In short, we had our parochial mass, holidays and Sundays, with the necessary instructions; prayer evening and morning, and every other Christian exercise. Orison was offered with tranquillity in the midst of this solitude, where we saw no stranger for three months, at the end of which our men while hunting discovered a number of Iroquois coming to this place to hunt beaver. They used to visit us and found us in a very good cabin whose construction they admired, and afterward they brought every Indian who passed that way to see it. For that reason, we had built it in such a fashion that we could have defended ourselves for a long time against these barbarians, if the desire had entered their minds to come to insult us.

The winter was very severe all over Canada in the year 1669, especially in February, 1670. However, the deepest snow was not more than a foot, which began to cover the ground in the month of January, whilst at Montreal there is usually seen three feet and a half of it, which covers the ground during four months of the year. I believe we should have died of cold, if we had been in a place where the weather was as severe as in Montreal. For it turned out that all the axes were worthless, and we broke almost all of them; so that, if the wood we were cutting had been frozen as hard as it is in Montreal, we should have had no axes from the month of January; for the winter passed off with all possible mildness.

However, we could not help longing for the season of navigation, so as to get to the Pottawattamies at an early date, and that I might be able to return this year to Montreal, in order to send back to M. Dollier the things he would require in his mission.

On the 23rd of March, Passion Sunday, we all went to the lake shore to make and plant a cross in memory of so long a sojourn of Frenchmen as ours had been. We offered our prayers there, and seeing that where we were was almost clear of ice we resolved to set out on the 26th March, the day after Annunciation.

But as the river by which we had gone to the place of our wintering was not so exposed either to the wind or sun as the lake, it was still entirely frozen, so that it was necessary to portage all our baggage and our canoes as far as the lake, where we embarked after living in that place five months and eleven days.

We made six or seven leagues that day, and were met by so heavy a wind that we had to stop and wait two days, during which the wind continued so strong that, catching my canoe which my men had not taken care to fasten securely, it carried it out so far before we perceived it, that it was more than a good quarter of a league distant from the shore. Two men got into another canoe to go and rescue it, and actually reached it; but the violence of the wind came very near drowning them. Unable to manage their own canoe because of mine, which was playing at the sport of the wind and which they were unable to hold, they were obliged to cut the line with which they had attached it to their own, in order to save themselves. The wind was off land, therefore it did not appear to me very strong, so I thought they were letting the canoe go because they were not strong enough to bring it. I embarked accordingly with two men in the canoe that remained to us. We were no sooner far enough out to be caught by the wind than we knew well there was no means of saving my canoe. So I was constrained to let it go where the wind was carrying it and to get myself back to shore.

This accident caused us a great deal of trouble, for I had a large quantity of baggage. M. Dollier, who was going for the purpose of establishing himself, had his two canoes very heavily loaded. So there we were, consulting what we should do. At length we decided to withdraw one man from each of the remaining canoes and to put my baggage in their places. Thus, of nine men remaining, we went five by land and two in each canoe until we should reach the one that had been given me.

We reckoned on only two days' walking to reach it, so we made up our minds to suffer hardship for one of them, for the land route was very bad, because of four rivers that had to be crossed and a number of great gulches that the water from the snows and rains had scooped out in many places on its way to the lake—to say nothing of the difficulty there always is in walking in these woods, because of the obstructions caused by the trees that fall from time to time, either from age or being uprooted by the impetuosity of the winds. We set out accordingly, and decided it was necessary, in order to cross the rivers that we had to pass, to go a good distance into the woods, because the farther the rivers run into the woods the narrower they are, and, indeed, one usually finds trees, which, having fallen in every direction, form bridges over which one passes.

We plunged then about four leagues into the woods, loaded with provisions, ammunition, and our blankets. We passed the first river easily by this method, but when we came to the second, far from stopping in the woods, it widened in the form of a marsh and flowed with great rapidity. There is no safety in crossing the rivers of this country by fording unless one knows them well, because there are a great many quicksands, in which one sinks so far that it is impossible to get out. This river seems very deep, as in reality it is. When we reached its bank we held a council as to what we should do, and in the first place resolved to go on for some time longer towards its mouth, in order to cross it on a raft.

We slept that night on the bank of this river, about two leagues from its mouth, and it was at this place that we heard towards the east voices that seemed to us to be of men calling to each other. We ran to the river bank to see if it was not our men looking for us, and at the same time we heard the same voices on the south side. We turned our heads in that direction, but at last were undeceived, hearing them at the same time towards the west, which gave us to understand that it was the phenomenon commonly called the *hunting of Arthur*. I have never heard it, nor have any of those who were of our company, which was the reason we were deceived by it.

Next day we arrived at the mouth of the river, which was very deep and rapid, and bordered on both sides by large submerged meadows.[1] Notwithstanding the difficulty of the crossing, we resolved to make a raft to take all five of us over. This conveyance is very dangerous, for it is nothing but pieces of wood fastened together with ropes. We were an entire day preparing our wretched boat and putting it into the water, but that is the day we suffered most during our whole journey, for it snowed frightfully, with an extremely cold northeaster, so that there fell in fourteen or fifteen hours' time a good foot of snow. Notwithstanding this, as soon as the snow had ceased, we embarked on our machine with the water up to mid-leg, and landed in a meadow more than 200 paces wide, which we had to cross, loaded as we were, in mud, water, and snow up to the middle.

We pursued our way afterward as far as the shore of the great lake of which I spoke before, and, contrary to all expectation, found it still quite filled with floating ice, which made us think our people had not been able to set out upon it. We were by this time in Holy Week, and very glad to suffer something at that season in order to conform ourselves to our Lord; but we were afraid we should not succeed in rejoining our party before the approaching festival of Easter.

---

[1] Identified by Coyne as Big Creek, Norfolk County, Ontario.

Meanwhile we went and awaited them on a ridge of sand, which joins the peninsula of Lake Erie to the mainland, and separates the great from the little Lake Erie. As they must necessarily make a portage over this ridge,[1] we decided we could not miss them. We had no provisions left, and M. Dollier and myself had deprived ourselves of part of our share to give to our men, so that they might have more strength to go hunting, and God willed that they should kill a stag, which did us much honor, although it was very lean.

We went and camped near the animal, and next day our men found us at this place, where we met again with much joy, and resolved not to leave the place until we should receive the Easter sacrament together, which we did with much consolation.[2]

On Tuesday after Easter, we set out after hearing holy mass, and notwithstanding the ice which still lined the entire lake, we launched our canoes and proceeded, still five by land, for two days, to the place of the canoe. As the cold was still very severe, the game was still in the depth of the woods and did not come towards the shore of the great lake. Thus we were short of meat, and were five or six days eating nothing but a little Indian corn cooked in water.

We arrived at last at the place where our people had placed the canoe in question and we found it no longer there, because the Iroquois having come upon it during the winter, while hunting, had carried it off. I leave you to imagine whether we were embarrassed. We were without provisions, in a very severe season, at a place where there was no means of obtaining any at the time, and without being able to get away for lack of canoes. We could do nothing else than recommend the matter to God and prepare for great misery and suffering. We sent our people hunting for a day, and they did not see so much as one animal. We could not as yet strip bark to make a canoe, because the wood was not in sap, and would not become so for a month and a half, and we were unable to wait that time for want of provisions.

In short, we were in this perplexity when one of our men, going in search of dry wood to put on the fire, came upon

[1] Now called Long Point Portage; Little Lake Erie was Long Point Bay.
[2] Easter in 1670 fell on April 6.

the canoe that we wanted hidden between two large trees. The Indians had placed it on the other side of a river[1] and hidden it so well that it was impossible to find it without a special providence of God. Everybody was delighted over this discovery; and although we were without provisions, we thought we were in a condition to reach some good hunting spot soon. And in fact at the end of one day's travel we found ourselves in a place that appeared very suitable to put animals in and where there was plenty of game. We stopped there in the thought that we should not die of hunger, there being always a certainty of killing game enough to keep body and soul together, whilst the others were off looking for some animal.

Our men went hunting accordingly, and after missing their aim at a herd of more than two hundred does that they came upon, vented their wrath on a poor wolf, which they skinned and brought to camp, and which was just about to be put in the kettle, when one of our men on the look-out told us that he perceived on the other side of a little lake, on the shore of which we were encamped, a herd of twenty or thirty does. We rejoiced at this news, and after we had arranged a plan for securing them, they were surrounded from behind so successfully that they were obliged to take to the water. They were immediately overtaken with the canoes, so that not a single one should have escaped if we had desired: but we selected those that appeared to us the best, and killed ten, letting the rest go.

We loaded ourselves in this place with fresh and smoked meat, and proceeded as far as a long point, which you will find marked on the map of Lake Erie.[2] We landed there on a beautiful sand beach on the east side of the point. We had made that day nearly twenty leagues, so we were all very much tired. That was the reason why we did not carry all our packs up on the high ground, but left them on the sand and carried our canoes up on the high ground.

Night came on, and we slept so soundly that a great northeast wind rising had time to agitate the lake with so much violence that the water rose six feet where we were, and carried

[1] Probably Kettle Creek, of Elgin County, Ontario.
[2] Point Pelee, of Essex County, Ontario.

away the packs of M. Dollier's canoe that were nearest the water, and would have carried away all the rest if one of us had not awoke. Astonished to hear the lake roaring so furiously, he went to the beach to see if the baggage was safe, and seeing that the water already came as far as the packs that were placed the highest, cried out that all was lost. At this cry we rose and rescued the baggage of my canoe and of one of M. Dollier's. Pieces of bark were lighted to search along the river, but all that could be saved was a keg of powder that floated; the rest was carried away. Even the lead was carried away, or buried so deep in the sand that it could never be found. But the worst of all was that the entire altar service was lost. We waited for the wind to go down and the waters to retire, in order to go and search along the water, whether some débris of the wreck could not be found. But all that was found was a musketoon and a small bag of clothes belonging to one of our men; the rest was lost beyond recall. Even our provisions were all lost except what was in my canoe.

This accident put it out of our power to have the aid of the sacraments or to administer them to the rest. So we took counsel together to know whether we ought to stop with some tribe to carry on our mission there, or should return to Montreal for another altar service, and other goods necessary to obtain provisions, with a view to returning afterwards and establishing ourselves in some spot, and this suggestion seemed to us the best. As the route to the Ottawas seemed to us almost as short from the place where we were as the way we had come, and as we purposed to reach Sainte-Marie of the Sault, where the Ottawas assemble in order to descend in company, before they should leave, we thought we should descend with them more easily. Add to this, moreover, that we were better pleased to see a new country than to turn back.

We pursued our journey accordingly towards the west, and after making about 100 leagues on Lake Erie arrived at the place where the Lake of the Hurons, otherwise called the Fresh Water Sea of the Hurons, or Michigan, discharges into this lake. This outlet is perhaps half a league in width and turns sharp to the northeast, so that we were almost retracing our path. At the end of six leagues we discovered a place that is very remarkable, and held in great veneration by all the Indians of these countries, because of a stone idol that nature has formed there. To it they say they owe their good luck in sailing on Lake Erie, when they cross it without accident, and they propitiate it by sacrifices, presents of skins, provisions, etc., when they wish to embark on it. The place was full of camps of those who had come to pay their homage to this stone, which had no other resemblance to the figure of a man than what the imagination was pleased to give it. However, it was all painted, and a sort of face had been formed for it with vermillion. I leave you to imagine whether we avenged upon this idol, which the Iroquois had strongly recommended us to honor, the loss of our chapel. We attributed to it even the dearth of provisions from which we had hitherto suffered. In short, there was nobody whose hatred it had not incurred. I consecrated one of my axes to break this god of stone, and then having yoked our canoes together we carried the largest pieces to the middle of the river, and threw all the rest also into the water, in order that it might never be heard of again. God rewarded us immediately for this good action, for we killed a roebuck and a bear that very day.

At the end of four leagues we entered a small lake, about ten leagues in length and almost as many in width, called by M. Sanson the Salt Water Lake, but we saw no sign of salt in this lake.[1]

We entered the outlet of Lake Michigan, which is not a quarter of a league in width. At length, after ten or twelve leagues, we entered the largest lake in all America, called the Fresh Water Sea of the Hurons, or in Algonkin, "Michigan." It is 660 or 700 leagues in circumference. We travelled about 200 leagues on this lake, and were really afraid of being in want of provisions because the animals of this lake appear very unprolific. However, God did not will that we should lack in His service; for we were never more than a day without food. It is true that we happened several times to have

---

[1] Nicolas Sanson d'Abbeville's map of 1656 is here referred to. Lake St. Clair was spoken of as "Salt Water Lake" from the time of Champlain, possibly because of a knowledge of Michigan salines in the neighborhood. The present name was assigned by Father Hennepin, who passed through this lake August 12, 1679, the fête-day of Ste. Claire.

nothing left, and to pass an evening and a morning without having anything whatever to put in the kettle; but I did not see that anyone became discouraged or troubled on that account.   For we were so accustomed to see God aiding us mightily on these occasions, that we awaited with tranquillity the effects of His bounty, in the thought that He who nourished so many barbarians in these woods would not abandon His servants.

Although this lake is as large as the Caspian Sea, and much larger than Lake Erie, storms do not arise in it either so violent or so long, because it is not very deep.   Thus in many places, after the wind has gone down, it does not require more than five or six hours, whilst it will be necessary sometimes to wait one or two days until Lake Erie is calmed down.

We crossed this lake without any danger and entered the Lake of the Hurons,[1] which communicates with it by four mouths, each of them nearly two leagues in width.   At last we arrived on the 25th May, the Day of Pentecost, at Sainte-Marie of the Sault, the place where the Reverend Jesuit Fathers have made their principal establishment for the missions of the Ottawas and neighboring tribes.   They have had two men in their service since last year, who have built them a pretty fort, that is to say, a square of cedar posts twelve feet high, with a chapel and house inside the fort so that now they see themselves in the condition of not being dependent in any way on the Indians.   They have a large clearing well planted, from which they ought to gather a good part of their sustenance; they are even hoping to eat bread there within two years from now.   Before arriving here, we fell in with three canoes of Indians, with whom we arrived at the fort of the Fathers.   These men informed us of the custom they had when they reached the fort, of saluting it with several gunshots, which we also did very gladly.

We were received at this place with all possible charity. We were present at a portion of vespers on the day of Pentecost, and the two following days.   We received the communion with so much the more joy, inasmuch as for nearly a month and a half we had not been able to enjoy this blessing.

The fruit these Fathers are producing here is more for the

[1] Georgian Bay.

French, who are here often to the number of 20 or 25, than for
the Indians; for although there are some who have been
baptized, there are none yet that are good enough Catholics
to be able to attend divine service, which is held for the
French, who sing high mass and vespers on saints' days and
Sundays. The Fathers have, in this connection, a practice
which seems to me rather extraordinary, which is, that they
baptize adults not in danger of death, when they have manifested any good-will toward Christianity, before they are
capable either of confessing or of attending holy mass, or
keeping the other commandments of the Church; so that at
Pointe du Saint-Esprit, a place at the head of Lake Superior,
where the remnant of the Hurons retired after the burning
of their villages, the Father who passed the winter with them
told me that although there was a large portion of them who
had been baptized when the Fathers had been amongst the
Hurons, he had never yet ventured to say mass before them,
because these people regard this service as jugglery or witchcraft.

I saw no particular sign of Christianity amongst the Indians of this place, nor in any other country of the Ottawas,
except one woman of the nation of the Amikoues, who had
been instructed formerly at the French settlements, and who,
being as she thought in danger of death, begged M. Dollier
to have pity on her. He reminded her of her old instructions
and the obligation she was under of confessing herself, if she
had offended God since her last confession, a very long time
before, and he confessed her with great testimonies of joy on
both sides.

When we were with the Fathers we were still more than
300 leagues from Montreal, to which, however, we wished to
proceed at once, in order to be able to return at an early day
to some of the Ottawa tribes and winter there, and in the following spring to go in search of the River Ohio and the races
settled there, in order to carry the Gospel to them.

We learned that two days previously a fleet of 30 Ottawa
canoes had set out for Montreal, and that there was still another of Kilistinons which was to leave shortly. As we were
not certain at what time the latter were to come, and knew,
besides, the trouble there is in being obliged to follow Indians,

we judged it more convenient to look out for a guide to conduct us to Montreal, because the routes are more difficult and toilsome than can be imagined. We succeeded in finding one at an expense of 25 or 30 crowns' worth of goods, which we simply had to promise, so we took leave of Fathers d'Ablon and Marquette, who were then at this place, it being the 28th of May.

Hitherto the country of the Ottawas had passed in my mind, and in the minds of all those in Canada, as a place where there was a great deal of suffering for want of food. But I am so well persuaded of the contrary that I know of no region in all Canada where they are less in want of it. The nation of the Saulteaux, or in Algonkin Waoüitiköungka Entaöuakk or Ojibways, amongst whom the Fathers are established, live from the melting of the snows until the beginning of winter on the bank of a river nearly half a league wide and three leagues long, by which Lake Superior falls into the Lake of the Hurons. This river forms at this place a rapid so teeming with fish, called white fish, or in Algonkin *attikamegue*, that the Indians could easily catch enough to feed 10,000 men. It is true the fishing is so difficult that only Indians can carry it on. No Frenchman has hitherto been able to succeed in it, nor any other Indian than those of this tribe, who are used to this kind of fishing from an early age. But, in short, this fish is so cheap that they give ten or twelve of them for four fingers of tobacco. Each weighs six or seven pounds, but it is so big and so delicate that I know of no fish that approaches it. Sturgeon is caught in this small river, close by, in abundance. Meat is so cheap here that for a pound of glass beads I had four minots of fat entrails of moose, which is the best morsel of the animal. This shows how many these people kill. It is at these places that one gets a beaver robe for a fathom of tobacco, sometimes for a quarter of a pound of powder, sometimes for six knives, sometimes for a fathom of small blue beads, etc. This is the reason why the French go there, notwithstanding the frightful difficulties that are encountered.

In going there from Montreal it is necessary to ascend a river[1] in which thirty portages must be made in order to

[1] Ottawa River.

avoid a like number of falls or rapids, in which, if one ran them, he would incur the danger of losing a thousand lives. From this river, which is as large as the River St. Lawrence, one passes, half by land and half by water, the space of twenty-five or thirty leagues, to get to the Lake of the Nipissings, from which one descends by French River, where there are four or five more waterfalls, to the Lake of the Hurons.

The greatest difficulty is in descending; for if one does not know exactly where the landings are, to make the port-ages, he runs the risk of being swallowed up in the falls and perishing, to say nothing of the difficulty of the portages, which are generally amongst stones and gravel. One often ventures into the less difficult channels, in which if the man who steers the canoe or the man in front were to fail sometimes by the thickness of a silver crown to pass between rocks and whirlpools that are found in these channels, the canoe would be wrecked or fill with water, and one would see himself swallowed up in places that look horrible. This is only too common, and a Jesuit brother who descended after us, wrecked his canoe in one of these channels; and few canoes are seen belonging to Indians who have made the Montreal trip which are not well patched. God protected us so especially that no harm happened to us, although of forty-five or fifty portages that are made going up, we saved seventeen or eighteen coming down. However, we had a very good guide and men who were not novices in these channels.

We arrived at last at Montreal on the 18th of June, after twenty-two days of the most fatiguing travelling that I have ever done in my life. Moreover, I was attacked towards the end of the journey with a tertian fever, which somewhat moderated the joy I should have had in arriving at Montreal, on seeing myself at last back in the midst of our dear brethren, if I had been in full health. We were received by everybody, and especially by the Abbé de Queylus, with demonstrations of particular kindness. We were looked upon rather as per-sons risen from the dead than as common men.

Everybody desired me to make the map of our journey, which I have done accurately enough; however, I recognize rather serious faults in it still, which I will correct when I have time. I send it to you such as it is, and beg you to have the goodness to accept it, because I have made it just now for you. I have marked in it nothing but what I saw. Thus you will find only one side of each lake, since their width is so great that one cannot see the other. I have made it as a marine chart, that is to say, the meridians do not converge near the poles, because I am more familiar with these maps than with the geographical ones, and, moreover, the former are commonly more exact than the others.[1]

[1] Faillon, *Histoire de la Colonie Française en Canada*, III. 305 (1866), gives a reproduction of this map and says that it is in the Archives de la Marine at Paris. Parkman, *La Salle*, pp. 449–450, describes it. Harrisse, in his *Notes sur la Nouvelle France* (1872), No. 200, says that he could not find it there, and it is not in De la Roncière's *Catalogue* of the manuscripts of the Marine. There is a copy of it, made in 1856 from the original at Paris, in the Library of Parliament at Ottawa. This is reproduced and compared with other copies by James H. Coyne in the Ontario Historical Society's *Papers and Records*, IV.

THE PAGEANT OF 1671

INTRODUCTION

SEVENTEENTH-CENTURY France had imperial ambitions. Louis XIV. and his great minister Colbert aimed not only at domination in Europe, but at empire in North America. At the instigation of the intendant, Jean Talon, the royal court determined to lay claim to all the territory discovered by French enterprise and all the valleys traversed by French priests or traders, and to assert supremacy over all the aborigines dwelling therein. In the summer of 1670 plans were set on foot for a pageant of possession to impress the Indian tribesmen, and to proclaim to the world the right of France to the great interior of the North American Continent.

The site chosen was the Jesuit mission of Sault Ste. Marie, the centre of missionary enterprise in the Northwest, whose location at the head of the Great Lakes made it appropriate and commanding. Talon, newly returned from a visit to France, brought orders for the arrangement of the pageant. The titular head of the expedition was a French soldier of fortune who had crossed to Canada on the same vessel with the intendant. Simon François Daumont, Sieur de St. Lusson, owes his place in history to the memory of this one event. Upon its conclusion he was sent with dispatches to the King, and never returned to the New World.

The other chief actors in the pageant, however, were men of experience in Western exploration, and of skill in the management of Indians. Nicolas Perrot, lately arrived at Quebec (1670) after five years among the tribes around Green Bay, was chosen translator and Indian agent for the expedition; Louis Jolliet, soon to start on his famed voyage of dis-

covery, likewise accompanied Sieur de St. Lusson; while at
Sault Ste. Marie four Jesuits of great experience in Indian
affairs awaited the cortège. Contrary to the usual custom
of inland voyaging the expedition left Montreal in the autumn;
therefore the winter was passed at Manitoulin Islands, and
in the early spring runners were sent out to notify the Northern tribes to come and participate in the proposed ceremony.
Perrot himself went to Green Bay, whence he accompanied
to the designated place chiefs of the Potawatomi, Menominee,
Winnebago, and Sauk Indians—those of the other bay tribes
attending only by proxy. Upon Perrot's arrival early in June
at the Jesuits' house at the Sault, he found delegates from
fourteen different tribes assembled, awaiting the pleasure of
the King's ambassador.

In solemn conclave the ceremony took place in the lovely
mid-June of the Northern lakes, beside the foaming waters
of the straits, with dark pines and hemlocks standing attentive. St. Lusson, clad in the gorgeous uniform of a French
officer of the seventeenth century, ascended a small height
on which the cross and the arms of New France had been
planted. Jesuits and voyageurs gathered around him while
with bared head and flashing sword he announced the purpose
of the concourse, amidst the hymns of the missionaries, the
whoops of the savages, and the salvos of musketry from all
assembled. With quaint old mediæval rites of twig and turf,
the King's representative proclaimed thrice in a loud voice
the annexation by the "Most High, Most Mighty and Most
Redoubtable Monarch Louis the XIV. of the Name, Most
Christian King of France and Navarre" of all countries discovered or to be discovered between the Northern, Western,
and Southern Seas—a realm that in all its length and breadth
included an empire many times the size and richness of the
home land of France and Navarre. After the ceremony had
been carefully explained to the assembled Indians papers were

drawn up and signed by all the white men present. Father Allouez then arose and in fitting phrase adapted to Indian understanding declared to the assembled chieftains the greatness and power of the sovereign under whose dominion they had passed. St. Lusson followed with a martial address, and the ceremony terminated with a huge bonfire, which lighted the depths of the dark wilderness with its fitful gleams—strange emblem of the brief sovereignty of France in the New World, that flamed so brightly for a time, and so quickly died away.

There are three contemporaneous accounts of the great pageant at Sault Ste. Marie. Of these the first is the official state paper or minutes of the ceremony. This was published in Pierre Margry, *Découvertes el Établissements des Français dans l'Amérique Septentrionale*, I. 96–99. It appeared in English form in the *New York Colonial Documents*, IX. 803–804, from which it was reprinted in *Wisconsin Historical Collections*, XI. 26–28. This records the names of the tribes whose representatives were present, and gives a résumé of St. Lusson's speech and the signatures of the participants—the Jesuits, Perrot, and Jolliet, and the fifteen voyageurs and soldiers who accompanied the expedition.

The second account is that of Nicolas Perrot in his *Mémoire*, first published in France in 1868, first translated in full in E. H. Blair, *Indian Tribes of the Upper Mississippi and the Great Lakes Region* (Cleveland, 1911). Perrot relates how Talon enlisted his services for the expedition in the summer of 1670, and describes the winter passed on Manitoulin Island where the Chippewa of the vicinity snared more than two thousand four hundred moose. He tells of his spring journey to the Bay of Puans (Green Bay) partly by sledge and partly by canoe, describes the summoning of the tribes, and the departure of the delegation for Sault Ste. Marie, gives a brief notice of the ceremony, and concludes in story-tellers' fashion, "After that, all those peoples returned to their respective abodes, and lived many years without any trouble in that quarter."

The third contemporary account, which we have chosen to present here, is given by the Jesuit missionaries in part third of the *Relation* of 1670–1671. This was published in Paris at the Cramoisy shop in 1672; the English translation that we reproduce is from Thwaites, *Jesuit Relations*, IV. 105–115.

THE PAGEANT OF 1671

Taking Possession, in the King's Name, of all the Countries Commonly Included under the Designation Outaouac.

IT is not our present purpose to describe this ceremony in detail, but merely to touch on matters relating to Christianity and the welfare of our missions, which are going to be more flourishing than ever after what occurred to their advantage on this occasion.

When Monsieur Talon, our intendant, returned from Portugal, and after his shipwreck, he was commanded by the King to return to this country; and at the same time received his Majesty's orders to exert himself strenuously for the establishment of Christianity here, by aiding our missions, and to cause the name and the sovereignty of our invincible monarch to be acknowledged by even the least known and the most remote nations. These commands, reinforced by the designs of the minister, who is ever equally alert to extend God's glory, and to promote that of his King in every land, were obeyed as speedily as possible. Monsieur Talon had no sooner landed than he considered means for insuring the success of these plans, choosing, to that end, Sieur de Saint Lusson, whom he commissioned to take possession, in his place and in his Majesty's name, of the territories lying between the east and the west, from Montreal as far as the South Sea, covering the utmost extent and range possible.

For this purpose, after wintering on the Lake of the Hurons, Monsieur de Saint Lusson repaired to Sainte Marie du Sault early in May of this year, 1671. First, he summoned the surrounding tribes living within a radius of a hundred leagues, and even more; and they responded through their ambassadors, to the number of fourteen nations. After making all necessary preparations for the successful issue of the whole undertaking to the honor of France, he began, on June fourth[1] of the same year, with the most solemn ceremony ever observed in these regions.

[1] This day is incorrect; according to the official minutes the ceremony occurred on June 14, 1671.

For, when all had assembled in a great public council, and a height had been chosen well adapted to his purpose, overlooking, as it did, the village of the people of the Sault, he caused the Cross to be planted there, and then the King's standard to be raised, with all the pomp that he could devise.

The Cross was publicly blessed, with all the ceremonies of the Church, by the superior of these missions; and then, when it had been raised from the ground for the purpose of planting it, the *Vexilla*[1] was sung.   Many Frenchmen there present at the time joined in this hymn, to the wonder and delight of the assembled savages; while the whole company was filled with a common joy at the sight of this glorious standard of Jesus Christ, which seemed to have been raised so high only to rule over the hearts of all these poor peoples.

Then the French escutcheon, fixed to a cedar pole, was also erected, above the Cross; while the *Exaudiat*[2] was sung, and prayer for his Majesty's sacred person was offered in that far-away corner of the world.   After this, Monsieur de Saint Lusson, observing all the forms customary on such occasions,[3] took possession of those regions, while the air resounded with repeated shouts of "Long live the King!" and with the discharge of musketry, to the delight and astonishment of all those peoples, who had never seen anything of the kind.

After this confused uproar of voices and muskets had ceased, perfect silence was imposed upon the whole assemblage; and Father Claude Allouez began to eulogize the King, in order to make all those nations understand what sort of a man he was whose standard they beheld, and to whose sover-

---

[1] This hymn, *Vexilla Regis Prodeunt*, now a part of the Roman Breviary, was written by Venantius Fortunatus in the latter part of the sixth century.

[2] The twentieth Psalm.

[3] According to the official minutes these customary ceremonies consisted in shouting aloud three times, "In the name of the Most High, Most Mighty and Most Redoubtable Monarch Louis, the Fourteenth of the Name, Most Christian King of France and Navarre, we take possession of the said place of St. Marie of the Falls as well as of Lakes Huron and Superior, the island of Caientonon (Manitoulin) and of all other countries, rivers, lakes and tributaries, contiguous and adjacent thereunto, as well discovered as to be discovered, which are bounded on the one side by the Northern and Western Seas and on the other side by the South Sea including all its length and breadth; Raising at each of the said three times a sod of earth whilst crying *Vive le Roy*."

eignty they were that day submitting. Being well versed in
their tongue and in their ways, he was so successful in adapt-
ing himself to their comprehension as to give them such an
opinion of our incomparable monarch's greatness that they
have no words with which to express their thoughts upon the
subject.

"Here is an excellent matter brought to your attention,
my brothers," said he to them, "a great and important
matter, which is the cause of this council. Cast your eyes
upon the Cross raised so high above your heads: there it
was that Jesus Christ, the Son of God, making himself man
for the love of men, was pleased to be fastened and to die,
in atonement to his Eternal Father for our sins. He is the
master of our lives, of Heaven, of Earth, and of Hell. Of
Him I have always spoken to you, and His name and word I
have borne into all these countries. But look likewise at that
other post, to which are affixed the armorial bearings of the
great captain of France whom we call King. He lives beyond the sea; he is the captain of the greatest captains, and
has not his equal in the world. All the captains you have
ever seen, or of whom you have ever heard, are mere children
compared with him. He is like a great tree, and they, only
like little plants that we tread under foot in walking. You
know about Onnontio, that famous captain of Quebec. You
know and feel that he is the terror of the Iroquois, and that
his very name makes them tremble, now that he has laid
waste their country and set fire to their villages. Beyond the
sea there are ten thousand Onnontios like him, who are only
the soldiers of that great captain, our Great King, of whom I
am speaking. When he says, 'I am going to war,' all obey
him; and those ten thousand captains raise companies of a
hundred soldiers each, both on sea and on land. Some embark in ships, one or two hundred in number, like those that
you have seen at Quebec. Your canoes hold only four or five
men, or, at the very most, ten or twelve. Our ships in France
hold four or five hundred, and even as many as a thousand.
Other men make war by land, but in such vast numbers that,
if drawn up in a double file, they would extend farther than
from here to Mississaquenk,[1] although the distance exceeds

---

[1] The present island of Mackinac.

twenty leagues. When he attacks, he is more terrible than the thunder: the earth trembles, the air and the sea are set on fire by the discharge of his cannon; while he has been seen amid his squadrons, all covered with the blood of his foes, of whom he has slain so many with his sword that he does not count their scalps, but the rivers of blood which he sets flowing. So many prisoners of war does he lead away that he makes no account of them, letting them go about whither they will, to show that he does not fear them. No one now dares make war upon him, all nations beyond the sea having most submissively sued for peace. From all parts of the world people go to listen to his words and to admire him, and he alone decides all the affairs of the world. What shall I say of his wealth? You count yourselves rich when you have ten or twelve sacks of corn, some hatchets, glass beads, kettles, or other things of that sort. He has towns of his own, more in number than you have people in all these countries five hundred leagues around; while in each town there are warehouses containing enough hatchets to cut down all your forests, kettles to cook all your moose, and glass beads to fill all your cabins. His house is longer than from here to the head of the Sault," that is, more than half a league, "and higher than the tallest of your trees; and it contains more families than the largest of your villages can hold."

The Father added much more of this sort, which was received with wonder by those people, who were all astonished to hear that there was any man on earth so great, rich, and powerful.

Following this speech, Monsieur de Saint Lusson took the word, and stated to them in martial and eloquent language the reasons for which he had summoned them, and especially that he was sent to take possession of that region, to receive them under the protection of the great King whose panegyric they had just heard, and to form thenceforth but one land of their territories and ours. The whole ceremony was closed with a fine bonfire, which was lighted toward evening, and around which the *Te Deum* was sung to thank God, on behalf of those poor peoples, that they were now the subjects of so great and powerful a monarch.

THE MISSISSIPPI VOYAGE OF JOLLIET AND MARQUETTE, 1673

INTRODUCTION

FROM the days of Champlain the thoughts of the founders of New France had been haunted by the mystery of the Mississippi. Its discovery was the burning question of the day, and the successful accomplishment of that discovery has been ascribed to many of the early explorers. Nicolet is supposed to have visited westward-flowing streams that led ultimately to the Mississippi. Radisson no doubt crossed the great river somewhere in its upper reaches. Perrot, before the voyage of Marquette, was cognizant of its existence. La Salle, after leaving Dollier de Casson and Galinée at the head of Lake Ontario in 1669, may have ventured as far as the mouth of the Ohio. Allouez, in the same year, first mentioned the Mississippi by its present name. Whatever these earlier explorers may have accomplished, the first recorded voyage on the Mississippi is that of Jolliet and Marquette, who among their contemporaries stood accredited as the discoverers of the great river.

By 1673, the year of their departure, the time was ripe for a definite voyage of discovery. From Indian descriptions and the vague suggestions of early travellers and traders, all New France believed in the existence of a great river draining to the west or south, beyond the rim of the Great Lakes. Expectation of immediate access to the South Sea had diminished, and a route to China was less eagerly sought than a vast new hinterland to explore and occupy.

Count de Frontenac, who in 1672 came to New France as vice-regent for Louis XIV., had the imperial imagination of the great Frenchmen of his time. The pageant of St. Lusson, at the outlet of the greatest of the Great Lakes, was to his mind a prophecy to be fulfilled by the annexation of the great interior valleys stretching north, west, and south, whose only boundaries should be the oceans, and whose perpetual sovereign should dwell in France. True, the Spaniards were somewhere in this vast domain, but just where no one knew, and Frontenac cared little, since Louis XIV. was already planning to annex their crown to his own.

The road that led to the great river was well known to Canadians. Perrot had traded up and down its length as far as the Mascoutin village; Allouez and Dablon had several times mounted the rapids of the lower Fox and gone far on the way to the portage; it only remained to choose qualified voyagers and prepare them for the journey. The choice fell upon Louis Jolliet, partly perhaps because of his Canadian birth, certainly because of his successful journey of 1668–1669, as narrated in Galinée above, and his connection with St. Lusson in the pageant of 1671. With all such enterprises it was customary that a priest should be associated. That the gentle Jacques Marquette was chosen for this mission seems to have been a response to his longing "to obtain from God the grace of being able to visit the nations who dwell along the Mississippi River," of which he had heard so frequently in his northern missions of St. Esprit de Chequamegon and St. Ignace de Michilimackinac.

Marquette seems to have been one of those gifted beings to whom the satisfaction of desires is granted, because in themselves the desires are so pure and altruistic. Born at Laon (1637), he cherished from childhood ideals of a religious life. Entering the Jesuit order in 1654, his longing to be sent to a foreign mission was gratified by a voyage to Canada in 1666. Thence he was detailed in 1669 to replace Allouez on the shores of the Chequamegon Bay. Two years later he followed his neophytes to Mackinac, where upon the northern side of the strait he built the mission of St. Ignace. Thence he set forth for the Mississippi journey, never to return to his northern home, but to obtain his last and final wish to die a martyr to the cause he loved.

The accident of the loss of the journals of Jolliet made those of his fellow discoverer doubly valued, and secured his fame forever. The story is a pleasant one, of gentle rivers, wide landscapes, friendly Indians for the most part—an uneventful chronicle save for the vast significance of the discovery. Although perhaps the courage required for the voyage has been exaggerated, it is certain that the Indians tried to dissuade the travellers by tales of fierce enemies and horrid monsters. Instead, however, were only timid savages pacified or reassured by the powerful calumet, and painted dragons on the high cliffs that frowned as the canoes slipped by. Still more to be dreaded, once familiar shores were left behind, had been unknown rapids and falls, which, however, proved to be almost non-existent, lost in the full current of the onward-moving stream. The wide entrances of the two great tributaries—the Missouri and Ohio—were located and mapped; and finally at the Arkansas village, when the course of the great stream had been clearly determined as descending to the Mexican Gulf, the return journey was begun. Continued along the Illinois River, past the Kaskaskia Indian village, and over the Des Plaines-Chicago portage, skirting the western shore of Lake Michigan to Sturgeon Bay, the momentous voyage ended, the last of September, at the mission house at De Pere.

Thence Jolliet hastened to report to the governor at Quebec, while Father Marquette among his trusted and eager friends set himself to writing the story of the journey which we here present.

The autograph manuscripts of his account of his two voyages were kept for a century and a half in the Jesuit convent

at Montreal.   An abridged form of Marquette's journal was
early sent to Paris and published there in 1681 by Melchisédec
Thévenot in his *Recueil de Voyages*.   The Catholic historian
John G. Shea first made known to historians the original
manuscripts, publishing them with an English translation in
1852.   Several other editions followed, until in 1899 Dr.
R. G. Thwaites in *Jesuit Relations and Allied Documents*,
LIX., printed the definitive edition from the original docu-
ments, lent him by their custodian Father Arthur E. Jones of
St. Mary's College, Montreal.   We reprint from this edition,
LIX. 87–163, the record of the Mississippi voyage; that of
the final voyage follows.

THE MISSISSIPPI VOYAGE OF JOLLIET AND MARQUETTE, 1673

Of the first Voyage made by Father Marquette toward New Mexico, and how the Idea thereof was conceived.[1]

THE Father had long premeditated this undertaking, influenced by a most ardent desire to extend the kingdom of Jesus Christ, and to make him known and adored by all the peoples of that country. He saw himself, as it were, at the door of these new nations when, as early as the year 1670, he was laboring in the mission at the Point of St. Esprit, at the extremity of Lake Superior, among the Outaouacs;[2] he even saw occasionally various persons belonging to these new peoples, from whom he obtained all the information that he could. This induced him to make several efforts to commence this undertaking, but ever in vain; and he even lost all hope of succeeding therein, when God brought about for him the following opportunity.

In the year 1673, Monsieur the Count de Frontenac, our governor,[3] and Monsieur Talon, then our intendant, recognizing the importance of this discovery—either that they might seek a passage from here to the Sea of China, by the river that discharges into the Vermillion, or California Sea; or because they desired to verify what has for some time been

[1] This introduction was written by Father Claude Dablon, superior of the mission.

[2] For this mission, see Allouez's narrative, pp. 115–118, *ante.* Marquette superseded the former at La Pointe du St. Esprit in the autumn of 1669.

[3] Louis de Buade, Count de Frontenac, was the greatest governor of New France during the seventeenth century. Born in 1620, he entered the army at the age of fifteen, and was in active service for many years. In 1672 he was sent to Canada as governor-general. Recalled ten years later because of dissensions with the Jesuits, he was again in 1689 sent to save the colony from destruction by the Iroquois. In 1696 he invaded their territory, compelled them to peace, and returned triumphant. He died at Quebec, November 28, 1698.

said concerning the two kingdoms of Theguaio and Quivira,[1] which border on Canada, and in which numerous gold mines are reported to exist—these gentlemen, I say, appointed at the same time for this undertaking Sieur Jolyet, whom they considered very fit for so great an enterprise; and they were well pleased that Father Marquette should be of the party.

They were not mistaken in the choice that they made of Sieur Jolyet, for he is a young man, born in this country, who possesses all the qualifications that could be desired for such an undertaking. He has experience and knows the languages spoken in the country of the Outaouacs, where he has passed several years. He possesses tact and prudence, which are the chief qualities necessary for the success of a voyage as dangerous as it is difficult. Finally, he has the courage to dread nothing where everything is to be feared. Consequently, he has fulfilled all the expectations entertained of him; and if, after having passed through a thousand dangers, he had not unfortunately been wrecked in the very harbor, his canoe having upset below Sault St. Louys, near Montreal, where he lost both his men and his papers, and whence he escaped only by a sort of miracle, nothing would have been left to be desired in the success of his voyage.

Section 1.   Departure of Father Jacques Marquette for the Discovery of the Great River called by the Savages Missisipi, which leads to New Mexico.

The feast of the Immaculate Conception of the Blessed Virgin[2]—whom I have always invoked since I have been in this country of the Outaouacs, to obtain from God the grace of being able to visit the nations who dwell along the Missisipi River—was precisely the day on which Monsieur Jollyet arrived with orders from Monsieur the Count de Frontenac,

[1] The reference is to sixteenth-century Spanish accounts of explorations north from Mexico. Theguaio or Tiguex was a pueblo of New Mexico; see, in the present series, in the volume entitled *Spanish Explorers in the Southern United States*, 1528–1543, Mr. Frederick W. Hodge's edition of the *Journey of Coronado*, pp. 312–324. Quivira was the region sought by Coronado (Southern Kansas); *ibid.*, p. 337, note. See also the New Mexico section of Professor Herbert E. Bolton's *Spanish Exploration in the Southwest*, 1542–1706, in the same series.

[2] This feast falls on December 8.

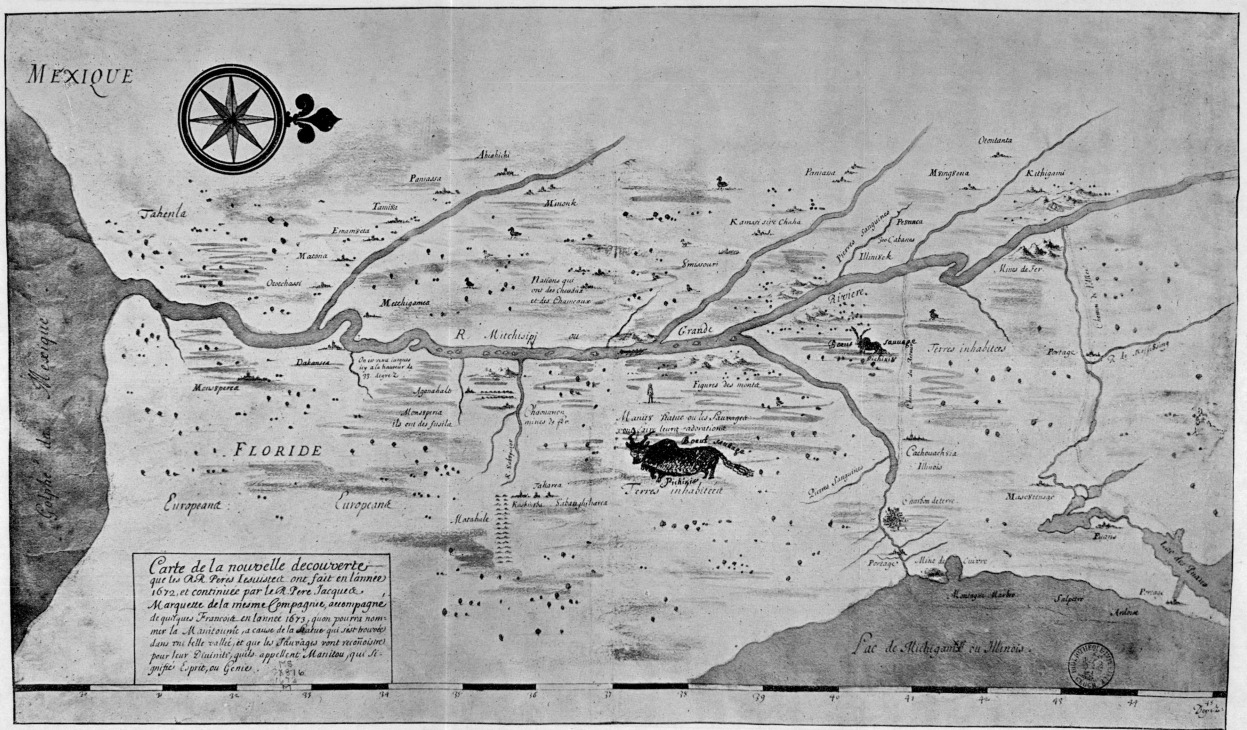

CONTEMPORARY MAP MADE TO ILLUSTRATE MARQUETTE'S DISCOVERIES

From the original in the Bibliothèque Nationale, Paris

our governor, and Monsieur Talon, our intendant, to accomplish this discovery with me.   I was all the more delighted at this good news, since I saw that my plans were about to be accomplished; and since I found myself in the blessed necessity of exposing my life for the salvation of all these peoples, and especially of the Ilinois, who had very urgently entreated me, when I was at the Point of St. Esprit, to carry the word of God to their country.

We were not long in preparing all our equipment, although we were about to begin a voyage, the duration of which we could not foresee.   Indian corn, with some smoked meat, constituted all our provisions; with these we embarked—Monsieur Jollyet and myself, with five men—in two bark canoes, fully resolved to do and suffer everything for so glorious an undertaking.

Accordingly, on the 17th day of May, 1673, we started from the mission of St. Ignace at Michilimakinac, where I then was.[1] The joy that we felt at being selected for this expedition animated our courage, and rendered the labor of paddling from morning to night agreeable to us.   And because we were going to seek unknown countries, we took every precaution in our power, so that, if our undertaking were hazardous, it should not be foolhardy.   To that end, we obtained all the information that we could from the savages who had frequented those regions; and we even traced out from their reports a map[2] of the whole of that new country; on it we indicated the rivers which we were to navigate, the names of the peoples and of the places through which we were to pass, the course of the great river, and the direction we were to follow when we reached it.

Above all, I placed our voyage under the protection of the Blessed Virgin Immaculate, promising her that, if she granted us the favor of discovering the great river, I would

[1] The mission of St. Ignace, founded by Marquette in 1671, was on the north shore of the Straits of Mackinac. It was maintained throughout the seventeenth century. See Thwaites, "The Story of Mackinac," in *Wis. Hist. Colls.*, XIV. 1–16.

[2] This map, which is preserved with Marquette's manuscript in St. Mary's College, Montreal, was drawn, as Marquette says, from Indian information before the voyage was undertaken. See "Marquette's Map" in *Wis. Hist. Soc. Proceedings*, 1906, pp. 183–193.

give it the name of the Conception, and that I would also make the first mission that I should establish among those new peoples, bear the same name. This I have actually done, among the Ilinois.[1]

Section 2.   The Father visits, in passing, the Tribes of the Folle Avoine.   What that Folle Avoine is.   He enters the Bay des Puants;   some Particulars about that Bay.   He arrives among the Fire Nation.

With all these precautions, we joyfully plied our paddles on a portion of Lake Huron, on that of the Ilinois and the Bay des Puants.

The first nation that we came to was that of the Folle Avoine.[2] I entered their river, to go and visit these peoples to whom we have preached the Gospel for several years, in consequence of which, there are several good Christians among them.

The wild oat, whose name they bear because it is found in their country, is a sort of grass, which grows naturally in the small rivers with muddy bottoms, and in swampy places. It greatly resembles the wild oats that grow amid our wheat. The ears grow upon hollow stems, jointed at intervals; they emerge from the water about the month of June, and continue growing until they rise about two feet above it. The grain is not larger than that of our oats, but it is twice as long, and the meal therefrom is much more abundant. The savages gather and prepare it for food as follows. In the month of September, which is the suitable time for the harvest, they go in canoes through these fields of wild oats; they shake its ears into the canoe, on both sides, as they pass through. The grain falls out easily, if it be ripe, and they obtain their supply in a short time. But, in order to clean it from the straw, and to remove it from a husk in which it is enclosed, they dry

---

[1] The name "Conception" for the Mississippi appears only on the map drawn by Marquette before the voyage. The name applied to the Illinois mission persisted—it was known throughout its existence as the Mission of the Immaculate Conception.

[2] The French name for the Menominee tribe, for whom see p. 76, note 1, *ante.*

it in the smoke, upon a wooden grating, under which they maintain a slow fire for some days. When the oats are thoroughly dry, they put them in a skin made into a bag, thrust it into a hole dug in the ground for this purpose, and tread it with their feet—so long and so vigorously that the grain separates from the straw, and is very easily winnowed. After this, they pound it to reduce it to flour, or even, without pounding it, they boil it in water, and season it with fat. Cooked in this fashion, the wild oats have almost as delicate a taste as rice has when no better seasoning is added.[1]

I told these peoples of the Folle Avoine of my design to go and discover those remote nations, in order to teach them the mysteries of our holy religion. They were greatly surprised to hear it, and did their best to dissuade me. They represented to me that I should meet nations who never show mercy to strangers, but break their heads without any cause; and that war was kindled between various peoples who dwelt upon our route, which exposed us to the further manifest danger of being killed by the bands of warriors who are ever in the field. They also said that the great river was very dangerous, when one does not know the difficult places; that it was full of horrible monsters, which devoured men and canoes together; that there was even a demon, who was heard from a great distance, who barred the way, and swallowed up all who ventured to approach him; finally that the heat was so excessive in those countries that it would inevitably cause our death.

I thanked them for the good advice that they gave me, but told them that I could not follow it, because the salvation of souls was at stake, for which I would be delighted to give my life; that I scoffed at the alleged demon; that we would easily defend ourselves against those marine monsters; and, moreover, that we would be on our guard to avoid the other dangers with which they threatened us. After making them pray to God, and giving them some instruction, I separated from them. Embarking then in our canoes, we arrived

---

[1] Marquette's description of the wild rice (*zizania aquatica*) is very accurate. It formed an important article of food for Wisconsin tribesmen and is still harvested in inland lakes. See A. E. Jenks, "Wild Rice Gatherers of the Upper Lakes," in U. S. Bureau of Ethnology *Report*, XIX. 1072 *ff*.

shortly afterward at the bottom of the Bay des Puantz, where our Fathers labor successfully for the conversion of these peoples, over two thousand of whom they have baptized while they have been there.

This bay bears a name which has a meaning not so offensive in the language of the savages; for they call it *la Baye Sallée*[1] rather than Bay des Puans, although with them this is almost the same and this is also the name which they give to the sea. This led us to make very careful researches to ascertain whether there were not some salt-water springs in this quarter, as there are among the Hiroquois, but we found none. We conclude, therefore, that this name has been given to it on account of the quantity of mire and mud which is seen there, whence noisome vapors constantly arise, causing the loudest and most continual thunder that I have ever heard.

The bay is about thirty leagues in depth and eight in width at its mouth; it narrows gradually to the bottom, where it is easy to observe a tide which has its regular ebb and flow, almost like that of the sea. This is not the place to inquire whether these are real tides; whether they are due to the wind, or to some other cause; whether there are winds, the precursors of the moon and attached to her suite, which consequently agitate the lake and give it an apparent ebb and flow whenever the moon ascends above the horizon. What I can positively state is, that, when the water is very calm, it is easy to observe it rising and falling according to the course of the moon; although I do not deny that this movement may be caused by very remote winds, which, pressing on the middle of the lake, cause the edges to rise and fall in the manner which is visible to our eyes.[2]

We left this bay to enter the river that discharges into it; it is very beautiful at its mouth, and flows gently; it is full of bustards, ducks, teal, and other birds, attracted thither by the wild oats, of which they are very fond. But, after ascending the river a short distance, it becomes very difficult of passage, on account of both the currents and the sharp rocks, which cut the canoes and the feet of those who are obliged

[1] Salt Bay.
[2] This phenomenon was noted by many early travellers. The tides in the Great Lakes are small, but noticeable at certain points.

to drag them, especially when the waters are low. Nevertheless, we successfully passed those rapids; and on approaching Machkoutens, the Fire Nation, I had the curiosity to drink the mineral waters of the river that is not far from that village.[1] I also took time to look for a medicinal plant which a savage, who knows its secret, showed to Father Alloues with many ceremonies. Its root is employed to counteract snake-bites, God having been pleased to give this antidote against a poison which is very common in these countries. It is very pungent, and tastes like powder when crushed with the teeth; it must be masticated and placed upon the bite inflicted by the snake. The reptile has so great a horror of it that it even flees from a person who has rubbed himself with it. The plant bears several stalks, a foot high, with rather long leaves; and a white flower, which greatly resembles the wallflower.[2] I put some in my canoe, in order to examine it at leisure while we continued to advance toward Maskoutens, where we arrived on the 7th of June.

Section 3. *Description of the Village of Maskoutens; what passed there between the Father and the Savages. The French begin to enter a New and Unknown Country, and arrive at Missisipi.*

Here we are at Maskoutens.[3] This word may, in Algonquin, mean "the Fire Nation," which, indeed, is the name given to this tribe. Here is the limit of the discoveries which the French have made, for they have not yet gone any farther.

This village consists of three nations who have gathered there—Miamis, Maskoutens, and Kikabous. The former are the most civil, the most liberal, and the most shapely. They wear two long locks over their ears, which give them a pleasing appearance. They are regarded as warriors, and rarely

[1] For the location of this spring and illustration of its present condition see *Wis. Hist. Soc. Proceedings*, 1906, p. 168. It was southeast of the present town of Berlin, in Green Lake County, Wisconsin.

[2] Sufficient indications are not given by Marquette to enable botanists to identify this plant, which may be one of several "snake roots" found in this vicinity.

[3] This village was located not far from the spring mentioned above. See Perrot's description, *ante*, pp. 84–88.

undertake expeditions without being successful. They are very docile, and listen quietly to what is said to them; and they appeared so eager to hear Father Alloues when he instructed them that they gave him but little rest, even during the night. The Maskoutens and Kikabous are ruder, and seem peasants in comparison with the others. As bark for making cabins is scarce in this country, they use rushes; these serve them for making walls and roofs, but do not afford them much protection against the winds, and still less against the rains when they fall abundantly. The advantage of cabins of this kind is, that they make packages of them, and easily transport them wherever they wish, while they are hunting.[1]

When I visited them, I was greatly consoled at seeing a handsome Cross erected in the middle of the village, and adorned with many white skins, red belts, and bows and arrows, which these good people had offered to the great Manitou (this is the name which they give to God). They did this to thank him for having had pity on them during the winter, by giving them an abundance of game when they most dreaded famine.[2]

I took pleasure in observing the situation of this village. It is beautiful and very pleasing; for, from an eminence upon which it is placed, one beholds on every side prairies, extending farther than the eye can see, interspersed with groves or with lofty trees. The soil is very fertile, and yields much Indian corn. The savages gather quantities of plums and grapes, wherewith much wine could be made, if desired.

No sooner had we arrived than we, Monsieur Jollyet and I, assembled the elders together; and he told them that he was sent by Monsieur our governor to discover new countries, while I was sent by God to illumine them with the light of the holy Gospel. He told them that, moreover, the sovereign Master of our lives wished to be known by all the nations; and that in obeying His will I feared not the death to which

[1] The rushes are woven into mats which are easily rolled up and transported.

[2] This cross is supposed by some commentators to have been the symbol of a "Medicine" society among the Indians. It seems more natural to regard it as the sign of Allouez's mission, which the superstitious savages regarded as a "manitou."

I exposed myself in voyages so perilous. He informed them
that we needed two guides to show us the way; and we gave
them a present, by it asking them to grant us the guides.
To this they very civilly consented; and they also spoke to
us by means of a present, consisting of a mat to serve us as a
bed during the whole of our voyage.

On the following day, the tenth of June, two Miamis who
were given us as guides embarked with us, in the sight of a
great crowd, who could not sufficiently express their astonishment at the sight of seven Frenchmen, alone and in two
canoes, daring to undertake so extraordinary and so hazardous an expedition.

We knew that, at three leagues from Maskoutens, was a
river which discharged into Missisipi.[1] We knew also that
the direction we were to follow in order to reach it was west-
southwesterly. But the road is broken by so many swamps
and small lakes that it is easy to lose one's way, especially as
the river leading thither is so full of wild oats that it is difficult to find the channel. For this reason we greatly needed
our two guides, who safely conducted us to a portage of 2,700
paces, and helped us to transport our canoes to enter that
river; after which they returned home, leaving us alone in
this unknown country, in the hands of Providence.[2]

Thus we left the waters flowing to Quebeq, four or five
hundred leagues from here, to float on those that would
thenceforward take us through strange lands. Before embarking thereon, we began all together a new devotion to the
blessed Virgin Immaculate, which we practised daily, addressing to her special prayers to place under her protection both
our persons and the success of our voyage; and, after mutually encouraging one another, we entered our canoes.

The river on which we embarked is called Meskousing.[3]
It is very wide; it has a sandy bottom, which forms various

---

[1] There is some mistake in the distance stated. Father Arthur E. Jones
thinks it is intended for "three leagues from Maskoutens" River. See *Wis.
Hist. Soc. Proceedings*, 1906, pp. 175–182.

[2] The Fox-Wisconsin portage at the site of Portage, Wisconsin, has now
been cut by a government canal. In 1895 there was erected here on the old
portage route a monument to Marquette.

[3] A variant for the name Wisconsin.

shoals that render its navigation very difficult. It is full of islands covered with vines. On the banks one sees fertile land, diversified with woods, prairies, and hills. There are oak, walnut, and basswood trees; and another kind, whose branches are armed with long thorns. We saw there neither feathered game nor fish, but many deer, and a large number of cattle. Our route lay to the southwest, and, after navigating about thirty leagues, we saw a spot presenting all the appearances of an iron mine; and, in fact, one of our party who had formerly seen such mines, assures us that the one which we found is very good and very rich. It is covered with three feet of good soil, and is quite near a chain of rocks, the base of which is covered by very fine trees.[1] After proceeding 40 leagues on this same route, we arrived at the mouth of our river; and, at 42 and a half degrees of latitude, we safely entered Missisipi on the 17th of June, with a joy that I cannot express.[2]

Section 4. Of the Great River called Missisipi; its most notable Features; of various Animals, and especially the Pisikious or Wild Cattle, their Shape and Nature; of the First Villages of the Ilinois, where the French arrived.

Here we are, then, on this so renowned river, all of whose peculiar features I have endeavored to note carefully. The Missisipi River takes its rise in various lakes in the country of the northern nations. It is narrow at the place where Miskous empties; its current, which flows southward, is slow and gentle. To the right is a large chain of very high mountains, and to the left are beautiful lands; in various places, the stream is divided by islands. On sounding, we found ten brasses of water. Its width is very unequal; sometimes it is three-quarters of a league, and sometimes it narrows to three arpents.[3] We gently followed its course, which runs toward the south and southeast, as far as the 42nd degree of latitude.

[1] The traces of a mine seen here were probably those of the lead mines of southwestern Wisconsin.

[2] In 1910 a monument to Marquette was dedicated at Prairie du Chien, near the point where he entered the Mississippi.

[3] *I. e.*, about 600 feet.

Here we plainly saw that its aspect was completely changed. There are hardly any woods or mountains; the islands are more beautiful, and are covered with finer trees. We saw only deer and cattle, bustards, and swans without wings, because they drop their plumage in this country. From time to time, we came upon monstrous fish, one of which struck our canoe with such violence that I thought that it was a great tree, about to break the canoe to pieces. On another occasion, we saw on the water a monster with the head of a tiger, a sharp nose like that of a wildcat, with whiskers and straight, erect ears; the head was gray and the neck quite black; [1] but we saw no more creatures of this sort. When we cast our nets into the water we caught sturgeon, and a very extraordinary kind of fish. It resembles the trout, with this difference, that its mouth is larger. Near its nose, which is smaller, as are also the eyes, is a large bone shaped like a woman's busk, three fingers wide and a cubit long, at the end of which is a disk as wide as one's hand. This frequently causes it to fall backward when it leaps out of the water. [2] When we reached the parallel of 41 degrees 28 minutes, following the same direction, we found that turkeys had taken the place of game; and the *pisikious*, or wild cattle, that of the other animals. [3]

We call them "wild cattle," because they are very similar to our domestic cattle. They are not longer, but are nearly as large again, and more corpulent. When our people killed one, three persons had much difficulty in moving it. The head is very large; the forehead is flat, and a foot and half wide between the horns, which are exactly like those of our oxen, but black and much larger. Under the neck they have a sort of large dewlap, which hangs down; and on the back is a rather high hump. The whole of the head, the neck, and a portion of the shoulders, are covered with a thick mane like

---

[1] The first monster was a catfish (*silurus Mississippiensis*), which grows to great size in western rivers; the second a wildcat, called by the Canadians *pichou du sud*.

[2] This has been identified as the *polyodon spatula*, a very rare Mississippi River fish, called by the French inhabitants *le spatule*.

[3] The buffalo or American bison. Marquette has drawn a picture of one of these animals on his map. See article cited in note 2 on p. 229, *ante*.

that of horses; it forms a crest a foot long, which makes them hideous, and, falling over their eyes, prevents them from seeing what is before them. The remainder of the body is covered with a heavy coat of curly hair, almost like that of our sheep, but much stronger and thicker. It falls off in summer, and the skin becomes as soft as velvet. At that season, the savages use the hides for making fine robes, which they paint in various colors. The flesh and the fat of the *pisikious* are excellent, and constitute the best dish at feasts. Moreover, they are very fierce; and not a year passes without their killing some savages. When attacked, they catch a man on their horns, if they can, toss him in the air, and then throw him on the ground, after which they trample him under foot, and kill him. If a person fire at them from a distance, with either a bow or a gun, he must, immediately after the shot, throw himself down and hide in the grass; for if they perceive him who has fired, they run at him, and attack him. As their legs are thick and rather short, they do not run very fast, as a rule, except when angry. They are scattered about the prairie in herds; I have seen one of four hundred.

We continued to advance, but, as we knew not whither we were going, for we had proceeded over one hundred leagues without discovering anything except animals and birds, we kept well on our guard. On this account, we make only a small fire on land, toward evening, to cook our meals; and, after supper, we remove ourselves as far from it as possible, and pass the night in our canoes, which we anchor in the river at some distance from the shore. This does not prevent us from always posting one of the party as a sentinel, for fear of a surprise. Proceeding still in a southerly and south-south-westerly direction, we find ourselves at the parallel of 41 degrees, and as low as 40 degrees and some minutes,—partly southeast and partly southwest,—after having advanced over 60 leagues since we entered the river, without discovering anything.

Finally, on the 25th of June, we perceived on the water's edge some tracks of men, and a narrow and somewhat beaten path leading to a fine prairie. We stopped to examine it; and, thinking that it was a road which led to some village of savages, we resolved to go and reconnoitre it. We therefore

left our two canoes under the guard of our people, strictly
charging them not to allow themselves to be surprised, after
which Monsieur Jollyet and I undertook this investigation—
a rather hazardous one for two men who exposed themselves,
alone, to the mercy of a barbarous and unknown people. We
silently followed the narrow path, and, after walking about
two leagues, we discovered a village on the bank of a river,
and two others on a hill distant about half a league from the
first.[1] Then we heartily commended ourselves to God, and,
after imploring His aid, we went farther without being perceived, and approached so near that we could even hear the
savages talking. We therefore decided that it was time to
reveal ourselves. This we did by shouting with all our energy,
and stopped, without advancing any farther. On hearing
the shout, the savages quickly issued from their cabins, and
having probably recognized us as Frenchmen, especially when
they saw a black gown—or, at least, having no cause for dis-
trust, as we were only two men, and had given them notice
of our arrival—they deputed four old men to come and
speak to us. Two of these bore tobacco-pipes, finely ornamented and adorned with various feathers. They walked
slowly, and raised their pipes toward the sun, seemingly offering them to it to smoke, without, however, saying a word.
They spent a rather long time in covering the short distance
between their village and us. Finally, when they had drawn
near, they stopped to consider us attentively. I was reassured
when I observed these ceremonies, which with them are performed only among friends; and much more so when I saw
them clad in cloth, for I judged thereby that they were our
allies. I therefore spoke to them first, and asked them who
they were. They replied that they were Ilinois; and, as a
token of peace, they offered us their pipes to smoke. They
afterward invited us to enter their village, where all the people
impatiently awaited us. These pipes for smoking tobacco
are called in this country *calumets*. This word has come so
much into use that, in order to be understood, I shall be obliged to use it, as I shall often have to mention these pipes.

[1] The site of these villages has not been definitely determined. It was
formerly supposed that they were on Des Moines River; some Iowa archaeolo-
gists, however, locate them on the river of that name.

Section 5.   How the Ilinois received the Father in their Village.

At the door of the cabin in which we were to be received
was an old man, who awaited us in a rather surprising atti-
tude, which constitutes a part of the ceremonial that they
observe when they receive strangers.   This man stood erect,
and stark naked, with his hands extended and lifted toward
the sun, as if he wished to protect himself from its rays, which
nevertheless shone upon his face through his fingers.   When
we came near him, he paid us this compliment : "How beautiful the sun is, O Frenchman, when thou comest to visit us!
All our village awaits thee, and thou shalt enter all our cabins
in peace."   Having said this, he made us enter his own, in
which were a crowd of people ; they devoured us with their
eyes, but, nevertheless, observed profound silence.   We
could, however, hear these words, which were addressed to us
from time to time in a low voice : "How good it is, my brothers,
that you should visit us."

After we had taken our places, the usual civility of the
country was paid to us, which consisted in offering us the
calumet.   This must not be refused, unless one wishes to be
considered an enemy, or at least uncivil ; it suffices that one
make a pretense of smoking.   While all the elders smoked
after us, in order to do us honor, we received an invitation on
behalf of the great captain of all the Ilinois to proceed to his
village where he wished to hold a council with us.   We went
thither in a large company, for all these people, who had
never seen any Frenchmen among them, could not cease
looking at us.   They lay on the grass along the road ; they
preceded us, and then retraced their steps to come and see
us again.   All this was done noiselessly, and with marks of
great respect for us.

When we reached the village of the great captain, we saw
him at the entrance of his cabin, between two old men, all
three erect and naked, and holding their calumet turned
toward the sun.   He harangued us in a few words, congratulating us upon our arrival.   He afterward offered us his calumet, and made us smoke while we entered his cabin, where
we received all their usual kind attentions.

Seeing all assembled and silent, I spoke to them by four presents that I gave them. By the first, I told them that we were journeying peacefully to visit the nations dwelling on the river as far as the sea. By the second, I announced to them that God, who had created them, had pity on them, inasmuch as, after they had so long been ignorant of Him, He wished to make himself known to all the peoples; that I was sent by Him for that purpose; and that it was for them to acknowledge and obey Him. By the third, I said that the great captain of the French informed them that he it was who restored peace everywhere; and that he had subdued the Iroquois. Finally, by the fourth, we begged them to give us all the information that they had about the sea, and about the nations through whom we must pass to reach it.

When I had finished my speech, the captain arose, and, resting his hand upon the head of a little slave[1] whom he wished to give us, he spoke thus: "I thank thee, black gown, and thee, O Frenchman," addressing himself to Monsieur Jollyet, "for having taken so much trouble to come to visit us. Never has the earth been so beautiful, or the sun so bright, as to-day; never has our river been so calm, or so clear of rocks, which your canoes have removed in passing; never has our tobacco tasted so good, or our corn appeared so fine, as we now see them. Here is my son, whom I give thee to show thee my heart. I beg thee to have pity on me, and on all my nation. It is thou who knowest the great Spirit who has made us all. It is thou who speakest to Him, and who hearest His word. Beg Him to give me life and health, and to come and dwell with us, in order to make us know Him." Having said this, he placed the little slave near us, and gave us a second present, consisting of an altogether mysterious calumet, upon which they place more value than upon a slave. By this gift, he expressed to us the esteem that he had for Monsieur our governor, from the account which we had given of him; and, by a third, he begged us on behalf of all his nation not to go farther, on account of the great dangers to which we exposed ourselves.

---

[1] Slavery among North American Indians arose from the treatment of captives taken in war. The position of slaves was not as a rule seriously different from that of other members of the tribe, except that they could be disposed of by their masters at will.

I replied that I feared not death, and that I regarded no happiness as greater than that of losing my life for the glory of Him who has made all. This is what these poor people cannot understand.

The council was followed by a great feast, consisting of four dishes, which had to be partaken of in accordance with all their fashions. The first course was a great wooden platter full of *sagamité*, that is to say, meal of Indian corn boiled in water, and seasoned with fat. The master of ceremonies filled a spoon with sagamité three or four times, and put it to my mouth as if I were a little child. He did the same to Monsieur Jollyet. As a second course, he caused a second platter to be brought, on which were three fish. He took some pieces of them, removed the bones therefrom, and, after blowing upon them to cool them, he put them in our mouths as one would give food to a bird. For the third course, they brought a large dog, that had just been killed; but, when they learned that we did not eat this meat, they removed it from before us. Finally, the fourth course was a piece of wild ox, the fattest morsels of which were placed in our mouths.

After this feast, we had to go to visit the whole village, which consists of fully three hundred cabins. While we walked through the streets, an orator continually harangued to oblige all the people to come to see us without annoying us. Everywhere we were presented with belts, garters, and other articles made of the hair of bears and cattle, dyed red, yellow, and gray. These are all the rarities they possess. As they are of no great value, we did not burden ourselves with them.

We slept in the captain's cabin, and on the following day we took leave of him, promising to pass again by his village, within four moons. He conducted us to our canoes, with nearly six hundred persons who witnessed our embarkation, giving us every possible manifestation of the joy that our visit had caused them. For my own part, I promised, on bidding them adieu, that I would come the following year, and reside with them to instruct them. But, before quitting the Ilinois country, it is proper that I should relate what I observed of their customs and usages.

Section 6. Of the Character of the Ilinois; of their Habits and Customs; and of the Esteem that they have for the Calumet, or Tobacco-pipe, and of the Dance they perform in its Honor.

When one speaks the word "Ilinois," it is as if one said in their language, "the men," as if the other savages were looked upon by them merely as animals. It must also be admitted that they have an air of humanity which we have not observed in the other nations that we have seen upon our route. The shortness of my stay among them did not allow me to secure all the information that I would have desired; among all their customs, the following is what I have observed.

They are divided into many villages, some of which are quite distant from that of which we speak, which is called Peouarea.[1] This causes some difference in their language, which, on the whole, resembles Allegonquin, so that we easily understood each other. They are of a gentle and tractable disposition; we experienced this in the reception which they gave us. They have several wives, of whom they are extremely jealous; they watch them very closely, and cut off their noses or ears when they misbehave. I saw several women who bore the marks of their misconduct. Their bodies are shapely; they are active and very skillful with bows and arrows. They also use guns, which they buy from our savage allies who trade with our French. They use them especially to inspire, through their noise and smoke, terror in their enemies; the latter do not use guns, and have never seen any, since they live too far toward the west. They are warlike, and make themselves dreaded by the distant tribes to the south and west, whither they go to procure slaves; these they barter, selling them at a high price to other nations, in exchange for other wares. Those very distant savages against whom they war have no knowledge of Europeans; neither do they know anything of iron, or of copper, and they have only stone knives. When the Ilinois depart to go to war, the whole village must be notified by a loud shout, which is uttered at the doors of their cabins, the night and the

[1] The Peoria were a branch of the Illinois whose later home was on the Illinois River near the lake of their name.

morning before their departure. The captains are distinguished
from the warriors by wearing red scarfs. These are made,
with considerable skill, from the hair of bears and wild cattle.
They paint their faces with red ochre, great quantities of which
are found at a distance of some days' journey from the village.
They live by hunting, game being plentiful in that country,
and on Indian corn, of which they always have a good crop;
consequently, they have never suffered from famine. They
also sow beans and melons, which are excellent, especially
those that have red seeds. Their squashes are not of the best;
they dry them in the sun, to eat them during the winter and
the spring. Their cabins are very large, and are roofed and
floored with mats made of rushes. They make all their
utensils of wood, and their ladles out of the heads of cattle,
whose skulls they know so well how to prepare that they use
these ladles with ease for eating their sagamité.

They are liberal in cases of illness, and think that the effect
of the medicines administered to them is in proportion to the
presents given to the physician. Their garments consist only
of skins; the women are always clad very modestly and very
becomingly, while the men do not take the trouble to cover
themselves. I know not through what superstition some
Ilinois, as well as some Nadouessi, while still young, assume
the garb of women, and retain it throughout their lives.
There is some mystery in this, for they never marry and glory
in demeaning themselves to do everything that the women do.
They go to war, however, but can use only clubs, and not
bows and arrows, which are the weapons proper to men.
They are present at all the juggleries, and at the solemn dances
in honor of the calumet; at these they sing, but must not
dance. They are summoned to the councils, and nothing can
be decided without their advice. Finally, through their profession of leading an extraordinary life, they pass for Manitous,
that is to say, for spirits, or persons of consequence.[1]

There remains no more, except to speak of the calumet.
There is nothing more mysterious or more respected among
them. Less honor is paid to the crowns and sceptres of kings
than the savages bestow upon this. It seems to be the god

---

[1] These persons were known as "berdashes," their condition had some religious significance, and they received certain especial honors.

of peace and of war, the arbiter of life and of death. It has
but to be carried upon one's person, and displayed, to enable
one to walk safely through the midst of enemies, who, in the
hottest of the fight, lay down their arms when it is shown.
For that reason, the Ilinois gave me one, to serve as a safe-
guard among all the nations through whom I had to pass
during my voyage. There is a calumet for peace, and one for
war, which are distinguished solely by the color of the feathers
with which they are adorned; red is a sign of war. They
also use it to put an end to their disputes, to strengthen their
alliances, and to speak to strangers. It is fashioned from a
red stone, polished like marble,[1] and bored in such a manner
that one end serves as a receptacle for the tobacco, while the
other fits into the stem; this is a stick two feet long, as thick
as an ordinary cane, and bored through the middle. It is
ornamented with the heads and necks of various birds, whose
plumage is very beautiful. To these they also add large
feathers—red, green, and other colors—wherewith the whole
is adorned. They have a great regard for it, because they
look upon it as the calumet of the Sun; and, in fact, they
offer it to the latter to smoke when they wish to obtain a calm,
or rain, or fine weather. They scruple to bathe themselves
at the beginning of summer, or to eat fresh fruit, until after
they have performed the dance, which they do as follows:

The calumet dance, which is very famous among these
peoples, is performed solely for important reasons; sometimes to strengthen peace, or to unite themselves for some
great war; at other times, for public rejoicing. Sometimes
they thus do honor to a nation who are invited to be present;
sometimes it is danced at the reception of some important
personage, as if they wished to give him the diversion of a
ball or a comedy. In winter, the ceremony takes place in a
cabin; in summer, in the open fields. When the spot is selected, it is completely surrounded by trees, so that all may
sit in the shade afforded by their leaves, in order to be protected from the heat of the sun. A large mat of rushes, painted

[1] This peculiar red pipestone is now known as "catlinite" in honor of George
Catlin, who was said to be the first white person to visit (in 1836) the sacred
quarry in the present Pipestone County in southwest Minnesota. See his
North American Indians, II. 164–177.

in various colors, is spread in the middle of the place, and serves as a carpet upon which to place with honor the god of the person who gives the dance; for each has his own god, which they call their Manitou. This is a serpent, a bird, or other similar thing, of which they have dreamed while sleeping, and in which they place all their confidence for the success of their war, their fishing, and their hunting. Near this Manitou, and at its right, is placed the calumet in honor of which the feast is given; and all around it a sort of trophy is made, and the weapons used by the warriors of those nations are spread, namely: clubs, war-hatchets, bows, quivers, and arrows.

Everything being thus arranged, and the hour of the dance drawing near, those who have been appointed to sing take the most honorable place under the branches; these are the men and women who are gifted with the best voices, and who sing together in perfect harmony. Afterward, all come to take their seats in a circle under the branches; but each one, on arriving, must salute the Manitou. This he does by inhaling the smoke, and blowing it from his mouth upon the Manitou, as if he were offering to it incense. Every one, at the outset, takes the calumet in a respectful manner, and, supporting it with both hands, causes it to dance in cadence, keeping good time with the air of the songs. He makes it execute many differing figures; sometimes he shows it to the whole assembly, turning himself from one side to the other. After that, he who is to begin the dance appears in the middle of the assembly, and at once continues this. Sometimes he offers it to the sun, as if he wished the latter to smoke it; sometimes he inclines it toward the earth; again, he makes it spread its wings, as if about to fly; at other times, he puts it near the mouths of those present, that they may smoke. The whole is done in cadence; and this is, as it were, the first scene of the ballet.

The second consists of a combat carried on to the sound of a kind of drum, which succeeds the songs, or even unites with them, harmonizing very well together. The dancer makes a sign to some warrior to come to take the arms which lie upon the mat, and invites him to fight to the sound of the drums. The latter approaches, takes up the bow and arrows, and the war-hatchet, and begins the duel with the other, whose sole defense is the calumet. This spectacle is very pleasing, especially as all is done in cadence; for one attacks, the other defends himself; one strikes blows, the other parries them; one takes to flight, the other pursues; and then he who was fleeing faces about, and causes his adversary to flee. This is done so well, with slow and measured steps, and to the rhythmic sound of the voices and drums, that it might pass for a very fine opening of a ballet in France. The third scene consists of a lofty discourse, delivered by him who holds the calumet; for, when the combat is ended without blood-shed, he recounts the battles at which he has been present, the victories that he has won, the names of the nations, the places, and the captives whom he has made. And, to reward him, he who presides at the dance makes him a present of a fine robe of beaver-skins, or some other article. Then, having received it, he hands the calumet to another, the latter to a third, and so on with all the others, until every one has done his duty; then the president presents the calumet itself to the nation that has been invited to the ceremony, as a token of the everlasting peace that is to exist between the two peoples.

Here is one of the songs that they are in the habit of singing. They give it a certain turn which cannot be sufficiently expressed by note, but which nevertheless constitutes all its grace.

Ninahani, ninahani, ninahani, nani ongo.[1]

Section 7. Departure of the Father from the Ilinois; of the Painted Monsters which he saw upon the Great River Missisipi; of the River Pekitanoui. Continuation of the Voyage.

We take leave of our Ilinois at the end of June, about three o'clock in the afternoon. We embark in the sight of all the people, who admire our little canoes, for they have never seen any like them.

We descend, following the current of the river called

---

[1] The music for this chant is published in Thwaites, *Jesuit Relations*, LIX. 311.

Pekitanoui, which discharges into the Mississipy, flowing from the northwest. I shall have something important to say about it, when I shall have related all that I observed along this river.[1]

While passing near the rather high rocks that line the river, I noticed a simple which seemed to me very extraordinary. The root is like small turnips fastened together by little filaments, which taste like carrots. From this root springs a leaf as wide as one's hand, and half a finger thick, with spots. From the middle of this leaf spring other leaves, resembling the sconces used for candles in our halls; and each leaf bears five or six yellow flowers shaped like little bells.

We found quantities of mulberries, as large as those of France; and a small fruit which we at first took for olives, but which tasted like oranges; and another fruit as large as a hen's egg. We cut it in halves, and two divisions appeared, in each of which eight to ten fruits were encased; these are shaped like almonds, and are very good when ripe. Nevertheless, the tree that bears them has a very bad odor, and its leaves resemble those of the walnut-tree. In these prairies there is also a fruit similar to hazelnuts, but more delicate; the leaves are very large, and grow from a stalk at the end of which is a head similar to that of a sunflower, in which all its nuts are regularly arranged. These are very good, both cooked and raw.[2]

While skirting some rocks, which by their height and length inspired awe, we saw upon one of them two painted monsters which at first made us afraid, and upon which the boldest savages dare not long rest their eyes. They are as large as a calf; they have horns on their heads like those of deer, a horrible look, red eyes, a beard like a tiger's, a face somewhat like a man's, a body covered with scales, and so long a tail that it winds all around the body, passing above the head and going back between the legs, ending in a fish's tail. Green, red, and black are the three colors composing

---

[1] The Missouri River takes its present name from an Indian tribe that formerly dwelt upon its banks. The word by which Marquette knew it was an Indian word for "Muddy."

[2] These fruits have been identified respectively as the cactus or prickly pear, the persimmon, and the chincapin.

the picture. Moreover, these two monsters are so well painted that we cannot believe that any savage is their author; for good painters in France would find it difficult to paint so well, and besides, they are so high up on the rock that it is difficult to reach that place conveniently to paint them. Here is approximately the shape of these monsters, as we have faithfully copied it.[1]

While conversing about these monsters, sailing quietly in clear and calm water, we heard the noise of a rapid, into which we were about to run. I have seen nothing more dreadful. An accumulation of large and entire trees, branches, and floating islands, was issuing from the mouth of the river Pekistanouï, with such impetuosity that we could not without great danger risk passing through it. So great was the agitation that the water was very muddy, and could not become clear.

Pekitanouï is a river of considerable size, coming from the northwest, from a great distance; and it discharges into the Missisipi. There are many villages of savages along this river, and I hope by its means to discover the Vermillion or California Sea.

Judging from the direction of the course of the Missisipï, if it continue the same way, we think that it discharges into the Mexican Gulf. It would be a great advantage to find the river leading to the Southern Sea, toward California; and, as I have said, this is what I hope to do by means of the Pekitanouï, according to the reports made to me by the savages. From them I have learned that, by ascending this river for five or six days, one reaches a fine prairie, twenty or thirty leagues long. This must be crossed in a north-westerly direction, and it terminates at another small river, on which one may embark, for it is not very difficult to transport canoes through so fine a country as that prairie. This second river flows toward the southwest for ten or fifteen leagues, after which it enters a lake, small and deep, which

---

[1] These pictographs on a rock near Alton, Illinois, were called "piasa," and supposed to represent the "thunder bird." They were quite distinct when described by Stoddard in 1803; when visited in 1838 only one could be seen, of which traces were discernible as late as 1848, soon after which the rock was quarried down.

flows toward the west, where it falls into the sea.   I have
hardly any doubt that it is the Vermillion Sea, and I do not
despair of discovering it some day, if God grant me the grace
and the health to do so, in order that I may preach the Gospel
to all the peoples of this new world who have so long grovelled
in the darkness of infidelity.

Let us resume our route, after escaping as best we could
from the dangerous rapid caused by the obstruction which I
have mentioned.

Section 8.   *Of the New Countries discovered by the Father.
Various Particulars.   Meeting with some Savages.   First
News of the Sea and of Europeans.   Great Danger avoided
by means of the Calumet.*

After proceeding about twenty leagues straight to the
south, and a little less to the southeast, we found ourselves
at a river called Ouaboukigou,[1] the mouth of which is at
the 36th degree of latitude.   Before reaching it, we passed by
a place that is dreaded by the savages, because they believe
that a manitou is there, that is to say, a demon, that devours
travellers; and the savages, who wished to divert us from our
undertaking, warned us against it.   This is the demon: there
is a small cove, surrounded by rocks twenty feet high, into
which the whole current of the river rushes; and, being pushed
back against the waters following it, and checked by an
island near by, the current is compelled to pass through a
narrow channel.   This is not done without a violent struggle
between all these waters, which force one another back, or
without a great din, which inspires terror in the savages, who
fear everything.   But this did not prevent us from passing,
and arriving at Waboukigou.   This river flows from the lands
of the East, where dwell the people called Chaouanons in so
great numbers that in one district there are as many as twenty-
three villages, and fifteen in another, quite near one another.
They are not at all warlike, and are the nations whom the
Iroquois go so far to seek, and war against without any reason; and, because these poor people cannot defend them-

[1] The present Ohio River was usually known as the Wabash (Ouaboukigou)
below its confluence with the latter stream.

selves, they allow themselves to be captured and taken like
flocks of sheep; and, innocent though they are, they nevertheless sometimes experience the barbarity of the Iroquois, who
cruelly burn them.

A short distance above the river of which I have just
spoken are cliffs, on which our Frenchmen noticed an iron
mine, which they consider very rich. There are several veins
of ore, and a bed a foot thick, and one sees large masses of it
united with pebbles. A sticky earth is found there, of three
different colors—purple, violet, and red. The water in which
the latter is washed assumes a bloody tinge. There is also
very heavy, red sand. I placed some on a paddle, which was
dyed with its color, so deeply that the water could not wash
it away during the fifteen days while I used it for paddling.

Here we began to see canes, or large reeds, which grow on
the bank of the river; their color is a very pleasing green;
all the nodes are marked by a crown of long, narrow, and
pointed leaves. They are very high, and grow so thickly
that the wild cattle have some difficulty in forcing their way
through them.

Hitherto, we had not suffered any inconvenience from
mosquitoes; but we were entering into their home, as it were.
This is what the savages of this quarter do to protect themselves against them. They erect a scaffolding, the floor of
which consists only of poles, so that it is open to the air in
order that the smoke of the fire made underneath may pass
through, and drive away those little creatures, which cannot
endure it; the savages lie down upon the poles, over which
bark is spread to keep off rain. These scaffoldings also serve
them as protection against the excessive and unbearable heat
of this country; for they lie in the shade, on the floor below,
and thus protect themselves against the sun's rays, enjoying
the cool breeze that circulates freely through the scaffolding.

With the same object, we were compelled to erect a sort
of cabin on the water, with our sails as a protection against
the mosquitoes and the rays of the sun. While drifting down
with the current, in this condition, we perceived on land some
savages armed with guns, who awaited us. I at once offered
them my plumed calumet, while our Frenchmen prepared
for defense, but delayed firing, that the savages might be the

first to discharge their guns. I spoke to them in Huron, but they answered me by a word which seemed to me a declaration of war against us. However, they were as frightened as we were; and what we took for a signal for battle was an invitation that they gave us to draw near, that they might give us food. We therefore landed, and entered their cabins, where they offered us meat from wild cattle and bear's grease, with white plums, which are very good. They have guns, hatchets, hoes, knives, beads, and flasks of double glass, in which they put their powder. They wear their hair long, and tattoo their bodies after the Hiroquois fashion. The women wear head-dresses and garments like those of the Huron women. They assured us that we were no more than ten days' journey from the sea; that they bought cloth and all other goods from the Europeans who lived to the east; that these Europeans had rosaries and pictures; that they played upon instruments; that some of them looked like me, and had been received by these savages kindly. Nevertheless, I saw none who seemed to have received any instruction in the faith; I gave them as much as I could, with some medals.[1]

This news animated our courage, and made us paddle with fresh ardor. We thus push forward, and no longer see so many prairies, because both shores of the river are bordered with lofty trees. The cottonwood, elm, and basswood trees there are admirable for their height and thickness. The great numbers of wild cattle, which we heard bellowing, led us to believe that the prairies are near. We also saw quail on the water's edge. We killed a little parroquet, one half of whose head was red, the other half and the neck yellow, and the whole body green.[2] We had gone down to near the 33rd degree of latitude having proceeded nearly all the time in a southerly direction, when we perceived a village on the water's edge called Mitchigamea.[3] We had recourse to our

[1] The explorers were now in the Chickasaw country; but the similarity of this band with the Iroquois, their language and customs, would indicate that they were either Tuscarora or Cherokee—both tribes of Iroquoian origin.

[2] A small species of paroquet was very abundant in the Mississippi and Ohio valleys in early days.

[3] The Michigamea Indians were of Algonquian origin, allied to the Illinois, from whom they were temporarily separated. Their habitat was probably above

patroness and guide, the blessed Virgin Immaculate; and we greatly needed her assistance, for we heard from afar the savages who were inciting one another to the fray by their continual yells. They were armed with bows, arrows, hatchets, clubs, and shields. They prepared to attack us, on both land and water; part of them embarked in great wooden canoes, some to ascend, others to descend the river, in order to intercept us and surround us on all sides. Those who were on land came and went, as if to commence the attack. In fact, some young men threw themselves into the water, to come and seize my canoe; but the current compelled them to return to land. One of them then hurled his club, which passed over without striking us. In vain I showed the calumet, and made them signs that we were not coming to war against them. The alarm continued, and they were already preparing to pierce us with arrows from all sides, when God suddenly touched the hearts of the old men, who were standing at the water's edge. This no doubt happened through the sight of our calumet, which they had not clearly distinguished from afar; but as I did not cease displaying it, they were influenced by it, and checked the ardor of their young men. Two of these elders even, after casting into our canoe, as if at our feet, their bows and quivers, to reassure us, entered the canoe, and made us approach the shore, whereon we landed, not without fear on our part. At first, we had to speak by signs, because none of them understood the six languages which I spoke. At last, we found an old man who could speak a little Ilinois.

We informed them, by our presents, that we were going to the sea. They understood very well what we wished to say to them, but I know not whether they apprehended what I told them about God, and about matters pertaining to their salvation. This is a seed cast into the ground, which will bear fruit in its time. We obtained no other answer than that we should learn all that we desired at another large village, called Akamsea, which was only eight or ten leagues

St. Francis River, in the neighborhood of the present Big Lake that takes its name from this tribe—Michigame, or Big Lake. About the end of the seventeenth century the Michigamea were driven north and coalesced with the Kaskaskia branch of the Illinois.

lower down.[1]   They offered us sagamité and fish, and we
passed the night among them, with some anxiety.

*Section 9.   Reception given to the French in the Last Village
which they saw.   The Manners and Customs of those Savages.   Reasons for not going farther.*

We embarked early on the following day, with our interpreter; a canoe containing ten savages went a short distance
ahead of us.   When we arrived within half a league of the
Akamsea, we saw two canoes coming to meet us.   He who
commanded stood upright, holding in his hand the calumet,
with which he made various signs, according to the custom
of the country.   He joined us, singing very agreeably, and
gave us tobacco to smoke; after that, he offered us sagamité,
and bread made of Indian corn, of which we ate a little.   He
then preceded us, after making us a sign to follow him slowly.
A place had been prepared for us under the scaffolding of the
chief of the warriors; it was clean, and carpeted with fine
rush mats.   Upon these we were made to sit, having around
us the elders, who were nearest to us; after them, the warriors; and, finally, all the common people in a crowd.   We
fortunately found there a young man who understood Ilinois
much better than did the interpreter whom we had brought
from Mitchigamea.   Through him, I spoke at first to the whole
assembly by the usual presents.   They admired what I said
to them about God and the mysteries of our holy Faith.
They manifested a great desire to retain me among them,
that I might instruct them.

We afterward asked them what they knew about the sea.
They replied that we were only ten days' journey from it—
we could have covered the distance in five days; that they
were not acquainted with the nations who dwelt there, because their enemies prevented them from trading with those
Europeans; that the hatchets, knives, and beads that we saw

[1] Akamsea was a village of the Quapaw tribe, of the great Siouan stock,
allied to the tribes of the Missouri and upper Mississippi regions.   The name
Akamsea means "down-stream people" and their early habitat is supposed to
have been on the Ohio.   The village visited by Marquette appears to have been
above the Arkansas River, near the site where De Soto died in 1541.

were sold to them partly by nations from the East, and partly by an Ilinois village situated at four days' journey from their village westward. They also told us that the savages with guns whom we had met were their enemies, who barred their way to the sea, and prevented them from becoming acquainted with the Europeans, and from carrying on any trade with them; that, moreover, we exposed ourselves to great dangers by going farther, on account of the continual forays of their enemies along the river, because, as they had guns and were very warlike, we could not without manifest danger proceed down the river, which they constantly occupy.

During this conversation, food was continually brought to us in large wooden platters, consisting sometimes of saga-mité, sometimes of whole corn, sometimes of a piece of dog's flesh. The entire day was spent in feasting. These people are very obliging and liberal with what they have; but they are wretchedly provided with food, for they dare not go and hunt wild cattle, on account of their enemies. It is true that they have an abundance of Indian corn, which they sow at all seasons. We saw at the same time some that was ripe, some other that had only sprouted, and some again in the milk, so that they sow it three times a year. They cook it in great earthen jars, which are very well made. They have also plates of baked earth which they use in various ways. The men go naked, and wear their hair short; they pierce their noses, from which, as well as from their ears, hang beads. The women are clad in wretched skins; they knot their hair in two tresses which they throw behind their ears, and have no ornaments with which to adorn themselves. Their feasts are given without any ceremony. They offer the guests large dishes, from which all eat at discretion and offer what is left to one another. Their language is exceedingly difficult, and I could succeed in pronouncing only a few words notwith-standing all my efforts. Their cabins, which are made of bark, are long and wide; they sleep at the two ends, which are raised two feet above the ground. They keep their corn in large baskets made of canes, or in gourds as large as half-barrels. They know nothing of the beaver. Their wealth consists in the skins of wild cattle. They never see snow in their country, and recognize the winter only through the rains, which there fall more frequently than in summer. We ate no other fruit there than watermelons. If they knew how to till their soil, they would have fruits of all kinds.

In the evening, the elders held a secret council, in regard to the design entertained by some to break our heads and rob us; but the chief put a stop to all these plots. After sending for us, he danced the calumet before us, in the manner I have already described, as a token of our entire safety; and, to relieve us of all fear, he made me a present of it.

Monsieur Jolliet and I held another council, to deliberate upon what we should do—whether we should push on, or remain content with the discovery which we had made. After attentively considering that we were not far from the Gulf of Mexico, the basin of which is at the latitude of 31 degrees 60 minutes, while we were at 33 degrees 40 minutes, we judged that we could not be more than two or three days' journey from it; and that, beyond a doubt, the Missisipi River discharges into the Florida or Mexican Gulf, and not to the east in Virginia, whose sea-coast is at 34 degrees latitude,—which we had passed, without, however, having as yet reached the sea,—or to the west in California, because in that case our route would have been to the west, or the west-southwest, whereas we had always continued it toward the south. We further considered that we exposed ourselves to the risk of losing the results of this voyage, of which we could give no information if we proceeded to fling ourselves into the hands of the Spaniards who, without doubt, would at least have detained us as captives. Moreover, we saw very plainly that we were not in a condition to resist savages allied to the Europeans, who were numerous, and expert in firing guns, and who continually infested the lower part of the river. Finally, we had obtained all the information that could be desired in regard to this discovery. All these reasons induced us to decide upon returning; this we announced to the savages, and, after a day's rest, made our preparations for it.

Section 10.   *Return of the Father and of the French.   Baptism
of a Dying Child.*

After a month's navigation, while descending Missisipi
from the 42nd to the 34th degree, and beyond, and after
preaching the Gospel as well as I could to the nations that I
met, we start on the 17th of July from the village of the Akensea, to retrace our steps.   We therefore reascend the Missisipi which gives us much trouble in breasting its currents.
It is true that we leave it, at about the 38th degree, to enter
another river, which greatly shortens our road, and takes us
with but little effort to the Lake of the Ilinois.[1]

We have seen nothing like this river that we enter, as regards its fertility of soil, its prairies and woods; its cattle,
elk, deer, wildcats, bustards, swans, ducks, parroquets, and
even beaver.   There are many small lakes and rivers.   That
on which we sailed is wide, deep, and still, for 65 leagues.
In the spring and during part of the summer there is only one
portage of half a league.   We found on it a village of Ilinois
called Kaskasia,[2] consisting of 74 cabins.   They received us
very well, and obliged me to promise that I would return to
instruct them.   One of the chiefs of this nation, with his
young men, escorted us to the Lake of the Ilinois, whence, at
last, at the end of September, we reached the Bay des Puantz,
from which we had started at the beginning of June.

Had this voyage resulted in the salvation of even one soul,
I would consider all my troubles well rewarded, and I have
reason to presume that such is the case.   For, when I was returning, we passed through the Ilinois of Peouarea, and during
three days I preached the Faith in all their cabins; after
which, while we were embarking, a dying child was brought
to me at the water's edge, and I baptized it shortly before it
died, through an admirable act of Providence for the salvation
of that innocent soul.

[1] The Illinois River, leading via the Chicago portage to Lake Michigan,
then frequently called Lake of the Illinois.

[2] The Kaskaskia village, removed later to the stream bearing that name in
southern Illinois.   In Marquette's time it was on the Illinois, not far from the
present village of Utica in La Salle County.

MARQUETTE'S LAST VOYAGE, 1674–1675

INTRODUCTION

For a year Father Marquette recuperated at the mission of St. François Xavier. Then, in the autumn of 1674, there came to him from Canada the permission he so passionately desired to found a mission among the Illinois Indians. He embarked on Lake Michigan in the late autumn of 1674, but the rigors of an early winter and the weakness of disease incapacitated the Father for his chosen work. Nevertheless he struggled on, and wintered on the site of Chicago, teaching and baptizing such stray savages as came his way. As soon as spring opened he hastened to the Illinois village, where he spent Easter with his red children, after which his two attendants sought to take him home to St. Ignace. Day by day with patient devotion they paddled the sick man in his canoe along the eastern shore of the great lake. Finally, May 18, 1675, at the mouth of the river that now bears his name, they carried him reverently to land and his spirit escaped to the immortals. Two years later some Ottawa to whom he had ministered transplanted his remains to the chapel he had built at St. Ignace. To-day Marquette's statue in the Capitol at Washington typifies Wisconsin's remembrance of the discoverer, missionary, and martyr, Jacques Marquette.

The history of his manuscripts has been recounted in the introduction to the preceding piece. We reprint here, from Dr. Thwaites's edition of the *Jesuit Relations*, LIX. 165–211, Marquette's unfinished journal of his final voyage, and the general account of this last expedition and of his death, by Father Dablon, superior of the Jesuits in Canada, in a contemporary relation, of which the manuscript is in the archives of their College of St. Mary in Montreal.

MARQUETTE'S LAST VOYAGE, 1674–1675

Unfinished Journal of Father Jacques Marquette, addressed to the Reverend Father Claude Dablon, Superior of the Missions.

+

My Reverend Father, Pax Christi.

Having been compelled to remain at St. Francois[1] throughout the summer on account of an ailment, of which I was cured in the month of September, I awaited there the return of our people from down below,[2] in order to learn what I was to do with regard to my wintering. They brought me orders to proceed to the mission of La Conception among the Ilinois. After complying with Your Reverence's request for copies of my journal concerning the Missisipi River, I departed with Pierre Porteret and Jacque [*blank*], on the 25th of October, 1674, about noon. The wind compelled us to pass the night at the outlet of the river,[3] where the Poutewatamis were assembling; for the elders would not allow them to go in the direction of the Ilinois, lest the young men, after collecting robes with the goods that they brought from below, and after hunting beaver, might seek to go down in the spring; because they have reason to fear the Nadouessi.

October 26. On passing the village, we found only two cabins of savages, who were going to spend the winter at La Gasparde. We learned that five canoes of Poutewatamis, and four of Ilinois, had started to go to the Kaskaskia.

27. We were delayed in the morning by rain; in the afternoon, we had fine, calm weather, so that at Sturgeon Bay we joined the savages, who travelled ahead of us.

---

[1] The mission of St. François Xavier at De Pere, Wisconsin.

[2] The ordinary term for lower Canada, whence the trading canoes went each year.

[3] Fox River, emptying into Green Bay.

28. We reached the portage.[1] A canoe that had gone ahead prevented us from killing any game. We began our portage and slept on the other shore, where the stormy weather gave us much trouble. Pierre did not arrive until an hour after dark, having lost his way on a path where he had never been. After the rain and thunder, snow fell.

29. Being compelled to change our camping-ground, we continued to carry our packs. The portage covers nearly a league, and is very difficult in many places. The Ilinois assemble in the evening in our cabin, and ask us not to leave them, as we may need them, and they know the lake better than we do. We promise them this.

30. The Ilinois women complete our portage in the morning. We are delayed by the wind. There are no animals.

31. We start, with tolerably fair weather, and sleep at a small river. The road by land from Sturgeon Bay is very difficult. Last autumn, we were travelling not far from it when we entered the forest.

November 1. After I said holy mass, we came for the night to a river, whence one goes to the Poutewatamis by a good road. Chachagwessiou, an Ilinois greatly esteemed among his nation, partly because he engages in the fur trade, arrived at night with a deer on his back, of which he gave us a share.

2. After holy mass, we travel all day in very fine weather. We kill two cats, which are almost nothing but fat.

3. While I am ashore, walking on fine sand, the whole water's edge being covered with grass similar to that which is hauled up by the nets at St. Ignace, I come to a river which I am unable to cross.[2] Our people enter it, in order to take me on board; but we are unable to go out, on account of the waves. All the other canoes go on, excepting one, which came with us.

4. We are delayed. There seems to be an island out in the lake, for the game go there at night.

5. We had considerable difficulty in getting out of the river at noon. We found the savages in a river, where I seized the opportunity of instructing the Ilinois, on account of a feast that Nawaskingwe had just given to a wolfskin.

---

[1] Sturgeon Bay portage through the Door County peninsula, Wisconsin.

[2] Probably Sheboygan River, Wisconsin.

6.   We performed a good day's journey.   While the savages were hunting, they discovered some tracks of men, and this compelled us to stay over on the following day.

9.   We landed about two o'clock, because there was a good camping-ground.   We were detained there for five days, on account of the great agitation of the lake, although without any wind; and afterward of the snow, which was melted on the following day by the sun, and a breeze from the lake.

15.   After proceeding a sufficient distance, we camp at a favorable place, where we are detained three days.   Pierre mends a savage's gun. Snow falls at night, and thaws during the day.

20.   We sleep near the bluffs, and are very poorly sheltered.   The savages remain behind while we are delayed two days and a half by the wind.   Pierre goes into the woods, and finds the prairie twenty leagues from the portage.   He also goes through a fine canal which is vaulted, as it were, to the height of a man, in which there is water a foot deep.

23.   After embarking at noon, we experienced some difficulty in reaching a river.[1]   Then the cold began, and more than a foot of snow covered the ground; it has remained ever since.   We were delayed for three days, during which Pierre killed a deer, three bustards, and three turkeys, which were very good.   The others proceeded to the prairies.   A savage discovered some cabins, and came to get us.   Jacques went there on the following day, with him; two hunters also came to see me.   They were Maskoutens, to the number of eight, or nine cabins, who had separated from the others in order to obtain subsistence.   With fatigues almost impossible to Frenchmen, they travel throughout the winter over very bad roads, the land abounding in streams, small lakes, and swamps.   Their cabins are wretched; and they eat or starve, according to the places where they happen to be.   Being detained by the wind, we noticed that there were great shoals out in the lake, over which the waves broke continually.   Here I had an attack of diarrhœa.

27.   We had some trouble in getting out of the river; then, after proceeding about three leagues, we found the savages, who had killed some cattle, and three Ilinois who

[1] Milwaukee River.

had come from the village. We were delayed there by a wind from the land, by heavy waves from the lake, and by cold.

December 1. We went ahead of the savages, so that I might celebrate holy mass.

3. After saying holy mass, we embarked, and were compelled to make for a point, so that we could land, on account of floating masses of ice.

4. We started with a favoring wind, and reached the river of the portage, which was frozen to the depth of half a foot; there was more snow there than elsewhere, as well as more tracks of animals and turkeys.

Navigation on the lake is fairly good from one portage to the other, for there is no crossing to be made, and one can land anywhere, unless one persist in going on when the waves are high and the wind is strong. The land bordering it is of no value, except on the prairies. There are eight or ten quite fine rivers. Deer-hunting is very good, as one goes away from the Poutewatamis.

12. As we began yesterday to haul our baggage in order to approach the portage, the Ilinois who had left the Poutewatamis arrived, with great difficulty. We were unable to celebrate holy mass on the day of the Conception, owing to the bad weather and cold.[1] During our stay at the entrance of the river, Pierre and Jacques killed three cattle and four deer, one of which ran some distance with its heart split in two. We contented ourselves with killing three or four turkeys, out of many that came around our cabin because they were almost dying of hunger. Jacques brought in a partridge that he had killed, exactly like those of France except that it had two ruffs, as it were, of three or four feathers as long as a finger, near the head, covering the two sides of the neck where there are no feathers.

14. Having encamped near the portage, two leagues up the river, we resolved to winter there, as it was impossible to go farther, since we were too much hindered and my ailment did not permit me to give myself much fatigue.[2] Several Ilinois passed yesterday, on their way to carry their furs to

[1] See p. 228, note 2, *ante*.

[2] A large cross has been erected in the southwestern district of Chicago to commemorate the site of Marquette's winter quarters in 1674–1675.

Nawaskingwe; we gave them one of the cattle and one of the deer that Jacque had killed on the previous day. I do not think that I have ever seen any savages more eager for French tobacco than they. They came and threw beaver-skins at our feet, to get some pieces of it; but we returned these, giving them some pipefuls of the tobacco because we had not yet decided whether we would go farther.

15. Chachagwessiou and the other Ilinois left us, to go and join their people and give them the goods that they had brought, in order to obtain their robes. In this they act like the traders, and give hardly any more than do the French. I instructed them before their departure, deferring the holding of a council until the spring, when I should be in their village. They traded us three fine robes of ox-skins for a cubit of tobacco; these were very useful to us during the winter. Being thus rid of them, we said the mass of the Conception. After the 14th, my disease turned into a bloody flux.

30. Jacque arrived from the Ilinois village, which is only six leagues from here; there they were suffering from hunger, because the cold and snow prevented them from hunting. Some of them notified La Toupine[1] and the surgeon that we were here; and, as they could not leave their cabin, they had so frightened the savages, believing that we should suffer from hunger if we remained here, that Jacque had much difficulty in preventing fifteen young men from coming to carry away all our belongings.

January 16, 1675. As soon as the two Frenchmen learned that my illness prevented me from going to them, the surgeon came here with a savage, to bring us some blueberries and corn. They are only eighteen leagues from here, in a fine place for hunting cattle, deer, and turkeys, which are excellent there. They had also collected provisions while waiting for us; and had given the savages to understand that their cabin belonged to the black gown; and it may be said that they have done and said all that could be expected of them. After the surgeon had spent some time here, in order to perform his devotions, I sent Jacque with him to tell the Ilinois

---

[1] Pierre Moreau *dit* La Toupine was a noted wood-ranger of the seventeenth century, who had been a soldier in the garrison of Quebec. He was with St. Lusson at Sault Ste. Marie in 1671, and died at Quebec as late as 1727.

near that place that my illness prevented me from going to see them; and that I would even have some difficulty in going there in the spring, if it continued.

24. Jacque returned with a sack of corn and other delicacies, which the French had given him for me. He also brought the tongues and flesh of two cattle, which a savage and he had killed near here. But all the animals feel the bad weather.

26. Three Ilinois brought us, on behalf of the elders, two sacks of corn, some dried meat, pumpkins, and twelve beaverskins: first, to make me a mat; second, to ask me for powder; third, that we might not be hungry; fourth, to obtain a few goods. I replied: first, that I had come to instruct them, by speaking to them of prayer, etc.; second, that I would give them no powder, because we sought to restore peace everywhere, and I did not wish them to begin war with the Muiamis; third, that we feared not hunger; fourth, that I would encourage the French to bring them goods, and that they must give satisfaction to those who were among them for the beads which they had taken as soon as the surgeon started to come here. As they had come a distance of twenty leagues, I gave them, in order to reward them for their trouble and for what they had brought me, a hatchet, two knives, three clasp-knives, ten brasses of glass beads, and two double mirrors, telling them that I would endeavor to go to the village, for a few days only, if my illness continued. They told me to take courage, and to remain and die in their country; and that they had been informed that I would remain there for a long time.

February 9. Since we addressed ourselves to the Blessed Virgin Immaculate, and commenced a novena with a mass, at which Pierre and Jacque, who do everything they can to relieve me, received communion, to ask God to restore my health, my bloody flux has left me, and all that remains is a weakness of the stomach. I am beginning to feel much better, and to regain my strength. Out of a cabin of Ilinois, who encamped near us for a month, a portion have again taken the road to the Poutewatamis, and some are still on the lake-shore, where they wait until navigation is open. They bear letters for our Fathers of St. François.

20. We have had opportunity to observe the tides coming in from the lake, which rise and fall several times a day; and, although there seems to be no shelter in the lake, we have seen the ice going against the wind. These tides made the water good or bad, because that which flows from above comes from prairies and small streams. The deer, which are plentiful near the lake-shore, are so lean that we had to abandon some of those which we had killed.

March 23. We killed several partridges, only the males of which had ruffs on the neck, the females not having any. These partridges are very good, but not like those of France.

30. The north wind delayed the thaw until the 25th of March, when it set in with a south wind. On the very next day, game began to make its appearance. We killed thirty pigeons, which I found better than those down the great river; but they are smaller, both old and young. On the 28th, the ice broke up, and stopped above us. On the 29th, the waters rose so high that we had barely time to decamp as fast as possible, putting our goods in the trees, and trying to sleep on a hillock. The water gained on us nearly all night, but there was a slight freeze, and the water fell a little, while we were near our packages. The barrier has just broken, the ice has drifted away; and, because the water is already rising, we are about to embark to continue our journey.

The Blessed Virgin Immaculate has taken such care of us during our wintering that we have not lacked provisions, and have still remaining a large sack of corn, with some meat and fat. We also lived very pleasantly, for my illness did not prevent me from saying holy mass every day. We were unable to keep Lent, except on Fridays and Saturdays.

31. We started yesterday and travelled three leagues up the river without finding any portage. We hauled our goods probably about half an arpent. Besides this discharge, the river has another one by which we are to go down. The very high lands alone are not flooded. At the place where we are, the water has risen more than twelve feet. This is where we began our portage eighteen months ago. Bustards and ducks pass continually; we contented ourselves with seven. The ice, which is still drifting down, keeps us here, as we do not know in what condition the lower part of the river is.

April 1.　As I do not yet know whether I shall remain next summer in the village, on account of my diarrhœa, we leave here part of our goods, those with which we can dispense, and especially a sack of corn.　While a strong south wind delays us, we hope to go to-morrow to the place where the French are, at a distance of fifteen leagues from here.

6.　Strong winds and the cold prevent us from proceeding.　The two lakes over which we passed are full of bustards, geese, ducks, cranes, and other game unknown to us.　The rapids are quite dangerous in some places.　We have just met the surgeon, with a savage who was going up with a canoe-load of furs; but, as the cold is too great for persons who are obliged to drag their canoes in the water, he has made a cache of his beaver-skins, and returns to the village to-morrow with us.　If the French procure robes in this country, they do not disrobe the savages, so great are the hardships that must be endured to obtain them.[1]

[Addressed: "To my Reverend Father, Father Claude Dablon, Superior of the Missions of the Society of Jesus in New France.　Quebec."]

[Endorsed: "Letter and Journal of the late Father Marquette."]

[Endorsed: "Everything concerning Father Marquette's Voyage."]

ACCOUNT OF THE SECOND VOYAGE AND THE DEATH OF FATHER JACQUES MARQUETTE

The mission of the Ilinois was founded in the year 1674, after the first voyage which Father Jacques Marquet made to discover new territories and new peoples who are on the great and famous river Missisipi.

The year following, he made a second voyage in order to establish there the mission; it is that one which we are about to relate.

---

[1] This was Marquette's last entry.　The succeeding part of the relation, describing his last voyage, death, and burial, was written by Father Dablon.

*Section 1.   Narrative of the Second Voyage that Father Marquet
     made to the Ilinois.   He reaches them, notwithstanding his
     Illness, and begins the Mission of La Conception.*

Father Jacques Marquette, having promised the Ilinois
on his first voyage to them, in 1673, that he would return to
them the following year, to teach them the mysteries of our
religion, had much difficulty in keeping his word.   The great
hardships of his first voyage had brought upon him a bloody
flux, and had so weakened him that he was giving up the
hope of undertaking a second.   However, his sickness de-
creased; and, as it had almost entirely abated by the close
of the summer in the following year, he obtained the permission of his superiors to return to the Ilinois and there begin
that fair mission.

He set out for that purpose, in the month of November
of the year 1674, from the Bay des Puants, with two men, one
of whom had made the former voyage with him.   During a
month of navigation on the Lake of the Ilinois, he was tolerably well; but, as soon as the snow began to fall, he was again
seized with his bloody flux, which compelled him to halt in
the river which leads to the Ilinois.   It was there that they
constructed a cabin in which to pass the winter, amid such
inconveniences that, his malady increasing more and more,
he saw clearly that God was granting to him the favor which
he had so many times besought from Him; and he even told
his two companions very plainly that he would certainly die
of that malady, and during that voyage.   Duly to prepare
his soul, despite the severe indisposition of his body, he began
this so severe winter sojourn by the retreat of St. Ignatius,
which he performed with every feeling of devotion, and many
celestial consolations; and then he passed the whole of the
remaining time in holding communion with all Heaven, having, in these deserts, no intercourse with the earth except
with his two companions.   He confessed them and administered communion to them twice in the week, and exhorted
them as much as his strength permitted him.   A short time
after Christmas, that he might obtain the favor of not dying
without having taken possession of his dear mission, he in-

vited his companions to make a novena in honor of the Immaculate Conception of the Blessed Virgin. His prayer was answered, against all human probability; and, his health improving, he prepared himself to go to the village of the Ilinois as soon as navigation should open, which he did with much joy, setting out for that place on the 29th of March. He spent eleven days on the way, during which time he had occasion to suffer much, both from his own illness, from which he had not entirely recovered, and from the very severe and unfavorable weather.

On at last arriving at the village, he was received as an angel from Heaven. After he had assembled at various times the chiefs of the nation, with all the old men, that he might sow in their minds the first seeds of the Gospel, and after having given instruction in the cabins, which were always filled with a great crowd of people, he resolved to address all in public, in a general assembly which he called together in the open air, the cabins being too small to contain all the people. It was a beautiful prairie, close to a village, which was selected for the great council; this was adorned, after the fashion of the country, by covering it with mats and bearskins. Then the Father, having directed them to stretch out upon lines several pieces of Chinese taffeta, attached to these four large pictures of the Blessed Virgin, which were visible on all sides. The audience was composed of 500 chiefs and elders, seated in a circle around the Father, and of all the young men, who remained standing. They numbered more than 1500 men, without counting the women and children, who are always numerous, the village being composed of five or six hundred fires. The Father addressed the whole body of people, and conveyed to them ten messages, by means of ten presents which he gave them. He explained to them the principal mysteries of our religion, and the purpose that had brought him to their country. Above all, he preached to them Jesus Christ, on the very eve [of that great day] on which he had died upon the Cross for them, as well as for all the rest of mankind; then he said holy mass. On the third day after, which was Easter Sunday,[1] things being prepared in the same manner as on Thursday, he celebrated the holy mys-

[1] April 14, 1675.

teries for the second time; and by these two, the only sacrifices ever offered there to God, he took possession of that land in the name of Jesus Christ, and gave to that mission the name of the Immaculate Conception of the Blessed Virgin.

He was listened to by all those peoples with universal joy; and they prayed him with most earnest entreaty to come back to them as soon as possible, since his sickness obliged him to return. The Father, on his side, expressed to them the affection which he felt for them, and the satisfaction that they had given him; and pledged them his word that he, or some other of our Fathers, would return to carry on that mission so happily inaugurated. This promise he repeated several times, while parting with them to go upon his way; and he set out with so many tokens of regard on the part of those good peoples that, as a mark of honor, they chose to escort him for more than thirty leagues on the road, vying with each other in taking charge of his slender baggage.

Section 2.   The Father is compelled to leave his Ilinois Mission.
His Last Illness.   His Precious Death in the Heart of the Forest.

After the Ilinois, filled with great esteem for the Gospel, had taken leave of the Father, he continued his journey, and shortly after reached the Lake of the Ilinois, upon whose waters he had to journey nearly a hundred leagues, by an unknown route, whereon he had never before travelled; for he was obliged to coast along the southern shore of the lake, having come by the northern.[1] But his strength was so rapidly diminishing that his two men despaired of being able to bring him alive to the end of their journey. Indeed, he became so feeble and exhausted that he was unable to assist or even to move himself, and had to be handled and carried about like a child.

Meanwhile, he preserved in that condition an admirable equanimity, resignation, joy, and gentleness, consoling his dear companions and encouraging them to suffer patiently all the hardships of that voyage, in the assurance that God

---

[1] This southern or rather eastern route was taken by voyagers in order to take advantage of the currents setting northwardly.

would not abandon them after his death.   It was during this voyage that he began to make more special preparation for death.   He held communion, sometimes with our Lord, sometimes with his holy Mother, or with his guardian angel, or with all Paradise.   He was often overheard repeating these words, *Credo quod redemptor meus vivit;* or *Maria, Mater Gratiæ, Mater Dei, memento mei.*[1]   In addition to the spiritual exercise, which was read to him every day, he requested toward the close that they would read to him his meditation preparatory for death, which he carried about with him.   He recited every day his breviary; and although he was so low that his sight and strength were greatly enfeebled, he continued to do so to the last day of his life, despite the remonstrance of his companions.

Eight days before his death, he was thoughtful enough to prepare the holy water for use during the rest of his illness, in his agony, and at his burial; and he instructed his companions how it should be used.

The evening before his death, which was a Friday, he told them, very joyously, that it would take place on the morrow.   He conversed with them during the whole day as to what would need to be done for his burial: about the manner in which they should inter him; of the spot that should be chosen for his grave; how his feet, his hands, and his face should be arranged; how they should erect a Cross over his grave.   He even went so far as to counsel them, three hours before he expired, that as soon as he was dead they should take the little hand-bell of his chapel, and sound it while he was being put under ground.   He spoke of all these things with so great tranquillity and presence of mind that one might have supposed that he was concerned with the death and funeral of some other person, and not with his own.

Thus did he converse with them as they made their way upon the lake, until, having perceived a river, on the shore of which stood an eminence that he deemed well suited to be the place of his interment, he told them that that was the place of his last repose.[2]   They wished, however, to proceed

[1] "I know that my Redeemer liveth," and "Mary, Mother of Grace, Mother of God, remember me."

[2] Now known as Pere Marquette River, at whose mouth is the city of Ludington, Michigan.

farther, as the weather was favorable, and the day was not far advanced; but God raised a contrary wind, which compelled them to return, and enter the river which the Father had pointed out. They accordingly brought him to the land, lighted a little fire for him, and prepared for him a wretched cabin of bark. They laid him down therein, in the least uncomfortable way that they could; but they were so stricken with sorrow that, as they have since said, they hardly knew what they were doing.

The Father, being thus stretched on the ground in much the same way as was St. Francis Xavier, as he had always so passionately desired, and finding himself alone in the midst of these forests, for his companions were occupied with the disembarkation, he had leisure to repeat all the acts in which he had continued during these last days.

His dear companions having afterward rejoined him, all disconsolate, he comforted them, and inspired them with the confidence that God would take care of them after his death, in these new and unknown countries. He gave them the last instructions, thanked them for all the charities which they had exercised in his behalf during the whole journey, and entreated pardon for the trouble that he had given them. He charged them to ask pardon for him also, from all our Fathers and brethren who live in the country of the Outaouacs. Then he undertook to prepare them for the sacrament of penance, which he administered to them for the last time. He gave them also a paper on which he had written all his faults since his own last confession, that they might place it in the hands of the Father Superior, that the latter might be enabled to pray to God for him in a more special manner. Finally, he promised not to forget them in Paradise. And, as he was very considerate, knowing that they were much fatigued with the hardships of the preceding days, he bade them go and take a little repose. He assured them that his hour was not yet so very near, and that he would awaken them when the time should come, as, in fact, two or three hours afterward he did summon them, being ready to enter into the agony.

They drew near to him, and he embraced them once again, while they burst into tears at his feet. Then he asked for holy water and his reliquary; and having himself removed his crucifix, which he carried always suspended round his neck, he placed it in the hands of one of his companions, begging him to hold it before his eyes. Then, feeling that he had but a short time to live, he made a last effort, clasped his hands, and, with a steady and fond look upon his crucifix, he uttered aloud his profession of faith, and gave thanks to the Divine Majesty for the great favor which he had accorded him of dying in the Society, of dying in it as a missionary of Jesus Christ, and, above all, of dying in it, as he had always prayed, in a wretched cabin in the midst of the forests and bereft of all human succor.

After that, he was silent, communing within himself with God. Nevertheless, he let escape from time to time these words, *Sustinuit anima mea in verbo ejus;* [1] or these, *Mater Dei, memento mei*—which were the last words that he uttered before entering his agony, which was, however, very mild and peaceful.

He had prayed his companions to put him in mind, when they should see him about to expire, to repeat frequently the names of Jesus and Mary, if he could not himself do so. They did as they were bidden; and, when they believed him to be near his end, one of them called aloud, "Jesus, Mary!" The dying man repeated the words distinctly, several times; and as if, at these sacred names, something presented itself to him, he suddenly raised his eyes above his crucifix, holding them riveted on that object, which he appeared to regard with pleasure. And so, with a countenance beaming and all aglow, he expired without any struggle, and so gently that it might have been regarded as a pleasant sleep.

His two poor companions, shedding many tears over him, composed his body in the manner which he had prescribed to them. Then they carried him devoutly to burial, ringing the while the little bell as he had bidden them; and planted a large Cross near to his grave, as a sign to passers-by.

When it became a question of embarking, to proceed on their journey, one of the two, who for some days had been so heartsick with sorrow, and so greatly prostrated with an internal malady, that he could no longer eat or breathe except with difficulty, bethought himself, while the other was making

[1] "My soul hath endured in his word."

all preparations for embarking, to visit the grave of his good Father, and ask his intercession with the glorious Virgin, as he had promised, not doubting in the least that he was in Heaven. He fell, then, upon his knees, made a short prayer, and having reverently taken some earth from the tomb, he pressed it to his breast. Immediately his sickness abated, and his sorrow was changed into a joy which did not forsake him during the remainder of his journey.

Section 3.   What occurred at the Removal of the Bones of the late Father Marquette, which were taken from his Grave on the 19th of May, 1677, the same Day as that on which he died in the Year 1675.[1] A Brief Summary of his Virtues.

God did not permit that a deposit so precious should remain in the midst of the forest, unhonored and forgotten. The savages named Kiskakons,[2] who have been making public profession of Christianity for nearly ten years, and who were instructed by Father Marquette when he lived at the Point of St. Esprit, at the extremity of Lake Superior, carried on their last winter's hunting in the vicinity of the Lake of the Ilinois. As they were returning in the spring, they were greatly pleased to pass near the grave of their good Father, whom they tenderly loved; and God also put it into their hearts to remove his bones and bring them to our church at the mission of St. Ignace at Missilimakinac, where those savages make their abode.

They repaired, then, to the spot, and resolved among themselves to act in regard to the Father as they are wont to do toward those for whom they profess great respect. Accordingly, they opened the grave, and uncovered the body; and, although the flesh and internal organs were all dried up, they found it entire, so that not even the skin was in any way injured. This did not prevent them from proceeding to dissect it, as is their custom. They cleansed the bones and exposed them to the sun to dry; then, carefully laying them

---

[1] May 18, 1675, was the true date of his death, since Dablon expressly relates that it befell on Saturday.

[2] For the Kiskakon Ottawa see p. 121, note 1, *ante*.

in a box of birch-bark, they set out to bring them to our mission of St. Ignace.[1]

There were nearly thirty canoes which formed, in excellent order, that funeral procession. There were also a goodly number of Iroquois, who united with our Algonquin savages to lend more honor to the ceremonial. When they drew near our house, Father Nouvel, who is its Superior, with Father Piercon, went out to meet them, accompanied by the Frenchmen and savages who were there; and having halted the procession, he put the usual questions to them, to make sure that it was really the Father's body which they were bringing. Before conveying it to land, they intoned the *De profundis*[2] in the presence of the thirty canoes, which were still on the water, and of the people who were on the shore. After that, the body was carried to the church, care being taken to observe all that the ritual appoints in such ceremonies. It remained exposed under the pall, all that day, which was Whitmonday, the 8th of June; and on the morrow, after having rendered to it all the funeral rites, it was lowered into a small vault in the middle of the church, where it rests as the guardian angel of our Outaouas missions. The savages often come to pray over his tomb. Not to mention more than this instance, a young girl, aged nineteen or twenty years, whom the late Father had instructed, and who had been baptized in the past year, fell sick, and applied to Father Nouvel to be bled and to take certain remedies. The Father prescribed to her, as sole medicine, to come for three days and say a *pater* and three *ave's* at the tomb of Father Marquette. She did so, and before the third day was cured, without bleeding or any other remedies.

Father Jaques Marquette, of the province of Champagne, died at the age of thirty-eight years, of which twenty-one were passed in the Society—namely, twelve in France and nine in Canada. He was sent to the missions of the upper Al-

---

[1] The site of this mission chapel and the remains of Marquette were discovered two hundred years after his burial by the priest of the village, Rev. Edward Jacker. The remnants of a birch-bark box, a number of bones, and part of a skull were unearthed. Most of these relics are now in the possession of Marquette University at Milwaukee.

[2] Psalm 130.

gonquins, who are called Outaouacs; and labored therein with the zeal that might be expected from a man who had proposed to himself St. Francis Xavier as the model of his life and death. He resembled that great saint, not only in the variety of barbarian languages which he mastered, but also by the range of his zeal, which made him carry the faith to the ends of this new world, and nearly 800 leagues from here into the forests, where the name of Jesus Christ had never been proclaimed.

He always entreated God that he might end his life in these laborious missions, and that, like his dear St. Xavier, he might die in the midst of the woods, bereft of everything. Every day, he interposed for that end both the merits of Jesus Christ and the intercession of the Virgin Immaculate, for whom he entertained a singular tenderness.

Accordingly, he obtained through such powerful mediators that which he solicited with so much earnestness; since he had, like the apostle of the Indies, the happiness to die in a wretched cabin on the shore of Lake Ilinois, forsaken by all the world.

We might say much of the rare virtues of this noble missionary: of his zeal, which prompted him to carry the Faith so far, and proclaim the Gospel to so many peoples who were unknown to us; of his gentleness, which rendered him beloved by all, and made him all things to all men—a Frenchman with the French, a Huron with the Hurons, an Algonquin with the Algonquins; of the childlike candor with which he disclosed his heart to his superiors, and even to all kinds of persons, with an ingenuousness which won all hearts; of his angelic chastity; and of his uninterrupted union with God.

But that which apparently predominated was a devotion, altogether rare and singular, to the Blessed Virgin, and particularly toward the mystery of her Immaculate Conception. It was a pleasure to hear him speak or preach on that subject. All his conversations and letters contained something about the Blessed Virgin Immaculate—for so he always called her. From the age of nine years, he fasted every Saturday; and from his tenderest youth began to say the little office of the Conception, inspiring every one with the same devotion. Some months before his death, he said every day with his two men a little corona of the Immaculate Conception which he had devised as follows: After the *credo*, there is said once the *pater* and *ave*, and then four times these words: *Ave Filia Dei Patris, ave Mater Filii Dei, ave Sponsa Spiritus Sancti, ave Templum totius Trinitatis: per sanctam Virginitatem et Immaculatam Conceptionem tuam, purissima Virgo, emunda cor et carnem meam: in nomine Patris, et Filii, et Spiritus Sancti,*[1] —concluding with the *Gloria Patri*, the whole repeated three times.

He never failed to say the mass of the Conception, or, at least, when he could do so, the prayer of the Conception. He hardly meditated upon anything else day and night. That he might leave us an ever-enduring testimony of his sentiments, it was his desire to bestow on the mission of the Ilinois the name of La Conception.

So tender a devotion toward the Mother of God merited some singular grace; and she accorded him the favor that he had always requested—to die on a Saturday. His companions never doubted that she appeared to him at the hour of his death, when, after pronouncing the names of Jesus and Mary, he suddenly raised his eyes above his crucifix, holding them fixed on an object which he regarded with extreme pleasure, and a joy that showed itself upon his features; and they had, at that time, the impression that he had rendered up his soul into the hands of his good Mother.

One of the last letters that he wrote to the Father Superior of the missions before his great voyage, is sufficient evidence that such were his sentiments. He begins it thus: "The Blessed Virgin Immaculate has obtained for me the favor of reaching this place in good health, and with the resolve to correspond to the intentions which God has respecting me, since He has assigned me to the voyage toward the south. I have no other thought than that of doing what God wills. I dread nothing —neither the Nadoissis, nor the reception awaiting me among the nations, dismay me. One of two things will happen: either God will punish me for my crimes and cowardice, or

---

[1] "Hail, Daughter of God the Father; hail, Mother of God the Son; hail, Bride of the Holy Spirit; hail, Temple of the whole Trinity; by thy Holy Virginity and Immaculate Conception, most pure Virgin, cleanse my heart and flesh; in the name of the Father, and of the Son, and of the Holy Ghost."

else He will give me a share in his Cross, which I have not yet carried since my arrival in this country. But this Cross has been perhaps obtained for me by the Blessed Virgin Immaculate, or it may be death itself, that I may cease to offend God. It is that for which I try to hold myself in readiness, surrendering myself altogether into His hands. I entreat Your Reverence not to forget me, and to obtain for me of God that I may not remain ungrateful for the favors which He heaps upon me."

There was found among his papers a manuscript entitled "The directing Care of God over a Missionary," in which he shows the excellence of that vocation, the advantages which it affords for self-sanctification, and the care that God takes of Gospel laborers. One sees in this little abstract the spirit of God which possessed him.

MEMOIR ON LA SALLE'S DISCOVERIES, BY TONTY, 1678–1690 [1693]

INTRODUCTION

ROBERT CAVELIER DE LA SALLE, whose name is indissolubly associated with the valley of the Mississippi, although he was unfortunate in his life and in his death has been fortunate in his biographers both contemporary and recent. About none of the French explorers has so large an amount of documentary material collected. Every detail of his plans and activities after 1678 has been told and retold. His own letters and memorials to the court have been preserved in the French archives, and were in 1879 printed in three volumes by Pierre Margry. In addition to these materials we have the accounts of two of the chaplains of his expedition—the garrulous, lively, popular reminiscences of Father Louis Hennepin, whose work appeared in edition after edition; the accurate, painstaking narrative of Father Zénobe Membré, who accompanied La Salle in his earlier and later attempts at penetrating the Mississippi Valley. For La Salle's last expedition, his tragic death, and the return of the remnant of his people there are numerous sources—the narratives of his brother Jean Cavelier and Henri Joutel being those best known. But among all who acted with La Salle in his ambitious plans for founding an empire in the heart of America, no one is more justly entitled to credence than his faithful lieutenant and friend Henri de Tonty.

Tonty was the son of an Italian banker, Lorenzo Tonti, from whom the tontine system of insurance takes its name. Having been concerned in Masaniello's Neapolitan conspiracy of 1647, Lorenzo fled from his native land to France, where he found service under the Italian premier Cardinal Mazarin. Henri was born probably near Naples and was a babe when he was carried to the French court. At the age of eighteen or nineteen he entered the French service; he took part in seven campaigns, lost his right hand in battle, and was taken prisoner. After the treaty of Nymwegen in 1678 his regiment was disbanded, and he returned to Versailles, where he was presented to La Salle, then a suppliant for permission to colonize the valley of the Mississippi.

It has been well said that of all that La Salle obtained on his journey to France in 1678—the support of the king, the interest of his ministers, and substantial help for the expenses of his project—none were of more worth than the allegiance of the young Italian lieutenant, whose services he secured upon this occasion. Through all the following years of danger, toil, misfortune, and calumny, Tonty was the one companion who comprehended and seconded all La Salle's far-reaching plans, and was ever his efficient and faithful supporter. Even after his superior's death, Tonty continued his efforts to carry out those plans, to rescue La Salle's memory from obloquy and to secure his fortune and his fame

Left by La Salle, in 1682, in charge of his interests in Illinois, Tonty maintained with great ability the Fort of St. Louis upon "The Rock" on the Illinois River, pacified his Indian colonists, introduced agriculture, prosecuted the fur trade. His journeys took him from the mouth of the Mississippi to the land of the Assiniboin on the Red River of the North; from his seigniory in Arkansas to the French capital on the St. Lawrence. Deprived at last by royal edict of his Fort St. Louis, some time about the close of the seventeenth century he sought the South and joined his fortunes with those of the Canadian founder of Louisiana. There, not far from Mobile, the great lieutenant of La Salle died, September 6, 1704.

Tonty wrote two accounts of his experiences in North America. The first covers the five years, 1678–1683, and exists in two copies in the Bibliothèque Nationale in Paris. It is published in Pierre Margry, *Découvertes et Établissements des Français dans l'Ouest de l'Amérique Septentrionale*, I. 573–616. The second or longer narrative, covering the years 1678–1691, was sent in 1693 to Count de Pontchartrain, then minister of the colonies. It is published in Pierre Margry, *Relations et Mémoires Inédits* (Paris, 1867), pp. 1–36. It first appeared in an English translation in Thomas Falconer, *On the Discovery of the Mississippi*, etc. (London, 1844). The same translation was used by Benjamin F. French in *Louisiana Historical Collections*, part I. 52–66, and is reprinted in *Illinois Historical Collections*, I. 128–164, from which we reprint with many textual corrections. This second memoir of Tonty formed the basis of a spurious work entitled, *Dernières Découvertes dans l'Amérique Septentrionale de Monsieur de la Salle par Chevalier de Tonti, Gouverneur du Fort St. Louis aux Illinois* (Paris, 1697). This was Englished in 1698, and issued in London. Tonty during his lifetime protested the authorship. This spurious memoir should not be confounded with the genuine memoir addressed to the Count de Pontchartrain, which remained in the French archives until the nineteenth century. This latter has seemed to the editors the best brief connected account, by a participant and survivor, of La Salle's explorations in the Mississippi Valley, his plans for settlement and exploitation, and his premature and tragic death.

MEMOIR ON LA SALLE'S DISCOVERIES, BY TONTY, 1678–1690 [1693]

Memoir Sent in 1693, on the Discovery of the Mississippi and the Neighboring Nations by M. de la Salle, from the Year 1678 to the Time of His Death, and by the Sieur de Tonty to the Year 1691.

AFTER having been eight years in the French service, by land and by sea, and having had a hand shot off in Sicily by a grenade,[1] I resolved to return to France to solicit employment. At that time the late M. Cavelier de La Salle came to court, a man of great intelligence and merit, who sought to obtain leave from the court to explore the Gulf of Mexico by traversing the countries of North America. Having obtained of the King the permission he desired through the favor of the late M. Colbert and M. de Seignelai, the late Monseigneur the Prince of Conti,[2] who was acquainted with him and who honored me with his favor, sent me to ask him to be allowed to accompany him in his long journeys, to which he very willingly assented.

We sailed from Rochelle on the 14th of July, 1678, and arrived at Quebec on the 15th of September following. We recruited there for some days, and after having taken leave of M. the Count de Frontenac, governor general of the country, ascended the St. Lawrence as far as Fort Frontenac, 120 leagues from Quebec, on the banks of the Lake of Frontenac, which is about 300 leagues around;[3] and after staying there

---

[1] Tonty had this hand replaced by one of metal which he usually wore covered with a glove. He is said to have used this as a weapon with much effect among enemy Indians, who called him *Bras de Fer* (Iron Arm).

[2] Colbert was the prime minister of Louis XIV., Seignelay Colbert's son; the (second) prince of Conti was a prominent courtier who had married a daughter of the king.

[3] Count de Frontenac built this post in 1673 and two years later granted it as a seigniory to La Salle. The Indian name for the site was Cataraqui, at the modern town of Kingston. La Salle rebuilt the fort in stone, and it was main-

286

four days, we embarked in a boat of forty tons to cross this
lake, and on Christmas day we found ourselves opposite a
village called Tsonnontouan,[1] to which M. de La Salle sent
some canoes to procure Indian corn for our subsistence. From
thence we sailed towards Niagara, intending to look for a
suitable place above the Falls where a boat might be built.
The winds were so contrary that we could not approach it
nearer than nine leagues, which determined us to go by land.
We found there some cabins of the Iroquois, who received
us well. We slept there, and the next day we went three
leagues further up to look for a good place to build a boat.[2]
There we encamped.

The boat in which we came was lost on the coast through
the obstinacy of the pilot, whom M. de La Salle had ordered
to bring it ashore. The crew and the things in it were saved.
M. de La Salle determined to return to Fort Frontenac over
the ice, and I remained in command at Niagara with a Recollect
Father[3] and thirty men. The bark was completed in the
spring. M. de La Salle joined us with two other Recollect
Fathers and several men, to aid in bringing this bark up, on
account of the rapids, which I was not able to ascend on account of the weakness of my crew. He directed me to wait
for him at the extremity of Lake Erie, at a place called Detroit,
120 leagues from Niagara, to join there some Frenchmen
whom he had sent off the last autumn. I went in advance in
a bark canoe, and when we were near Detroit the ship came up.[4]

tained until captured in 1758 by the English. Lake Ontario was frequently
called Lake Frontenac.

[1] The village of the Seneca near the Genesee River.

[2] This shipyard has been identified near the mouth of Cayuga Creek at a
village now called La Salle.

[3] This Recollect priest was Louis Hennepin, born about 1640 in Belgium.
Fond of adventure, he travelled in Europe, officiated as chaplain in the Netherlands during war, and embarked in 1675 for New France, becoming the next year
chaplain at Fort Frontenac. Having accompanied La Salle to Illinois, he was
sent with an exploring party to the upper Mississippi, captured by the Sioux,
and carried past the Falls of St. Anthony, to which he gave the present name.
Rescued by Duluth, he returned to Canada and sailed for Europe, where he published several accounts of his journeys, all designed to give prominence to his
own achievements. For his rescue by Duluth, see the succeeding document.

[4] This first sailing vessel on the upper lakes was called the *Griffin*, in honor
of Frontenac's armorial bearings.

We got into it, and continued our voyage as far as Missili-makinak, where we arrived at the end of August, having crossed two lakes larger than that of Frontenac.

We remained there some days to rest ourselves, and as M. de La Salle intended to go to the Illinois, he sent me to the Sault Sainte-Marie, where Lake Superior discharges it-self into Lake Huron, to look for some of his men who had deserted, and himself set sail on the Lake of the Islinois. Having arrived at Poutouatamis, an Islinois village,[1] the calumet was sung, a ceremony of theirs during which large presents are given and received, and in which a post is placed in the midst of the assembly, where those who wish to make known their great deeds in war, striking the post, declaim on the deeds they have done. This ceremony regularly takes place in the presence of those with whom they wish to make alliance, and the calumet is among the savages the symbol of peace. M. de La Salle sent his ship back to Niagara to fetch the things he wanted, and, embarking in a canoe, continued his voyage to the Miamis River. There he commenced build-ing a house.[2]

In the meantime I came up with the deserters,[3] and kept on my way to within thirty leagues of the Miamis River, where I was obliged to leave my men, in order to hunt, our provisions failing us. I then went on to join M. de La Salle. When I arrived he told me he wished that all the men had come with me in order to proceed to the Islinois. I retraced my way to find them. But the wind increasing, we were forced to land, and the violence of the waves was such that our canoe was upset. We were, however, saved, but everything that was in the canoe was lost, and for want of provisions we lived for three days on acorns. I sent word of what had hap-pened to M. de La Salle. He directed me to join him. I went in my little canoe. As soon as I arrived we ascended twenty-

---

[1] There seems to be some hiatus here. La Salle set sail from Michilimackinac for Green Bay, on which there was a Potawatomi (not an Illinois) village.

[2] The present St. Joseph River, emptying into Lake Michigan at its south-eastern extremity. La Salle's fort at the mouth of the stream was named for the Miami Indians, who had recently removed thither from Wisconsin.

[3] Tonty, having apprehended the deserters, came down the eastern shore of the lake, while La Salle and the main body of the expedition proceeded in canoes along the western and southern shores to St. Joseph River.

five leagues, as far as the portage,[1] where the men whom I had left behind joined us. We made the portage, which is about two leagues in length, and came to the source of the Islinois River. We embarked there and descended the river for 100 leagues. When we arrived at the village of the savages, they were absent hunting and as we had no provisions we opened some caches[2] of Indian corn.

During this journey some of our Frenchmen, fatigued, determined to leave us, but that night was so cold that their plan was broken up. We continued our route, in order to join the savages, and found them thirty leagues below the village. When they saw us they thought we were Iroquois, and therefore put themselves on the defensive and made their women run into the woods; but when they recognized us, the women with their children were called back and the calumet was danced to M. de La Salle and me, in order to mark their desire to live in peace with us. We gave them some merchandise for the corn which we had taken in their village.

This was on the 3d of January, 1679.[3] It was necessary to fortify ourselves for the winter. Applying ourselves to it, we made a fort which was called Crèvecœur.[4] Part of our people deserted and they even put poison into our kettle. M. de La Salle was poisoned, but he was saved by some antidote a friend had given to him in France. The desertion of these men gave us less annoyance than the effect which it had on the minds of the savages, for the enemies of M. de La Salle had spread a report among the Islinois that we were friends of the Iroquois, who are their greatest enemies. The effect this produced will be seen hereafter.

M. de La Salle commenced building a boat to descend the

---

[1] The location of the portage from the St. Joseph to the Kankakee—the southern branch of the Illinois—has been found by recent investigations of local historians to be above the city of South Bend, in St. Joseph County, Indiana.

[2] A cache was a kind of underground storehouse used by Indians and woodsmen to conceal provisions and goods.

[3] This date should be January 3, 1680; probably it is given according to an earlier method, that made the year begin March 1 instead of January 1.

[4] Early commentators supposed that the fort received its name, Crèvecœur (heartbreak), from the distressing circumstances of the leader of the expedition. It is now thought to have been named for a fortress in the Netherlands captured by Turenne, in July, 1672.

river.   He sent a Recollect Father with the Sieur Acau[1]
to explore the nation of the Sioux,[2] 400 leagues from the
Islinois, toward the north, on the Mississipy River, a river
that runs not less than 800 leagues to the sea without rapids,
and having determined to go himself by land to Fort Frontenac, because he had heard nothing of the bark which he had
sent to Niagara, he gave me the command of this place and
left us on the 22d of March with five men.   On his road he
met with two men, whom he had sent in the autumn to Missilimakinak to obtain news of his bark.   They assured him
that it had not come down, and he therefore determined to
continue his journey.[3]   These two men were sent to me with
orders to go to the old village to visit a rock and to build a
strong fort upon it.[4]

Whilst I was absent all my men deserted.   They took away
everything that was finest and most valuable, and left me with
two Recollects and three Frenchmen, newly arrived from
France, stripped of everything and at the mercy of the savages.[5]   All that I could do was to draw up an authentic account of the affair and send it to M. de La Salle.   He lay in
wait for them on Lake Frontenac, took some of them and
killed the others.   After this he returned towards the Islinois.
As for his bark, it has never been heard of.[6]

[1] Michel Accault, the leader of the expedition of three to the Sioux country,
was a native of Poitiers.   He was captured by the Sioux, rescued by Duluth,
and settled permanently in Illinois, where he married a woman of the Illinois
tribe.   The Recollect was Louis Hennepin, for whom see p. 287, note 3, *ante*.

[2] The country of the Sioux was about the headwaters of the Mississippi
and westward.   For its discovery and exploration, see the succeeding narrative
of Duluth.

[3] This winter journey of La Salle, overland through northern Illinois, Indiana, southern Michigan, southern Ontario to the fort at Niagara is proof of
the tremendous determination and physical endurance of the explorer.

[4] This rock, known throughout the French régime as "Le Rocher," is
situated on the southern bank of the Illinois, not far from the village of Utica.
It is locally known as "Starved Rock."

[5] While Tonty had gone to survey the site for the new fort, his men destroyed Fort Crèvecœur, stole the ammunition and goods, and left in writing the
statement, "We are all savages."   The two friars with Tonty were Gabriel
de La Ribourde and Zénobe Membré.

[6] The fate of the *Griffin* has never been known.   Probably it foundered in
one of the autumn gales.

In the meanwhile, the Islinois were greatly alarmed at seeing a party of 600 Iroquois. It was then near the month of September. The desertion of our men and the journey of M. de La Salle to Fort Frontenac made the savages suspect that we were betraying them. They severely reproached me respecting the arrival of their enemies. As I was recently come from France and was not then acquainted with their manners, this embarrassed me and determined me to go to the enemy with necklaces[1] to tell them that I was surprised they had come to make war upon a nation dependent on the Governor of New France, and that M. de La Salle, whom he esteemed, governed these peoples. An Islinois accompanied me, and we separated ourselves from the body of the Islinois, who were 400 in number, and were already fighting with the enemy. When I was within gun-shot the Iroquois fired a great volley at us, which compelled me to tell the Islinois to retire. He did so. When I had come up to them, these wretches seized me, took the necklace from my hand, and one of them, reaching through the crowd, plunged a knife into my breast, wounding a rib near the heart. However, having recognized me, they carried me into the midst of their camp and asked me what I came for. I gave them to understand that the Islinois were under the protection of the King of France and of the Governor of the country, and that I was surprised that they wished to break with the French, and to postpone peace.

All this time skirmishing was going on on both sides, and a warrior came to give notice to the chief that their left wing was giving way, and that they had recognized some Frenchmen among the Islinois, who were shooting at them. On this they were greatly irritated against me and held a council concerning what they should do with me. There was a man behind me with a knife in his hand, who every now and then lifted up my hair. They were divided in opinion. Tegancouti, chief of the Tsonnontouan, wished positively to have me burnt. Agonstot, chief of the Onontagués,[2] as a friend of M. de La Salle, wished to have me set at liberty. He carried his point. They agreed that, in order the better to deceive the

---

[1] Strings of wampum, which were used by the Indians in peace negotiations.
[2] The Onondaga tribe of the Iroquois confederacy.

Islinois, they should give me a necklace of porcelain beads to show to them that they also were children of the Governor, and that they all ought to unite and make a good peace.

They sent me to deliver their message to the Islinois. I had much difficulty in reaching them on account of the great quantity of blood I had lost, both from my wound and from my mouth. On my way I met the Fathers Gabriel de la Ribourde and Zénoble Membré, who were coming to look after me. They expressed their joy that these barbarians had not put me to death. We went together to the Islinois, to whom I reported the sentiments of the Iroquois, adding, however, that they must not altogether trust them. They retired within their village, but seeing the Iroquois present themselves always in battle array they felt obliged to rejoin their wives and children, three leagues off. They left us there: namely, the two Recollect Fathers, the three Frenchmen, and myself.

The Iroquois made a fort in the village and left us in a cabin at some distance from their fort. Two days later, the Islinois appearing on the hills near the Iroquois, the Iroquois thought that we had had some conference together, which led them to bring us inside their fort. They pressed me to go and find the Islinois and induce them to come and make a treaty of peace. They gave me one of their own nation as a hostage. I went with Father Zénobe.[1] The Iroquois remained with the Islinois, and one of the latter came with me. When we got to the fort, instead of mending matters, he spoilt them entirely by saying to the enemy that they had in all only 400 men and that the rest of their young men were gone to war, and that if the Iroquois really wished to make peace with them they were ready to give them a quantity of beaver skins and some slaves which they had. The Iroquois called me to them and loaded me with reproaches; they told me that I was a liar to have said that the Islinois had 1,200 warriors, and several tribes of allies who had given them as-

---

[1] The name is variously spelled Zénobe, Zénoble, Zénobie. It is the French form of the Latin Zenobius; the first spelling is the usual one. Father Zénobe Membré accompanied La Salle on his three principal expeditions, was left in the dwelling on the coast of Texas (1686), and perished with the remnant of La Salle's colony.

sistance. Where were the sixty Frenchmen who, I had told them, were at the village? I had much difficulty in getting out of the scrape.

The same evening they sent back the Islinois to tell his nation to come the next day to within half a league of the fort and that they would there conclude the peace, which in fact was done, at noon. The Islinois having come to the meeting-place, the Iroquois gave them presents of necklaces and merchandise. The first necklace signified that the Governor of New France was not angry at their having come to molest their brothers; the second was addressed to M. de La Salle with the same meaning, and by the third, accompanied with merchandise, they bound themselves by oath to a strict alliance, that hereafter they should live as brothers. They then separated and the Islinois believed, after these presents, in the sincerity of the peace, which induced them to come several times into the fort of the enemies, where, some Islinois chiefs having asked me what I thought, I told them they had everything to fear, that there was among these barbarians no good faith, and that I knew that they were making canoes of elm bark and that consequently they were intending to pursue them, and that they should take advantage of the time and retire to some distant nation, for they were most assuredly betrayed.

The eighth day after their arrival, on the 10th of September, they called me and Father Zénoble to council, and having made us sit down, they placed six packets of beaver skins before us and addressing me they said that the two first packets were to inform M. de Frontenac that they would not eat his children and that he should not be angry at what they had done; the third was to serve as a plaster for my wound; the fourth was oil to rub on my own and the Recollect father's limbs, on account of the journeys we had taken; the fifth, that the sun was bright; the sixth, that we should depart the next day for the French settlements. I asked them when they would go away themselves. Murmurs arose among them. Some of them answered me that they would eat some of the Islinois before they went away; upon which I kicked away their presents, saying that there was no use in making presents to me, I would have none of them, since they designed to eat the children of the governor. An Abenakis[1] who was with them, and who spoke French, told me that the men were irritated, and the chiefs rising drove me from the council.

We went to our cabin, where we passed the night on our guard, resolved to kill some of them before they should kill us, for we thought that we should not live out the night. However, at daybreak they directed us to depart, which we did. After making five leagues in the canoe, we landed to dry some peltries, which were wet. While we were repairing our canoe, Father Gabriel told me he was going aside to pray. I advised him not to go away, because we were surrounded by enemies. He went about 1,000 paces off and was taken by forty savages, of the nation called Kikapous, who carried him away and broke his head. Finding that he did not return, I went to look for him with one of my men. Having discovered his trail, I found it cut by several others, which joined and ended at last in one.

I brought back this sad news to the Father Zénoble, who was greatly grieved at it. Towards evening we made a great fire, hoping that perhaps he might return; and we went over to the other side of the river, where we kept a good lookout. Towards midnight we saw a man appear, and then many others.

The next day we recrossed the river to look for our equipment, and after waiting till noon we embarked and reached the Lake of the Islinois by short journeys, always hoping to meet with the good Father. After having sailed on this lake till All Saints' Day we were wrecked, twenty leagues from the village of Poutouatamis.[2] Our provisions failing us, I left a man to take care of our things and went off by land, but, as I had a fever constantly on me, and my legs were swollen, we did not arrive at the village of Poutouatamis till St. Martin's Day.[3] During this time we lived on nothing but wild garlic, which we were obliged to grub up from under the snow. When we arrived we found no savages; they had gone to

---

[1] The Abenaki Indians were from Maine and the eastern provinces of Canada.

[2] November 1, 1680. The location of this Potawatomi village is not certainly known; it appears to have been the one on the lake shore mentioned in 1698 by St. Cosme as being on the eve of abandonment. See p. 344, note 4, *post*.

[3] November 14.

their winter quarters. So we were obliged to go into their wilds, where we obtained hardly as much as two handfuls of Indian corn a day and some frozen gourds, which we piled up in a cabin at the water's side.

Whilst we were gleaning in the wilds, a Frenchman[1] whom we had left at the cache came to the cabin where we had left our little store of provisions. He thought we had put them there for him, and therefore did not spare them. We were very much surprised, as we were starting off for Missilimakinak, to find him in the cabin. He had arrived three days before. We had much pleasure in seeing him, and much regret to see our provisions partly consumed. We did not delay to embark, and after two leagues' sail, the wind having arisen offshore, I came to land. We saw a fresh trail and I directed that it should be followed. It was that of the Poutouatamis village, who had made a portage to the Bay of the Puans. The next day, weak as we were, we carried our little canoe and all our things into this bay, to which there is a league of portage.[2] We embarked in a creek called Sturgeon Creek, and turned to the right at hazard, not knowing where to go. After sailing for a league we found the same number of cabins, which led us to expect soon to find the savages.

Five leagues from this place we were stopped by the wind for a week, which compelled us to consume the few provisions we had collected together, and we were without anything. At last we held a council to see what we should do, and despairing of being able to come up with the savages, every one asked to return to the village, since there was wood there, so that we might die warm. The wind lulling, we embarked and set off. On entering Sturgeon's Creek we saw a fire and went to it. It was made by savages, who had just gone away. We thought they were gone to their village and determined to go there, but the creek having frozen in the night, we could not proceed in our canoe. We made shoes of

---

[1] Sieur de Boisrondet, one of Tonty's party who had been lost for several days.

[2] The Sturgeon Bay portage, across Door County peninsula, Wisconsin. It is now cut by a canal. See Marquette's journey across this portage, p. 263, ante.

the late Father Gabriel's cloak, having no leather. We were
to have started in the morning. One of my men being very
ill from having eaten some pare-flesche,[1] in the evening,
as I was urging our starting two Outawas savages came up,
who led us to where the Poutouatamis were. We found some
Frenchmen there, who received us kindly. I spent the winter
with them, and Father Zénoble left us to pass the winter with
the Jesuit fathers at the end of the bay.[2]

When I left this place in the spring for Missilimakinak
we had hardly recovered from the miseries which we had
suffered from hunger and cold during thirty-four days. We
reached Missilimakinak about Corpus Christi in 1680.[3] M. de
La Salle arrived some time afterwards, on his way to seek us
at the Illinois, with M. de La Forest.[4] He was very glad
to see us again, and notwithstanding all reverses, we made
new preparations to continue the exploration which he had
undertaken. I therefore embarked with him for Fort Frontenac, to bring things that we should need for the expedition.
Father Zénoble accompanied us thither. When we came to
Lake Frontenac, M. de La Salle went forward, and I waited
for his boat at the village of Teyagon.[5] When it arrived
there I embarked for the Islinois. When we came to the
Miamis River I assembled some Frenchmen and savages for
the exploration, and M. de La Salle joined us in December.

We went in canoes to the River Chicaou, where there is a
portage which joins that of the Islinois. The rivers being frozen we made sledges and dragged our baggage to a point thirty
leagues below the village of Islinois, and there, finding the
navigation open, we arrived at the end of January at the River

---

[1] Dried meat or leather.

[2] At the mission of St. François Xavier, at the site of De Pere, Wisconsin.
This mission was established by Father Claude Allouez. See pp. 142–146, *ante*.

[3] 1681. In that year Corpus Christi fell on June 5.

[4] La Salle had just come from the Illinois, where he had been to seek Tonty
and his men, and found only the ruins of the fort, and the destruction caused by
the Iroquois. In great desolation he retraced his way to Mackinac, there to be
cheered by finding Tonty and a few of his men safe and well.

Guillaume de La Forest had commanded for La Salle at Fort Frontenac.
He later became Tonty's partner at Fort St. Louis in Illinois. In 1710 he was
commandant at Detroit, where he died four years later.

[5] La Salle on this journey took the Toronto portage. The village where
he left Tonty was probably on an island in Lake Simcoe.

Mississipy.[1] The distance from Chicaou is estimated at 140 leagues. We descended this river and found, six leagues below, on the right, a great river, which comes from the west. There are numerous nations above. We slept at its mouth. The next day we went on to the village of the Tamaroas, six leagues off on the left.[2] There was no one there, all the people being at their winter quarters in the woods. We made our marks to inform the savages that we had passed, and continued our route as far as the River Ouabache, which is eighty leagues from that of the Islinois. It comes from the east and is more than 500 leagues in length. It is by this river that the Iroquois advance to make war against the nations of the south. Continuing our voyage, we came to a place, about sixty leagues from there, which was named Fort Prudhomme, because one of our men, of that name, lost himself there when out hunting and was nine days in the woods without food.[3] As they were looking for him they fell in with two Chicachas savages, whose village was three days' journey from there, in the lands along the Mississipy. They have 2,000 warriors, the greatest number of whom have flat heads, which is considered a beauty among them, the women taking pains to flatten the heads of their children, by means of a cushion which they put on their foreheads and bind with a band to the cradle, and thus make their heads take this form, and when they are fat their faces are as big as a large soup-plate. All the nations on the seacoast have the same custom.[4]

M. de La Salle sent back one of them with presents to his village, so that, if they had taken Prudhomme, they might

[1] The boat carrying the exploring party entered the Mississippi from the Illinois, February 6, 1682.

[2] The great river coming from the west was the Missouri. Somewhere below it on the Illinois side was the village of the Tamarois, a division of the Illinois tribe. The Tamarois afterward removed to the neighborhood of Cahokia and coalesced with the Cahokia branch of the Illinois Indians.

[3] For the use of the name "Ouabache" for the Ohio River, see p. 250, note 1, ante. Pierre Prud'homme was the armorer of La Salle's expedition. The fort called by his name was located on the Third Chickasaw Bluff, near the present city of Memphis.

[4] The custom of intentional deformation of the heads of children was found among a few Indian tribes: the Natchez and neighboring tribes near the Gulf of Mexico, and a few tribes in the Pacific Northwest. The French called the Chickasaw *Têtes Plats*.

send him back, but we found him on the tenth day, and as the Chicachas did not return, we continued our route as far as the village of Capa, fifty leagues off. We arrived there in foggy weather, and as we heard the beating of the drum we crossed over to the other side of the river, where in less than half an hour we made a fort. These savages, having been informed that we were coming down the river, came in their canoes to look for us. We made them land, and sent two Frenchmen as hostages to their village. The chief visited us with the calumet, and we went to visit them. They regaled us for five days with the best they had, and after having danced the calumet to M. de La Salle, they conducted us to the village of Tongengan, of their nation, eight leagues from Capa. These received us in the same manner, and from thence they went with us to Toriman, two leagues further on, where we met with the same reception.[1]

It should be remarked that these villages, with another called Osotouy, which is six leagues to the right descending the river, are commonly called Arkansas. The first three villages are situated on the Great River. M. de La Salle erected the arms of the king there. They have cabins made with the bark of cedar; they have no worship, adoring all sorts of animals. Their country is very beautiful, having abundance of peach, plum, and apple trees. Vines flourish there. Buffaloes, deer, stags, bears, turkeys, are very numerous. They even have domestic fowls. They have very little snow during the winter, and the ice is not thicker than an *écu*.[2] They gave us guides to conduct us to their allies, the Taensas, sixty leagues distant.[3]

The first day we began to see and to kill alligators, which

---

[1] "Cappa" was the village visited by Marquette and Jolliet in 1673, that formed the extent of their voyage. See p. 254, note 1, *ante*. The other two villages were neighboring residences of the Quapaw tribe.

[2] The coin he had in mind was most likely the three-livre piece, nearly as large as an American silver dollar.

[3] The Taensa was a small tribe closely allied in language and customs to the Natchez. La Salle was the first of the French explorers to visit their village. See account of the mission established for this tribe in Introduction to St. Cosme's *Narrative*, p. 339, *post*. The French commandants of Louisiana had various dealings with this tribe, and in 1764 the Taensa removed to Red River rather than become subject to the English. About the close of the eighteenth century they merged with other tribes.

are numerous, and from fifteen to twenty feet long. When we had arrived opposite to the village of the Taenças, M. de La Salle ordered me to go to it and inform the chief of his arrival. I went with our guides. We had to carry a bark canoe for ten arpents, and to launch it on a small lake[1] on which their village was placed. I was surprised to find their cabins made of mud and covered with cane mats. The cabin of the chief was forty feet square, the wall about ten feet high and a foot thick, and the roof, which was of a dome shape, about fifteen feet high. I was not less surprised when, on entering, I saw the chief seated on a camp bed, with three of his wives at his side, surrounded by more than sixty old men, clothed in large white cloaks, which are made by the women out of the bark of the mulberry tree, and are tolerably well worked. The women were clothed in the same manner, and every time the chief spoke to them, before answering him, they howled and cried out several times—"Oh! Oh! Oh!"—to show their respect for him, for their chiefs are held in as much consideration as our kings. No one drinks out of the chief's cup, nor eats out of his dishes; no one passes before him; when he walks they clean the path before him. When he dies they sacrifice his principal wife, his principal house-steward, and a hundred men of the nation, to accompany him into the other world.

They have a form of worship, and adore the sun. They have a temple opposite the house of the chief, and similar to it, except that three eagles are placed on this temple who look towards the rising sun. The temple is surrounded with strong mud walls, in which are fixed spikes on which they place the heads of their enemies whom they sacrifice to the sun. At the door of the temple is a block of wood, on which is a great shell plaited round with the hair of their enemies in a plait as thick as an arm and about twenty fathoms long. The inside of the temple is bare; there is an altar in the middle, and at the foot of the altar three logs of wood are placed end to end, and a fire is kept up day and night by two old medicine-men, who are the directors of their worship. These old men showed me a small cabinet in the middle of the wall, made of mats of cane. When I wished to see what was inside, the

[1] Lake St. Joseph, in Tensas Parish, Louisiana.

old men prevented me, giving me to understand that their God was there; but I have since learnt that it is the place where they keep all their treasure, such as fine pearls which they fish up in the neighborhood, and European merchandise.

At the last quarter of each moon all the cabins make an offering of a dish of the best food they have, which is placed at the door of the temple. The old men take care to carry it away and to make a good feast of it with their families. Every spring they make a clearing, which they name "the field of the spirit," where all the men work to the sound of the drum. In the autumn the Indian corn of this field is harvested with ceremony and stored in magazines until the moon of June in the following year, when all the village assemble, and invite their neighbors to the feast to eat it. They do not leave the ground until they have eaten it all, making great rejoicings the whole time. This is all I learnt of this nation. The three villages below have the same customs.

Let us return to the chief. When I was in his cabin he told me with a smiling countenance the pleasure he felt at the arrival of the French. I saw that one of his wives wore a pearl necklace. I presented her with ten yards of blue glass beads in exchange for it. She made some difficulty, but the chief having told her to let me have it, she did so. I carried it to M. de La Salle, giving him an account of all that I had seen and told him that the chief intended to visit him the next day—which he did. He would not have done this for savages, but the hope of obtaining some merchandise induced him to act thus. He came the next day to our cabins, to the sound of the drum and the music of the women, who had embarked in wooden canoes. The savages of the river use no other boats than these. M. de La Salle received him with much politeness, and gave him some presents; they gave us, in return, plenty of provisions and some of their robes. The chief returned well satisfied. We stayed during the day, which was the 21st of March. We took an observation and found ourselves at 31 degrees of latitude.[1]

We left on the 22nd, and slept on an island ten leagues from there. The next day we saw a canoe. M. de La Salle

---

[1] This observation was more than a degree out of the way, the true latitude being somewhat more than 32°.

ordered me to chase it, which I did, and when I was just on
the point of taking it, more than 100 men appeared on the
banks of the river, with bows bent, to defend their people.
M. de La Salle shouted to me to come back, which I did.
We went on and encamped opposite them. Afterwards, M.
de La Salle expressing to me a wish to meet them peacefully,
I offered to carry to them the calumet. I embarked, and
crossed to the other side. At first they joined their hands,
as a sign that they wished to be friends; I, who had but one
hand, told our men to do the same thing.

I made the chief men among them cross over to M. de
La Salle, who accompanied them to their village, three leagues
inland, and passed the night there with some of his men.
The next day he returned with the chief of the village where
he had slept, who was a brother of the great chief of the
Naché; he conducted us to his brother's village, situated on
a hill-side near the river, at six leagues distance.[1] We were
very well received there. This nation counts more than
3,000 warriors. These men cultivate the ground as well as
hunt, and they fish as well as the Taensa, and their customs
are the same. We departed thence on Good Friday, and
after a voyage of twenty leagues, encamped at the mouth of a
large river, which comes in from the west.[2] We continued
our journey, and crossed a great canal, which went towards
the sea on the right.

Thirty leagues further on we saw some fishermen on the
bank of the river, and sent to reconnoitre them. It was
the village of the Quinipissa, who let fly arrows upon our
scouts, who retired in consequence, as ordered.[3] As M. de
La Salle did not wish to fight against any nation, he made us
embark. Twelve leagues from this village, on the left, we
found that of the Tangibao.[4] Not a week before, this vil-

[1] The village of the Natchez Indians at the time of La Salle's voyage is
thought to have been about three miles from the present city of that name upon
St. Catherine's Creek.

[2] Red River. Good Friday in 1682 fell on March 27.

[3] The Quinipissa were a tribe of Choctaw, found in St. Charles Parish not
far above New Orleans. They are identical with the Acolapissa, among whom
Iberville found a letter that Tonty on his second voyage had left for La Salle.

[4] The Tangipahoa were a tribe (now extinct) related to the Creek Indians.
Their name is perpetuated in a river and parish north of Lake Pontchartrain.

lage had been totally destroyed. Dead bodies were lying one on another and the cabins were burnt. We proceeded on our course, and after going forty leagues, arrived at the sea on the 7th of April.

M. de La Salle sent canoes to inspect the channels. Some went to the channel on the right hand, some to the left, and M. de La Salle chose that in the centre. In the evening each made his report, that is to say, that the channels were very fine, wide, and deep. We encamped on the right bank, erected the arms of the King, and returned several times to inspect the channels. The same report was made.

This river is 800 leagues long, without rapids, to wit, 400 from the country of the Sioux, and 400 from the mouth of the Islinois River to the sea. The banks are almost uninhabitable, on account of the spring floods. The woods are chiefly poplar, the country one of canes and briars and of trees torn up by the roots; but a league or two from the river, is the most beautiful country in the world, prairies, open woods of mulberry trees, vines, and fruits that we are not acquainted with. The savages gather the Indian corn twice in the year. In the lower course of the river, the part which might be settled, is where the river makes a course north and south, for there, in many places, every now and then it has bluffs on the right and left.

The river is only navigable for ships as far as the village of Nadesche, for above that place the river winds too much; but this would not prevent one's setting out from the country above with pirogues and flatboats, to proceed from the Ouabache to the sea. There are but few beavers, but to make amends, there is a large number of buffaloes or bears, large wolves, stags, *sibolas*,[1] hinds, and roe deer in abundance; and some lead mines, with less than one-third refuse. As these savages are stationary, and have some habits of subordination, they might be obliged to make silk in order to procure necessaries for themselves, if the eggs of silkworms were brought to them from France, for the forests are full of mulberry trees. This would be a valuable trade.

As for the country of the Islinois, the river runs 100 leagues from Fort St. Louis, to where it falls into the Mississipy.

---

[1] Cibola (*sibola*) was the Spanish term for the buffalo.

It may be said to contain the finest lands ever seen. The climate is the same as that of Paris, though in the 40th degree of latitude. The savages there are quick, agile, and brave, but extremely lazy, except in war, when they think nothing of seeking their enemies at a distance of 500 or 600 leagues from their own country. This they constantly show in the country of the Iroquois, whom, at my instigation, they continually harass. Not a year passes in which they do not take a number of prisoners and scalps.

A few pieces of pure copper, whose origin we have not yet sought, are found in the river of the Islinois. Polygamy prevails in this nation, and is one of the great hindrances to the introduction of Christianity, with the fact of their having no form of worship of their own. The nations lower down would be more easily converted, because they adore the sun, which is their sole divinity. This is all that I am able to relate of those parts.

Let us return to the sea coast, where, provisions failing, we were obliged to leave sooner than we wished, in order to seek provisions in the neighboring villages. We did not know how to get anything from the village of the Quinipissa, who had received us badly as we went down the river. We lived on potatoes until six leagues from their village, when we saw smoke. M. de La Salle went to reconnoitre at night. Our people reported that they had seen some women. We went there at daybreak and taking four of the women, encamped on the other bank, opposite their village. One of the women was sent with merchandise, to show this tribe that we had no evil design against them and wished for their alliance and for provisions. She made her report. One of them came immediately and invited us to encamp on the other bank, which we did. We sent back the three other women, keeping, however, constant guard. They brought us some provisions in the evening, and the next morning, at daybreak, the scoundrels attacked us.

We vigorously repulsed them, and by ten o'clock had smashed their canoes, and, but for the fear of using up our ammunition for the future, we should have attacked their village. We left in the evening in order to reach the village of the Nachés where we had left a quantity of grain as we passed down. When we arrived there the chief came out to meet us. M. de La Salle made them a present of the scalps we had taken from the Quinipissa. They had already heard the news, for they had resolved to betray and kill us. We went up to their village armed, and, as we saw no women there, we had no doubt of their having some evil design. In a moment we were surrounded by more than 1,500 men. They brought us something to eat, and we ate with our guns in our hands. As they are afraid of firearms, they did not dare to attack us. The chief of the nation begged M. de La Salle to go away, as his young men had not much sense, which we very willingly did—the game not being equal, we having only fifty men, French and savages. We then went on to the Taença, and then to the Akansas, where we were very well received.

From thence we came to Fort Prudhomme, where M. de La Salle fell dangerously ill, which obliged him to send me forward, with five others, to arrange his affairs at Missilimakinak. In passing toward the Ouabache, I found four Iroquois, who told us that there were 100 men of their nation coming on after them. This gave us some alarm, for there is no pleasure in meeting warriors on one's road, especially when they have been unsuccessful. I left them and at about twenty leagues from the Tamaroas, we saw smoke. I ordered our people to prepare their arms, and we resolved to advance, expecting to meet the Iroquois. When we were near the smoke, we saw some canoes, which made us think that they could only be Islinois or Tamaroas. They were in fact the latter. As soon as they saw us, they came out of the wood in great numbers to attack us, taking us for Iroquois.

I presented the calumet to them. They laid down their arms and conducted us to their village without doing us any harm. The chiefs held a council, and, taking us for Iroquois, had already resolved to burn us; and, but for some Islinois who were among them, we should have fared ill. They let us proceed. We arrived about the end of June,[1] at the River Chicacou, and, by the middle of July, at Missilimakinak. M. de La Salle, having recovered, joined us in September. Resolving to go to France, he ordered me to go and collect

[1] 1682.

together the French who were on the River Miamis to construct the Fort of St. Louis in the Islinois. I left with this design, and when I arrived at the place, M. de La Salle, having changed his mind, joined me. They set to work at the fort, and it was finished in March, 1683.

During the winter I gave all the nations notice of what we had done to defend them from the Iroquois, at whose hands they had lost 700 people in the preceding years. They approved of our good intentions, and established themselves, to the number of 300 lodges, at the Fort—Islinois and Miamis and Chaouanons.[1]

M. de La Salle departed for France in the month of September, leaving me to command the fort. He met on his way the Chevalier de Bogis, whom M. de La Barre[2] had sent with letters ordering M. de La Salle to Quebec. He had no trouble in getting him to make the journey, as he found him on the road. M. de La Salle wrote to me to receive M. de Bogis well, which I did.

The winter passed, and on the 20th of March, 1684, being informed that the Iroquois were about to attack us, we prepared to receive them well, and dispatched a canoe to M. de La Durantaye, governor of Missilimakinak,[3] to ask him for assistance, in case the enemy should hold out against us a long time. The savages appeared on the 21st. We repulsed them with loss. After six days' siege they retired with some slaves which they had made in the neighborhood, who afterwards escaped and came back to the fort.

M. de La Durantaye, with Father Daloy,[4] a Jesuit, arrived at the fort with about sixty Frenchmen, whom they were bringing to our assistance, and, more particularly, to inform

[1] This concentration of Indian tribes had an important influence on aboriginal geography and economy. The various villages clustered around Fort St. Louis are located on Franquelin's "Map of Louisiana" of 1684.

[2] Antoine Le Febvre de La Barre superseded Count Frontenac in 1682 as governor-general of New France. He reversed as far as possible all the plans of the latter, and replaced La Salle's men with his own officers, one of whom was Chevalier de Baugis (Bogis). The latter was recalled after a year in Illinois.

[3] Olivier Morel, Sieur de La Durantaye, came to Canada as officer in the Carignan regiment in 1665. He commanded in the Northwest 1683–1690; he died in 1717.

[4] Father Claude Allouez, for whom see ante.

me of the orders of M. de La Barre, to leave the place, and
that M. de Bogis was in possession of a place belonging to M.
de La Salle. I obeyed orders, and went to Montreal, and thence
to Quebec, where M. de La Forest, who had accompanied M.
de La Salle to France, returned by order of M. de La Salle
with a lettre de cachet, by which M. de La Barre was directed
to deliver up to M. de La Forest the lands belonging to the
Sieur de La Salle, and which were occupied by others to his
prejudice.

As he brought me news that M. de La Salle was sailing by
way of the islands to find the mouth of the Mississipy, and
had at court obtained a company[1] for me, and sent me orders
to go and command at Fort St. Louis, as captain of foot, and
governor, we took our measures together, and formed a company of 20,000 livres to maintain the fort.

M. de La Forest went away in the autumn, for Fort Fron-
tenac, and I began my journey to the Islinois. Being stopped
by the ice, however, I was obliged to halt at Montreal, where
I passed the winter. M. de La Forest arrived there in the
spring. We took new measures. He embarked for Fort
Frontenac, and I for the Islinois, where I arrived in June.[2]
M. le Chevalier de Bogis retired, according to the orders that
I brought him from M. de La Barre.

The Miamis having seriously defeated the Islinois, it
cost us 1,000 dollars in presents to reconcile these two nations,
which I did not accomplish without great trouble. In the
autumn I embarked for Missilimakinak, in order to obtain
news of M. de La Salle. I heard there that M. le Marquis de
Denonville[3] had succeeded M. de La Barre; and by a letter
which he did me the honor to write to me, he expressed his
wish to see me, that we might take measures for the war
against the Iroquois, and informed me that M. de La Salle
was engaged in seeking the mouth of the Mississipy in the

---

[1] La Salle secured a commission for Tonty as captain of a company in the
colonial troops.

[2] 1685.

[3] Jacques René de Brisay, Marquis Denonville, was governor of Canada
from 1685 to 1689. His well-known expedition of 1687 against the Iroquois
was only a partial success, and led to fresh hostilities in 1689, which forced
Denonville's retirement, and the return of Frontenac.

Gulf of Mexico. This made me resolve to go in search of him
and aid him, with a number of Canadians that I should take
to him, and as soon as I should have found him, to return
to execute the orders of M. de Denonville.

I embarked, therefore, for the Islinois, on St. Andrew's
Day,[1] but, being stopped by the ice, I was obliged to leave my
canoe and to proceed by land. After going 120 leagues I
arrived at the Fort of Chicacou, where M. de La Durantaye
commanded; and from thence I came to Fort St. Louis, where
I arrived in the middle of January, 1685.[2] I departed thence
on the 16th of February, with thirty Frenchmen and five
Islinois and Chaouanons for the sea, which I reached in Holy
Week,[3] after having passed the tribes described above, by
whom I was very well received. I sent out one canoe towards
the coast of Mexico, and another towards Carolina, to see if
they could discover anything. They each sailed about thirty
leagues, in either direction, but were obliged to stop for want
of fresh water. They reported to me that where they had
been the land began to rise. They brought me a porpoise
and some oysters. As it would take us five months to reach
the French settlements, I proposed to my men, that if they
would trust me, we should follow the coast as far as Menade,
and that by this means we should arrive shortly at Montreal,
declaring that we should not lose our time, because we might
discover some fine country and might even take some prize
on our way.[4] Part of my men were willing to adopt my plan,
but the rest were opposed to it, so I decided to return the way
I came.

The tide does not rise more than two feet perpendicularly
on the sea coast; the land is very low at the entrance of the
river. We encamped in the place where M. de La Salle had
erected the arms of the King. As they had been thrown down
by the floods, I took them five leagues farther up, and placed
them in a higher situation. I put a silver écu[5] in the hollow
of a tree to serve as a mark of time and place. We left this

---

[1] November 30, 1685.   [2] Meaning 1686.   [3] April 7–14.

[4] It was a daring plan conceived by Tonty to skirt the coast all the way to
New York (Menade or Manhattan Island) in the small canoes used for river and
lake transportation.

[5] See p. 298, note 2, ante.

place on Easter Monday. When we came opposite the Quinipissa Village, the chiefs brought me the calumet and declared the sorrow they felt at the treachery they had perpetrated against us on our first voyage. I made an alliance with them.

Forty leagues higher up, on the right, we discovered an inland village, with whom we also made an alliance. These are the Ouma,[1] the bravest savages of the river. When we were at Akansas, ten of the Frenchmen who accompanied me asked for settlements on the River Akansas, on a seigniory that M. de La Salle had given me on our first voyage. I granted the request to some of them. They remained there and built a house surrounded with stakes.[2] The rest accompanied me to the Islinois, in order to get what they wanted. I arrived there on St. John's Day.[3] I made two chiefs of the Islinois embark with me in my canoe, to go and receive the orders of M. de Denonville, and we arrived at Montreal by the end of July.

I left that place at the beginning of September to return to the Islinois. I came there in December, and I directly sent some Frenchmen to our savage allies to declare war against the Iroquois, inviting them to assemble in good season at the fort. They did so in the month of April, 1686.[4] The Sieur de La Forest was already gone in a canoe with thirty Frenchmen, and he was to wait for me at Detroit till the end of May. I gave our savages a dog feast, and after having declared to them the will of the King and of the Governor of New France, I set out on April 17 with sixteen Frenchmen and a guide of the Miami nation.

We encamped half a league from the fort, to wait for the savages who might wish to follow us. I left twenty Frenchmen at the fort and the Sieur de Bellefontaine to command there during my absence. Fifty Chaouanons, four Loups, and

---

[1] This is a tribe of the Choctaw nation, usually known as the Huma. Apparently La Salle, in 1682, had passed their village without seeing it.

[2] Thus was founded the oldest existing French settlement in the Mississippi Valley. It was later known as Aux Arcs, although technically named the fort and mission of St. Étienne. The Americans called it Arkansas Post. It is on the Arkansas River in the present Arkansas County.

[3] June 24, 1686.   [4] This should be 1687.

seven Miamis came to join me at night; and the next day
more than 300 Islinois came, but they went back again,
with the exception of 149. This did not prevent me from continuing my route; and after 200 leagues of journey by land,
we came, on the 19th of May, to Fort Detroit. We there
made some canoes of elm wood. I sent one of them to Fort
St. Joseph, which was at the harbor of Detroit, thirty leagues
from where we were, to give Sieur Dulud, the commander
of this fort, information of my arrival.[1] The Sieur de Beau-
vais de Tilly, his lieutenant, joined me, and afterwards the
Sieur de La Forest, then the Sieurs de La Durantaye and Dulud. I made the French and the savages line up along the
road, and, after the Sieur de La Durantaye had saluted us,
we returned the salute. They had with them 300 English,
whom they had taken on Lake Huron, who had come there to
trade.[2] It was the Sieur de La Durantaye who commanded
the party that captured them. We made more canoes, and
coasted along Lake Erie to Niagara, where we made a fort
below the portage to wait there for news. On our way we
took thirty more Englishmen, who were going to Missilimakinak, commanded by Major Grégoire,[3] who was bringing back some Huron and Outawas slaves taken by the Iroquois. Had it not been for these two strokes of good luck
our affairs would have turned out badly, as we were at war
with the Iroquois, and the English, from the great quantity
of brandy and merchandise which they had with them, would
have gained over our allies, and thus we should have had all
the savages and the English upon us at once.

I sent the Sieur de La Forest to inform M. the Marquis

[1] Fort St. Joseph, located about where Fort Gratiot now stands, was built
by Daniel Greysolon, Sieur Duluth, in 1686. During the winter of 1687-1688 it
was commanded by Baron Lahontan, who destroyed it in August, 1688. For
Duluth, see the following narrative.

[2] A company of English and Dutch traders from Albany had been assured
by the Iroquois that the tribesmen at Mackinac were ready to secede from the
French alliance. The capture of their caravan was of immense importance to
the trade of Canada.

[3] Major Patrick Macgregory, a Scottish immigrant to Maryland (1684),
who entered the fur-trade at Albany. After release from captivity (1688) he
was killed in Leisler's revolt (1691). See Charles M. Andrews, *Narratives of the
Insurrections* (Original Narratives Series), p. 248.

de Denonville of everything. He was at Fort Frontenac, and he joined us at Fort des Sables.[1] The large boat coming, and bringing us provisions, the Marquis sent us word by it that he expected to arrive by the 10th of July at the Marsh, which is seven leagues from the Sonnontouans.

The Poutouatamis, Hurons, and Outawas joined us there, and built some canoes. There was an Iroquois slave among the Hurons. Because of some foolish words he spoke of the French I proposed to have him put to death. They paid no attention to my proposal, and, twelve leagues on our march, he ran away and gave our enemies information of our approach, and of the marks which our savages bore, which did us great harm in the ambuscade, as will be seen.

On the 10th we arrived at the marsh of Fort des Sables, and the army from below arrived at the same time. I received orders to take possession of a certain position, which I did with my company and savages. We then set about building a fort. On the 11th I went with fifty men to reconnoitre the road, three leagues from camp. On the 12th the fort was finished, and we set off for the village. On the 13th, half a league from the clearing, we found an ambuscade. My company, who were the advance guard, forced it. We lost there seven men, of whom my lieutenant was one, and two of my people.[2] We were occupied for seven days in cutting down the corn of four villages. We returned to Fort des Sables, then embarked, and went to build a fort at Niagara.[3]

From thence I was going back to Fort St. Louis with my cousin, the Sieur Dulud, who was returning to his post with eighteen soldiers and some savages. Having made half the portage, which is two leagues in length, as we were about to make the rest, some Hurons who were at the rear, perceived some Iroquois. They came and gave us warning. There were only forty of us, and we thought the enemy strong. We agreed to fall back with our ammunition towards the fort and

---

[1] A temporary post at the mouth of Irondequoit River, New York.

[2] This Seneca ambuscade occurred west and north of the present site of Victor, New York. The French loss was much greater than Tonty mentions; he enumerates only the losses in his own division.

[3] This fort was a temporary structure at the mouth of Niagara River.

get an escort. We marched all night, and as the Sieur Dulud
could not leave his detachment, he begged me to go to the
Marquis, while he placed himself in ambush in a very good
position. I embarked, and when I came to the fort, the
Marquis was reluctant to give me any men, inasmuch as the
militia had gone away and he had only some infantry remaining to escort him; however, he sent a captain named Clément
de Valrenne and fifty men to support us. He stayed at the
portage whilst we crossed it. We embarked, and when clear
of the land we perceived the Iroquois on the banks of the lake.
We crossed Lake Erie, and I left the Sieur Dulud at his post
at Detroit, and went on from there in company with the
Reverend Father Gravier[1] as far as Missilimakinak, and
thence on to Fort St. Louis.

There I found M. Cavelier, a priest, his nephew, and the
Reverend Father Anastatius, a Recollect, and two men.
They concealed from me the assassination of M. de La Salle;
and upon their assuring me that he had remained at the Gulf
of Mexico in good health, I received them as if they had been
M. de La Salle himself, and lent them more than 700 francs.
M. Cavelier, brother of M. de La Salle, departed in the spring,
1687, to give an account of his voyage at court.[2] M. de La
Forest came here in the autumn, and went away in the fol-
lowing spring.

On the 7th of September, one named Couture[3] brought to
me two Akansas, who danced the calumet to me, and informed
me of the death of M. de La Salle, with all the circumstances
which they had heard from the lips of M. Cavelier, who had
fortunately discovered a house I had built at the Akansas,
where the said Couture had stayed with three Frenchmen.
The former told me that the fear of not obtaining from me

[1] Jacques Gravier, a Jesuit recently arrived in New France. In 1688 he
succeeded Allouez in the Illinois mission, where he served many years.

[2] Jean Cavelier, a Sulpitian priest, accompanied his brother, La Salle, on
his last fateful expedition to the mouth of the Mississippi. After the latter's
assassination in March, 1687, Cavelier with his young nephew, Father Anastase
Douay, Henri Joutel, and Tessier, the pilot, made his way to Fort St. Louis,
and ultimately to France. Cavelier and his company passed the winter of 1687–
1688 at Fort St. Louis, and left in the spring of 1688.

[3] Couture was from Rouen, a carpenter by trade. He came to Illinois in
1683 with Baugis, and formed the Arkansas settlement in 1686.

what he desired had made him conceal the death of his brother, of which he had told them.

M. Cavelier had told me that the Cadadoquis had one day proposed to accompany him if he would go and fight against the Spaniards.[1] He had objected that there were only fourteen Frenchmen. They replied that their nation was numerous, that they only wanted a few musqueteers, that the Spaniards had much money, of which they would be the masters; that, as for themselves, they only wished to keep the women and children as slaves. Then Couture told me that a young man whom M. Cavelier had left at the Akansas had assured him that this was true. Not wishing to undertake anything without the consent of the Governor of Canada, I sent the said Couture to the French remaining at Nicondiché,[2] to get all the information he could. He set off, and at 100 leagues from the fort was wrecked and, having lost everything, returned.

In the interval M. de Denonville directed me to let the savages do as they liked, and to do nothing against the Iroquois, and informed me that war was declared against Spain. This caused me to resolve to go to the Naodiches, to execute what M. Cavelier had not ventured to undertake, and to bring back M. de La Salle's men, who had remained on the sea coast not knowing of the misfortune that had befallen him. I set off on the 3d of December, and joined my cousin, who was gone on before, and who was to accompany me, as he expected that M. de La Forest would come and take the command in my absence; but as he did not come I sent my cousin back to command the fort.

I bought a boat larger than my own. We embarked five Frenchmen, one Chaouanon, and two slaves. We arrived on the 17th at a village of the Islinois at the mouth of their

---

[1] The Kadohadacho (Cadadoquis) were the principal tribe of the Caddo, who were the northern confederacy of the southern division of the Caddoan stock. Their village was located on Red River, not far from the present Texarkana. For the Spaniards in this region during La Salle's time see *Texas Historical Quarterly*, V. 171–205.

[2] Nicondiché (Naodiches, Naouadiche) was Notedache, a village of the Cenis tribe, known to ethnologists as the Hasinai. Thither the remains of La Salle's party had repaired after his murder. It was located on San Pedro Creek, a western branch of the Neches River, in the northeastern part of Houston County, Texas.

river. They had just come from fighting the Osages,[1] where they had lost thirteen men, but brought back 130 prisoners. We reached the village of the Kapa on the 16th of January, where we were received with much joy, and for four days there was nothing but dancing, feasting, and masquerading after their manner. They danced the final calumet for me, which confirmed the last alliance.

On the 20th I came to the Tongenga. They wished to entertain us as the Kapa had done; but being in haste I put them off until another time. I did the same with the Torimans, where I arrived on the 22d. Leaving my crew I set off the next day for Ossotoué, where my commercial house is. These savages had not yet seen me, as they lived on a branch of the river coming from the west. They did their best, giving me two women of the Cadadoquis nation, to which I was going. I returned to Torimans on the 26th, and bought there two pirogues. We went away on the 27th. On the 29th, finding one of our men asleep when on duty as sentinel, I reprimanded him, and he left me. I sent two of my people to the Coroa,[2] to seek some Frenchmen and appoint them a rendezvous at the lower part of their river, in order to spare myself the fatigue of dragging our goods six leagues inland. The Frenchman with whom I had quarrelled made with them a third.

We camped opposite the rivers. Some Taença coming from the Akansas found us there. On the 2nd,[3] having reached the place of meeting, my Chaouanon went out hunting on the other side of the river, where he was attacked by three Chachouma.[4] He killed one of them, and was slightly wounded by an arrow on the left breast. On the 4th, the rest of the party having arrived, we set out down stream. On the 5th, being opposite the Taença, the men whom I had sent to the

---

[1] The Osage were a large and important tribe whose habitat was on the Big and Little Osage rivers, in the present states of Missouri and Arkansas.

[2] The Koroa were a small tribe located on the Mississippi below the Natchez, with whom La Salle in 1682 made alliance. Later they merged with the Yazoo and ultimately with the Choctaw. In customs they resembled the Natchez and Taensa, near whom they dwelt, although their language was reported to be different.

[3] Of February, 1690.

[4] The Chakchiuma Indians dwelt on the Yazoo, and were allied to the Chickasaw, with whom they later merged.

Coroa not having brought any news of the two Frenchmen whom I was anxious about, I sent them to the Naché. They found that this nation had killed our two men. They retired as well as they could, making the savages believe that we were numerous.

They arrived on the 8th of February. We set off on the 12th with thirty Taença, and after a voyage of twelve leagues to the northwest[1] we left our pirogue, made twenty leagues' portage, and on the 17th of February, 1690, came to the village of the Nachicoche. They made us stay at the place which is in the midst of the three villages called Nachicoche, Ouasita, and Capiche.[2] All the chiefs of the three nations assembled, and before they began to speak, the thirty Taença who were with me got up, and leaving their arms went to the temple, to show the nations how sincerely they wished to make a firm peace. After having taken their God to witness they asked for their friendship. I made them some presents in the name of the Taença. Peace having been concluded, they remained some days in the village to traffic for salt, which these nations got from a salt lake in the neighborhood.

After the departure of the Taença the villages where I was gave me guides to the Yataché; and after ascending the river, always towards the northwest, about thirty leagues, we found fifteen cabins of Naché, who received us pretty well. We arrived on the 16th of March at the Yataché, about forty leagues from thence. The three villages of Yataché, Nadao, and Choye are together.[3] When they knew of our arrival they came three leagues to meet us with refreshments. On their joining us, we went together to their villages. The chief made many feasts for us. I gave presents to them, and asked for guides to the Cadodaquis.

They were very unwilling to give us any, as they had murdered three ambassadors only four days before, who went

[1] On the Red River.

[2] Three tribes of Caddoan stock located near the site of the present town of Natchitoches, Louisiana.

[3] The Yataché were the tribe usually known as Yatasi. They were of Caddoan stock and lived near the present site of Shreveport, Louisiana. The Nadao may have been the Nadaco (Anadarko), a related tribe who later dwelt west of the Yatasi between the Sabine and the Neches. The Choye are not identified.

to them to make peace. However, by dint of entreaties, and assuring them that no harm should happen to their people, they granted me five men, and we got to the Cadodaquis on the 28th. At the place where we were encamped we discovered the trail of men and horses. The next day some horsemen came to reconnoitre us, and after speaking to the wife of the chief of their nation, whom I was bringing back with me, carried back the news to their nation. The next day a woman, who governed this nation, came to visit me with the principal persons of the village. She wept over me, demanding revenge for the death of her husband, and of the husband of the woman whom I was bringing back, both of whom had been killed by the Osages. As one takes advantage of everything, I promised that their death should be avenged. We went together to their temple. After the priests had invoked their God for a quarter of an hour they conducted me to the cabin of their chief. Before entering they washed my face with water, which is a ceremony among them.

During the time I was there I learnt from them that eighty leagues off there were the seven Frenchmen whom M. Cavelier had left. I hoped to accomplish my purpose by rejoining them, but the Frenchmen who had accompanied me, tired of the voyage, being unwilling to go further, told me so. As they were unmanageable persons over whom I could exercise no authority in this distant country I was obliged to give way, and all that I could do was to engage one of them, with a savage, to accompany me to the village of the Naouadiche, where I hoped to find the Frenchmen. I told those who abandoned me, that to prevent the savages knowing this, they must say that I had sent them to carry back the news of my arrival, so that the savages should not suspect our disunion.

The Cadodaquis are united with two other villages called Natchitoches and Nasoui. They are situated on the Red River. All the nations of this river speak the same language. Their cabins are covered with straw, and they are not assembled in villages, but their huts are distant one from the other. Their fields are beautiful. They have fish and game in abundance, but few cattle. They wage cruel war, hence their villages are but thinly populated. I never found that they did any work except to make very fine bows, in which they trade

with distant nations. The Cadodaquis possess about thirty
horses, which they call *cavalis*.[1] The men and women are tat-
tooed in the face, and all over the body. They call this river
the Red River, because in fact it deposits a sand which makes
the water as red as blood. I am not acquainted with their
manners, having only seen them in passing.

I left this place on the 6th of April, directing our route
southwards, with a Frenchman, a Chaouanon, a little slave
of mine, and five of their savages, whom they gave me as
guides to the Naouadiche. When I went away, I left in the
hands of the wife of the chief a small box, in which I had put
some ammunition. On our road we found some Naouadiché
savages hunting, who assured me that they had left the Frenchmen at their habitations. This gave me great pleasure,
hoping to succeed in my whole object by finding them. On
the 19th the Frenchman with me was lost. I sent the savages
who were with me to look for him. He came back on the
21st, and told me that, having lost our trail, he was near
drowning in crossing a little river on a log. His bag having
slipped off, all our powder was lost, which very much annoyed
us as we were reduced to sixty rounds of ammunition.

On the 23d we slept half a league from the village, and the
chiefs came to visit us at night. I asked them about the
Frenchmen. They told me at first that they were at their
village. Arriving there the next day and seeing no one, when
they desired to give me the calumet I refused, until I should
see the Frenchmen. Seeing that I was determined, they told
me that the Frenchmen had accompanied their chief to fight
the Spaniards seven days' journey away from their village;
that the Spaniards, having espied them, had surrounded them
with their cavalry, and that their chief having spoken in their
favor the Spaniards had given them horses and arms. Others
told me that the Quanouatino had killed three of them, and
that the four others were gone in search of iron arrow-heads.
I no longer doubted that they had murdered them. So I told
them that they had killed the Frenchmen. Directly all the
women began to cry, and thus I saw that what I had said to
them was true. I would not, therefore, accept the calumet.
I told the chief I wanted four horses for my return, and having

[1] *Cf.* Spanish *caballo.*

given him seven hatchets and a string of large glass beads, they gave me the next day four Spanish horses, two of which were marked on the haunch with an R and a crown above it, and another with an N. Horses are very common among them. There is not a cabin which has not four or five. As this nation is sometimes at peace and sometimes at war with the neighboring Spaniards, they take advantage of a war to carry off their horses.

We harnessed ours as well as we could, and departed on the 29th, greatly vexed that we could not continue our route as far as M. de La Salle's camp, not having been able to obtain guides from this nation to take us there, though not more than eighty leagues away, and also being without ammunition, owing to the accident which I have related.

It was at the distance of three days' journey from hence that M. de La Salle was murdered. I will say a word, in passing, of what I have heard of his misfortune.

M. de La Salle having landed beyond the Mississipy, on the side toward Mexico, about eighty leagues from the mouth of the river,[1] and having lost his vessels on the coast, saved a part of the cargo, and began to march along the seashore, in search of the Mississipy. Meeting with many obstacles to his plans on account of the bad roads, he resolved to go to the Islinois by land. So he loaded several horses to carry what was necessary. The Recollect Father Anastatius,[2] M. Cavelier, the priest, his brother; M. Cavelier, his nephew; M. de Morangé, his relative;[3] MM. du Haut and Lanquetot,[4] and several Frenchmen accompanied him, with a Chaouanon savage.

[1] The site of La Salle's lost colony on the coast of Texas has recently been discovered by Professor Herbert E. Bolton. It was located on Garcitas River in Victoria County, Texas. See his article in the *Mississippi Valley Historical Review*, II. 166–182.

[2] Anastase Douay, a Recollect friar, accompanied La Salle as one of the chaplains of his final expedition. After his return to France with La Salle's brother, he wrote an account of the expedition which was published in Chrestien Le Clercq, *Premier Établissement de la Foy dans [la Nouvelle France* (Paris, 1691). Father Anastase afterward returned to Louisiana as chaplain for Iberville.

[3] Crevel de Moranget was a nephew of La Salle.

[4] The name is spelled Liotot, Lanctot, and as printed here. He was the surgeon of La Salle's expedition, who was embarked at La Rochelle, having given no previous account of his history.

When three days' journey from the Naouadiche, finding himself short of provisions, he sent M. de Morangé, his servant, and the Chaouanon, to hunt in a small wood with orders to return in the evening. When they had killed some buffaloes, they stopped to dry the meat. M. de La Salle was uneasy, so he asked the Frenchmen who among them would go and look for them. Du Haut and Lanquetot had for a long time determined to kill M. de La Salle, because, during the journey he had made along the seacoast, he had compelled the brother of Lanquetot, who was unable to keep up, to return to camp, and as he was returning alone he was massacred by the savages. This caused Lanquetot to swear that he would never forgive his brother's death. And as in long journeys there are always many discontented persons in a company, he easily found partisans. He offered, therefore, with them, to search for M. de Morangé, in order to have an opportunity to execute their design.

Having found the men, he told them that M. de La Salle was uneasy about them; but, they declaring that they could not set off till the next day, it was agreed to sleep there. After supper they arranged the order of the watch, that it should begin with M. de Morangét; after him was to follow the servant of M. de La Salle, and then the Chaouanon. After they had kept their watch and were asleep, the others massacred them, as persons attached to M. de La Salle. Toward daybreak they heard the reports of pistols, which were fired as signals by M. de La Salle, who was coming with the Recollect Father in search of them. The wretches, suspecting that it was he, lay in wait for him, placing M. du Haut's servant in front. When M. de La Salle came near, he asked where M. de Morangé was. The servant, keeping on his hat, answered that he was behind. As M. de La Salle advanced to remind him of his duty, he received three balls in his head, and fell down dead (March 19, 1687). I do not know whether the Recollect Father could do anything, but it is agreed that he was frightened, and, thinking that he also was to be killed, threw himself on his knees before the murderers, and begged for a quarter of an hour to prepare his soul. They replied that they were willing to spare his life.

They went on together to where M. Cavelier was, and, as

they advanced, shouted, "Down with your arms." M. Cavelier, on hearing the noise, came forward, and, when told of the death of his brother, threw himself on his knees before the murderers, making the same request that had been made by the Recollect Father. They granted him his life. He asked to go and bury the body of his brother, but they refused.[1]

Such was the end of one of the greatest men of this age, a man of an admirable spirit, and capable of undertaking all sorts of explorations. This murder much grieved the three Naoudiche whom M. de La Salle had found hunting, and who had accompanied him to the village. After the murderers had committed this crime, they seized all the baggage of the deceased, and the rest of the Frenchmen continued their journey to the village of the Naouadiche, where they found two Frenchmen domesticated among the savages, who had deserted in M. de La Salle's time.[2]

After staying some days in this village, the savages proposed to them to go to war against the Quanouatino, to which the Frenchmen agreed, lest the savages should illtreat them. As they were ready to set off for war, an English buccaneer,[3] whom M. de La Salle had always liked, begged of the murderers that, as the savages were soon going to war, they would give him and his comrades some shirts. They flatly refused, which offended the Englishman, and he could not help expressing this to his comrades. They agreed together to make a second demand, and if refused, to revenge the death of M. de La Salle.

This they did some days afterwards. The Englishman, taking two pistols in his belt, accompanied by a Frenchman with a gun, went deliberately to the cabin of the murderers, whom they found outside shooting with bows and arrows.

Lanquetot bade them good day, and asked how they were. They answered that they were pretty well, that as for his

[1] Professor Bolton concludes in the article noted above, p. 317, note 1, that La Salle's death occurred on Brazos River just above the mouth of the Navasota.

[2] These Frenchmen were Ruter, a Breton seaman, and Grollet, from La Rochelle.

[3] This man, whose name was Hiens, is called by some authorities a German. La Salle took him into his party in the West Indies.

party it was not necessary to ask how they did, as they were always eating turkeys and good venison. Then the Englishman asked if they would not give some ammunition and shirts, as they had taken possession of everything. They replied that M. de La Salle was their debtor, and that what they had taken was theirs. "You will not, then?" said the Englishman. "No," replied they. On which the Englishman said to one of them, "You are a wretch; you murdered my master," and firing his pistol killed him on the spot. Du Hault tried to get into his cabin, but the other Frenchman shot him also with a pistol, in the loins, which threw him on the ground. M. Cavelier and Father Anastase ran to his assistance. Du Haut had hardly time to confess himself, for the father had but just given him absolution when he was finished by another pistol-shot at the request of the savages, who could not endure that he should live after having killed their chief. The Englishman took possession of everything. He gave a share to M. Cavelier, who, having found my abode at the Akansas, went from thence to the Islinois. The Englishman, with five companions, remained at the Naouadiche.

We reached the Cadodaquis on the 10th of May. We stayed there to rest our horses, and went away on the 17th, with a guide who was to take us to the village of the Coroas. After four days' journey he left us, in consequence of an accident which happened to us in crossing a marsh. As we were leading our horses by the bridle, he fancied he was pursued by an alligator, and this led him to try to climb a tree in the midst of this little marsh. In doing this, he entangled the halter of my horse, which was drowned. This induced him to leave us without saying anything, lest we should punish him for the loss of the horse. This left us in great difficulty respecting the road which we were to take.

I forgot to say that the savages who have horses use them both for war and for hunting. They make pointed saddles, wooden stirrups, and body-coverings of several skins, one over the other, as a protection from arrows. They arm the breasts of their horses with the same material, a proof that they are not very far from the Spaniards.

When our guide was gone I told our Chaouanon to take the lead; he said in answer that since he was accompanying

me that was my affair; and as I was unable to change his purpose I was obliged to act as guide.   I directed our course to
the southeast, and after about forty leagues' march, crossing
seven rivers, we found the river of the Coroas.   We made a
raft to explore the other side of the river, but, finding there no
dry land, we were compelled to resolve to abandon our horses,
as it was impossible to take them on, upon account of the great
inundation.

In the evening, as we were preparing to depart, we saw
some savages.   We called to them in vain—they ran away,
and we were unable to come up with them.   Two of their
dogs came to us, which with our two, we embarked the next
day on our rafts, and left our horses.   We crossed fifty leagues
of flooded country.   The water, where it was least deep,
reached half-way up the leg; and in all this tract we found
only one little island of dry land, where we killed a bear and
dried its flesh.   It would be difficult to give an idea of the
trouble we had to get out of this miserable country, where
it rained night and day.   We were obliged to sleep on the
trunks of two great trees, placed together, to make our fires
on the trees, [to make] rafts on entering every new field, to
eat our dogs, and to carry our baggage across large tracts
covered with reeds.   In short, I never suffered so much in my
life as in this journey to the Mississipy, which we reached on
the 11th of July.

Finding where we were, and that we were only thirty
leagues from the Coroas, we resolved to go there, although
we had never set foot in that village.   We arrived there on
the evening of the 14th.   We had not eaten for three days,
as we could find no animal, on account of the great flood.   I
found at this village two of the Frenchmen who had abandoned me.   The savages received me very well, and were concerned at the troubles which we had had, for during the week
they did not cease to make good cheer for us, sending men
every day to hunt and fish, and not sparing their chickens
and turkeys.   I set out on the 20th, and arrived on the 31st
at the Akansas, where the fever fastened on me, which obliged
me to stay there till the 11th of August, when I left that
place, and it continued with me to the Islinois, where I arrived in the month of September.

I should not know how to describe the beauty of all the countries that I have mentioned, and, if I had worked them, I would say for what purposes they might be utilized. As for the Mississipy, it might produce every year peltries to the amount of 2,000 crowns, and abundance of lead and of timber for ships. Commerce in silk might be established there, and a port to harbor ships and form a base for the Gulf of Mexico. Pearls will be found, and even if wheat could not be had below, the upper river would furnish it, and one could furnish the islands[1] with what they need, such as lumber, vegetables, grain, and salt beef.

If I had not been in haste to compose this narrative, I might have put into it many details which would have pleased the reader, but the loss of my memoranda in my voyages brings it about that this narrative is not written as I should have wished.

HENRY DE TONTY.

[1] The French possessions in the West Indies.

MEMOIR OF DULUTH ON THE SIOUX COUNTRY
1678–1682

INTRODUCTION

THE heroic age of French exploration in the Northwest would be incomplete without an account of the adventures of Daniel Greysolon, Sieur Duluth, the peer of Perrot and La Salle. Duluth was a native of St. Germain-en-Laye, a suburb of Paris. His family was allied to that of Tonty, who spoke of him as his cousin. This family alliance gave Duluth access to the court, and advanced him in his chosen career of arms to a place in the King's Guard—an honor reserved for youth of noble families alone. Just what his military services were we do not know, save that he participated as squire to a great noble in the bloody battle of Seneff in 1674, and escaped unharmed while his patron was sorely wounded.

Duluth had before this battle made a visit to New France, where several of his relatives had preceded him and held offices in the colony. After his feat of arms he returned to the new country, whose great rivers and vast silences seemed ever to call him to solve their mysteries, and to whose exploration he devoted twenty years of his mature life. It was in 1678 that the resolution to explore the Sioux country came to him in his quiet home among the river-side gardens of old Montreal. Perchance a hint dropped by the great Count de Frontenac determined the future career of the young soldier; perchance, the lure of the wilderness life directed his vagrant fancy. At all events, he determined to see for himself the great fresh-water seas of the northern country, and to push beyond toward the setting sun, and the possible hope of a route to the Vermillion Sea.

After having circled the lofty and picturesque shores of Lake Superior he found his way through the tangle of lakes, streams, and marshes that constitute the headwaters of the Mississippi, and planted the arms and emblems of the French monarch in the heart of the country of the great Sioux tribe. The alliance with this tribe was to bring unlimited wealth in furs to the young colony along the St. Lawrence, for the Sioux were a great people, of many branches, whose territory abounded in beaver and other valuable peltry.

Duluth next visited the country of the Assiniboin, far northwest of Lake Superior, and having made peace between them and their neighbors diverted the stream of the rich northern fur trade from the channels leading to the English posts on Hudson Bay to those leading to the Great Lakes and the Ottawa.

On one of his expeditions into the Siouan territory, he was astonished and annoyed to learn that the tribe was holding as prisoners three Frenchmen, one of whom was a Recollect friar, chaplain of La Salle's expedition. Without a moment's hesitation Duluth changed his plans for farther westward exploration, and set out to rescue the captives from the hands of his quondam friends. Spurning the calumets with which they met him, he sternly demanded why they had violated their treaty with the French, and from the cowed and repentant chief he carried off Father Hennepin and his two voyageurs.

Like Nicolas Perrot, Duluth was a master of the art of Indian domination. Mingling sternness with kindness, and always meting out a rude justice, he secured an ascendancy over the savage mind that proved of vital importance to the colony of New France. He composed the difficulties between warring tribes, imposed a *Pax Gallica* upon the northern country, and made its ways safe for every French wanderer through the forests of the great Northwest.

Halted in this daring and beneficent labor by the petty criticism and condemnation of small-minded officials, Duluth was obliged to return to the colony to justify his actions, and to clear himself of the charge of being a *coureur des bois*. His patron Frontenac had him arrested, in reality for the purpose of keeping him safe from machinations of his enemies. Soon Duluth was permitted to return again to the great territory he had explored, whose reservoirs of wealth he had tapped for the sake of New France, and whose inhabitants he swayed by the force of truth and justice. In 1686 he was sent by the governor of that time to build a post on the straits between Lakes Erie and Huron in order to intercept the Dutch and English traders that were trying to break the monopoly of the French with the Northwestern tribes. At this Fort St. Joseph, somewhere on the St. Clair River, the wild tribes of the West gathered for Denonville's expedition against the Iroquois in 1687. Thither came Perrot with the tribes of the Mississippi and Wisconsin, and thither Tonty led his gathered forces from the Illinois. Great must have been the satisfaction of these explorers and governors of the great Western hinterland to meet and relate tales of adventure and plan for future growth and progress.

After Denonville's disastrous failure, and the return of Frontenac in 1689 as governor of the distracted colony, it was to Tonty, Perrot, and Duluth that the great governor turned to maintain the French empire in the West and keep the ascendancy over its numerous tribesmen. It was Duluth's part to spend more years among the Sioux, to explore the west and northwest shores of Superior, and to build a fort upon Lake Nipigon. In 1696 he was called to command at Fort Frontenac on the northern shore of Lake Ontario, after having been promoted to a captaincy in the colonial troops.

After the death of Frontenac, Duluth returned to Montreal, where his latter years were quietly spent. His death in 1710 was a release for his brave spirit.

Thus passed away a nobleman of old and new France.

He had annexed an empire to the colony, had secured it by forts on Lake Superior, Lake Nipigon, and the River St. Clair; he had threaded the portages from Lake Superior to the Mississippi, had discovered the headwaters of that stream and the sources of Lake Winnipeg; he had turned back the threatening English invasion of the Northwest, and by firmness, decision, good judgment, and sacrifice had saved to New France a seventy years' tenure of the Upper Country. Singularly modest in the midst of boasters, always a nobleman in his treatment of both friends and rivals, this "gentleman of the King's Guard" was equally at home in the haunts of pleasure or the savage wilderness, in the palace at Versailles, or the council-house of the Sioux. His memory is perpetuated by the noble city that bears his name at the head of the mighty lake he delighted to traverse.

The brief account which we here publish of Duluth's early experiences in the Northwest was a memoir addressed by him to the French minister of marine in 1685. The manuscript is in the archives of the Ministry of the Marine at Paris; it has been printed by Henry Harrisse, *Notes pour Servir à l'Histoire de la Nouvelle France* (Paris, 1872), pp. 177–181; also in Margry, *Découvertes et Établissements des Français dans l'Amérique Septentrionale* (Paris, 1886), VI. 20–25. It appeared first in English form in John G. Shea, *A Description of Louisiana by Father Louis Hennepin* (New York, 1880), pp. 374–377, from which we here reprint.

MEMOIR OF DULUTH ON THE SIOUX COUNTRY, 1678–1682

Memoir of the Sieur Daniel Greyselon du Luth on the Exploration of the Country of the Nadouecioux, of which he gives a very detailed Narrative.

To my Lord the Marquis de Seignelay:[1]
My Lord:

AFTER having made two voyages from here to New France, where everyone believed that it was impossible to explore the country of the Nadouecioux,[2] nor to have any commerce with them, both because of their distance, which is 800 leagues from our settlements, and because they are at war generally with all sorts of tribes, this difficulty caused me to make the resolve to go among them, which I could not put into execution at that time, my affairs having obliged me to come back here, whence, after having made the campaign of Franche Comté, and of the battle of Senef, where I had the honor to be a gendarme of the guard of his Majesty and squire of Monsieur de Lassay,[3] our ensign, I set out to return to Quebec, where I had no sooner arrived, than the desire I already had to carry out this plan increased, and I began to take my measures to make myself known on the part of the savages, who having assured me of their friendship, and for

---

[1] Seignelay (1651–1691), eldest son of Colbert, was minister of marine from 1683 to 1690.

[2] The Sioux Indians, living in northwest Wisconsin and in Minnesota. See p. 24, note 1, *ante.*

[3] The battle of Seneff occurred August 11, 1674, between the forces of the United Netherlands and those of Louis XIV. The French general was the great Condé, one of whose aides-de-camp was Armand de Madaillan de Lesparre, Marquis de Lassay. The latter had two horses shot under him and was thrice wounded in this affray. It is interesting to remember that succoring the wounded in the Flemish ranks was the Recollect monk Louis Hennepin, whom a few years later Duluth was to meet in the depth of the American wilderness.

proof of it given three slaves whom I had asked of them only in order that they might come with me, I set out from Montreal with them and seven Frenchmen on the first of September of the year 1678, to attempt the exploration of the Nadouecioux and the Assénipoualaks[1] who were unknown to us, and to cause them to make peace with all the nations around Lake Superior who dwell in the dominion of our invincible monarch.

I do not believe that such an expedition can give anyone ground to accuse me of having disobeyed the King's orders of the year 1676, since he merely forbade all his subjects to go into the depths of the woods to trade there with the savages.[2] This I have never done, nor even been willing to take any presents from them, though they have several times thrown them to me, which I have always refused and left, in order that no one might be able to accuse me of having carried on any indirect traffic.

On the second of July, 1679, I had the honor to set up the arms of his Majesty in the great village of the Nadouecioux called Izatys,[3] where no Frenchman had ever been, nor to the Songaskitons and Houetbatons,[4] distant 26 leagues from the first, where also I set up the arms of his Majesty in the same year 1679.

On the 15th of September, having made with the Assenipoulaks and all the other nations of the North a rendezvous at the extremity of Lake Superior to cause them to make peace with the Nadouecioux their common enemy, they all appeared there, where I had the good fortune to gain their esteem and their friendship, to bring them together, and in order that peace might last longer among them, I believed

---

[1] For this tribe, now known as the Assiniboin, see p. 133, note 2, *ante*.

[2] This edict was one of several issued by the King against the *coureurs des bois*, illegal traders with the Indian tribesmen.

[3] Hennepin called the Sioux tribe who captured him "Issati." The village in which Duluth placed the King's arms, no doubt with ceremonies similar to those of St. Lusson at Sault Ste. Marie, is supposed to have been situated on the shore of Lake Mille Lac in northern Minnesota.

[4] These were two branches of the Eastern Sioux; the term "Songaskitons" is translated by some as the "village of the fort," by others the "strong or brave" ones; the "Houetbatons" are known to ethnologists as the Wahpeton, interpreted as the "village of the river." See *Wis. Hist. Coll.*, XVI. 193, 194.

that I could not better cement it than by causing marriages to be made mutually between the different nations. This I could not carry out without much expenditure. During the following winter I caused them to hold meetings in the forest, at which I was present, in order to hunt together, feast, and thus draw closer the bonds of friendship.

A still greater expense arose from the presents which I had to make in order to cause the savages to come to Montreal, who had been diverted from this by the Openagos and Abenakis[1] under incitement from the English and the Flemings[2] who made them believe that the pestilence was in the settlements of the French, and that it had gone up as far as Nipissinguie, where the greater part of the Nipissiriniens had died of it.[3]

In June, 1680, not having been satisfied with having made my exploration by land, I took two canoes, with a savage who was my interpreter, and with four Frenchmen, to seek a means of making it by water. For this purpose I entered into a river which has its mouth eight leagues from the extremity of Lake Superior on the south side,[4] where after having cut down some trees and broken through about one hundred beaver dams, I went up the said river, and then made a carry of half a league to reach a lake,[5] which emptied into a fine river, which brought me to the Mississippi, where I learned, from eight lodges of Nadouecioux whom I met, that the Reverend Father Louis Henpin, Recollect, now at the convent of St. Germain, had with two other Frenchmen[6]

[1] For the Abenaki, see p. 294, note 1, *ante*. The name Openagos is a variant of Abenaki; it is sometimes applied to the Passamaquoddy branch of this tribe.

[2] Duluth uses the term "Flemings" to denote the dwellers in the Low Countries generally; the reference is to the Dutch of the colony of New York, who were the rivals of the French in the Western fur trade.

[3] The pestilence was doubtless smallpox, which was very fatal among the Indians. For Lake Nipissing and the tribe of that name, see p. 15, note 4, *ante*.

[4] The stream now known as the Bois Brulé, or simply the Brulé, in Douglas County, Wisconsin.

[5] The portage is to Upper Lake St. Croix. See description of this portage in recent times, in *Wis. Hist. Coll.*, XX. 405, 406, notes 32 and 34.

[6] For Father Louis Hennepin, see p. 287, note 3, *ante*. His companions were Antoine du Gay Auguel, known from his birthplace as "le Picard"; and Michel Accault, a native of Poitiers, for whom see p. 290, note 1, *ante*.

been seized and taken away as slaves for more than three hundred leagues by the Nadouecioux themselves.

This news surprised me so much that, without hesitating, I left two Frenchmen with these above mentioned eight lodges of savages, together with the goods which I had for making presents, and took one of the said savages, to whom I gave a present in order that he should conduct me with my interpreter and two Frenchmen to the place where the said Reverend Father Louis was, and as it was eighty good leagues I went in my canoe two days and two nights, and the next day at ten o'clock in the morning I met him with about 1000 or 1100 souls. The want of respect that was being shown to the said Reverend Father provoked me, and I let them know it, telling them that he was my brother, and I put him in my canoe to go with me into the villages of the said Nadouecioux, to which I took him. There, a week after having arrived, I caused a council to be held, setting forth the ill-treatment which they had bestowed both upon the said Reverend Father and upon the other two Frenchmen who were with him, seizing them and leading them away as slaves, and even taking the priestly robes of the said Reverend Father.[1] I caused two calumets (which they had danced to us) to be given back to them in recognition of the insult they had done us, these being the things most esteemed among them for pacifying affairs, saying to them that I took no calumets from people who, after having seen me, having received my peace-gifts, and having been constantly for a year with Frenchmen, kidnapped them when they were coming to see them.

Each one sought to excuse himself in the council, but their excuse did not prevent me from saying to the Reverend Father Louis that he must come with me toward the Outagamys,[2] which he did, I informing him that it would be

---

[1] The vanity of Hennepin did not allow him to admit that he was a captive and a slave, the cruel sport of the Indians. He represented that he accompanied Duluth because of the latter's pleasure in his society, and his desire for his companionship. See Hennepin, *New Discovery* (ed. Thwaites, Chicago, 1903), pp. 293-305.

[2] The Fox Indians, dwelling at this time on the river of their name. See p. 76, note 2, and p. 81, note 1, *ante*.

striking a blow at the French nation in a new exploration, to
suffer insult of this sort without showing resentment of it,[1]
though my plan had been to penetrate then to the sea of the
west-northwest coast, which is believed to be the Vermillion
Sea, whence the savages who had gone to war in that direction gave salt to three Frenchmen whom I had sent to explore
and who brought me some of the said salt, having reported to
me that the savages had told them that it was only twenty
days' journey from where they were to the discovery of the
great lake whose water is not good to drink.[2] This is what
makes me believe that it would not be at all difficult to find
it, if one were willing to give permission to go there. Nevertheless I preferred to retrace my steps, letting them know of
the just indignation I had against them, rather than remain
after the violence they had done to the said Reverend Father
and to the two Frenchmen who were with him, whom I put
in my canoes, and brought them to the Michelimakinak mission of the reverend Jesuit fathers,[3] where wintering together,
I learned that, far from being approved in what I had done,
using up my goods and risking my life every day, I was treated
as the chief of a party, although I have never had more than
eight men with me.[4] It was not necessary to say more, to
compel me, on the 29th of March of the year 1681, to set out
over the ice with the said Reverend Father and the two other
Frenchmen, causing my canoe and our provisions to be dragged
along, to come the sooner to our settlements and to make known
the correctness of my conduct, never having been disposed to
depart from the obedience which is due to the orders of the
King.

Accordingly, three months before the arrival of the am-
nesty which his Majesty has been pleased to accord to his
subjects who had disobeyed his orders, I reached our settle-

[1] Duluth recognized the necessity of rendering the lives of Frenchmen
secure among such a horde of savages. See his punishment of Indian murderers
related in *Wis. Hist. Coll.*, XVI. 114–125.

[2] This is by some historians considered a probable reference to Great Salt
Lake.

[3] For the foundation of this mission, see p. 229, note 1, *ante*.

[4] See La Salle's complaints of Duluth in *Wis. Hist. Coll.*, XVI. 107–110.
It should be remembered, in this connection, that La Salle could brook no rivals.

ments without Monsieur the Intendant's[1] having been willing to hear what request I had to present.

As to the manner in which I lived during my journey, it would be superfluous to enlarge upon this subject, and to weary your Excellency by a long discourse, being persuaded that thirteen original letters from the Reverend [Father] Nouvel, superior of the missions to the Outaouas,[2] the Reverend Father Enjalran, missionary of St. Francis of Borgia,[3] the Reverend Father Bailloquet, missionary of Ste. Marie du Sault,[4] and the Reverend Father Pierson, missionary to the Hurons at St. Ignace,[5] all Jesuits, will for the rest suffice to inform your Excellency faithfully and amply.

[1] Duluth is thought to have been acting for the governor, Count de Frontenac, who was in opposition to the intendant, Jacques de Muelles. The former's protection was probably the source of the latter's enmity.

[2] Henri Nouvel, born in 1624, entered the Jesuit order in 1648 and was sent to Canada in 1662. He served in lower Canada for seven years, and in 1669 was sent to the Ottawa mission. He was superior for the years 1672–1680 (with an interregnum in 1678–1679), and again from 1688 to 1695. The date of his death is uncertain.

[3] Jean Enjalran, born in 1639, came to Canada in 1676, and the following year was sent to the Ottawa mission, where he served for many years. From 1681 to 1688 he was superior of the mission; in 1687, having accompanied as chaplain Denonville's Iroquois expedition, he was seriously wounded. After a visit to France, he returned to the Mackinac mission, where he was in service as late as 1706. He died, probably in France, in 1718. The mission to the Algonquian tribes at Mackinac was known as St. Francis Borgia.

[4] Pierre Bailloquet came to Canada in 1647; he was assigned to the Ottawa mission in 1673, and spent five years among the Indians of the Manitoulin Islands. Afterward he was stationed at Sault Ste. Marie and at Mackinac, and died in the Ottawa country June 7, 1692.

[5] Philippe Pierson was a native of Flanders, who came to Canada in 1666. In 1673 he went to the St. Ignace mission at Mackinac, where he resided ten years. The final years of his ministry were spent among the Sioux, whence he returned to die at Quebec in 1688.

THE VOYAGE OF ST. COSME, 1698–1699

INTRODUCTION

THE seventeenth century had but barely turned into its second half when a group of five young men of religious tendencies met in Paris and formed an ascetic brotherhood, who dwelt together and stimulated one another to noble deeds. From this group sprang the Société des Missions Étrangères —a society still in active existence after two and a half centuries' mission work in foreign lands. One of the group of five was a young nobleman of a great family closely allied to the royal house—François Laval de Montmorency. In his zeal to carry the message of the Gospel to distant lands, he sought the colony of New France, where he became the first Canadian bishop. His experiences in Paris led him to found in Quebec a seminary for the training of priests and missionaries, which was under the auspices of the Paris Seminary, and allied with the movement for foreign missions.

Several years, however, passed before Laval obtained the opportunity he sought to establish Indian missions in the heart of the American continent. The Jesuits had pre-empted the field, and the Sulpitians and Franciscans likewise had entered into a friendly rivalry to effect the conversion of the North American Indians. The discoveries and explorations of La Salle and Tonty had, however, made known a large number of tribes in the lower Mississippi Valley, that were to all appearance of a docile and receptive disposition, and furnished to the eager missionaries a virgin soil to cultivate. Laval thereupon chose three of his Seminary priests to inaugurate the work in the far Southwest, and sent them forth in the summer of 1698 to begin new missions among yet pagan tribes of aborigines.

The expedition of the Seminary mission was very well equipped. It is said that the cost was over 10,000 livres, a large share of which was furnished by the head of the company, François Jolliet de Montigny, whom Laval named vicar-general of the enterprise. Accompanying him were Father Antoine Davion, who had been since 1690 in the Canadian field, and Father Jean François Buisson de St. Cosme, a native of New France who had seen missionary service in Acadia. Another Canadian, Rev. Dominic Thaumer de la Source, accompanied them, together with several lay brothers, and the usual complement of voyageurs and engagés.

At Mackinac they were fortunate enough to fall in with Henri Tonty, commandant in the Illinois, whose services to the reverend fathers were inestimable. Leaving the post and mission at the Straits early in September, they made their way along the western shore of Lake Michigan, regretfully abandoned the Fox-Wisconsin route because of the hostile Fox Indians, and after vainly essaying a portage from Root River of Racine to the Fox River of the Illinois, coasted along until the latter part of October brought them to Chicago. There the Seminary fathers were the guests of the Jesuits who had preceded them, and had established at this favorable site a mission for the Miami Indians. Thence, after a few days' rest, the little company of priests and their companions made their way to the Illinois River, and spent some time among the populous villages of the Illinois Indians, lying along the banks of the river of their name.

In these villages Tonty was a welcome and honored guest, and for his sake the priests were received for the most part with courtesy and kindness. Some of the tribesmen deprecated their visits to the Indians of the Mississippi and attempted to place obstacles in their way. The strength of their retinue and the vigor of Tonty's support forbade serious opposition, and the only hindrance was the early formation of an ice bridge, which after some delay they broke by the impact of wooden canoes.

Once upon the Mississippi, the days were passed in gently drifting down the stream, admiring the wooded bluffs and grassy islands, enjoying the abundance of game that thronged the banks and the new and unknown kinds of fruits that supplied them with abundant food. Strange peoples, too, flocked to the water's edge to see the canoes of the white men pass by. At all the villages Tonty's presentation of the calumet of peace opened the way for an honorable reception.

At the site of the old Kappa village near the mouth of the Arkansas—the village of Marquette's farthest south on his voyage of 1673—the expedition halted. Tonty after visiting his post on the Arkansas River returned at once to the Illinois. The priests, however, remained in order to seek for favorable locations for missions among the tribes still farther southward along the Mississippi.

By the returning party, under Tonty's protection, letters were sent to the Bishop of Quebec, informing him of the success of the enterprise and the plans for further action. Among these letters was that of St. Cosme, which we here present for its vivid detailed description of the inland journey from Michilimackinac of the northern lakes to Arkansas Post on the southwestern rivers.

To follow the fortunes of our travellers farther, we learn that Davion was left among the Tonica tribesmen to begin his mission. They, however, proved so inhospitable that he was soon obliged to retire to the fort at Mobile. In 1704 he returned to his post, and labored among these Indians for eighteen years. Then, worn with age and hardships, he withdrew to New Orleans, and in 1727 returned to die in his native France.

Montigny attempted a mission for the Taensas tribe, but was soon discouraged by their lack of response to his appeals.

In 1700 he returned to France, and after serving as missionary in China for several years, was made director of the Société des Missions Étrangères at Paris, and devoted his later life to the superintendency of all the foreign fields.

For St. Cosme, the simple-hearted Canadian priest, was reserved a sadder fate. He first began his mission work among the Cahokia and Tamarois tribe, located near the site of the present Cahokia in Illinois. A few years later (the exact date is in doubt), on his way down the Mississippi to some of the lower missions, he was set upon and murdered by a dis-appointed war-party of the Chitimacha Indians. The mis-sion he had founded among the Cahokia was maintained by his colleague Thaumer de la Source until about 1721, when it was made over to the Jesuits, and the Seminary missions ceased to exist in the Mississippi Valley.

Iberville, who had in the meanwhile annexed Louisiana to the crown of France, took summary vengeance on the mur-derers of St. Cosme by a retaliatory expedition against the Chitimacha, and the execution of the guilty chiefs.

The letter that St. Cosme wrote, January 2, 1699, from the Arkansas post to Bishop Laval in Quebec has reposed in the archives of Laval University to this day. There it was dis-covered about the middle of the nineteenth century by John Gilmary Shea, the Catholic historian, and published by him simultaneously in French and in English. The French version was included in Shea's Cramoisy series under the title, *Re-lation de la Mission du Mississippi du Séminaire de Québec en 1700* (New York, 1861), the St. Cosme letter being supple-mented by shorter letters from Montigny and La Source. The English version was published by Joel Munsell at Albany in the same year, under the title *Early Voyages up and down the Mississippi*. With the letters of the Seminary priests Shea included in this latter volume Jean Cavelier's account of the death of La Salle; a letter from Father Gravier, a Jesuit

missionary; the voyage of Pierre Charles Le Sueur to discover
mines in Minnesota; and the narrative of Father Guignas,
who, in 1728, escaped from Fort Beauharnois among the Sioux.
In publishing the letter of St. Cosme, Shea had recourse to a
transcript of the original manuscript that had been made for
Francis Parkman, of Boston. The transcriber had evidently
been inexpert, and unable correctly to decipher the somewhat
crabbed and peculiar writing of Father St. Cosme. The
original manuscript being accessible in the University of Laval
at Quebec, Dr. R. G. Thwaites, about 1898, had a careful
transcript made and the translation collated by Col. Craw-
ford Lindsay, official translator for the Quebec province.
This translation has been kindly put at our disposal by Dr.
M. M. Quaife, the present superintendent of the Wisconsin Historical Society. He has also permitted us to see, and compare
with Colonel Lindsay's translation, a photostatic copy of a
transcript in the possession of the Chicago Historical Society.
Using this, we have made a few minor changes in our text.
We believe, therefore, that the translation we here present
has been made from a correct text of the original letter, and
that it will solve some of the difficulties that have been raised
by the text as previously published by Shea. Mgr. A. E.
Gosselin, rector of Laval University, has kindly furnished
tracings of certain names, in the original manuscript, the
reading of which was doubtful.

With this final narrative of our series we are brought to
the closing years of the seventeenth century. The era of exploration and adventure now merged in the era of exploitation.
For sixty years longer France held the great interior valley
of North America. Then it passed into other hands, and at
present only a few hamlets and a few French-speaking people
remain to remind us of the French régime in the American
Northwest.

THE VOYAGE OF ST. COSME, 1698–1699

Letter of M. Jean Frs. Buisson de St. Cosme, Priest of the Seminary of Quebec.

In the Akansças country, this 2nd January 1699.

My Lord,

THE last letter that I had the honor of writing to you was from Michilimakinac,[1] whence we started on the fourteenth of September, journeying overland to meet our canoe, which had rounded the Pointe aux Iroquois and had gone to wait for us at the village of the Outaouacs, which village contains about three hundred men.[2] God grant that they may respond to the care taken and the labors performed by the Reverend Jesuit Fathers for their instruction; but they seem less advanced in Christianity than the Illinois, who, we are told, have only recently had missionaries. We left that village on the 15th of September to the number of eight canoes: four for the River of the Miamis under the Sieur de Vincenne;[3] our three canoes and that of Monsieur de Tonty,[4] who, as I have already written you in my last, had resolved to ac-

---

[1] Father Jacques Gravier, who was one of the Jesuit missionaries at Mackinac, writes September 20, 1698: "Father de Careil and myself are charmed with the good judgment, the zeal, and the modesty that Monsieur de Montigny, Monsieur de St. Cosme, and Monsieur Davion have displayed in the conferences that we have had together during the seven days they spent here." *Jesuit Relations,* LXV. 59.

[2] Now called Point St. Ignace. For a map of this period showing the location of the Ottawa (Outaouac) village, see R. G. Thwaites (ed.), *Lahontan's New Voyages* (Chicago, 1905), I. 36.

[3] This is one of the earliest notices of Jean Baptiste Bissot, sieur de Vincennes, the founder of the French post among the Miami Indians. Vincennes was an officer in the regiment of Carignan that came to New France in 1665. Early in the eighteenth century he was dwelling in the Miami village on the site of the present Fort Wayne, Indiana, and there in 1719 he died. His nephew founded the Indiana city of Vincennes. The river of the Miami was the present St. Joseph River, Michigan.

[4] For this officer, see Introduction to his *Memoir,* pp. 283–285, *ante.*

A PORTION OF FRANQUELIN'S GREAT MAP OF 1688 (DÉPÔT DES CARTES, PARIS)
From a copy in the Library of Congress

company us to the Acansças.[1] I cannot sufficiently express, my lord, the obligations we owe him. He conducted us to the Acansças; he procured us much pleasure during the voyage; he greatly facilitated our passage through many nations, securing us the friendship of some and intimidating others—I mean the nations who through jealousy or the desire to pillage us sought to oppose our passage. He not only did his duty as a brave man but he also performed those of a zealous missionary, entering into all our views, exhorting the savages everywhere to pray and to listen to the missionaries. He soothed the minds of our servants in their petty whims; he supported by his example the devotional exercises that the journey allowed us to perform and frequently attended the sacraments.

It would be useless for me, my lord, to give you a description of Lake Mictpgan,[2] on which we embarked on leaving the fort of the Outaouacs.   This route is fairly well known. We should have gone by the south side, which is much finer than the north, but as it is the route usually followed by the Iroquois, who, not long before, had made an attack on the soldiers and savages proceeding to the country of the Miamis, this compelled us to take the north side, which is not so agreeable nor so well stocked with game, though it is easier, I believe, in the autumn because one is sheltered from the northwest winds. On the 21st of the month we reached the traverse of the Bay of the Puants,[3] which is distant forty leagues from Michilimakinac. We camped on an island called L'Isle du Détour because at that spot the lake begins to trend to the south.[4] We were windbound on that island for six days, during which our people occupied themselves in setting nets and caught great quantities of white fish, which are excellent eating and a very plentiful manna that fails not along that lake, where there is a dearth of meat almost all the time.

[1] For this post, see p. 308, note 2, *ante.* In 1689 Tonty gave a site at this post for the establishment of a mission.

[2] The orthography of the proper names in this document is very peculiar. It may be due to a crabbed hand-writing, which is difficult to decipher; but the manuscript seems clearly to give this form of spelling for the word Michigan.

[3] The place where the mouth of Green Bay must be crossed.

[4] Still known as Point Detour, the southeastern end of Delta County, Michigan, opposite Summer Island.

On the 28th we crossed from island to island. The Bay of
the Puants is about twenty or thirty leagues long. One
passes on the right hand another small bay called that of the
Noquest.[1] The Bay of the Puants is inhabited by several
savage tribes: the Noquest, the Folles Avoine, the Renards,
the Poûtoûatamis and the Saki.[2] The Jesuit Fathers have
a mission at the bottom of that bay.[3] We should have liked
very much to pass by the bottom of that bay and it would
have greatly shortened our journey. A small river has to be
ascended wherein there are only three leagues of rapids and
which is about sixty leagues long; then by means of a short
portage one reaches the River Ouiskonsin, which is a very fine
one, and by going down it one takes only two days to reach
the Miçissipi. In truth there is a distance of two hundred
leagues from the spot where this river falls into the Missiçipi
to the place where the River of the Illinois discharges into
the same Miçissipi; the current however is so strong that the
distance is sooner passed. But the Renards, who live on that
little river that one ascends on leaving the bay to reach Ouiskonsin, will not allow any persons to pass lest they might go
to the Sioux, with whom they are at war, and consequently
have already pillaged several Frenchmen who tried to go
that way. This compelled us to take the route by way of
Chikagou.

On the 29th of September we arrived at the village of the
Poûs, distant about twenty leagues from the crossing of the
bay.[4] There had formerly been a very large village here,
but after the death of the chief a portion of the savages had
gone to live in the bay and the remainder were preparing to
go there when we passed. We stopped in that village. On the
30th we purchased some provisions which we needed. We
started on the 31st[5] and on the 4th of October we came upon

[1] Both Big and Little Bay de Noquet are northern arms of Green Bay in
Delta County, Michigan. The city of Escanaba lies on the latter bay.

[2] The Noquet, Menominee, Fox, Potawatomi, and Sauk Indians.

[3] The mission of St. François Xavier at De Pere, Wisconsin, for which see
the Introduction to Allouez's Journal, p. 97.

[4] The site of this Potawatomi (Poûs) village has not been positively determined. It was on the Lake Michigan side of the Door County peninsula; the
distances would seem to indicate that it was not far from the present Kewaunee,
Wisconsin.   [5] *Sic.*

another small village of Poûx, on a small river, where Reverend
Father Marais had spent the winter with some Frenchmen
and had planted a cross.[1]   We stayed there for the remainder
of the day.   We left on the 5th and after being windbound
for two days we started and after two days of heavy wind
we reached Milouakik on the 9th.[2]   This is a river where there
is a village which has been a large one, consisting of Mas-
coutins, of Renards, and also of some Poux.   We stayed
there two days, partly on account of the wind and partly to
recruit our men a little, because there is an abundance of duck
and teal in the river.

On the eleventh of October we started early in the morning
from the fort of Milouakik, and at an early hour we reached
Kipikaoui, about eight leagues farther.[3]   Here we separated
from Monsieur de Vincenne's party, which continued on its
route to the Miamis.   Some savages had led us to hope that
we could ascend this river and after a portage of about two
leagues might descend by another river called Pesioui[4]
which falls into the River of the Illinois about 25 or 30 leagues
from Chikagou, and that we should thereby avoid all the
portages that had to be made by the Chikagou route.   We
passed by this river [Root] which is about ten leagues in length
to the portage[5] and flows through agreeable prairies, but as
there was no water in it we judged that there would not be
any in the Peschoui either, and that instead of shortening our
journey we should have been obliged to go over forty leagues
of portage roads ; this compelled us to take the route by way of
Chikagou which is distant about twenty leagues.

[1] This appears to have been on the site of the present Manitowoc, Wisconsin.
The priest was probably Father Gabriel Marest of the Jesuit order, who came to
Canada in 1694.   His first service was as chaplain to Iberville's expedition of
1695 to Hudson Bay, where Marest was captured by the English.   As soon as
he was exchanged he returned to New France, and was sent to the Illinois mission, where he remained until his death in 1714.

[2] Milwaukee.

[3] The present site of Racine, Wisconsin, at the mouth of Root River.

[4] The present Fox River of Illinois, which was called on Franquelin's map
of 1684 the Pestekouy.   One of its affluents is still known as Lake Pistakee, in
Lake County, Illinois.

[5] The portage is from the upper waters of Root River to Muskego Lake in
the southeastern part of Waukesha County, Wisconsin, thence by its outlet into
Fox River.

We remained five days at Kipikaoui, leaving on the 17th and after being windbound on the 18th and 19th we camped on the 20th at a place five leagues from Chikagou. We should have arrived there early on the 21st but the wind which suddenly arose on the lake compelled us to land half a league from Chikagou. We had considerable difficulty in landing and in saving our canoes; we all had to jump into the water. One must be very careful along the lakes, and especially Lake Mixcigan, whose shores are very low, to take to the land as soon as possible when the waves rise on the lake, for the rollers become so high in so short a time that one runs the risk of breaking his canoe and of losing all it contains. Many travellers have already been wrecked there. We, Monsieur de Montigny, Davion, and myself, went by land to the house of the Reverend Jesuit Fathers while our people remained behind.[1] We found there Reverend Father Pinet and Reverend Father Binneteau,[2] who had recently arrived from the Illinois country and was slightly ill.

I cannot describe to you, my lord, with what cordiality and manifestations of friendship these Reverend Fathers received and embraced us while we had the consolation of residing with them. Their house is built on the bank of a small river, with the lake on one side and a fine and vast prairie on the other. The village of the savages contains over a hundred and fifty cabins, and a league up the river is still another village almost as large. They are all Miamis. Reverend Father Pinet usually resides there except in winter, when the savages are all engaged in hunting, and then he goes to the Illinois. We saw no savages there; they had already started for their

[1] For the Jesuit mission at Chicago, known as that of the Guardian Angel, see M. M. Quaife, *Chicago and the Old Northwest* (Chicago, 1913), pp. 40–42.

[2] Pierre François Pinet was born at Périgueux, France, November 11, 1660. He entered the Jesuit order in 1682 and was sent to Canada twelve years later. He was first stationed at Mackinac, and in 1696 founded the mission at Chicago. He was obliged to leave in 1697, but returned the following year. In 1700 he abandoned the Chicago mission and settled among the Tamarois Illinois, where he died in 1704. Some authorities state that he died at Chicago July 16, 1704.

Julien Binneteau came as missionary to Canada in 1691. He was two years at an Acadian mission, went West in 1695, and the next year was sent to the Illinois mission, where his death, December 24, 1699, was due to an illness contracted while following his neophytes in their hunting expeditions.

hunt. If one may judge of the future from the short time that Reverend Father Pinet has passed in this mission, we may believe that if God will bless the labors and the zeal of that holy missionary there will be a great number of good and fervent Christians. It is true that but slight results are obtained with reference to the older persons, who are hardened in profligacy, but all the children are baptized, and the jugglers even, who are the most opposed to Christianity, allow their children to be baptized. They are also very glad to let them be instructed. Several girls of a certain age and also many young boys have already been and are being instructed, so that we may hope that when the old stock dies off, they will be a new and entirely Christian people.

On the 24th of October the wind fell and we sent for our canoes with all our effects, and finding that the water was extraordinarily low, we made a cache in the ground with some of them and took only what was absolutely necessary for our journey, intending to send for the remainder in the spring. We left Brother Alexandre in charge thereof, as he agreed to remain there with Father Pinet's man. We started from Chikagou on the 29th, and slept about two leagues from it on the little river[1] that afterward loses itself in the prairies. On the following day we began the portage, which is about three leagues in length when the waters are low, and is only one-fourth of a league in the spring, for then one can embark on a small lake[2] that discharges into a branch of the river of the Illinois, and when the waters are low a portage has to be made to that branch. On that day we got over half our portage, and would have gone still further, when we perceived that a little boy given us by Monsieur de Muis,[3] and who had set out alone although he was told to wait, was lost. We had not noticed it because all our people were busy. We were obliged to stop to look for him; everybody went and

---

[1] The south fork of Chicago River.

[2] Mud or Portage Lake. For an early map of this region, see *Wis. Hist. Coll.*, XVIII. 146.

[3] Nicolas Daneaux, sieur de Muy, came to Canada in 1685 and served with distinction in King William's War (1689–1697). After the commencement of the colony of Louisiana, he was in 1707 chosen governor, but died on his way to assume his post.

several gun-shots were fired, but he could not be found. It was a rather unfortunate accident; we were pressed for time, owing to the lateness of the season, and the waters being very low, we saw quite well, that as we were obliged to carry our baggage and our canoe, it would take a long time to reach the Illinois. This compelled us to separate. Messieurs de Montigny, de Tonty, and Davion continued the portage on the following day, while I with four other men went back to look for the little boy. While retracing my steps I met Fathers Pinet and Binneteau, who were on the way to the Illinois with two Frenchmen and a savage. We looked for the boy during the whole of that day also, without finding him. As it was the day before the feast of All Saints,[1] I was compelled to go to Chikagou for the night with our people. After they had heard mass and performed their devotions early in the morning, they spent the whole of that day also looking for the little boy without getting sight of him. It was very difficult to find him in the long grass, for this country consists of nothing but prairies with a few groves of trees. We were afraid to set fire to the long grass lest we might burn the boy. Monsieur de Montigny had told me to remain only one day, because the cold weather pressed us, and this compelled me to proceed, after giving orders to Brother Alexandre to seek him and to take some Frenchmen who were at Chikagou.[2]

I started in the afternoon of the 2nd of November. I crossed the portage and passed the night at the river or branch[3] of the River of the Illinois. We descended the river as far as an island. During the night we were surprised to see a slight fall of snow, and on the following day the river was frozen over in several places. We had therefore to break the ice and haul the canoe, because there was no open water. This compelled us to leave our canoe and go by land to seek Monsieur de Montigny, whom we met on the following day, the 5th of the month, at the Isle aux Cerfs. They had already gone over two leagues of portage. We still had four

---

[1] All Saints' Day is November 1.

[2] The boy came in to the mission house thirteen days after he was lost. He was utterly exhausted and out of his mind. See letter of Thaumer de la Source in Shea, *Early Voyages* (Albany, 1861), p. 85.

[3] The River Des Plaines.

leagues to do, as far as Mont Joliet. This took us three days, and we arrived on the 8th of the month.

From the Isle à la Cache to the said Mont Jolliet, a distance of seven leagues, everything has to be portaged, as there is no water in the river except in the spring. The banks of this river are very agreeable; they consist of prairies bounded by small hills and very fine thickets; there are numbers of deer in them and along the river are great quantities of game of all kinds, so that after crossing the portage one of our men, while taking a walk, procured enough to provide us with an abundant supper as well as breakfast on the following day. Mont Jolliet is a very fine mound of earth in the prairie to the right, descending a little. It is about thirty feet high. The savages say that at the time of the great deluge one of their ancestors escaped, and that this small mountain is his canoe which he upset there.

On leaving Mont Jolliet we proceeded about two leagues by water. We remained two whole days at our short portage, about a quarter of a league in length. As one of our men named Charbonneau had killed several turkeys and bustards in the morning, together with a deer, we were very glad to give our people a good meal and to let them rest for a day. On the tenth we made the short portage and found half a league of water, after which two men carried the canoe for about a league, the others walking behind, each carrying his load; and we then embarked for a league and a half. We slept at a short portage, five or six arpents in length. On the eleventh, after making the short portage, we came to the river Teatiki,[1] which is the true river of the Illinois, that which we descended being only a distant branch. We put all our baggage in the canoe, which two men paddled, while Monsieur de Tonty and ourselves, with the remainder of our men, proceeded by land, walking all the time through fine prairies. We came to the village of the Peangichias,[2] Miamis who formerly dwelt at the falls of the Miçipi and who have for some years been settled at this place. There was no one in

---

[1] The present Kankakee River.

[2] This tribe was known to American settlers as the Piankeshaw. It was a branch of the Miami that later removed to the lower Wabash, and settled in the neighborhood of Vincennes.

the village, for all had gone hunting. That day we slept near
Massane,[1] a small river which falls into the River of the Illinois. On that day we began to see oxen, and on the morrow two of our men killed four; but as these animals are in
poor condition at this season we contented ourselves with
taking the tongues only. These oxen seem to me to be larger
than ours; they have a hump on their backs; their legs are
very short; the head is very large and so covered with long
hair that it is said a bullet cannot penetrate it. We afterward saw some nearly every day during our journey as far
as the Acansças.

After experiencing considerable difficulty during three
days in carrying and hauling our baggage in the canoe, owing
to the river being rapid, low, and full of rocks, we arrived
on the 15th of November at the place called the Old Fort.
This is a rock on the bank of the river, about a hundred
feet high, whereon Monsieur de la Salle had caused a fort to
be built, which has been abandoned,[2] because the savages
went to reside about twenty-five leagues further down. We
slept a league above it, where we found two cabins of savages; we were consoled on finding a woman who was a thoroughly good Christian. The distance between Chicagou and
the fort is considered to be about thirty leagues. There we
commenced the navigation, that continues to be always good
as far as the fort of Permetaoui,[3] where the savages now are
and which we reached on the 19th of November. We found
there Reverend Father Binetot and Reverend Father Marais
who, owing to their not being laden when they left Chigaou,
had arrived six or seven days before us. We also saw Reverend Father Pinet there. All the Reverend Jesuit Fathers
gave us the best possible reception. Their sole regret was to
see us compelled to leave so soon on account of the frost.
We took there a Frenchman who had lived three years with
the Acansças and who knows a little of their language.

This mission of the Illinois seems to me the finest that the
Reverend Jesuit Fathers have up here, for without counting

[1] Now known as Mazon Creek in Grundy County, Illinois.
[2] Fort St. Louis on the rock called Le Rocher. See Tonty's *Narrative*,
p. 290, note 4, *ante*.
[3] This post was on Peoria Lake, whose early name was Pimetoui.

all the children who are baptized, a number of adults have abandoned all their superstitions and live as thoroughly good Christians; they frequently attend the sacraments and are married in church. We had not the consolation of seeing all these good Christians often, for they were all scattered down the bank of the river for the purpose of hunting. We saw only some women savages married to Frenchmen, who edified us by their modesty and their assiduity in going to prayer several times a day in the chapel. We chanted high mass in it, with deacon and sub-deacon, on the feast of the Presentation of the most Blessed Virgin,[1] and after commending our voyage to her and having placed ourselves under her protection we left the Illinois on the 22nd of November—we had to break the ice for two or three arpents to get out of Lake Pemsteoui. We had four canoes: that of Monsieur de Tonty, our two, and another belonging to five young voyageurs who were glad to accompany us, partly on account of Monsieur de Tonty, who is universally beloved by all the voyageurs, and partly also to see the country. Reverend Fathers Binneteau and Pinct also came with us a part of the way, as they wished to go and spend the whole winter with their savages.

On the first day after our departure we came to the cabin of Rouenssas, the most notable of the Illinois chiefs and a very good Christian.[2] He received us with the politeness, not of a savage but of a well-bred Frenchman. He led us to his cabin and made us sleep there. He presented us with three deer, one of which he gave to Monsieur [de Tonty], another to the Father, and the third to us. We learned from him that the Chaouanons, the Chikachas, and the Kakinanpols[3] had attacked the Kaoukias,[4] an Illinois tribe about five or six leagues below the mouth of the river of the Illinois along the Miçissipi, and that they had killed ten men and taken nearly one hundred slaves, both women and children. As this Rouensa is very quick-witted, we thought we should give

---

[1] November 21.

[2] This chief, usually called Rouensa or Roinsac, was head of the Kaskaskia branch of the Illinois. He removed about the beginning of the eighteenth century to the Kaskaskia River, where the village was frequently called Rouensac.

[3] The Shawnee, the Chickasaw, and possibly the Kickapoo.

[4] The Cahokia, a branch of the Illinois, who lived in the bottom lands opposite the site of St. Louis.

him some presents, to induce him to facilitate our passage
through the Illinois tribes, not so much for this first voyage
as for the others, when we should not be so strong; for all
these nations up here are very suspicious and easily become
jealous when we go to other nations. We therefore presented
him with a collar,[1] to show him that we formed an alliance
with him and with all his nation, and that as he was a Christian he should have no greater pleasure than in seeing the
other nations participate in the happiness he enjoyed, and
for that reason he was obliged to facilitate as much as he could
the designs of the missionaries who were going to instruct
them. We afterward gave them a small present of powder.

On the 28th, after saying our masses, when Roüensas and
his family received communion at Monsieur de Montigny's,
we left and came to a small village of savages, on disembarking at which the chief, named L'Ours,[2] told us that it was not
advisable that we should go into the Miçissipi country. But
Monsieur won him over or intimidated him by his words,
telling him that we were sent by the Master of Life and the
great Master of Prayer to instruct the savages whither we were
going, and that he was hired by the Governor to accompany
us, so that if he molested us he attacked the very person of our
Governor. The chief made no answer to these words. We
embarked and on the 24th we slept at another village of
several cabins where we found one Tiret, a chief who was
formerly famous in his nation but who has since been abandoned by nearly all his people. He made several complaints
to Monsieur de Tonty, who reproached him, saying that it
was his evil conduct that earned him the hatred of his people;
that he had long before told him to give up his jugglery—for
he is a famous sorcerer—and to pray; but that he had not
yet done so. He afterward went to the prayers, and the
savage promised him that he would be instructed on the following day.

On the 25th of the month we parted from Father Pinet,
who remains in this village to spend the winter, for there are
a good many savages here who pray, and on the 26th we came

---

[1] "Collar" was the French term for the belt of wampum beads, with which
the Indians sealed alliances and treaties with the whites and with other tribes.
[2] The Bear.

to a village whose chief was away hunting with all the young men. Some old men came to meet us, weeping for the death of their people killed by the Chaouanons. We went to their cabins, and they told us that we ought not to pass by the Chaouchias with the Chaouanons, to whom, they said, Monsieur de Tonty had given arms and who had attacked them. Monsieur de Tonty replied that he had left the Illinois country more than three years before and could not have seen the Chaouanons to give them arms. But the savages persisted in saying several things without reason, and we saw very well that they were evil-minded, and that we should leave as soon as possible, before the arrival of the young men who were to return the following morning. Therefore we went out abruptly, and when Monsieur de Tonty told them he feared not the men, they said that they pitied our young men, who would all be killed. Monsieur de Tonty replied that they had seen him with the Iroquois and knew what he could do and how many men he could kill.[1] It must be confessed that all these savages have a very high esteem for him. He had only to be in one's company to prevent any insult being offered. We embarked at once, and went to sleep at a place five or six leagues from that village.

On the following day we were detained for some hours, owing to quantities of ice drifting down the river, and on the 28th we landed at a village consisting of about twenty cabins, where we saw the woman chief. This woman enjoys great repute in her nation, owing to her wit and her great liberality and because, as she has many sons and sons-in-law who are good hunters, she often gives feasts, which is the way to acquire the esteem of the savages and of all their nations in a short time. We said mass in this village in the cabin of a soldier named La Viollette, who was married to a savage and whose child Monsieur de Montigny baptized. Monsieur de Tonty related to the woman chief what had been said to us in the last village. She disapproved of it all, and told him that the whole of her tribe were greatly rejoiced at seeing him once more, as well as us, but that they regretted that they could not be sure of seeing him again and of having him longer with them.

[1] See pp. 291–294, *ante*, for Tonty's experiences among the Iroquois.

We left this village and travelled about eight leagues between the 29th of November and the 3rd of December. We were detained at the same place by the ice, which completely barred the river. During that time we had an abundance of provisions, for no one need fast on that river, so great is the quantity of game of all kinds: swans, bustards, or duck. The river is bordered by a belt of very fine timber, which is not very wide, so that one soon reaches beautiful prairies, containing numbers of deer. Charbonneau killed several while we were detained, and others killed some also. Navigation is not very easy on this river when the water is low. We were sometimes obliged to walk with a portion of our people, while the others propelled the canoes, not without trouble, for they were often obliged to get into the water, which was already very cold. While we were detained, Reverend Father Binnetost, whom we had left at the village of the woman chief, came to see us, and after spending a day with us he returned to the village for the feast of St. Xavier.[1] On that day a heavy gale broke up a portion of the ice and we procceded about a league. On the following day we obtained some wooden canoes, at a place where there were five cabins of savages, and after breaking with them about three or four arpents of ice that barred the river, that was as much as four fingers thick and could bear a man's weight, we afterward had free navigation to the Miçissipi, which we reached on the 5th of December after journeying about eighty leagues from the fort of Pemiteouit.

The Miçissipi is a fine, large river flowing from the north. It divides into several channels at the spot where the River of the Illinois falls into it, forming very beautiful islands. It winds several times, but seems always to keep its course to the south as far as the Acansças. It is bordered by very fine woods. The banks on both sides seem about thirty feet high, which does not prevent its overflowing them far into the woods in the spring, when the waters are high, with the exception of some hills or very high places that are sometimes met with. All along the river are numbers of oxen, bears, deer, and also a great many turkeys. We were always so well supplied with meat, while descending the river as far as the Acansças, that

[1] December 3.

we passed many herds of oxen without attempting to fire at them.

On the 6th of December we embarked on the Micissipi, and after proceeding about six leagues we came to the great River of the Myssouries, which flows from the west, and is so muddy that it dirties the waters of the Micissipi, which until they meet that river are very clear. It is reported that there are great numbers of savages on the upper part of that river. Three or four leagues lower down we saw, on the left bank, a rock on which some figures are painted and for which the savages are said to have a certain veneration.[1] They are now nearly effaced. We camped that day at the Kaouchias, who were still in grief in consequence of the attack made upon them by the Chikachas and the Chaouanons. On our arrival they all began to weep. They did not seem to us to be so evil-intentioned or so wicked as some Illinois savages had sought to make us believe. The poor people excited our pity more than our fears.

On the following day about noon we reached the Tamarois. These savages had received timely warning of our arrival through some of the Kaoukias, who carried the news to them, and as a year before they had molested Monsieur de Tonty's men, they were afraid and all the children and women fled from the village. The chief came with some of his people to receive us on the water's edge and to invite us to their village, but we did not go, because we wished to prepare for the feast of the Conception. We camped on the other side of the river on the right bank. Monsieur de Tonty went to the village, and after re-assuring them to some extent, he brought the chief, who begged us to go and see him in his village. We promised to do so and on the following day, the feast of the Conception,[2] after saying our masses, we went with Monsieur de Tonty and seven of our men well armed. They came to meet us and led us to the chief's cabin. All the women and children were there, and no sooner had we entered the cabin than the young men and the women broke away a portion of it to see us. They had never seen black gowns, except for a few days Reverend Father Gravier, who

---

[1] See p. 249, note 1, *ante*.
[2] December 8.

had made a journey to their country. They gave us food and we gave them a small present, as we had done to the Kaouchias. We told them that it was to show them that our hearts were without guile, and that we wished to effect an alliance with them, so that they might give a good reception to our people who would pass there and supply them with food. They received the gift with many thanks and after that we returned to our camp.

The Tamarois were camped on an island about [*blank in MS.*] lower than the village, probably in order to obtain wood more easily than in their village, which is on the edge of a prairie and some distance away, probably through fear of their enemies. We were unable to ascertain whether they were very numerous; there seemed to be a great many of them, although the majority of their people were away hunting. There would be enough for a rather fine mission, by bringing to it the Kaouchias, who live quite near, and the Mcchigamias, who live a little lower down the Miçissipi, and who are said to be pretty numerous. We did not see them because they had gone into the interior to hunt. The three villages speak the Illinois languages.

We left the Tamarois in the afternoon of the 8th of December. On the 10th we saw a hill at a distance of about three arpents from the Miçissipi, on the right side going down. After being detained for some time on the 11th by rain, we arrived early on the 12th at Cap St. Antoine,[1] where we spent the remainder of the day and the whole of the next, collecting gum which we needed. There are many pines between Cap St. Antoine and a river lower down, and this is the only place where I saw any between Chikagou and the Acansças. Cap St. Antoine is a rocky bluff on the left bank going down. Some arpents below it is another rock on the right bank, which projects into the river and towards an island or rather a rock about one hundred feet high, which makes the river turn very short and narrows the channel,

---

[1] Cape St. Antoine appears to have been just above the Grand Eddy in Perry County, Missouri. The present name of the creek entering at this point—Cape Cinq Homme Creek—is a corruption of the name St. Cosme, by which it appears on early maps. It seems, therefore, to have been named for our narrator.

causing a whirlpool in which it is said canoes are lost during the high waters. On one occasion fourteen Miamis perished there. This has caused the spot to be dreaded by the savages, who are in the habit of offering sacrifices to that rock when they pass there. We saw none of the figures that we were told we should find there. We ascended this island or rock with some difficulty by a hill and we planted a fine cross on it, chanting the hymn *Vexilla Regis*,[1] while our people fired three discharges from their guns. God grant that the Cross, that has never yet been known in this place, may triumph here, and that our Lord may abundantly spread the merits of His Holy Passion, so that all these savages may know and serve him. Canes begin to be seen at Cap St. Antoine. There is also a kind of a tree, as large as and similar to the linden, which exudes a sort of sweet-scented gum. Along the Miçissipi also grow a number of fruit-trees unknown in Canada, some of whose fruit we still found occasionally on the trees. I forgot to state that as soon as we were on the Micissipi we no longer perceived that it was the winter season, and the further we descended the river the greater we found the heat. The nights however are cool.

We left Cap St. Antoine on the 14th of December and on the 15th we slept a league above the Ouabache.[2] This is a large and fine river on the left of the Miçissipi, which flows from the north; it is said to be five hundred leagues in length and to take its source near the Sonontoûans.[3] By this river one goes to the country of the Chaouanons who trade with the English.[4] On the 16th we left the Ouabache, and nothing particular happened to us nor did we observe anything remarkable until we reached the Akansças, except that we killed a certain bird almost as large as a swan, with a beak about a foot long and a throat of extraordinary size. Some are said to have throats large enough to hold a bushel of corn. The one we killed was small and its throat could easily have contained half a bushel of corn. It is said that this bird

---

[1] See p. 218, note 1, *ante*.   [2] Ohio; see p. 250, note 1.

[3] The habitat of the Seneca (Sonontouans) was on the headwaters of the Allegheny River.

[4] The present Cumberland River was formerly known as the Shawnee (Chaouanon) River.

places itself in a current and by opening its great beak it catches the fish which it stuffs into its throat.[1] Our French called this bird Chictek. On the 22nd we came to a small river[2] on the left going down, which is said to be the road leading to the Chikachas, a numerous tribe. It is believed that the distance from this small river to their villages is not great.

On the 24th we camped early, in order that our people might prepare for the great festival of Christmas. We erected a small chapel and chanted a high mass at midnight, at which all our French performed their devotions. Christmas Day was spent in saying our masses, all of which were attended by our people, and in the afternoon we chanted vespers. We were greatly surprised to see the earth tremble about one o'clock in the afternoon, and though the earthquake did not last long it was severe enough and was easily felt by everybody.[3]

On the following day we started at a somewhat late hour, because we were obliged to wait for a little savage whom Monsieur de Tonty had brought with him, and who on the previous day had gone to the woods to look for fruit and had lost himself. We thought he might have been captured by some Chicachas or Acansças warriors; this compelled us to watch and be on guard all night. But we were greatly rejoiced when we saw him return next day. We started and slept at the place where the Kappas, a tribe of the Acansças, formerly dwelt.

On St. John's day,[4] after travelling about five leagues, we observed some wooden canoes and a savage at the water's edge. As we were near and feared that he would take to flight on seeing us, one of our men took the calumet and sang. He was heard in the village, which was close by. Some fled, while the others brought the calumet and came to receive us at the water's edge. On approaching us they rubbed us and then rubbed themselves, which is a mark of attention among sav-

---

[1] This is the pelican (*pelecanus erythrorhynchos*).

[2] The present Wolf River of Tennessee, at whose mouth stands Memphis. This was known to the French explorers as Rivière à Margot.

[3] This was the region of the great earthquake of 1811.

[4] December 27.

ages. They took us on their shoulders and carried us into
the cabin of a chief. A hill of heavy soil had to be ascended,
and as he who carried me was sinking under the burden, I
feared that he would let me fall, so I got down in spite of him
and walked up the hill. But as soon as I reached the top I
was compelled to get on his back to be carried to the cabin.
The young men brought all our things into the same cabin.
Some time afterward they came to sing the calumet for us,
and in the evening of the following day they carried us to
another cabin, where they made Monsieur de Tonty and the
three of us sit on bear-skins; four chiefs each took a calumet
that they had placed before us, and the others began to sing
and beat drums made of earthenware jars over which a skin
is stretched. Each holds in his hand a gourd containing seeds
that make a noise, and as they sing in accord with the sound
of the drum and the rattle of the gourds, the result is a music
that is not the most agreeable. During this harmony a savage who stood behind us bleated. We were soon tired of this
ceremony, which they perform for all strangers to whom they
wish to show consideration, and it must be endured unless
one wishes to be deemed evil-hearted or as harboring wicked
designs. After remaining a certain time, we put some of our
people in our place, and they had the pleasure of hearing the
lullaby throughout the night. On the following day they
made us a present of a little slave and of some skins, for which
we paid with a present of knives and other things that they
prize highly.

We were greatly consoled at seeing ourselves at the seat
of our missions, but we were deeply afflicted at finding this
nation of the Acansças, formerly so numerous, entirely destroyed by war and by disease. Not a month had elapsed
since they had rid themselves of smallpox, which had carried
off most of them. In the village are now nothing but graves,
in which they were buried two together, and we estimated
that not a hundred men were left. All the children had died,
and a great many women. These savages seem to be of a
very kind disposition. We were invited at every moment
to feasts. Their honesty is extraordinary. They transported
all our effects to a cabin where they remained two days without anybody taking a thing, and even without a single article

being lost.   One of our people forgot his knife in a cabin and a savage at once took it to him.   Polygamy is not common among them.   We saw however in the village of the Kappas one of those wretches who from their youth dress as girls and pander to the most shameful of all vices.   But this infamous man was not of their nation; he belonged to the Illinois, among whom the practice is quite common.   The savages have an abundance of corn, of beans, and of pumpkins.   As to meat, though they are in a country teeming with game, we found none in their villages, owing to the fact that they were weakened by disease and in continual dread of their enemies. They make houses like the Hurons, making use of great earthenware pots instead of kettles, and of very well made jars for holding water.   I have not yet seen savages so well formed. They are quite naked except that when they go out they wear a buffalo robe.   The women and girls are partly naked, as among the Illinois.   They wear a deer-skin hung over one shoulder.

We remained two days and a half in this village, and after planting a Cross in it, which we told the savages was to be the sign of our union, we left on the 30th of November [December] for their other village, about nine leagues distant from this one. We were deeply grieved to have to part from Monsieur de Tonty, who was unable to come with us for various reasons. He would greatly have liked to accompany us to the other nations whither we were going, but his affairs compelled him to return as soon as possible to the Illinois country.   He is the man who best knows these regions; he has twice gone down to the sea; he has been far inland to the most remote tribes, and is beloved and feared everywhere.   If it be desired to have discoveries made in this country, I do not think the task could be confided to a more experienced man than he.   I have no doubt, my lord, that your Grace will deem it a pleasure to acknowledge the obligations we owe him.

We slept at the mouth of the river of the Acansças,[1] which is a fine one and distant two hundred and fifty or three hundred leagues from that of the Illinois.   On the following day we reached the village at an early hour.   Six savages came to meet us with the calumet, and led us to the village with the

[1] The present Arkansas River.

same ceremonies as those observed at the first one. We passed two days there. This village seemed to be more populous than the first; there were more children in it. We told them that we were going further down, to their neighbors and friends; that they would see us often; that they would do well to live together, and that they would thereby more easily resist their enemies. They agreed to everything and promised that they would try to bring with them the Osages,[1] who had come from the River of the Missouris and were on the upper portion of this river. We started on the 2nd of January[2] and camped at the mouth of the river, where the French who were returning would allow us but one day for writing. I thought I should have more time to do so, as I hoped to go up from the Acansças to the Illinois, but, as we are going much further down, I am afraid the letters we shall write after this will not be received this year, for the persons by whom we wished to send them will have left before we can reach the Illinois. I therefore beg your Grace to excuse me if this one be somewhat badly expressed, as I am so greatly pressed for time that I cannot even write to one of our gentlemen, to whom I beg you to allow me to send greetings, and to commend myself to their holy prayers. I trust your Grace will be pleased to grant me the same favor, and to remember before our Lord him who remains, with very profound respect,

My lord,

Your Grace's very humble and very obedient servant,

J. F. BUISSON ST. COSME,

Priest, unworthy Missionary.

I have not time to reread this letter.

[1] For this tribe see p. 313, note 1, *ante.*   [2] 1699.

INDEX

Abenaki Indians, mission for, 160 n.; in Illinois, 294; in fur trade, 331; sketch, 294 n.

Acadia, missionary in, 338, 346 n.

Acansças Indians, see Quapaw Indians.

Accault (Acau), Michel, explorer, 290, 331; sketch, 290 n.

Acolapissa Indians, see Quinipissa Indians.

Agonstot, Onondaga chief, 291.

Akamsea, Quapaw village, Marquette at, 253–257; see also Quapaw Indians.

Akansas, see Arkansas Post.

Akensea Indians, see Quapaw Indians.

Albany, Dutch at, 21, 30, 309 n.

Alexandre, Brother, at Chicago, 347, 348.

Algonkin Indians, habitat, 11, 15 n.; intertribal relations, 15; hostilities with Iroquois, 58, 63, 64.

Algonquian stock, Indians of, 15 n., 19, 20, 23 n., 24 n., 36 n., 45 n., 73 n., 89 n., 95, 96, 252 n.; language, 24 n., 25 n., 69, 96, 123, 128, 130, 135, 158, 163, 164, 167, 170, 171, 184, 207, 243; commerce with, 109; missions for, 115, 160 n.

Alimouek Indians, see Illinois Indians.

Allegheny River, route to, 187 n.; Indians on, 357 n.

Alligators, La Salle sees, 298.

Allouez, Father Claude, explorer, 6; Lake Superior journey, 93–137, 224, 227 n.; Wisconsin journey, 140–160, 224, 233, 234 n.; in Illinois, 304, 311 n.; mentions the Mississippi, 130, 132, 136, 223; speeches, 109, 215, 218–220; sketch, 96.

Allumettes Island, in the Ottawa, 15 n.

Alton (Ill.), pictographs near, 249 n.

Amherstburg (Ont.), Indians at, 119 n.

Amickkoick Indians, see Beaver Indians.

Amikoue Indians, see Beaver Indians.

Anadardo Indians, see Nadao Indians.

Anastatius, Father, see Douay.

Andastes (Antastogué, Antastouais, Conestoga) Indians, intertribal relations, 181, 187, 192; sketch, 176 n.

André, Louis, Jesuit missionary, 160.

Apples, see Wild apples.

Appleton (Wis.), site, 150 n.

Arkansas, Indians in, 313 n.; St. Cosme, 342.

Arkansas Indians, see Quapaw Indians.

Arkansas Post, 8, 284, 308, 311, 320, 321, 339, 343 n.

Arkansas River, 7; settlement on, 8, 284, 308, 311, 339; Marquette reaches, 254 n., 339; St. Cosme at, 342, 360, 361; Indians on, 361.

Arpent, term defined, 150 n.

Assiniboin (Assinipoualac) Indians, described, 133, 134; Tonty among, 284; Duluth among, 326, 330; sketch, 134 n.

Assiniboine River, mouth, 133.

Attikamègue (Poissons-blancs) Indians, habitat, 134.

Auguel, Antoine du Gay, with Hennepin, 331, 332.

Bailloquet, Father Pierre, at Sault Ste. Marie, 334.

Barbue, see Catfish.

Barthélemy, ——, Sulpitian at Montreal, 169, 170.

Basswood-trees on the Wisconsin, 236; on the Mississippi, 252.

Baugis (Bogis), Chevalier de, in Illinois, 305, 306, 311 n.

Baye des Puants, see Green Bay.

Beans, Indians raise, 244, 360.

Bears, on the Ottawa route, 41; attack men, 133, 134; used as food, 148, 197, 204; on the Mississippi, 298, 302, 321, 354.

363

ORIGINAL NARRATIVES
OF EARLY AMERICAN HISTORY

REPRODUCED UNDER THE AUSPICES OF THE
AMERICAN HISTORICAL ASSOCIATION

GENERAL EDITOR, J. FRANKLIN JAMESON, PH.D., LL.D.

DIRECTOR OF THE DEPARTMENT OF HISTORICAL RESEARCH IN THE
CARNEGIE INSTITUTION OF WASHINGTON

Each volume octavo, cloth-bound, about 450 pages

$3.00 net.

VOLUMES PREVIOUSLY PUBLISHED

Each with Full Index, Maps and Facsimile Reproductions

The Northmen, Columbus, and Cabot, 985-1503
Edited by JULIUS E. OLSON, Professor of the Scandinavian Languages and Literatures in the University of Wisconsin, and EDWARD GAYLORD BOURNE, Ph.D., Professor of History in Yale University.

The Spanish Explorers in the Southern United States, 1528-1543
Edited by FREDERICK W. HODGE, of the Bureau of American Ethnology, and THEODORE H. LEWIS, of St. Paul.

Early English and French Voyages, Chiefly Out of Hakluyt, 1534-1608
Edited by the REV. DR. HENRY S. BURRAGE, of the Maine Historical Society.

Voyages of Samuel de Champlain, 1604-1618
Edited by W. L. GRANT, M.A. (Oxon.), Beit Lecturer on Colonial History in the University of Oxford.

Narratives of Early Virginia, 1606-1625
Edited by LYON GARDINER TYLER, LL.D., President of the College of William and Mary.

Bradford's History of Plymouth Plantation, 1606-1646
Edited by WILLIAM T. DAVIS, Formerly President of the Pilgrim Society.

Winthrop's Journal (History of New England), 2 vols., 1630-1649
Edited by DR. JAMES K. HOSMER, Corresponding Member of the Massachusetts Historical Society and of the Colonial Society of Massachusetts.

Narratives of New Netherland, 1609-1664
Edited by DR. J. F. JAMESON.

Johnson's Wonder-Working Providence of Sions Saviour in New England
Edited by DR. J. F. JAMESON.

Narratives of Early Maryland
Edited by CLAYTON COLMAN HALL, LL.B., A.M., of the Maryland Historical Society.

Narratives of Early Carolina
Edited by ALEXANDER S. SALLEY, JR., Secretary of the Historical Commission of South Carolina.

Narratives of Early Pennsylvania, Delaware and West Jersey
Edited by DR. ALBERT COOK MYERS.

The Journal of Jasper Danckaerts, 1679-1680
Edited by REV. B. B. JAMES, of Baltimore.

Narratives of the Indian Wars, 1675-1699
Edited by DR. CHARLES H. LINCOLN.

Narratives of the Witchcraft Cases, 1648-1706
Edited by PROFESSOR GEORGE L. BURR, of Cornell University.

Narratives of the Insurrections, 1675-1690
Edited by PROFESSOR CHARLES M. ANDREWS, of Yale University.

Spanish Exploration in the Southwest
Edited by PROFESSOR HERBERT E. BOLTON, of the University of California.

Early Narratives of the Northwest, 1634-1699
Edited by PROFESSOR LOUISE PHELPS KELLOGG, Ph.D., of the Research Department of the State Historical Society of Wisconsin.

WHAT EMINENT HISTORICAL SCHOLARS SAY OF THE SERIES

From the Preface of the General Editor, Dr. J. F. Jameson:

"At its annual meeting in December, 1902, the American Historical Association approved and adopted the plan of the present series, and the undersigned was chosen as its general editor. The purpose of the series was to provide individual readers of history, and the libraries of schools and colleges, with a comprehensive and well-rounded collection of those classical narratives on which the early history of the United States is founded, or of those narratives which, if not precisely classical, hold the most important place as sources of American history anterior to 1700.

"The plan contemplates, not a body of extracts, but in general the publication or republication of whole works or distinct parts of works. In the case of narratives originally issued in some other language than English, the best available translations will be used, or fresh versions made. The English texts will be taken from the earliest editions, or those having the highest historical value, and will be reproduced with literal exactness. The maps will be such as will give real help toward understanding the events narrated in the volume. The special editors of the individual works will supply introductions, setting forth briefly the author's career and opportunities, when known, the status of the work in the literature of American history, and its value as a source, and indicating previous editions; and they will furnish such annotations, scholarly but simple, as will enable the intelligent reader to understand and to estimate rightly the statements of the text."

Charles M. Andrews, Ph.D., Professor of History, Johns Hopkins University:
"The series is one of unquestioned importance in that it contains complete texts selected with excellent judgment of narratives valuable to every student and reader of American history. The series for this reason will always stand on a higher level than the ordinary source book, and will appeal to a much wider range of persons interested. Its value grows with each volume issued, not only because the amount of valuable text material is thereby increased, but also because the later volumes contain reprints of rarer and more indispensable narratives. Such reprints will be especially serviceable for class use where valuable originals could not be placed in the hands of students, and will be important additions to the libraries of small colleges which cannot afford generally to purchase rare and expensive texts."

George B. Adams, Ph.D., Litt.D., Professor of History in Yale University and President of the American Historical Association:
"I feel like congratulating you heartily on the impression which I am sure the volumes already published of the 'Original Narratives of Early American History' must make on all who examine them. They seem to me admirably done both from the editorial and the publishing side, and likely to be of constantly increasing usefulness to students, schools, and libraries, as time goes on."

Albert Bushnell Hart, Professor of History in Harvard University and First Vice-President of the American Historical Association:
"I have felt great interest in the series since its inception, and it is likely to be of considerable service to scholars, and particularly to libraries which can no longer find originals at the price within their means."

Max Farrand, Ph.D., Professor of History, Stanford University:
"The narratives chosen, the scholarly editing of those narratives, and the form in which they are presented, combine to render this an unusually good series. You have rendered a genuine service to American scholarship by thus placing within reach of every one, and in a serviceable form, documents which have hitherto been more or less inaccessible or unusable. The series is one which every student of American history must use, and he should have access to it either in his own library or in the library from which he draws his material."

William MacDonald, Ph.D., LL.D., Professor of American History in Brown University:
"For all historical study beyond the most elementary, the systematic and extended use of the sources is of course indispensable. The output of documentary material for the American Colonial Period has been these twenty years past very considerable, although vast quantities of significant documents still exist only in manuscript. In the field of narrative sources, however, republication has been far less frequent, and the scarcity of these originals, together with the high prices which copies command, have made it practically impossible for students who do not have access to the largest libraries to make more than occasional or incidental use of this kind of historical material.

"If the volumes of 'Original Narratives' thus far published are a sufficient indication — as I have no doubt they are — of what the series will be as a whole, a great gap in valuable material for the study of American origins will be worthily filled.

"The editorial work of the volumes shows a commendable union of care and restraint. The introductions both of the general editor and of the editors of the several volumes are sufficient without being too long, while the explanatory foot-notes are kept well within bounds. Mechanically, the volumes are well made, open easily in the hand, and are issued at a price which puts them within the reach of libraries and individuals of modest means.

'A series so well vouched for on the editorial side can need little commendation from other quarters, for the volumes are their own best commendation. As a teacher of American history to college classes, however, I am always glad to find valuable material for student use increase, and the 'Original Narratives' deserve, and I hope will receive, a cordial reception and a generous use."

Worthington C. Ford, Chief of Division of Manuscripts, Library of Congress, Washington, D. C.:

"I look upon it as one of the best series undertaken to encourage the study of American history. Not only is the original plan rarely intelligent, but the individual volumes prove the care and critical capacity of each editor. The volumes are not only our source books of American history, but they are also readable and in such convenient form that they should be in every library, and used as text books in the teaching of history."

Senator Henry Cabot Lodge, in the North American Review:

"In this volume on 'The Northmen, Columbus, and Cabot,' and as the prospectus indicates, in its successors, the selection could not be improved. Judging from this volume alone, it may also be said that nothing could be better than the editing. We have the best texts accompanied by brief but clear introductions, and explained by notes which are sufficient to guide and instruct and not sufficient to puzzle and encumber. In each case a short list of authorities is given which will direct those who wish to pursue their inquiries upon any one of the three subjects in the way in which they should go to find all the sources and the last works of modern research and antiquarian learning. The selection and editing could not in fact have been better done for the purpose which the editors had in view.

"If any one wishes to wrestle with the endless questions and controversies of the Columbian voyages, it is easy to plunge into the countless books upon the subject. Meantime the general reader, little concerned with dates and identification of places, but profoundly interested in the fact of America's discovery, can find in these letters and journals the man himself, and live over with him the triumph, one of the greatest ever won, and the tragedy, one of the most piteous ever endured.

"After all, there is nothing better than this that history can do for us, and very few histories can do it quite so well as an original narrative with all its errors and imperfections on its head, if we are only fortunate enough to possess one which has both literary quality and real human feeling."

A NECESSITY IN EVERY LIBRARY

The American Library Association Book List says of "Narratives of Early Virginia":

"A careful edition of the most readable original narratives having to do with the early history of Virginia. No better introduction to the use of source material could be given, and the general reader of history will find these accounts more fascinating than the latest historical novel. They should be found in every library that can afford to purchase them."